# PRO-INDEPENDENCE MOVEMENTS IN THE BASQUE COUNTRY and CATALUNYA

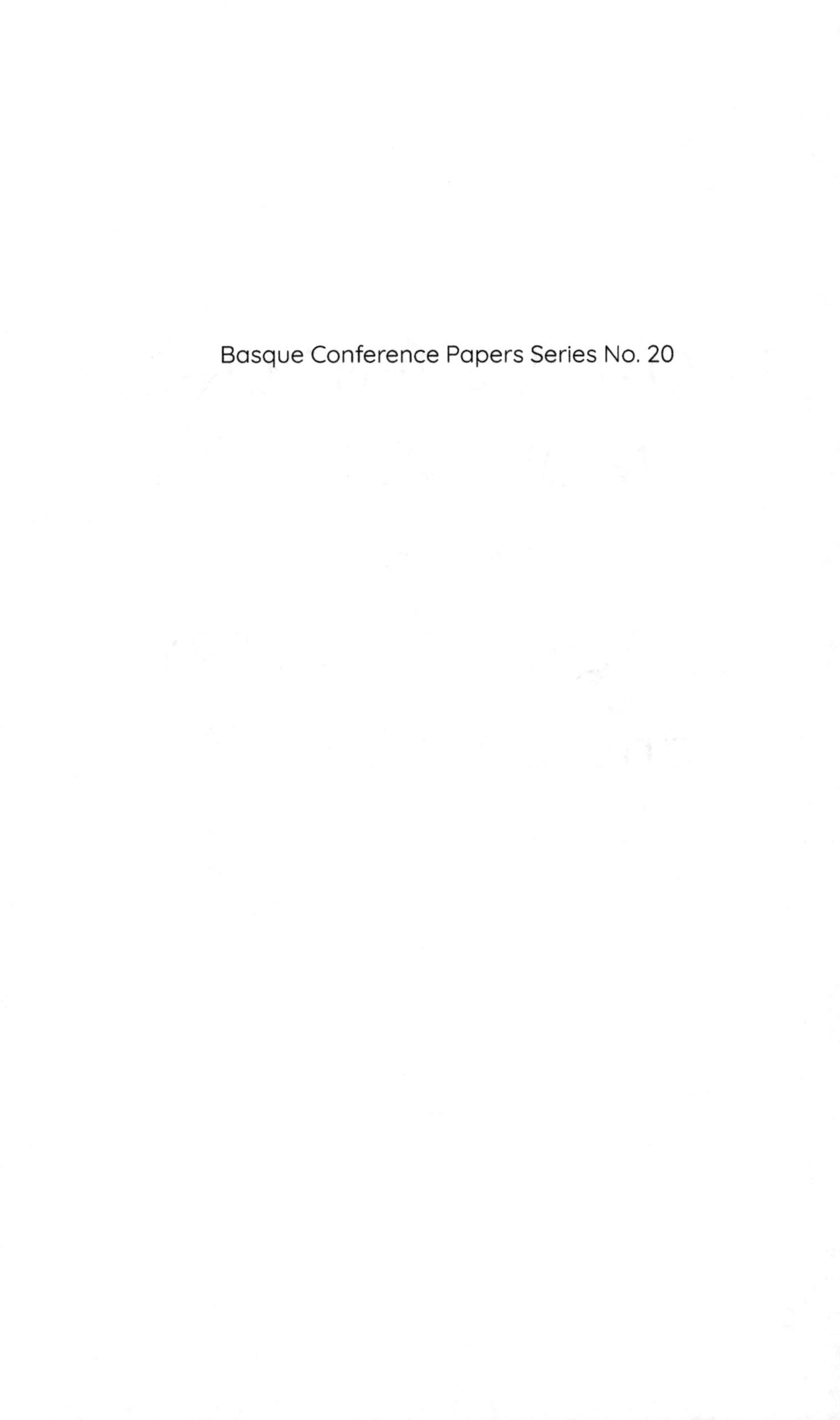

Basque Conference Papers Series No. 20

# PRO-INDEPENDENCE MOVEMENTS IN THE BASQUE COUNTRY and CATALUNYA

EDITED BY

XABIER IRUJO, QUERALT SOLE, AND
ANTONI SEGURA

This book was published with generous financial support from the Basque Government.

Center for Basque Studies
University of Nevada, Reno
1664 North Virginia St.
Reno, Nevada 89557 usa
http://basque.unr.edu


Series: Basque Conference Series No. 20
Series Editor: Xabier Irujo
ISBN-13: 978-1-949805-54-3


Cover design by Alissa Booth

Library of Congress Cataloging-in-Publication Data:
Names: Irujo Ametzaga, Xabier, editor. | Solé, Queralt, editor. | Segura, Antoni, editor.
Title: Pro-independence movements in the Basque Country and Catalunya / edited by Xabier Irujo, Queralt Sole, and Antoni Segura.
Description: Reno, Nevada : Center for Basque Studies, University of Nevada, Reno, [2022] | Series: Basque conference papers series ; no. 20 | Includes bibliographical references and index.
Identifiers: LCCN 2022016067 | ISBN 9781949805543 (paperback)
Subjects: LCSH: Autonomy and independence movements--Case studies. | País Vasco (Spain)--History--Autonomy and independence movements. | Pays Basque (France)--History--Autonomy and independence movements. | Catalunya (Spain)--History--Autonomy and independence movements. | Scotland--History--Autonomy and independence movements.
Classification: LCC JC311 .P736 2022 | DDC 320.54--dc23/eng/20220426
LC record available at https://lccn.loc.gov/2022016067

Printed in the United States of America

# Contents

## Hilari Raguer i Suñer

*In memoriam*

This book is dedicated to Hilari Raguer i Suñer, a very dear friend who left us on October 1, 2020. Without Hilari this book would have not been possible. He died before he could see it, but the present volume includes the papers presented at the symposium The Pro-Independence Movements in the Basque Country, Scotland, and Catalunya, organized by the universities of Barcelona and Nevada (Reno), held between June 19 and 20, 2019, at the Contemporary History Seminar in Barcelona. Nor would the volume *Nazi Juggernaut in the Basque Country and Catalunya* have seen the light, the result of a seminar held in the Benedictine monastery of l'Abadia de Montserrat between June 20 and 22, 2017, where Hilari was a monk.

Graduated in law from the University of Barcelona and later a political science student in Paris, Hilari, beyond his religious dedication, which led him to excel in biblical and liturgical studies, was a committed activist of the Catalan pro-independence movement. His book *Gunpowder and Incense: The Church and the Spanish Civil War* (1936-1939) placed him as one of the most outstanding researchers of the role of the Spanish Catholic Church during the Second Republic and the Francoist dictatorship. He was also an excellent biographer, and a great connoisseur of the history of the political party Unió Democràtica de Catalunya during the Republican period, which was the subject of his doctoral thesis. Moreover, he became a meeting point and the connection for Catalan historians of various generations and backgrounds.

As a result of that vocation to gather, debate, and exchange reflections with historians who have in common their interest in the dramatic recent history (from the Second Republic to the present day) of Catalunya and the Basque Country, Hilari created a solid bridge between historians of the Center for Basque Studies of the University of Nevada, Reno, and historians of the Department of History and Archeology of the University of Barcelona. Without Hilari, this fruitful link between Basque and Catalan researchers would not have occurred and the resultant manuscripts would not exist. Hilari has been the lifeblood of this academic relationship.

We dedicate this work to the person who has been our teacher and mentor, but above all a dear friend.

Xabier Irujo
Queralt Solé
Antonio Segura

# Prologue

*Xabier Irujo*

In the fall of 2013, Dr. Antoni Segura of the University of Barcelona organized the international conference, Formation of New States in the 21st Century World: The Pro-independence Processes in Quebec, Greenland, Flanders, Scotland, the Basque Country, and Catalunya. The conference gathered more than twenty scholars and a number of politicians. One of them was an MP of the Scottish National Party (SNP) at Westminster. We were having dinner at the Euskal Etxea restaurant by the Placeta de Montcada in Barcelona. Discussing the differences among the pro-independence movements and their achievements in Catalunya, the Basque Country, and Scotland, he told me: "Look, in the end, there is one basic difference between the Scottish and the Basque struggle for independence; we the Scottish have the cannons but don't have the balls, and you Basques have the balls but don't have the cannons." He previewed that the British government was going to allow a referendum on the Scottish independence movement (the British were going to provide the Scottish the cannon) because they knew that the SNP lacked the strength to win it; namely, the SNP did not have the votes (the cannonballs). Instead, the Basques did have the votes (or balls), and that was the reason why the Spanish and French governments were not going to allow a referendum on independence in the Basque Country. In 2013, a referendum on independence in Catalunya was not yet a project, but four years later things were going to change drastically. It turned out that the Catalans, like the Basques, had balls but did not have cannons.

From this perspective, it is the disallowance of the right for self-determination that stops Basques and Catalans from gaining independence. In 2021, that may be true for Scotland, too. These three European stateless nations—and many others—are seeking independence and want to create their own republics because, as the US Declaration of Independence says, "when in the Course of human events it becomes necessary for one people to dissolve the political bands which have connected them with another . . . ," nations have the right to pursue their freedom. As in 1776 in America, there are many politicians in Europe today holding that these truths are self-evident.

One of the first questions that arise, when approaching the debate on the independence of these stateless nations, is that Scotland, the Basque Country, and Catalunya are wealthy and prosperous lands, plentiful, and often to have living standards above the European's average. If people live well, why do they seek independence? The many origins, causes, and complex essence of the pro-independence movements are rooted in a distant history; the quests for independence of these three stateless nations are not briefs, but ancient chapters in the course of human history. It is not a mere question of interest, but a matter of individual and collective identity. Tacitus wrote the history of the conquest of Caledonia by the Roman general Gnaeus Julius Agricola. Calgacus confronted the Roman legions and before the Battle of Mons Graupius, deep into the Highlands, he gave a speech to his men. His words are those of Tacitus, but they reflect the aspirations of a nation to be free: "Now there is no people beyond us, nothing but tides and rocks and, more deadly than these, the Romans. It is no use trying to escape their arrogance by submission or good behavior. They have pillaged the world: when the land has nothing left for men who ravage everything, they scour the sea. If an enemy is rich, they are greedy, if he is poor, they crave glory. Neither East nor West can sate their appetite. They are the only people on earth to covet wealth and poverty with equal craving. They plunder, they butcher, they ravish, and call it by the lying name of 'empire.' They make a desert and call it 'peace.' " The drive to freedom is not a question of living standards and tax policies, but a question of living according to one's authority, according to one's identity, pursuing one's happiness in peace under one's rule of law.

Pro-independence movements are fueled mainly by the idea of the construction of nation-states. Troubles in Scotland started after the Treaty of Union in 1707, political distresses affected Catalunya after the Nueva Planta decrees were signed between 1707 and 1716, and political unrest unveiled in the Northern Basque Country after the unilateral decision of the French National Assembly to eliminate the Basque ancient laws and institutions in 1789. This process affected the Southern Basque Country starting in 1833 when the Spanish liberal movement set in motion the creation of a centralized Spanish state. The Acts of Union, the Nueva Planta decrees, and the decisions of the French

National Assembly marked the beginning of a highly turbulent historical, political, socioeconomic, and cultural cycle. For instance, although in the historical period between 1512 and 1789 the Basque people experienced episodes of violence—such as the persecution of women accused of witchcraft in Lapurdi (1609), the salt rebellion in Bizkaia (1631-1634), the Matalas rebellion in Zuberoa (1661), the king of Castile's attempt to eliminate the Basque customs (1717-1728), and the mutiny of 1766—for the most part, this period of three centuries was a peaceful one. In contrast, it will be from 1789 on when the Basque people faced the bloodiest process in their history: In the more than two hundred years between 1789 to 2022, the Basque people have lived through five fierce wars (1793-95, 1804-12, 1833-39, 1872-76, 1936-37) that add up to a total of twenty-two years of armed conflict; they have endured at least five serious revolutions or insurrections (1789-99, 1804, 1820-23, 1855, 1893); and a large number of despotic or dictatorial processes, with three peaks of cruelty (1877-81, 1923-31, 1936-75), add up to a total of forty- three years of dictatorship and terrorist activity. The death toll and the number of exiles and prison sentences are counted by the hundreds of thousands. In light of these historical events, it is obvious that the process that began in 1789 generated a bloodbath and that, even now, the majority of the Basque people are not satisfied with their current political status. The same thing may be said for Scotland and Catalunya.

Since the early nineteenth century, "reintegrationism" or "devolution" (the demand for the devolution or reintegration of historical rights, legislation, and institutions) became one of the political options with the greatest social support among Basques, Catalans, and Scottish. One key question to understand the pro-independence movement is that, historically, these three nations have enjoyed centuries of independence. The crystallization of different ideas and political positions conceived during centuries of unrest and political instability has generated a series of political positions currently divided into three main political blocs: the nationalist bloc (mostly pro-independence), the leftist bloc (federalist, or appealing for further decentralization), and the constitutional or unitarian bloc (centralist).

Starting in the new millennium, an increasing number of Scottish, Catalan, and Basque nationals believe that within a pluri-national state they will always be second-class citizens and their identity, their language, their ways of life, and the rest of the elements of their collective identity will disappear.

They have reasons to think this way. The political situation in these nations at present is that of a serious dysfunction between the cultural and sociological reality of the people and the political-economic status of the country, which constitutes the core of the political conflict. One of the key factors in defending independence is the preservation of the language and culture. For instance, because of the dismemberment of the nation into two states, the French Republic and the Spanish monarchy, the Basque Country and Catalunya, are divided into a number of diverse administrative entities. Given that the collective identity of these two nations is not politically recognized, the Basque and the Catalan languages suffer a decline in the number of speakers in some areas of their homeland. In fact, although the political-administrative reality of the Basque and Catalan people is that of a nation divided into two states and various administrative districts, the regulation of the use of the Basque and Catalan languages in the Basque Country and in Catalunya is fragmented into five dissimilar administrative realities:

- Within the Spanish political sphere, Basque and Catalan are co-official languages in the Autonomous Community of the Basque Country and Catalunya. However, Basque speakers are under three different statuses in the Historic Community of Navarre (the Basque language is not co-official in the south of this territory), and speakers of Catalan are subject to a different—and more restrictive—legislation in Valencia and the Balearic Islands.
- In the French Republic, Basque and Catalan simply did not officially exist until 1951, and both languages have been losing speakers since 1789, a linguistic process largely favored by the reinvigoration of a linguistic policy fueled by the neocolonial idea of the Francophonie promoted by the French institutions.
- In both states, outside the limits of the Basque and Catalan territories, these languages are not official, while Spanish and French are official in the entire realm (even in the times when no one spoke these "official languages").
- At the European level, the Basque language has been recognized as "a European language," but it does not enjoy the status of "a communitarian language" on an equal footing with the rest of the state languages of the continent. Ironically, Catalan has the legal status of a "communitarian language" not because it is a language spoken by millions of Catalans, but because it is the official language of the Principality of Andorra, a sovereign microstate with a population of 77,000.
- At the international level, Basque and Catalan enjoy the uncertain protection of the international legislation on linguistic diversity, but they are not among the languages officially recognized as working languages in international institutions.

This is a very irregular situation and continues to cause tension among

Basques and Catalans. As a consequence, according to many authors and the majority of the politicians in both nations, the most obvious solution for the official recognition of these languages, both nationally and internationally, is the constitution of a free and independent republic.

This book is the outcome of a conference held in Barcelona on June 19-21, 2019, on The Pro-Independence Movements in the Basque Country, Scotland, and Catalunya. It was organized by the Center for Basque Studies of the University of Nevada, Reno, and the Universitat de Barcelona.

Thirteen authors analyze, from different perspectives, the various aspects related to the origin, characteristics, development, and future projection of the Basque and Catalan political conflicts with references to the Scottish case. We have tried to answer some of the key questions around this issue: What is the origin of the pro-independence movements? What are the political and legal principles on which the pro-independence movements are based? What similarities and differences are there among the three pro-independence processes studied in this book? What transformations have occurred since their genesis over the last centuries? What have been and what are the aspirations of the groups that have supported independence? What social support have these movements historically had, and what support do they have today? What obstacles do they face? What part of the political spectrum has opposed the pro-independence movements? What legal obstacles must the pro-independence movements face to break through peacefully into the political arena of the Spanish, French, and British states? Can political independence be accommodated within the existing legal framework of the European Union? What would independence mean for the United Kingdom, Spain, France, and the whole of Europe or even the world at large should this happen? What socio-political, economic, and cultural ramifications result from the flowering of the pro-independence movements?

Dr. Alberto Spektorowski, in his chapter "From Rights to Necessity: Minority Nationalism, Democracy, and the Need for Self-Determination," claims that self-determination for minority nations in Europe is a political necessity for the future of Europe rather than a question of human rights. The author will try to demonstrate that minority nations fuse together democratic nationalism, liberalism, high economic performance, and are the best entities to deal with current pressing problems such as non-European immigration. Dr. Spektorowski defends that the best path to integration is through deep and recognized national identities. In short, according to the author, the only prospect of possible integration of "others" into polity is from the standpoint of a modern civic culture in the public sphere. The reason is that today more than ever, the region of minority nations constitutes a metaphor for an old desire for authentic identity that the democratic nation-state, fallen into disrepute, can no longer represent.

Dr. Xabier Ezeizabarrena's chapter, "Scottish Devolution and Basque Historical Rights: Toward Self-Determination & Cosovereignty," provides a legal and political comparative of the Basque claim for historical rights and the Scottish advocacy for devolution in order to establish a brief comparative approach linked with the concept of self-determination. The author underscores the potentials of these political frameworks to develop the concept of cosovereignty through mutual constitutional recognition within the UK and the Spanish state and even toward the European Union. In both cases, it is important to consider some historical data concerning the legal framework that explain and contextualize the claim for historical rights or "titles" and the demand for devolution.

In the chapter "The Literature of Peripheral Nationalisms: Late Nineteenth Century Western Europe from the Perspective of Political History and Culture," Dr. Francisco Letamendia defends that the literature of the peripheral European nationalisms of Western Europe differs from those of the early peripheral nationalisms of the Eastern empires, which were fed by the Enlightenment as early as the eighteenth century. Thus, Eastern European nations achieved independence in the twentieth century. As for Central Europe, the powerful state nationalism had the emergence of these peripheral nationalisms and their cultural production stifled (in Germany) or weakened (in Italy). In the old states of Western Europe, with nationalist movements differentiated from the "volkstaat" by their language and, in some cases, by their religion, their access to their own cultural and literary production was postponed until the end of the nineteenth century, and even into the twentieth century. The narrative of these nationalisms, within their diversity, share a certain number of characteristics that are the object of study of this chapter.

Dr. Xabier Irujo's chapter, "Independence as a Political Objective in the Basque Country (1789-2017)," is a journey through the history of the Basque independence movement. The origin of the independence movement in Euskal Herria dates back to 1855 but has its roots in the Carlist movement that sought full political reintegrationism (or devolution), which was generated, first, in the Northern Basque Country (Iparralde) after the French Revolution in 1789 and then in the four Basque territories of Hegoalde (the Southern Basque Country) by the beginning of the First Carlist War (1833-1839). That is, the author will show that the political pro-independence movement arises as a political program after the Basque territories lost their political independence between 1789 and 1841, and it will be fundamentally centered on the end of the Second Carlist War in 1876, when the first Basque nationalist parties were shaped and the first properly pro-independence political stream of thought emerged as a reaction to the loss of the ancient Basque laws and historical institutions. Between 1876 and 2022, Basque political nationalism in general, and the pro-independence movement in particular, has been gaining ground and today it constitutes one of the main axes of Basque politics, although its influence and roots vary in the three different administrations in which the Basque Country is divided today; namely, the Basque Autonomous Community and the Navarrese Historic Community in the Spanish state, and the Community of the Basque Country in the French Republic.

Dr. Igor Filibi's chapter, "Context and Political Innovations of the So-called Ibarretxe Plan (2001-2005)," illustrates how in an increasingly transnational international context, and within the framework of the European Union, there were new movements of self-determination based on shared sovereignty. The Proposal for a Political Statute attempted, on the basis of this concept, to find a new space in the debate over the political articulation of the Basque Country. In a climate of maximum confrontation and polarization, this project sought to transcend the limitations of the Spanish State of the Autonomies, attempting to build a political system based on the self-limitation of majorities and agreement between different national identities and political scales. However, despite its multiple innovations, the project was rejected without its terms even being negotiated.

In "The Basque Dream of Independence: Ideology and Organizations of the Basque Independence Movement," Dr. Iñigo Bullain offers the reader an approach to the historical and ideological grounds of the Basque pro-independence movement. The Basque nation being one of the oldest surviving nations in Europe, the historical background of its political status span more than one thousand years, from the origins of the Kingdom of Pamplona and later the Navarrese state to the Republic of Euzkadi in the twentieth century. This broad lapse of time has given way to diverse political interpretations, upon which the pro-independence movement has grounded its ideological basis. Dr. Bullain's study pays attention to the development and organization of the different pro-independence movements in modern times and analyzes the discourses of some of the personalities that have inspired it. The author provides a view of these movements in the aftermath of political violence and will offer a glimpse of its future in relation to the Catalan and Scottish cases.

During the years of the Franco dictatorship and the initial stage of the constitutional monarchy, the Catalanist movement's political approach was in the context of the Autonomous Community. In those years, the pro-independence movement was a minority sector of political Catalanism, although it did have significant presence in some social movements. Dr. Carles Santacana's chapter, "Catalan Nationalism and the Catalan Independence Movement under the Franco Dictatorship and the Restoration of Democracy (1939-2003)," analyzes Catalan resistance and the demand for the future recovery of political autonomy as the only possible political and social answer during the years of General Franco's dictatorship. Some people in exile raised the idea of going beyond that demand, relaunching the claim for self-determination, but the consolidation of the dictatorship made that impossible. Within the Spanish state, Catalanism was revived in the 1960s, combining legal and cultural initiatives with clandestine political activity. Dr. Santacana defends that, after 1978, the Catalanist movement achieved the restoration of autonomy as embodied in the Generalitat (the Catalan government), and for many years its main work was the consolidation of that institution. Explicitly pro-independence parties failed to achieve representation until Esquerra Republicana de Catalunya (ERC) transitioned from federalism to pro-independence in the late 1980s. It grew and became the third political force in 2003, and it was able to compel the drawing up of a new statute of autonomy, which started off a new stage for the whole of Catalan politics and Catalanism.

In "The Politicization of Catalanism and the Birth of the Catalan Independence Movement (1880-1939)," Drs. Giovanni C. Cattini and Daniel Roig offer a panoramic synthesis of the process of politicization that has characterized Catalanism since the late nineteenth century, when—after a long period of Catalan particularism among the popular classes, and a process of defending its own language as a language of culture during the so-called *Renaixença*—the first Catalan political groups were formed. This chapter is also a succinct analysis of how these same groups were to evolve, in turn, toward nationalist and pro-independence positions throughout the first third of the twentieth century. In fact, throughout that period Catalanism not only remained the cornerstone from which Catalan civil society mainly expressed itself; it also ended up laying bare some of the main flaws of the Spanish nationalization process: its territorial structures and the adoption of a model of Castilian-based cultural uniformity, insensitive to regional and historical singularities, and wary—and, on occasion, hostile—to the economic interests of the region and its elites, which were more in favor of an industrializing model than to the agricultural-based structure which was characteristic of the rest of the state.

In his chapter "The Catalan Independence Process Until the Referendum of October 1, 2017," Dr. Antoni Segura defends that Catalunya is a historic nation in the extreme northeast of the Iberian Peninsula, with its own language, culture, and political entity until the eighteenth century. Between 1714 and 1939, in the name of the Spanish political centralism, Catalunya lost its institutions. The restoration of democracy enabled a statute of autonomy in 1978 that at the beginning of the twenty-first century no longer satisfied the aspirations of self-government. In 2006, a new statute was approved in a referendum. The Spanish Constitutional Court blue-penciled it in 2010, and that gave rise to the political and sentimental rupture of a large part of the Catalans with Spain. The author defends that the process of political empowerment of the Catalan citizenship was originally based on the ideas of a Catalan "identity project" and the "right to decide" the political future of the nation. On October 1, 2017, a referendum took place that the Spanish government considered illegal, and which was brutally repressed by the police resulting in 1,066 people injured. On October 10, the Parliament of Catalunya proclaimed independence, a decision suspended by the Spanish government that rejected dialogue with the pro-independence Catalan government. On October 27, the Catalan executive unilaterally declared independence and the government of Madrid suspended the Catalan autonomy. Catalan politicians and elected members of government were forced into exile or were imprisoned. Nothing was solved, and the Catalan conflict still awaits some sort of political negotiation to be satisfactorily solved.

Drs. Teresa Abelló's and Queralt Solé's chapter, "Historical and Symbolic References in the Collective Imagination of the Catalan Independence Movement and New Symbols for the Twenty-First Century," focuses on the different symbols identified with Catalunya as a nation and with the Catalan defense of a collective identity and self-government. The first references date from the nineteenth century and relate to the Catalanist movement's attempt to change the dynamics of Catalunya's relationship with the Spanish state. The authors start by analyzing the origins of Catalanism in the late nineteenth century, a heterogeneous, plural movement that was embodied in political, social, and economic spheres, and which was the starting point for the subsequent pro-independence movement that has taken on many of the symbolic references of historical Catalanism.

Drs. Abelló's and Solé's work deals with the appearance, continuation, and transformation of various symbols (flag, anthem, national day, and other collective initiatives) and their adaptation to different sociopolitical situations, ranging from reformist positions to the most clearly pro-independence approaches, which have gained great momentum in today's society. Some dynamics, converted into symbols, remain constant: for instance, peaceful demands in urban areas; protest hymns that have survived generation after generation by being adapted by contemporary musical groups; and ballot boxes, a symbol of the struggle for self-government. A symbology, an expression of political and cultural identity, has survived the various political prohibitions, always claiming the Catalan language as an expression of collective identity shared through generations and over social changes.

In "Catalunya: The Challenges of Catalanism," Dr. Salvador Cardús i Ros summarizes the social and political process that has led to the rapid decay of a majority of Catalans from autonomism, a political movement that started after the end of the Spanish dictatorship in 1978, to the current pro-independence movements. The failure of the 2006 reform of the Catalan statute led certain Spanish politicians to think that it could end the national aspirations of the Catalans. But the policy of the central state provoked a reaction contrary to what was expected and accelerated the massive adherence to independence, rapidly growing from a mere 15 percent to about half of the Catalans. In addition, Dr. Cardús will show that, pro-independence or not, 80 percent of the Catalan population is currently in favor of the celebration of a referendum; namely, 80 percent of the Catalan people believe that the Catalans should have the right to self-determination. The attitude of the Spanish state to prohibit and harshly repress the holding of an agreed referendum has caused a political and legal conflict with serious and unforeseeable consequences. The present chapter reflects on the possible outcome of such a challenge.

From a general perspective, all these chapters illustrate an unstable political situation, in which the demands of a broad part of the citizenship or even majority sectors of society are being neglected, giving rise to an open conflict, waiting for a remedy that heals the wounds and allows the population to live according to their criteria, their will, and their identity.

I attended the Scottish National Party (SNP) congress on January 18, 1992. On that occasion, 2,500 party leaders participated in the Scotland Decide debate at Edinburgh's Usher Hall. I also attended the SNP conference in Perth in 1995, the year Roseanna Cunningham won elections in the Perth and Kinross districts with 40.4 percent of the vote. On the following November 30, St. Andrew's Day, the Scottish Constituent Convention, founded in 1987 to develop a scheme for the formation of a Scottish parliament, published the book *Scotland's Parliament, Scotland's Right*. Years later, once the Scottish government and parliament had been created and the SNP was in government, I was in Scotland when Alex Salmond said, "I ask for independence not because I think we are better but because I know we are as good as any other people."

The process currently under way in Scotland represents a good example of how to handle a political dialogue process in relation to holding a referendum on the constitutional future of a nation. The Scottish National Party defends the independence of Scotland. As Nicola F. Sturgeon, current prime minister of Scotland, told me once in the Basque Country, "Independence is not only a political issue, but also a social, cultural, and economic matter that is an effort to better serve the interests of Scottish citizens in particular and of Europeans in general."

The 2014 Scottish independence referendum was a lesson of democratic practice: The UK recognized the right of the Scottish people to choose their future within or outside of the Union. My Scottish friend was right, the British government knew that the Scottish people did not have the cannonballs. But still, in general terms, regardless of the outcome, the political process has been an exemplary model of the exercise of participatory democracy. The referendum on the political options for the constitutional future of Scotland provided the Scottish people in general, and each of the citizens of that nation in particular, the opportunity to express themselves and exercise their right of decision, because holding a referendum is a basic exercise of democracy. Beyond the result, holding a popular consultation helps reorient social efforts and generate new administrative channels to reach further social and political consensus because of a mature process of dialogue.

Ensuring that the people participate in a democratic process aimed at solving a political conflict is an essential responsibility of modern societies and a basic requirement of any democratic government. As citizens, we must reaffirm today an ancient European political tradition: sovereignty resides in the popular will. It is the people in an open assembly who are sovereign.

That said, one of the greatest obstacles to the resolution of the Basque and Catalan political conflicts is the lack of democratic political culture. Both the French Republic and the Spanish Monarchy are established political democracies, but they are in serious need of pushing a full expression of social democracy that will make possible the political dialogue that the British and Scottish governments were able to achieve. The violation of the right to self-determination, which has been considered by Basque political authorities as "political autism," represents the renunciation of formulating a diagnosis of the political conflict and the genesis of the pro-independence movement. It also means ignoring the popular will and, therefore, denying the right to self-determination as a fundamental right of humanity since, as expressed by the Spanish foreign minister José M. García-Margallo in 2012, "Organizing a referendum on self-determination equals a coup d'état." Criminalizing popular opinion and punishing the peaceful claim of a nation's right to decide does not offer a valid solution to human political conflicts and only extends the solution of the Basque, Catalan, and Scottish political conflicts.

Moreover, as my close friend Hilari Raguer once told me at the monastery of Montserrat, "The creation of a Basque, a Catalan, and a Scottish Republic in Europe is inevitable: it is a matter of time." These stateless nations will be independent states someday, as they were in the past. It is common sense, but most important it is a basic lesson of human rights: states should not be against the will of their people, and nations should become states, if their people's will be so. It won't be until we live in a world that respects all human rights that we can call ourselves "civilized," a world that respects and protects all political, economic, social, and cultural rights of us human beings. There will always be people claiming that this is a utopia, but we believe in the people's power, in the ability of the human spirit to make of this world a better place, where we all live united in diversity, respecting our differences in peace and mutual understanding.

## NOTES

1. Birley, Anthony R. (ed.), *Agricola and Germany* by Tacitus, Oxford University Press, Oxford, 22.

# 1

# From Rights to Necessity:

## Minority Nationalism, Democracy, and the Need for Self-Determination

*Alberto Spektorowski*

A full-fledged debate on democracy and self-determination had been raging on in the Western world for the last two decades. At first glance, that sounds strange, because the evidence shows that self-determination discourse has drastically and gradually declined in the last fifty years, reaching an unprecedented low in the 2000s (Abulof 2016, 8-9). Yet it seems that there is life after life. Indeed, as was noted by W. Connor, the perhaps unrealistic principle termed "self-determination of nations" is far from being exhausted as a significant force in international politics (Connor 1967). In current times, the debates that took place in Quebec, Scotland, the Basque Country, and especially Catalunya confirmed that the question of self-determination is living and kicking and especially important in several Western multinational democracies.

Yet, what seems to be clear is that the very idea of self-determination, and the desire of minority nations to separate from their parent states, are received with no enthusiasm by European liberal elites. Despite the fact that most substate nations demanding self-determination stick to liberal democratic values, are open societies, and all of them are pro-Europe; still their claims for self-determination are received with suspicion. The question is why such animosity against this type of substate-nationalism demands self-determination. The obvious and repeated assertion—the claim of governability, based on the idea that a greater number of states will make the Union ungovernable—is not nonsense, but it's still not convincing. A more powerful argument is the one that claims to reserve the right of self-determination to nations or regions that are oppressed by authoritarian states. The ensuing question is why there is a need for self-determination in the frame of a eurozone that tends to blur national boundaries. A European space is argued; it should be a cosmopolitan place open to immigrant communities, into where national identities, of all types, regional or national, should give way to a new whole liberal European identity.

At first glance, thus, this claim is at odds with the demand of self-determination of minority nations. For European political elites, the novelty of national self-determination expressed in holding "the people" as the supreme source of political legitimacy (Connor 2002) (Yack 2012) is useless and even dangerous. The very idea of "the right to have rights" is argued to be dependent on membership in a "national community," an ethno-national identity, and that might dash the "emancipatory hopes" that the idea of self-determination once inspired (Weitz 2015, 496). In this sense, many agree with US senator Daniel Patrick Moynihan's claim that due to ethnicity, "self-determination makes its way from the enlightenment of the eighteenth century to the darkness of the twentieth" (Moynihan 1993, 80). The very idea of nationalism, both in its civic or ethnic variant, was considered a contrast to Europe as an open space for newcomers.

Scholars such as Will Kymlicka suggest that modern liberal societies have to provide moral answers to minority nations demanding self-determination, as well as to immigrant cultures demanding to preserve their cultural dignity. Yet, as he himself stresses, the real challenge to a homogenous sense of national identity in these countries does not come to them in the first instance with immigrants, but with minority nationalism (Kymlicka 2011, 283). In an indirect way, Kymlicka is presenting the great dilemma into which modern democratic societies are immersed, which is how to define a common citizenship. Indeed, it seems to be clear that "if calls to promote a sense of common citizenship are controversial in traditional nation-states, they are even more so in multinational states where citizenship has already been pluralized to accommodate substate national groups" (Kymlicka 2011).

Yet to make things even more complicated, the question is whether there is a contradiction or opposition of interests between the accommodation of minority nationalism and the accommodation of immigrants into the nation. There is no doubt that European political and intellectual elites feel this is one of the most problematic issues at stake: Whether the multicultural arrangements, which could be applied to accommodate minority nations, may at the same time harm the rights of minorities within minority nations. Whether minority nations' defense of the right of self-determination could become a nightmare for immigrant communities (which would find it difficult to be integrated by strong national identities)?

This chapter opposes that view. In contrast to multicultural or cosmopolitan approaches, I suggest that the integration of immigrant minorities works better under strong national identities. In this sense, and despite logical fears which we do not neglect, I suggest that nowadays, because of massive immigration, receiving societies should display a strong sense of cultural collective identity in order to be open to newcomers. In short, the only prospect of possible integration of "others" into the polity is from the standpoint of a modern civic culture in the public sphere (Tamir 1992, 131).

Yet the question is: why can minority nations better fulfill that type of integration? The reason is that today, more than ever, the region or minority nation constitutes a metaphor for an old desire for authentic identity that the democratic nation-state, fallen into disrepute, can no longer represent (Dainotto 2000, 21). Against homogenizing nationalism, authentic minority nations could set a model of integration that could synthesize respect for diversity under a strong sense of national identity. As noted, a wide variety of liberals would feel uneasy about this. Yet, I suggest that it is the only possible course of action precisely because of two reasons. The first is that the European space is becoming more multicultural than ever, and the second is the rising up of a populist backlash against the multiculturalization of society. I suggest only minority nations constitute the best synthesis between liberal and national values, the necessary formula for the integration of the "other." In this sense, this chapter claims that, more than a right in itself, the new regional minority nationalism constitutes a European necessity.

## Self-Determination in Western Democracies. Why Now?

Precisely in times when the mounting dangers to the post–Cold War world order have reached a critical stage, and an emergent political contention focuses on the rise of populist reactions to immigration against distant political elites, the question liberal Europe asks is why nowadays wealthy regions ask for self-determination and separatism. While it is true that processes of separatism, such as those of Sweden and Norway and that of the Czechs and Slovaks, at different times may prove there is no inherent danger to democracy in the process of separatism, still the example of the deconstruction of Yugoslavia and the fratricide war against minorities remain to all a representation of the dangers involved in the process of self-determination and the ensuing process of "democratic homogenization." All in all, Europeans want less, not more, nationalism, and European liberals want more, not less, diversity in their societies.

At first glance thus far, the right of self-determination is reserved only for oppressed nations or oppressed regions in nondemocratic states. Indeed, for a long period of time, the very sense of minority nationalism was considered a backward idea. Minority nationalism was grasped as a phenomenon that may unfold in peripheral, undeveloped countries, and basically the phenomenon is condemned to disappear or be absorbed by economically advanced societies. As was remarked by Charles Tilly and Stein Rokkan, core regions used to combine economic and military power to expand their reach to adjacent areas and form a strong territorial nation-state. Capitalist coercion best represented by France and England, but also by Portugal, the Dutch Republic, and Piedmont, and which was the engine of Italian unification, did precisely that. This implied, among other things, that the nation-state would impose, at least theoretically, its highest culture to the regions it absorbed. As assumed by Montserrat Guibernau, the nation-state, even the liberal nation-state, has never been culturally neutral. It has basically imposed the culture of the majority into its parts (Guibernau 2006).

This model was consolidated during the post-world war period through the welfare state. Although the welfare state had been created before that time, it was during the post-war period when the automatic systems of redistribution between rich and poor citizens of the same state took an unprecedented magnitude. The center in general came to the aid of the poor regions. These times ended with the impact of globalization, yet paradoxically in current times, "in the midst of a civilization more and more cosmopolitan, more egalitarian and anonymous . . . an unavoidable regional resistance began to loom" (de Benoist 1993, 52). Cosmopolitan civilization however, implies, among other things, more immigration and more economic inequalities. Indeed, economic growth since the 1970s has been an engine for economic migration and the transformation of European societies into multicultural ones. At the time that modern democratic societies became increasingly diverse, liberal political philosophers made great efforts to meet the new social and moral challenges. Through the ideology of multiculturalism, liberals strove to give support to cultural claims of immigrant communities that established themselves in modern societies. Yet, at the same time, philosophers such as Kymlicka also assumed that liberals, in what looked like a prosperous postcommunist world, should also address claims from indigenous minorities, especially claims for self-determination.

The idea was to accept the plea of regions or minority nations to express their own identity. Indeed, liberal multiculturalists, especially those in the mold of Will Kymlicka and Charles Taylor, supported the right of "national minorities" to cultural autonomy. They believe multiculturalism provides a theoretical basis for demanding that states like Canada, Spain, Belgium, and Great Britain allow wide political and cultural rights to the Quebecois, Basques, Catalans,

Walloons, and Scots. In this sense, not only immigrant cultures should be respected by liberals, but authentic nations or regions that have been "conquered" or annexed by the liberal state should have a say in the new politics of identities. The question, however, is how such politics of identities should be politically expressed. Most liberals, understanding, maybe wrongly, that the post-communist era will be a post nation-state era, characterized by the adoption of a "post-national citizenship," considered the development of multi-identity frameworks, wherein different cultures could coexist one with another. In that sense, while multiculturalists could respect the idea of self-determination of minority nations, they were also quite aware of some of its dangers and challenges. Indeed, as Kymlicka (2001) himself admits, the fact that both groups, immigrants and national minorities, militate against cultural homogenization of the state does not stop their interests from conflicting (Kymlicka 2001, 278). While national minorities are natively rooted, immigrants are newcomers. While the former aspires to achieve territorial and cultural exclusiveness, the latter expects to be integrated into a receiving liberal democratic society. Though both may use a liberal right theory for their respective interests, the former also use an ethno-nationalist discourse. Given this background, it is not surprising that nationalists of large minority groups, such as Catalan, Quebecois, or Flemish nationalists, often endorse both Kymlicka's liberal multiculturalism and Charles Taylor's communitarianism. As Taylor notes, "the principle of individual rights to life, liberty, due process, and free speech are accepted as long as the Quebec government is free to guarantee the survival of French Quebecois culture" (Taylor 1994, 59).

Yet, liberal scholars wonder whether the idea of reserving the right of a minority nation to protect a national culture implies that a minority nation can impose its national culture on minorities within the minority nation. More worrying than that, is the other way around—whether an ethno-national society could be closed to immigrants and even be unwilling to integrate or assimilate them.

The Swiss example clearly shows how a multinational state, wherein the principle of democracy is used at the local level, can be especially difficult for unpopular minorities.

Can a Catalunyan, a Basque state, or a Quebecois do the same with its minorities? This is indeed a central question emerging in the debate about self-determination and secession. Different ideas address this point in a direct or indirect way. For several scholars, the very idea of globalization might contribute to domesticating self-determination and, in a certain sense, making statehood itself redundant (Talbott 2000). In any case, acts for self-determination and secession are complicated. As Ferran Requejo remarks, the outcomes of demands for secession vary according to factors both internal and external to the independence movements. Attaining statehood depends on the interaction between de facto effectiveness and recognition of the new political unit. The quest for recognition demands high levels of legitimacy, which are often "proven" via a referendum. In terms of effectiveness, it requires de facto control over the territory, which only seems possible in contexts in which the parent state is weak and/or the international community is involved (Requejo and Sanjaume-Calvet 2019, 11). Since international approval would be impossible to achieve if a liberal democratic mother state does not agree with self-determination of one of its parts, other solutions should be researched.

In this sense, stateless nations could then find peace and prosperity in regional solutions (Gottlieb, 1993). While the lack of popular sovereignty might leave a lot of space for minorities' freedom of action within minority nations, the idea is that, even holding popular sovereignty, minority nations within the frame of Europe will hardly be willing to repress minorities in their sovereign territory.

Yet despite voices in favor, political elites in Europe seemed reluctant to be convinced. They understand that some of the European states are unitary states, others are federal ones, some are multinational states, but none of the European nation-states are based on collective identities where the region is based on a specific ethnicity. Some states of the EU have been more respectful of the traditional, organically developed institutions of such regions (as in Germany and Spain), others much less so (such as Italy), but none have enshrined an ethnic character into EU regions, grounded in a feudal order predating the modern idea of the nation.

Indeed, only the 1918-born Yugoslav kingdom was officially called the "Kingdom of Serbs, Croats, and Slovenes," and despite the historical transformations it underwent, the argument goes, it was the persistence of this ethnic character that led to its tragic end.

Therefore, while the European Union has paid attention to regionalism and there is a charter of regions, European leaders have perceived the trap behind the question of regionalism or the development from regionalism into nationalism. The basic claim is that regions should not shift to nationalism. What European liberal elites are afraid of is precisely that minority nations or regional autonomies will become a new type of authentic exclusionist nationalism flourishing back. That is the reason why the relations of Europe's institutions with regionalism are expressed basically in the European Court of Human Rights.

"The fact that a group of persons calls for autonomy or even requests secession of part of the country's territory—thus demanding fundamental constitutional and territorial changes—cannot automatically justify a prohibition of its assemblies. Demanding territorial changes in speeches and demonstrations does not automatically amount to a threat to the country's territorial integrity and national security" (2021, 17). Ethno-regional parties are considered under the principle that "freedom of association involved the right of everyone to express, in a lawful context, their beliefs about their ethnic identity. However shocking and unacceptable certain views or words used might appear to the authorities, their dissemination should not automatically be regarded as a threat to public policy or to the territorial integrity of a country."

On the one hand, thus, European institutions provide a charter on regions and accept the discourse of ethno-regional parties as part of the liberal creed of freedom of speech. On the other hand, Europe is not ready to accept and support regional claims for self-determination, especially if that comes from regions within democratic states. The Catalans felt besieged by the European reaction to their claims.

While Catalans in favor of self-determination and separatism are not perceived as non-liberals or non-democrats, the European subtext is that regional self-determination is problematic and will hardly contribute to a more liberal Europe.

In that sense, while the Europe of the states is perceived as relying on liberal principles that project them from nation-states into a political and economic union, resting on the same philosophical basis, the same criteria could apparently not be applied for regions. For Europe's liberal elites, a return to regionalism is portrayed and interpreted as a shift to ethno-nationalist principles.

### What Is the Problem? Liberal Critics . . . Right-Wing Exclusionists' Hopes

As was noted by S. Benhabib, every new polity, in taking the form of a "nation-state," wants their culture to be hegemonic, and this entails a moral and political cost (Benhabib 2002, 150). For example, if a French-speaking majority in Quebec were to establish a nation-state in which they would stand as the central, national group that enforced criteria of political community (Salle 2007), this would create a difficult situation for immigrants. Similarly, Adrian Favell fears an intolerant-emergent English nationalism if the United Kingdom were to break up (Favell 1996) (McGarry, 1998, 215–32). Kymlicka, for example, explains that endorsing a post-ethno-nationalist stance, especially in response to immigration, is possible depending on a certain condition. Kymlicka gives the condition that sub-state nationalism should manage the volume of immigration into the structure. In other words, inclusiveness depends on demographic control by the national "majority,' which was the former minority (Kymlicka 2001). Indeed, it is likely that substate nationalism would become exclusionist if the demographic balance were to be challenged. It is only in this way that the cultural minority can crystallize and express its unique qualities. This is precisely why European liberal elites are not appeased by advocates of self-determination, and why a wide variety of New Right exclusionists are in favor of it. Building on the inconsistencies of liberal multiculturalism, neo-fascist New Rightists wish to radicalize the politics of identity. For the latter, the new identity expression of "white trash," while representing a total and violent response to immigrant identities, paradoxically relies on the same multicultural principles defended by liberal progressives. Indeed, the *identitary* road initiated in the 1980s by the French New Right is becoming a central asset for right-wing populist movements in Europe. European New Right employs a multiculturalist framework, which I define as a recognition/exclusionist one, in order to create a new discourse of "legitimate exclusionism" of non-authentic European immigrants (Spektorowski 2012). However, more interesting, the trend of legitimate exclusion does not depend on old-style colonialist and expansionist nationalism, but the opposite. For some analysts, this would be precisely an antinationalist method; however, it was conceived in order to exclude rather than integrate. Indeed, whereas earlier movements insisted on the indivisibility of France, Italy, or Belgium, for example, new national exclusionists may support the deconstruction of the old nation-state into its component regions. In this sense, the liberal European Union is not challenged by a resurgence of old state nationalism but by a post-national federalism which, although applauded by democratic and socialist intellectuals as we shall see, are also endorsed by neofascist right-wing political ideologues and by "right-wing anti-immigration parties" (de Winter 1998, 205).

Movements like the European Social Movement, a neo-neofascist Europe-wide alliance which emerged from the Italian Social Movement (bMSI), promote a pan-European nationalism clearly influenced by this thought. We are against [5.56] "particular nationalism" and proposed a European nation of nations, from Brest to Vladivostok, with Rome as its political capital, Paris as its cultural one, and Berlin as its economic one, and "they [Rome, Paris, and Berlin] must look to Moscow, the Third Rome, to bring peace and prosperity to the world." It is no question that movements such the Lega Nord in Italy and VlamsBelang—the right-wing Flemish party in Belgium—and even nationalist, non-separatist parties such as the Freedom Party in Austria have been influenced by this thought. One of the Lega Nord's most prominent intellectuals, Gianfranco Miglio, who also served in the *Lega'slist* as the senate for three terms, attempted to launch deep constitutional reform in Italy. Miglio, like de Benoist and other younger intellectuals of the New Right, was critical of the Weberian concept of the impersonal or neutral state, which legitimizes the capitalist meritocratic order. For example, he claims that there is a contradiction between the political state and the democratic state. Similar to other New Right intellectuals, Miglio contends that the nation-states in Europe have not been created by "nationalities," namely cultural and ethnic regions, but by "the authoritarian exercise of political power which has hegemonized those who were governed and made them into an [artificial] nation" (Miglio 1990). This modern nation-state is in contrast to the collective identity unfolding in smaller regions, since in the latter it has evolved naturally and has not been forced by state pressure. The regional nation is authentic and authentically represents the interests of its citizens. The authentic nation belongs to Europe, but to a Europe of its peoples, which for the later intellectuals and groups should contrast the liberal European Union. In Austria, for example, the 1997 program of the FPO supported the idea of European integration based on "a variety of peoples and ethnic groups, regions, nations and state units which have all grown up historically with shared values" (Program of the FPO 1997, Ch. 4). The Lega Nord, which meets the criteria of participatory democracy, feels more related to Austria and Mitteleuropa than to the Italian south. Also, the Flemish VlamsBelang in Belgium declared that it belongs to Europe—not to the liberal Maastricht-Europe, but to a new Europe that can accommodate their ethnic interests. Indeed, right-wing ethno-regionalist parties strive to keep their organic "productivist" communities intact as a way to protect their direct democracy. Since they understand that they can hardly survive economically and politically as independent entities, they prefer a confederal ethnic Europe of peoples over the liberal European Union. The common ground of this new Europeanism, however, is that they represent Europe's ethnic variety, a differentialist ethno-pluralism that will undermine liberal pluralism. By celebrating all authentic cultures in a differentialist spirit (Griffin 1998, 3), de Benoist and the European New Right assume that the ethno-regional trend is the source of a European post-colonial doctrine setting the basis for a new European renaissance, which promotes diversity as a way to exclusion. However, the question is whether it could be possible the other way around—how and whether a Europe of its regions could be precisely an open place for integration.

### The Positive Side of Self-Determination of Minority Nations or Regions

Several scholars and experts on non-state nationalism and regional nationalism had expressed, in a clear-cut way, that minority nationalism not only hardly remains the nationalism of the past, but that, in total contrast to the exclusionist perspective promoted by the New Right, it is precisely open and ready to integrate to the foreigner.

Indeed, the nationalism of Scots, Catalans, etc. should be distinguished from the negative narrow nationalism of the past (Laitin 2001, 103). Furthermore, in this new type of nationalism, the question of state sovereignty is removed and replaced with concepts of legal and constitutional pluralism (McCormick 1999). It is clear to all that minority nationalists tend to be in favor of the European Union, and that they differ radically from "old-style" sovereign nationalists.

With the same zeal, progressive movements had seen the positive side in the design of a new Europe in which the central factor would be authentic regions. Since the end of the 1990s, French ecologists have demanded recognition of regions instead of nation-states as primary political units in a new, decentralized, diverse, and democratic Europe (Les Verts 1991). They have also promoted a loose confederation of regions that are "culturally defined, historically developed, self-determined but intertwined" (Bomberg 1998, 66). From an empirical perspective, advocates of regional, non-state nationalism appropriately stress that ethno-regionalism in Europe does not lead to a regime of social exclusion (Anderson 1994, 9–10) (de Winter and Cachafeiro 2002) (Keating 1996, 2001) (Lynch 1996) (Newhouse 1997). Furthermore, what is generally seen is that policies in those units are benign toward immigrants. Several studies have demonstrated that linguistic policies in Catalunya or a rising Scottish self-consciousness have proven to be more integrating than alienating (Hussain and Miller, 2006) (Shafir 1992, 111). Democratic political parties such as the Catalunyan CyU, or Esquerra Republicana, the Scottish National Party, and the Basque PNV endorsed this criterion. They have supported European integration and defended federalism and subsidiarity, which enable solidarity on the one hand and diversity and difference on the other. They define themselves as nationalist and liberal or social-democratic. All of them aspire to advance self-determination and to be included in a liberal European Union, although the idea of a confederation of European peoples entices them as well. The Basque regional government, for example, is advancing a proposal of federalist integration in which the ideas of unity and diversity would contribute one to the other. The demand to Europe is to recognize the Basque region as a nation.

"At the time that the old nation state in Europe is in crisis, Europe should take into consideration subnational entities as the new organizational factor . . . The absence of any reference to regions in the White Book on the future of Europe of March 2017 proves that Europe is still dominated by the conviction that only existing states are the legitimate interlocutors in the decision-making process" (Gobierno Vasco 2018, 27). The Basque lehendakari added what were, according to his perspective, the sociopolitical reasons behind the necessity of approaching the vision of a European confederation of regions.

"The rise of populism is related to the growing perception by European populations, that they are governed by distant and centralizing powers. Either state officials or European elites are perceived as alien. Facing them we can place constitutional regions that might become catalysators of the new power of citizens" (Gobierno Vasco 2018, 28).

This is a compelling claim despite, as some scholars assert, that the Basque Country and Catalunya (Spain), PACA and Nord-Pas-de-Calais (France), and the Greek Islands have more populist potential than their respective national counterparts (Hawauert 2019, 307). This claim coincides with several studies that have already identified a close interdependence between regionalist and populist ideologies (van Kessel 2015).

Yet despite critics, the "Vision del future de Europa" promoted by the Basque government stresses what is obvious. In the context of increased social diversity, portions of the public are prone to understanding democracy through the lens of group memberships (Filindra 2018, 2). This can obviously lead to antiliberal populism; yet at the same time, this chapter claims that it is worth taking risks. A liberal version of national democracy is more likely to set a barrier against social frustration leading to populism and, as noted, it is precisely important as a tool for integration of foreigners and as a barrier against racism.

Regarding the first point, regions or minority nationalism become the new civil society in Europe, precisely in times of rebellion against neo-capitalism, and European political elites. For regional political elites, thus, the demand of their own regions for self-determination involves not only a national self-interest, but also a key for the redefinition of Europe as a new frame for democracy. Minority nations would transform the dependency in a multinational state into being part of a multinational Europe. Ireland is a case in point. Still, pundits may claim that there are no very clear differences between the right-wing Lega Nord's claim for self-determination within a new "Europe of its peoples" and Basque or Catalan nationalists' similar claim. As we stressed, Miglio's self-determination and idea of confederation proposed by the New Right are conceived in order to make the exclusion "of the other" a necessity. Yet the "Europes of the peoples," advanced by liberal nationalists, is founded in a different principle.

Here we enter into the second part of the equation. While the idea of a confederation of European peoples as a substitute to the liberal cosmopolitan and technocratic European Union can be similar to that promoted by left democratic or liberal nationalist parties, still there are strong differences about its meaning.

The later set the best frame for integration of "the other." Indeed, while several liberal voices claim that a post-national state sense of citizenship is better equipped for the integration of the other, I accept Will Kymlicka's claim that a post-national citizenship approach is hardly existent. States such as Canada, Spain, or the United Kingdom are not neutral amid historic national projects. They are connected to a national culture. In that sense, the very idea that they are post- national, while Catalunya or Scotland are national, does not hold. Yet more important than that, I suggest that minority national identities are better fitted for integration of newcomers than what old or multinational states are. In this point, this chapter agrees with Kymlicka's claim that "Pakistani support for the SNP in Scotland may be evidence of successful integration into the ethos and practice of multinational citizenship, whereas the almost total absence of immigrant support for secession in Quebec may be evidence of failed integration into multinational citizenship" (Kymlicka 2011, 283). Kymlicka aside, however, our idea of a liberal identity differs slightly from a multicultural one.

The idea advanced by liberal nationalists is that, when a strong identity is held at the public sphere, there is no problem to accept, respect, and even support minority identities within the country. Indeed, in his analysis and support for multinational states, Kymlicka admits that if a citizenship agenda is to be effective, we need a more multinational conception of citizenship and a more multicultural conception of multinationalism (Kymlicka 2011, 293). In our view, however, the idea of a liberal and inclusive national identity should be republican, namely one into which newcomers are welcomed but also demanded to integrate into an open republican identity. Learning the language, national traditions, and being part of society should be presented as a necessity for the newcomer as well as the receiver. Different from right-wing exclusionists who reject the very idea of assimilation/integration, thus a republican identity opens the gate to the "others," economic immigrants, refugees, etc. At the same time, different from liberal multiculturalists who harmonize the dominance of a national public sphere with the acceptance of cultural minorities to enhance their own culture, the republican identity puts more emphasis on integration into the historical national culture. That hardly means that the culture and religion of others should be totally ignored. However, the new receiving national culture should predominate. The nation-state should preserve a basic cultural frame that all citizens should perceive and accept as the dominant frame. Let's consider the most radical side of a democratic ethno-nationalism, as is the case of the Basque Country. Most analysts would define Basque nationalism as a classic ethno-nationalism profile, very near to what right-wing pundits would expect. If we gloss over the nationalist philosophy of Sabino Arana, the founder of Basque nationalism, there could be few doubts that a sense of anti-Spanish and antiforeigner racism could be seen. Arana looked nostalgically at the Basque past and first proposed a racially pure Basque nation with his motto "Euzkadi is the land of the Basques." He also drew on a previous tradition of myths, memories, and symbols that depicted Basques as a chosen and noble people who spoke a divine language. All these myths, which gave the Basques a distinct sense of identity, were mobilized by Arana in order to construct a radical project for the secession of the Basque Country. Indeed, the renewal of the nation would come when Basques achieved their political independence. The question, however, is whether non-Basques could be included within the nation and under what status. In order to answer this question, we can briefly examine how the idea of inclusion developed within ETA, which is probably the most radical form of Basque nationalism.

At first sight, ETA continued Arana's prescriptions. For several pundits, thus, ETA's nationalism could be portrayed as symbolic of what a radical type of exclusionist nationalism is. Yet that is hardly true. This is not the place to judge ETA's brand of violent struggle, but is specific to the idea of determining who could be considered as part of the nation. That might give us a sense of what a republican identity means. ETA hardly continues the anti-Makestism of Arana and hardly conceived the idea of a Basque race as the basis of a Basque sense of nationalism. Some of its prominent leaders, such as José Luis Álvarez Enparantza [*Txillardegi*], José María Benito del Valle, or Federico Krutwig Sagredo, did not even hold authentic Basque names as demanded by Arana as a key of belonging. In its letter of principles in its first assembly of May 1962, ETA explicitly rejected any connotation between Basque nationalism and racism. At the same time, it is important to stress and add that ETA's concept of nationality is hardly a liberal one. It was clear to all that "accepted foreigners," according to ETA prescriptions, could be those who share Basque's legitimate claim for self-determination, and those who are ready to learn Euzkera, which symbolizes the synthesis between a national language and a national culture. Consequently, the concept of Basque identity would be represented by the sociological act of *euskaldun*, a process of acculturalization. For several liberals, however, this linguistic criterion could be considered as another hidden way of exclusion according to racist basis. We suggest that this is hardly so. Learning of a language and a national culture is a condition, but it is hardly a racist barrier. Conditional inclusion is not based on a genealogical transmission, which is primarily a biological relation. It is a sociological transmission, which works through social practices and institutions (Patten 2011, 744). We suggest that it is difficult for a foreigner to become part of these social practices and institutions; but it is still possible and necessary, pending on the will and predisposition from the part of the receiver.

This conditional inclusion also rejects claims such as that of Krutwig Sagredo, who suggested that nonwhite people with no Indo-European lineage were not up to be assimilated. Needless to add to that, the very idea of considering that only Indo-Europeans are prone to assimilation is clearly associated with a racial view. The idea of conditional inclusion is color and culturally blind; all are welcomed into the republican identity. Whoever decides to be part of and contribute to the Basque people and nationalism, no matter religion or race, could be considered part of Basque nationality. In short, while the racist nation relies on the myth of biological links, and no one can apply to enter it, the republican melting pot model rejects ethnicity-based power sharing and advocates assimilation toward nationhood. The republican gates are open to all cultures and people from different religious backgrounds who are willing to be part of the nation, however, adapting theselves to the liberal values and behavior of the democratic majority. In this sense, this argument surpasses Avishai Margalit and Moshe Halbertal, who claim that liberal societies should grant minority cultures a right to preserve their own culture, even if, in some cases, it is an illiberal culture. Indeed for Margalit and Halbertal, "the state that may be granting a particular cultural group the opportunity to preserve its cultural homogeneity in a given region under certain circumstances may exact the price of preventing outsiders from living there" (Margalit-Halbertal 1994, 492). The republican nationalist model accepts the first part of the Margalit-Halbertal claim, regarding the right of self-determination, while it rejects the claim that belonging cannot be a voluntary act. It is and should be voluntary, under conditions that most human beings willing to be part of society can accomplish.

We are aware, however, that this change in criteria from ethnic exclusionism to a republican melting pot, while hardly racist, still could not be compatible with multicultural and neo-liberal theory models, which emphasize the idea of diversity and are conceived as a way to preserve ethnic, sectarian, religious, regional, and racial peculiarities and identities (Lijphart, 1969) (McGarry and O'Leary 2007). Scholars worried about the idea of cultural homogenization emphasize the requirement of protecting diversity. Yet our claim is, that while homogenization of national minorities into the nation is wrong, demands of integration into a national culture to immigrant minorities is necessary. I suggest that, nowadays, precisely because of massive immigration, conditional inclusion is necessary. We suggest that, even taking into account the tremendously bad experience Europe has had with nationalism, national integration is the opposite of national exclusion, and it is necessary precisely in order to prevent exclusion.

Thus, why is a nationally-sanctioned democratic public culture important? As several scholars have noted, because immigration is viewed negatively by large parts of the population, there is a need to facilitate integration of newcomers into a national public culture. Integrating newcomers would, according to David Miller and Michael Walzer, allow citizens to embrace and feel solidarity with the foreigner. Indeed, a hegemonic identity sanctioned by a national public culture is necessary for citizens to act on a basis other than strictly individualized strategic considerations (Miller 1989) (Walzer 1983). That is why, as several scholars suggest, Europeans should consider the value of preserving the foundational myth and narratives of the democratic civic community, to which immigrants should adapt. As Tamir explains, only the citizens' commitment to "mutual dependencies and responsibilities [embedded in a shared national identity] . . . invigorates the will to jointly pursue common ends" (Tamir 2019, 252). In more sense than one, this argument surpasses the classical justification for self-determination based on the democratic right of self-determination. Catalans and Spanish rely on their own interpretation of democracy. For Catalans, self-determination is directly related to their democratic right to decide, while for Spanish, defending democracy implied sticking to the constitution. In both cases, however, the debate was pulled out from the problematic concept of nationalism; or, the other way around, both parts blame the other of nationalism. In our account, however, both sides of nationalists' hold compelling claims about their definition of democracy. What turns the balance toward Catalunya as well as other minority nations is precisely the fact that Catalans and Basques are in better positions to synthesize liberalism with the mobilizationary spirit of authenticity. Nationalism used to carry democracy on its back and was the force behind movements of national liberation. Later on, during world war times, it was the force of destruction and division. Today it is the force that can precisely come to the help of democratic integration during times of expansive immigration. In summary, the reason why minority nations, through their self-determination, are preferable to the old nation-state is because the latter recover the spirit of authenticity that the old nation has lost, and that spirit is what allows the perfect synthesis for the integration of the others.

## Conclusion

It should be of no doubt why the new spirit of the Populist Right should be found in the idea of ethno-regionalism. They see the ethnic region as an old new unit wherein the seeds of organic nationalism will spurt again. They all see the very idea of organic nationalism as a clear road to alienate "foreigners," and they all see organic nationalism as the necessary unit to reform Europe as an exclusionary Europe that, at the same time, will be diverse and unitary. The concept of diversity implies diversity of ethno-national European peoples, which represents more than a narrow nationalism—a whole European nationalism. One of the latest critiques Marlene Wind stresses—that Catalan separatism represents the same spirit of reactionary tribalism—is featured in the vote for Brexit as well as in the democratic backsliding in Central and Eastern Europe. The common ground of these anti-globalism identity politics, accordingly, is putting cultural differences in front of dialogue collaboration and universal values (Wind 2020).

We reject this one-dimensional claim. Nationalist movements demanding the right for self-determination of regions such as Catalunya, the Basque Country, Scotland, and even Quebec defend liberal principles together with nationalism. They all envision a Europe of its peoples as a response to right-wing populism.

They conceived the nation as a new civil society, which allows peoples and leaders to interact in a meaningful way. Some of them aspire to secede from the state; however, not at all costs. The basic idea is to have the right to decide within the state and conform a federation of nations basically at the European level. In this chapter, I don't dismiss liberals' fears, especially those that suspect right-wing exclusionist appropriation of the right of self-determination. Yet, despite those basic fears, I suggest that it is worth trying. The European Union would have to change course in order to survive the increasing discontent against its bureaucratization and its mismanagement of the immigration challenge. Precisely, the very idea of enhancing a communitarian democratic nationalism fits perfectly well in the process of reception and integration of newcomers.

The question at that instance, thus, would be which Europe of the peoples will unfold: a right-wing exclusionist or a democratic inclusive Europe? The first would use ethnic roots and the national language to exclude, the latter would use the same elements to include. It will hardly be a multicultural integration, but it will be a national integration. In that case, paraphrasing Eugen Weber's famous book *From Peasants to Citizens* could mark the new trend: "From aliens to nationalists." Therefore, despite that newcomers' may grasp the idea of "Britishness" as a more open and civic identity compared to the more ethnic categories of English, Welsh, Scots, or Irish, I suggest that, in the long run, the idea of integration into national identities nowadays is the right balance, between reaffirming communities' long desire for identity and newcomers' search for political and social shelter.

## References


Abulof, Uriel. "We the Peoples? The Strange Demise of Self-Determination." *European Journal of International Relations* 22, no. 3 (September 2016): 536–565.

Banai, Ayelet. " 'Europe of the Regions' and the Problem of Boundaries in Liberal Democratic Theory," *Journal of Political Ideologies* 17, no. 1 (2012): 35–59.

Bomberg, Elizabeth. *Green Parties and Politics in the European Union*. New York: Routledge, 1998.

Connor, Walker. "Self-Determination: The New Phase," *World Politics* 20, no. 1 (1967): 30–53.

Connor, Walker. "Nationalism and Political Illegitimacy." In *Ethnonationalism in the Contemporary World: Walker Connor and the Study of Nationalism*, edited by Daniele Conversi, 24–49. New York: Routledge, 2002.

Dainotto, Roberto. *Place in Literature. Regions, Cultures, Communities.* Ithaca, London: Cornell University Press, 2000.

de Benoist, Alain. "The Idea of Empire," *Telos,* no. 98–99 (1993-1994): 81–98.

de Benoist, Alain. "Confronting Globalization," *Telos* 2, no. 108 (1996): 117–137.

de Winter, Lieven. "Conclusion: A Comparative Analysis of the Electoral Office and Policy Success of Ethnoregionalist Parties." In *Regionalist Parties in Western Europe,* edited by Lieven De Winter and Huri Tursan, 204–247. London: Routledge, 1998.

de Winter, Lieven, and Margarita Gomez-Reino Cachafeiro. "European Integration and Ethnoregionalist Parties," *Party Politics* 8, no. 4 (2002): 483–503.

European Court of Human Rights "Guide on Article 11 of the European Convention on Human Rights, Freedom of Assembly and Association," Art 72, 2021.

Favell, A. (1996) "Multicultural race relations in Britain—an exceptional case? Problems of interpretation and explanation." Paper presented at the European University Institute workshop on Immigration, Citizenship and Ethnic Conflict, Florence, Italy.

Filindra, Alexandra. "Of Regimes and Rhinoceroses: Immigration, Outgroup Prejudice, and the Microfoundations of Democratic Decline." In "Immigration and Populism," workshop held at Stanford University in 2018. https://fsi-live.s3.us-west-1.amazonaws.com/s3fs-public/filindra-of_regimes_and_rhinoceroses_0.pdf.

Gobierno Vasco. 2018. "Vision del futuro de Europa," https://www.euskadi.eus/contenidos/informacion/post_2020/es_def/adjuntos/Vision_del_Futuro_de_Europa.pdf.

Gottlieb, Gideon. *Nation against the State: A New Approach to Ethnic Conflicts and the Decline of Sovereignty.* New York: Council of Foreign Relations Press, 1993.

Guibernau, Montserrat. *The Identity of Nations*. Cambridge, UK, and Malden, MA: Polity, 2006. Van Hauwaert, Steven M., Christian H. Schimpf, and Régis Dandoy. "Populist Demand, Economic Development and Regional Identity Across Nine European Countries: Exploring Regional Patterns of Variance." *European Societies* 21, no. 2 (2019): 303–332.

Hussain, Asifa, and William Miller. *Multicultural Nationalism, Islamophobia, Anglophobia and Devolution*. Oxford: Oxford University Press, 2006.

Keating, Michael. *Nations against the State: The New Politics of Nationalism in Quebec, Catalunya and Scotland.* New York: St. Martin's Press, 1996.

Keating, Michael. *Plurinational Democracy: Stateless Nations in a Post-Sovereignty Era.* Oxford: Oxford University Press, 2001.

Krutwig, Federico. *Vasconia*. Pamplona: HerritarBerri, 2006.

Kymlicka, Will. *Politics in the Vernacular: Nationalism, Multiculturalism, and Citizenship.* New York: Oxford University Press, 2001.

Kymlicka, Will. "Multicultural Citizenship within Multination States." *Ethnicities* 11, no. 3 (September 2011): 281–302.

Laitin, David. "National Identities in the Emerging European State," in *Minority Nationalism and the Changing International Order*, eds. Michael Keating and John McGarry (Oxford, UK: Oxford University Press, 2001).

Les Verts. Langues et cultures des diffe´rents peuple de France: Verts et autonomistes agironsen concert. Verts Europe 32 (1991): 1–36.

Lijphart, Arend. *Democracies: Patterns of Majoritarian and Consensus Government in Twenty-One Countries.* New Haven: Yale University Press, 1984.

Lijphart, Arend. "Consociational Democracy," *World Politics* 21, no. 2 (1969): 207-275.

Louette, Jean-François. Drieu La Rochelle: Romans, récits, nouvelles (Édition sous la direction de Jean-François Louette avec la collaboration de Hélène Baty-Delalande, Julien Hervier, Nathalie Piégay-Gros). *Bibliothèque de la Pléiade* 578, 20 April (2012).

Lynch, Peter. *Minority Nationalism and European Integration.* Cardiff: University of Wales Press, 1996.

Margalit, Avishai, and Moshe Halbertal. "Liberalism and the Right to Culture," *Social Research* 71, no. 3 (Fall) (2004): 529–548.

McCormick, Neil. *Questioning Sovereignty: Law, State and Nation in the European Commonwealth.* Oxford: Oxford University Press, 1999.

McGarry, John. "'Orphans of Secession': National Pluralism in Secessionist Regions and Post-Secessionist States." In *National Self-Determination and Secession,* edited by Margaret Moore. New York: Oxford University Press, 1998.

McGarry, John, and Brendan O'Leary. "Iraq's Constitution of 2005: Liberal Consociation as Political Prescription," *International Journal of Constitutional Law* 5 (2007): 670–698.

McGarry, John, and Brendan O'Leary. "Consociational Theory, Northern Ireland's Conflict, and its Agreement. Part 1: What Consociationalists Can Learn from Northern Ireland," *Government and Opposition* 41, no. 1 (2006): 43.

Miller, David. *Market State and Community: The Foundations of Market Socialism.* Oxford: Oxford University Press, 1989.

Miglio, G. "Per una Italia federale," *Mondo Economico No. 20* (1990).

Moynihan, Daniel P. *Pandaemonium: Ethnicity in International Politics*. London: Oxford University Press, 1993.

Newhouse, John. "Europe's Rising Regionalism," *Foreign Affairs* 76, no. 1 (1997): 67–84.

Patten, Alan. "Rethinking Culture: The Social Lineage Account," *American Political Science Review* 105 (November 2011): 744.

Requejo, Ferran, and Marc Sanjaume-Calvet. "Independence Referendums: Catalunya in Perspective," *Catalan Social Sciences Review* 9 (2019): 1–18.

Salle, D. "The Quebec State and the Management of Ethnocultural Diversity: Perspectives on an Ambiguous Record." In *The Art of the State-III: Belonging? Diversity, Recognition and Shared Citizenship in Canada,* edited by Keith Banting, Thomas J. Courchene, and F. Leslie Seidle. Montreal: Institute for Research on Public Policy (2007).

Shafir, Gershon. "Relative overdevelopment and alternative paths of nationalism: a comparative study of Catalunya and the Baltic republics," *Journal of Baltic Studies*, vol. 23, no. 2, 1992.

Spektorowski, Alberto. "The French New Right: Multiculturalism of the Right and the Recognition/Exclusionism Syndrome," *Journal of Global Ethics* 8, no. 1 (April 2012): 41–61.

Talbott, Strove. "Self-Determination in an Interdependent World" *Foreign Policy* No. 118 (Spring 2000): 152–163.

Tamir, Yael. *Liberal Nationalism*. Princeton, NJ: Princeton University Press, 1992.

Tamir, Yael. *Why Nationalism*. Princeton, NJ: Princeton University Press, 2019.

Taylor, Charles. "The Politics of Recognition." In *Multiculturalism: Examining the Politics of Recognition*, edited by Amy Gutmann. Princeton, NJ: Princeton University Press, 1994.

Van Kessel, S. *Populist Parties in Europe: Agents of Discontent?* Basingstoke: Palgrave Macmillan, 2015.

Vial, P. *Dix Ans de Combat Culturel pour une Renaissance*. Paris: GRECE, 1977.

Walzer, Michael. *Spheres of Justice: A Defense of Pluralism and Equality*. New York: Basic Books, 1983.

Weitz, Eric D. "Self-Determination. How a German Enlightenment Idea Became the Slogan of National Liberation and Human Right" *The American Historical Review*, vol. 120, no. 2 (April 2015), 462–496.

Wind, Marlene. *The Tribalization of Europe: A Defense of Liberal Values*. Cambridge: Polity, 2020.

Yack, Bernard. *Nationalism and the Moral Psychology of Community*. Chicago: University of Chicago Press, 2012.

# 2

# Scottish Devolution and Basque Historical Rights:

## Toward Self-Determination & Cosovereignty

*Xabier Ezeizabarrena*

### Foreword

The legal and political process of devolution within the UK-Scottish relations contains similarities and the potential of remarkable comparative interest with the constitutional clauses of recognition of Basque historical rights or titles within the Spanish Constitution. Nowadays, the EU framework is suitable in both cases to ease and foster this interest within a background of progressive cosovereignty at the EU, particularly if we consider the open will of the Basque Country and Scotland to maintain and foster EU membership.

For the British case, the devolution process could be easily considered as the most recent of key moments in British "constitutional" history according to Wicks. This author has selected eight "key moments" as follows: the 1688 "glorious revolution," the 1707 Union of England and Scotland, Walpole's long tenure (1721-1742) as the first prime minister, the 1832 reform of Parliament, the Parliament Act 1911, the European Convention on Human Rights, the UK's accession to the European Communities, and the aforementioned devolution legislation of 1998.[1]

In 1976, Meadows stated the necessity to turn to the question of why devolution has become a political issue at this time. In general terms, the essence of the controversy is reflected in his following statement:

> Devolution! The very word contains a threat. The English pronounce it to rhyme with evolution, the Scots with revolution.[2]

However, authors like Bogdanor and Vogenauer recall the words of Dicey in his "Law of the Constitution," who underscored that:

> a British writer on the Constitution has good reason to envy professors who belong to countries such as France . . . or the United States, endowed with constitutions on which the terms are to be found in printed documents, known to all citizens and accessible to every man who is able to read. Britain remains, together with New Zealand and Israel, one of just three democracies which are still not "endowed" with a "written," or, more properly, a codified constitution.[3]

Nevertheless, written or codified, the principle of British parliamentary sovereignty:

> is no longer an unchallenged doctrine [. . .] and it is because there is scepticism concerning the value of the doctrine that voices have been heard calling for an enacted constitution. An enacted constitution would, however, have to confront at the outset the problem of whether or not the European Communities Act has limited the sovereignty of Parliament, and whether the practical limitation of sovereignty by the Human Rights Act and the devolution legislation should be registered in the Constitution. An enacted constitution would have to confront squarely the doctrine of the sovereignty of Parliament. We have been asked whether the enactment of a British constitution is feasible. Our answer is that there is no reason why it should not be feasible, no reason why, almost alone amongst democracies, Britain should be unable to enact a constitution. The problems involved in this enterprise are, however, formidable.[4]

In addition to the legal approach within the paper, there is also a different political consideration in the two situations. A nationalist party is ruling Scotland within the devolution process. Moreover, the 2011 elections in Scotland implied a clearer commitment toward a formal referendum on the independence of Scotland within the EU, considering the large absolute majority of the Scottish National Party with sixty-nine seats in the Scottish Parliament.

Meanwhile, the proposal designed by the former Basque government and parliament (approved by the Basque Parliament, December 2004) advocates direct participation by the Basque Country and Navarre in the EU,[5] not in independent terms, but in coordination with other Spanish interests and based upon the EU and constitutional principles of solidarity.[6] This would mean participation of the Basque Country and Navarre within the Committees of the Commission, and within the Council of Ministers as well as in the different working groups. These are examples of bodies with powers in the enactment of future treaties,[7] and in my view, a real example of a new path toward cosovereignty as stated within the proposal for a new Political Statute for the Basque Country approved by the Basque Parliament (PSBC).[8]

All these considerations are preliminary to the content of this study with a relatively brief approach between the devolution process in Scotland and the Basque case.

Therefore, it is important to analyze some data regarding the historical rights in the different territorial contexts of Euskal Herria (The Basque Land).[9] That is a legal constitutional framework which rules the main part of the public law relationship of the Basque territories with Spain—for example, the domestic structure of the Basque territories and their particularities vis-à-vis the common Spanish provinces.[10] If in the Basque case we are dealing with a constitutional provision (First Additional Clause of the Spanish Constitution), the Scottish case is based upon the idea of devolution—not necessarily written—but within the context of full historical national recognition of the Scottish nation.

According to Bengoetxea (2010), from the Basque viewpoint, the interest of the Scottish process is not new.[11] In his approach, it seems clear that Scotland is leading the path toward a higher degree of self-government within a general acceptance of it by the British establishment. In that sense, he underscores three advantages for the case of the UK, such as a strong democratic tradition, the absence of a written constitution and, therefore, the sovereignty of parliaments according to their own powers, together with an independent judiciary that normally avoids interfering in politics.

Bengoetxea (2010) recognizes two constitutional processes that may join together in the future. One refers to the National Conversation launched by the Scottish National Party (SNP), while the other relies on the report of the Calman Commission created by the Scottish Parliament without the participation of the SNP. The National Conversation implies a constitutional process for permanent consultation with Scottish society. And, thereby, Bengoetxea (2010) recognizes three different options:

1. To maintain the current process of devolution;
2. To increase Scottish self-government with new powers and, in particular, with financial and tax autonomy; and
3. To decide on independence, but sharing the sovereignty of the British Crown, the Sterling Pound, and the Commonwealth.

This third option is the one claimed by the SNP and the Scottish government, and it is the so-called "Independence in the EU." Meanwhile, the Calman

Commission delivered its report in June 2009 underscoring the necessity of a whole new tax and financial public system. In my view, there are two main legal backgrounds within the Scottish proposal and 2014 referendum:

1. The recognition of Scotland as a nation.
2. The example of Quebec.

Regarding the first item, there is a claim for the recognition of the right to self-determination based on the previous existence of Scotland as a nation. With regard to the example of Quebec, there are the principles and rules stated by the Supreme Court of Canada on the case of Quebec (Consultative Opinion, 8-20-1998). In both cases, there is a key role of concepts like negotiation, agreement, or treaty (1707) and referendum within the context of new or post-sovereignty, according to the ideas of Scottish academics such as Neil MacCormick or Michael Keating.

The proposal of the Scottish government is useful and remarkable in four main respects:

- The concept of democracy: because it is based on the principle of self-determination internationally recognized;
- The concept of "constitution": therefore, despite the absence of a written UK constitution, there is a mutual recognition of nations as stated and assumed by the 1707 Treaty;
- The social participation: due to the fact that the process is open to the whole society;
- The EU integration process: recognizing the clear will of participation within the EU structure according to the EU Treaties. This is indeed relevant concerning a potential new Scottish referendum due to the clear will of Scottish society to stay in the EU, and considering the English process for a Brexit in force.

This process toward the sovereignty of Scotland is clearly committed to the rules of democracy. In fact, one of its main characteristics is the acceptance by both parties of the core part of their nonwritten "constitutions": human rights and democratic principles. It is also important to underscore that a clear voice of the Scottish society would imply certain effects on close or similar situations throughout the EU; and, likewise, for the cases of Catalunya and the Basque Country. In Spain, for example, the approach of the Spanish government and the Constitutional Court made it unconstitutional for the Basque Parliament Act to call for a consultative referendum in 2008[12] as well as for Catalan efforts since 2012, even under very doubtful criminal proceedings against the Catalan government and its members. Therefore, what seems void in Spain, under the rules of a modern and written constitution, is perfectly viable without a written constitution and under precolonial rules. In my view, it seems to be a question of democratic culture and state vision from an old democracy like the one ruling for centuries in Great Britain.

### Note on Basque History

The singular nature of the "foral" (particular)[13] Basque regime has been always present within any historical analysis of our constitutional and legal background.[14] There is, in fact, a curious and relevant observation made by Loperena (1988)[15] regarding the very similar terms of the First Additional Clause of the Spanish Constitution (1978) and the Act of 10-25-1839.[16] If the Act of 10-25-1839 confirms the Basque and Navarre "Fueros" (Rights) through a common system, the First Additional Clause of the Constitution confirms and also respects the historical rights of the aforementioned territories.[17] This is relevant for a contemporary and practical interpretation of the perspectives arising from the concept of historical rights.[18, 19] We might be facing one of the most important paradoxical issues within Spanish constitutionalism.[20] In my view, the historical rights of the Basque Country constitute the logical path from the historic concept of "Fueros" to the constitutional integration of certain territories that maintained a voluntary, uninterrupted political and public will of political identity.[21] That is also very clearly seen in the case of Scotland.

The common background for both cases is the nature of agreement between two parties throughout history,[22] in Scotland since 1707.[23] Another interesting common consideration recognizes that situation from the state and EU perspectives. Herrero de Miñon (1987) has brilliantly demonstrated possible regimes for integration of the Basque historical rights within constitutional reality.[24] The words of Nieto Arizmendiarrieta (1999) are also clear in this regard.[25] My aim in the following pages is to mention, at least briefly, some of the possibilities of this singular legal institution at a domestic level, in order to go further into its particular integration in the EU. Therefore, the Basque and the Scottish examples are relevant in terms of identity, history, and recognition of public law toward cosovereignty or eventually sovereignty.

### A New Concept of Sovereignty

The Basque Proposal for a new Political Statute and the Scottish process led by the government of Scotland do have certain common grounds.

The legal and political structure of a state is not eternal.[26] Nowadays, the undeniable requirement of any democracy is the assumption and protection of human rights and democratic principles. A remarkable approach to these questions was the Proposal for a Political Statute for the Basque Country (PSBC) approved by the Basque Parliament (12-30-2004) but rejected afterward by the Spanish Parliament without any previous negotiation (February 2005).[27] Sharing sovereignty, democratic principles, and human rights were the essence of the PSBC.[28] In my opinion, the rest of the usual issues pending could perfectly become the subject of negotiation in any democratic system. In this regard, this was also the consideration made by the Supreme Court of Canada in 1998 regarding the case of Quebec.[29]

History in the British case and historical rights within the Spanish Constitution in the Basque case are suitable to push forward the proposal of sharing sovereignty, or even claiming for self-determination, within the context of protection and fulfillment of international human rights and within the EU. The "constitutional" background of written or customary historical rights is present in both cases despite important details of difference, to be the subject of mutual negotiation—inter alia, the basic elements of public constitutional law: organization, territory, and population. The political or legal approach to both cases must take into consideration the EU framework as a new relevant context of sovereignty or even post-sovereignty, according to the studies of MacCormick[30] or Keating.[31] These common main grounds are present in Scotland within the devolution process, particularly through the 1998 Scotland Act and notwithstanding the referendum proposed by the government of Scotland. Moreover, even within the context of the 1707 Act or Treaty of Union between England and Scotland, the Scottish nation maintained particular institutions and bodies, such as the judiciary, education, universities, the Presbyterian Church and its systems of civil and criminal law,[32] which weree based on Roman law but influenced as well by common law. In this regard, the legislative projects concerning Scotland have been historically considered and analyzed mainly by members of the Parliament coming from Scotland. Nevertheless, and even within the devolution process, the system adopted is clearly limited and under the control of Westminster. Actually, there is an essential principle of British constitutional law stating that Westminster Parliament is sovereign. No institution or body can abolish an act except the same Parliament, and this is the relevant one to intervene in any matter whatsoever. Hence, Article 28 of the 1998 Scotland Act assumed the competence of the Scottish Parliament to approve acts, while also stating the competence of the British Parliament to approve acts for Scotland.

### Basque Historical Titles at the EU[33]

The First Additional Clause of the Spanish Constitution states:

> La Constitución ampara y respeta los derechos históricos de los territorios forales. La actualización general de dicho régimen foral se llevará a cabo, en su caso, en el marco de la Constitución y de los Estatutos de Autonomía.[34]

According to the studies made by Herrero de Miñon and Fernandez (1998 and 1985), the Basque historical rights are more than a mere accumulation of competencies. They do represent a legal and political concept, previous to the current constitutional reality in Spain, which is also a common ground with Scotland. Historical rights cannot be derogated or deleted through any unilateral decision.[35] Cosovereignty is also present in this approach. Moreover, following the studies of Herrero de Miñon (1998), these titles are a constitutional recognition of the right of the Basque Country to self-determination in terms of a possible voluntary integration or a demand for a different political status.[36]

J. Cruz Alli (former president of Navarre), during his speech within the debate at the Spanish Senate on the General Commission of Autonomous Communities (1994), warned the Senate and the Spanish premier of the possible consequences arising from a breach of those agreements by the actions of the Spanish government, namely, against the common constitutional ground of the historical rights of the Basque Country and Navarre.[37] In this regard, the EU system is becoming gradually an institutionalized body, made up of the different member States' schemes moving toward integration. To get this into focus, we can use the institution of human rights as an example. There is a principle of mutual trust for the protection of human rights at member states. In fact, this is a core matter in our legal constitutional systems, so we might need a similar principle of mutual trust to recognize and assume the participation of nations like Scotland or the Basque Country within the EU. That would be, in particular, the case of entities with powers of legislation or that even are entitled with collective historical rights. These nations, therefore, do enjoy a material content of their competencies together with the relevant procedures for updating those competencies.[38] Thus, human rights represent a relevant part of the EU tradition with, at least, three sources of recognition and monitoring of human rights:

- EU law with the aforementioned limits.
- International law, particularly through the case law of the European Court of Human Rights.
- The domestic law of each member state.

This may serve as well to adopt similar approaches in cases where the historical rights of sub-state entities might be lacking in protection. This failure might also be considered as a breach of EU law. In fact, from the historic distance between the Spanish Constitutional Court and the Court of Justice of the European Union (CJEU), we are facing nowadays a mutual situation of linkages among human rights and the case law of both courts.

Therefore, in order to protect human rights, the domestic regime at the EU level is extremely important. Hence, the European bodies, member States and, eventually, the CJEU should also take up the challenge to define the extent to which Basque historical rights should be considered before the EU. In a word, to find those common grounds and limits would be a task of the CJEU, whose opinions would undoubtedly follow the grounds supported by the Spanish Constitutional Court, in direct enforcement of Article 10.2 of the Spanish Constitution.[39]

This conclusion may suggest to us some considerations in order to interpret the figure of Basque historical titles in relation to the EU system:

1. The CJEU made clear that European law has direct and prior enforcement effects. This means that any damage or impact caused by a member state to citizens and in breach of EU law will produce a liability to be assumed by the relevant member state in breach of EU law.
2. To enforce compliance with the aforementioned, the domestic courts do have a leading role—expressed at its highest level via Constitutional Courts or similar figures—in the constitutional monitoring of violations, together with the implementation of EU law. That is the task of domestic jurisdictions (i.e., the Spanish Constitutional Court, for the cases of human rights and Basque historical rights).[40]

However, the current reality does not provide real protection for those historical rights within the EU. This is due to a lack of political will at the Spanish domestic level. Meanwhile, some positive examples are represented by the cases of Germany, Belgium, and Austria and their sub-state regulations before the EU bodies to foster direct participation.

The implementation at the European level of the constitutional reality within every social, territorial, and legal scope is a key point to ease the distinction between these sub-state complexities that are not defined under the general concept of "regions." Domestic realities with a constitutional recognition within member states require a peculiar basis in order to implement their constitutional scope and singular approach. These are the case for entities with legislative powers, such as the Basque Country and Scotland, in accordance with their written or customary historical titles and entitled with some significant competencies.[41]

These ideas are alive nowadays, fifty years after the first Basque premier died in Paris. The deep Europeanism of José Antonio de Agirre Lekube is present throughout his thoughts and writings. Many of the thoughts and proposals in the EU were foreseen by Agirre Lekube as a pioneer statesman since the forties.[42] Moreover, Agirre Lekube made a clear forecast on the necessity of Europe underscoring the protection of human rights as a limit of any modern political system. In 1944, he wrote that:

> la garantía de los pueblos, principalmente de los pequeños, reside precisamente en estas más amplias estructuras supraestatales.

Only a year later, in his book, *Inglaterra y los Vascos,* Irujo recalls Saint Luis: "todas las libertades son solidarias." Therefore, Europe must be a space of civil rights and freedom. And following the thoughts of Aguirre, the Basque Country played and plays a key role throughout our historical rights, as a real exercise of sovereignty to be updated toward the EU.

Nowadays, Germany, Belgium, and Austria have constitutionally recognized sub-state participation at the EU. That is remarkable in those countries because the subsidiarity principle should become a requirement for the state/sub-state relationships at all levels. That would also imply a sense of respect for the national identities of the member states, which are in many cases plurinational, as quoted by Agirre Lekube. Meanwhile, the UK leaving the EU is becoming useful to reopen the debate of Scottish independence and eventual membership in the EU.

There are also substate proposals to ease the presence of one of its representatives within the state delegations negotiating regulations and treaties. In fact, that is the path followed by Germany, Belgium, and Austria, with representatives from the different regions of Länder, Wallonia, or Flanders. Within the Spanish context, historical rights legitimates similar possibilities for the Basque Country.[43] In my view, the example of historical rights is very useful to reconcile these approaches and to update the Europeanism of Agirre Lekube to the requirements of the present time.

### Some Pending Challenges

The Basque historical titles have been unable to present their peculiarities at the EU level, while some other sub-state entities are arranging useful frameworks and agreements within their member states. In the case of Euskal Herria, their respective scopes of competencies have been several times disregarded by the EU. Even though many authors assume the federal approach of the EU Treaties, that consideration is not easily seen from the viewpoint of the historical rights analyzed in this brief chapter.

The principle of respect for the national identities of the member states (Article 6 of the EU Treaty)[44] is a useful tool for granting the legitimacy of the Spanish constitutional agreement on historical rights in terms of a real path toward cosovereignty between Spain and the Basque territories. A similar theoretical approach would be useful for the Scottish case within the context of devolution of powers or customary "historical rights." A new referendum in Scotland may imply a step forward on the abolishment of the 1707 Act or Treaty of Union within a real exercise of self-determination, including EU membership for Scotland.

The so-called "useful constitutionalism," using the terms of Herrero de Miñon (2000) and Lluch (2000)[45] for Spain, requires an implementation of this question at the EU, and that is clearly—but only formally—granted by the Spanish Constitution.[46] Herrero de Miñon (2000) reaffirms his support for this proposal.[47] A similar approach is followed by Alli (2000), who suggested linkages to connect with the EU integration process.[48]

A new Proposal for a Political Statute to be approved by the Basque Parliament, assuming the right to self-determination through historical titles and bilateral negotiation,[49] could become a unique opportunity to resolve the situation of the Basque territories within the Spanish Constitution and, in particular, so far as the EU is concerned. The Scottish proposal led by the SNP will have an important test in terms of a new referendum on independence and EU membership.

## Bibliography

Alli, Juan Cruz. "Paz y Fueros. Los Derechos Históricos Como Instrumentos de Pacificación." In *Derechos Históricos y Constitucionalismo Útil.* Bilbao: Fundación BBV, 2000.

Alli, Juan Cruz. *La Cooperación Entre la C. A. del País Vasco y la Comunidad Foral de Navarra.* Donostia-San Sebastián: Fundación para el Estudio del Derecho Histórico de Vasconia, 2004.

Arrieta, Jon. "Las 'Imágenes' de los Derechos Históricos: Un Estado de la Cuestión." In *Derechos Históricos y Constitucionalismo Útil.* Bilbao: Fundación BBV, 2000.

Arrieta, Jon. "El 1707 Español y el Británico." In *Conciliar la Diversidad. Pasado y Presente de la Vertebración de España,* edited by Jon Arrieta and ASTIGARRAGA. The University of the Basque Country, 2009.

Bengoetxea, Joxerramon. "El Futuro de Euskadi y el Futuro de Europa. ¿Quién Tiene Miedo de Europa?" In *Jornadas de Estudio sobre la Propuesta Política para la convivencia del Lehendakari Ibarretxe.* Oñati: IVAP, 2003.

Bengoetxea, Joxerramon. *La Europa Peter Pan. El Constitucionalismo Europeo en la Encrucijada.* Oñati: IVAP, 2005.

Bogdanor, Vernon. *Devolution.* Oxford: Oxford University Press, 1979.

Bogdanor, Vernon. "Federalism and the Nature of the European Union." In *Whose Europe? National Models and the Constitution of the European Union,* edited by Kalypso Nicolaidis and Stephen Weatherill. Oxford: Oxford University Press, 2003.

Bogdanor, Vernon, and Stefan Vogenauer. "Enacting a British Constitution: Some Problems," *Public Law,* 2008.

Ezeizabarrena, Xabier. "Brief Notes on the Historical Rights of the Basque Country and Navarre with Regard to Community Law." *Ius Fori. Revista de la Facultad de Derecho de la Universidad del País Vasco,* no. 1 (1999).

Ezeizabarrena, Xabier. "Derechos Históricos y Derecho Comunitario ante la Propuesta del Lehendakari." In *Jornadas de Estudio sobre la Propuesta Política para la convivencia del Lehendakari Ibarretxe.* Oñati: IVAP, 2003.

Ezeizabarrena, Xabier. *Los Derechos Históricos de Euskadi y Navarra ante el Derecho Comunitario.* Donostia-San Sebastián: Eusko Ikaskuntza, 2003.

Ezeizabarrena, Xabier. "Europe & Co-sovereignty." *Oxford Magazine,* no. 226 (2004).

Ezeizabarrena, Xabier. *La Ciaboga Infinita. Una Visión Política y Jurídica del Conflicto Vasco.* Irun: Alberdania, 2005.

Ezeizabarrena, Xabier. "La Articulación del Federalismo Vasco en la UE y en las Relaciones Internacionales. Euskadi y Navarra ante la UE y las Relaciones Internacionales en la Ley 25/2014, de Tratados y otros Acuerdos Internacionales." *Europa de las Regiones y el futuro federal de Europa: Balance y perspectivas de la gobernanza multinivel de la UE,* Eurobasque, Dykinson, 2019.

Fernández, Tomas Ramon. *Los Derechos Históricos de los territorios forales.* Madrid: Civitas, 1985.

Feldman, David. "None, One or Several? Perspectives on the UK's Constitution(s)." Cambridge Law Journal, 64.2. (2005).

Gagnon, Alain. *Québec y el Federalismo Canadiense.* Madrid: CSIC, 1998.

García Ureta, Agustin. "La Transferencia de Poderes a las Regiones en el Reino Unido: el Caso de Escocia." *Revista Vasca de Administración Pública,* no. 55 (1999).

Herrero de Miñón, Miguel. "La Titularidad de los Derechos Históricos Vascos." *Revista de Estudios Políticos,* no. 58 (1987).

Herrero de Miñón, Miguel, and Ernest Lluch. "Constitucionalismo Útil." In *Derechos Históricos y Constitucionalismo Útil.* Bilbao: Fundación BBVA, 2000.

Herrero de Miñón, Miguel. "Autodeterminación y Derechos Históricos." In *Derechos Históricos y Constitucionalismo Útil.* Bilbao: Fundación BBVA, 2000.

Herrero de Miñón, Miguel. *Derechos Históricos y Constitución.* Madrid: Taurus, 2000.

Herrero de Miñón, Miguel. *El Valor de la Constitución.* Barcelona: Crítica, 2003.

Herrero de Miñón, Miguel. "España y Vasconia: Presente y Futuro (Consideraciones en Torno al Plan Ibarretxe)." *In Jornadas de Estudio Sobre la Propuesta Política para la Convivencia del Lehendakari Ibarretxe.* Oñati: IVAP, 2003.

Herrero de Miñón, Miguel. 2003. "El pacto con la Corona ¿ocasión perdida u opción abierta?" Un Homenaje al Profesor DE. Pablo Lucas Verdú (Estudios de Deusto, vol. 51/1 enero-junio 2003). Bilbao: Universidad de Deusto.

Herrero de Miñón, Miguel. *Constitución Española y Constitución Europea.* Madrid: Instituto de España, 2004.

Irujo, Manuel. *Inglaterra y los vascos.* Ekin, Buenos Aires, 1944.

Keating, Michael. "Self-Determination, Multinational States and the Transnational Order." In *The Implementation of the Right to Self-determination as a Contribution to Conflict Resolution.* Edited by Michael Van Der Walt Van Praage and Onno Seroo. Barcelona: UNESCO Catalunya, 1998.

Keating, Michael. "Reforging the Union: Devolution and Constitutional Change in the United Kingdom." *The Journal of Federalism,* 28.1 (1998).

Keating, Michael. "The Minority Nations of Spain and European Integration. A new framework for autonomy?" *Spanish Cultural Studies,* 1.1 (2000).

Keating, Michael. "So Many Nations, So Few States: Accommodating Minority Nationalism." In *The Global Era,* in A. Gagnon and J. Tully (eds), *Struggles for Recognition in Multinational Societies.* Cambridge: Cambridge University Press, 2001.

Keating, Michael. "Nations Without States: Minority Nationalism in the Global Era." In *Democracy and National Pluralism.* Edited by Ferran Requejo. London: Routledge, 2001.

Keating, Michael. "Europe's Changing Political Landscape: Territorial Restructuring and New Forms of Government." In *Convergence and Divergence in European Public Law.* Edited by Paul Beaumont, Carole Lyons, and Neil Walker. Oxford: Hart, 2002.

Keating, Michael. "Plurinational Democracy and the European Order." In *Jornadas de Estudio Sobre la Propuesta Política para la Convivencia del Lehendakari Ibarretxe.* Oñati: IVAP, 2003.

Keating, Michael. *The Independence of Scotland.* Oxford: Oxford University Press, 2009.

Locke, John. 1690. *Segundo tratado sobre el gobierno civil.* Madrid: Alianza Editorial, 1994.

Loughlin, John. "The Regional Question, Subsidiarity and the Future of Europe." In *Whose Europe? National Models and the Constitution of the European Union.* Edited by Kalypso Nicolaidis and Stephen Weatherill. Oxford: Oxford University Press, 2003.

Loperena, Demetrio. 2003. "Navarra y el nacionalismo compatible." In *Jornadas de Estudio Sobre la Propuesta Política para la Convivencia del Lehendakari Ibarretxe.* Oñati: IVAP, 2003.

MacCormick, Neil. *Questioning Sovereignty. Law, State and Nation in the European Commonwealth.* Oxford: Oxford University Press, 2002.

MacLean, Ian, and Alistair McMillan. *State of the Union.* Oxford: Oxford University Press, 2005.

MacKillop, Andrew, and Michael O'Siochru. *Forging the State: European State Formation and the Anglo-Scottish Union of 1707.* Dundee: Dundee University Press, 2008.

Mance, Lord. "Constitutional Reforms, the Supreme Court and the Law Lords." *Civil Justice Quarterly* 25 (2006).

Meadows, Martin. "Constitutional Crisis in the United Kingdom: Scotland and the Devolution Controversy." *The Review of Politics* 39, no. 1 (January 1977).

Mees, Ludger. *El profeta pragmático.* Alberdania, 2006.

Monreal, Gregorio. "La base foral del Plan del Lehendakari Ibarretxe." In *Jornadas de Estudio Sobre la Propuesta Política para la Convivencia del Lehendakari Ibarretxe.* Oñati: IVAP, 2003.

Nieto Arizmendiarrieta, Eduardo. "Reflexiones Sobre el Concepto de Derechos Históricos." *Revista Vasca de Administración Pública* 54 (1999).

Nicolaidis, Kalypso, and Stephen Weatherill. *Whose Europe? National Models and the Constitution of the European Union.* Oxford: Oxford University Press, 2003.

Reid, Stuart, and Janice Edwards. "The Scottish Legal System." *Legal Information Management* 9, no. 1 (2009).

Rousseau, Jean Jacques. 1762. *Del contrato social.* Madrid: Alianza Editorial, 1991.

Ross, A., and M. Salvador. "The Effect of Devolution on the Implementation of EC law in Spain and the UK." *European Law Review* 28, no. 2 (2003).

Scottish Government, 2007. "Choosing Scotland's Future. A National Conversation."

Tamayo, Virginia. *La Autonomía Vasca Contemporánea: Foralidad y estatutismo 1975-1979.* Oñati: IVAP, 1994.

Tierney, Stephen. "Reframing Sovereignty? Sub-State National Societies and Contemporary Challenges to the Nation State." *International & Comparative Law Quarterly* 54, no.1 (2005).

Tierney, Stephen. *Constitutional Law and National Pluralism.* 2006.

Tierney, Stephen. "Giving with One Hand: Scottish Devolution Within a Unitary State." *International Journal of Constitutional Law* 5 (2007): 730-753.

Urzainqui, Tomas, and Juan M. Olaizola. *La Navarra Marítima.* Pamplona: Pamiela, 1998.

Urzainqui, Tomas. *Recuperación del Estado Propio.* Pamplona: Nabarralde, 2002.

Urzainqui, Tomas. *Navarra sin Fronteras Impuestas.* Pamplona: Nabarralde, 2002.

Urzainqui, Tomas. *Navarra Estado Europeo.* Pamiela: Pamplona, 2004.

VV.AA. 2005. Derechos Históricos y co-soberanía en la UE. Donostia-San Sebastián: St. Antony's College Oxford-Sociedad de Estudios Vascos-Diputación Foral de Gipuzkoa.

VV.AA. 2008. "Sub-State entibies and co-sovereignty within the EU," RIEV Cuadernos 3, Xabier Ezeizabarrena and Jeremy MacClancy eds., Eusko Ikaskuntza.

Weatherill, Stephen, and Ulf Bernitz. *The Role of Regions and Sub-National Actors in Europe.* Oxford: Hart, 2007.

Whatley, Christopher A. *The Scots and the Union.* Edinburgh: Edinburgh University Press, 2006.

Wicks, Elizabeth. *The Evolution of a Constitution: Eight Key Moments in British Constitutional History.* London: Bloomsbury Academic Press, 2006.

Woehrling, José. "The Quebec Secession Reference: Pitfalls Ahead for the Federal Government." *Canada Watch,* no. 6 (October 1997).

Woehrling, José. "El Juicio del Tribunal Supremo de Canadá Sobre la Eventual Secesión de Québec." *Revista Vasca de Administración Pública,* no. 54 (1999): 405-436.

Woehrling, José. "The Supreme Court's Ruling on Quebec's Secession: Legality and Legitimacy Reconciled by a Return to Constitutional First Principles." In *Political Dispute and Judicial Review.* Edited by Hugh Mellon and Martin Westmacott. Scarborough: Nelson, 2000.

## NOTES

1 Elizabeth Wicks, *The Evolution of a Constitution: Eight Key Moments in British Constitutional History.* London: Bloomsbury Academic Press, 2006.

2 Martin Meadows, "Constitutional Crisis in the United Kingdom: Scotland and the Devolution Controversy," *The Review of Politics* 39, no. 1 (January 1997): 42-43. Moreover,

in my view, with the concept of recovering and updating sovereignty for Scotland through historical rights or titles.

3 Vernon Bogdanor and Stefan Vogenauer, "Enacting a British Constitution: Some Problems," *Public Law* (2008): 38.

4 Bogdanor and Vogenauer, "Enacting a British Constitution," 56.

5 Relations with Navarre and the Basque provinces within the French territory (Lapurdi, Basse Navarre, and Zuberoa) are also reflected by the Proposal for a new *Basque Statute* (PSBC) in articles 6 and 7. This is a direct implication arising from the recognition of Basque historical titles in the First Additional clause of the Constitution.

6 In the same sense, we have the opinion of Murillo de la Cueva, Enrique. 2000. Comunidades Autónomas y política europea, IVAP-Civitas, 133, 143, and 146. This author argues for a new implementation of autonomic participation based on the criteria of exclusive competencies related to interests affected by EU decisions.

7 See Murillo de la Cueva, Enrique. 2000. Comunidades Autónomas y política europea, IVAP-Civitas, 123 and 124.

8 Plenary session of 12-30-2004. Proposal rejected by the Spanish Parliament (February 2005).

9 Preface and articles 1 and 2 of the PSBC.

10 This is the point of view of many previous authors. Among them, T. R. Fernandez, 1985, in his work Los Derechos Históricos de los territorios forales, Madrid, as a true and fair view of the whole process.

11 Bengoetxea, Joxerramon. 2010. "Escocia: enseñanzas para el País Vasco," *El Diario Vasco,* 12-3.

12 Spanish Constitutional Court Judgment 103/2008 (STC 103/2008).

13 And, in that sense, based on historical rights within the constitution.

14 An important historic landmark was set by Antoine D'Abbadie, according to the studies made by Gregorio Monreal, in his interesting work "El ideario jurídico de Antoine d'Abbadie," *Euskonews & Media* no. 16, http://www.euskonews.com.

15 Loperena, Demetrio. 1988. "Derecho histórico y régimen local de Navarra." Pamplona: Gobierno de Navarra, 37.

16 Act of October 25, 1839:

"Artículo 1º. Se confirman los Fueros de las provincias Vascongadas y de Navarra sin perjuicio de la unidad Constitucional de la Monarquía.

Art. 2º. "El Gobierno tan pronto como la oportunidad lo permita, y oyendo antes a las provincias Vascongadas y a Navarra, propondrá a las Cortes la modificación indispensable que en los mencionados fueros reclame el interés general de las mismas, conciliándolo con el general de la Nación y de la Constitución de la Monarquía, resolviendo entretanto provisionalmente, y en la forma y sentido expresados, las dudas y dificultades que puedan ofrecerse, dando de ello cuenta a las Cortes."

17 Loperena, Demetrio. 1988. "Derecho histórico y régimen local de Navarra," op. cit., 37.

18 This is a concept that, in the French Basque Country, within a different perspective and without any constitutional clause, is also present in the words of Maite Lafourcade, with regard to the peculiar identity of the French-Basque territories ("Iparralde" in Basque). See her work, "Iparralde ou les provinces du Pays Basque nord sous l'ancien régime," Euskonews & Media no. 3, http://www.euskonews.com.

19 The act to "confirm the 'fueros,'" of October 25, 1839, was considered by a sector of Basque nationalism as an abolition ruling, even though its sense and aims were simply to adapt the particular regimes of the Basque territories to the new constitution.

20 An interesting example of this was quoted by Virginia Tamayo in her work *La Autonomía Vasca Contemporánea: Foralidad y estatutismo 1975-1979* (Oñati: IVAP, 1994), 617. The author recalls a relevant event from our "foral" and constitutional history, during the debate in the Spanish Parliament on the First Additional Clause of the Constitution, about the Basque historical rights. At that time, the representatives of the Spanish Socialist Party (PSOE) refused to concede more recognition of the historical rights of the Basque territories.

21 This is the core idea of the First Additional Clause of the Constitution and the PSBC.

22 Authors like Tomas Urzainqui clearly disagree with the idea of bilateral agreement, whereas they consider evident that the Basque territories were conquered through military and violent means at different moments of history. See his historical and legal works clarifying the identity of Navarre as the Historical Basque State, while "Euskal Herria" represents its cultural global identity, mainly through language. In other words, both are the same body with different titles:

Tomas Urzainqui and Juan M. Olaizola, *La Navarra Marítima* (Pamplona: Pamiela, 1998).

Tomas Urzainqui, *Recuperación del Estado Propio* (Pamplona: Nabarralde, 2002).

Tomas Urzainqui, *Navarra sin Fronteras Impuestas* (Pamplona: Pamiela, 2002).

Tomas Urzainqui, *Navarra Estado Europeo* (Pamplona: Pamiela, 2004).

23 1707 Treaty of Union between Scotland-England, Article 1: "that the Two Kingdoms of Scotland and England shall upon the first day of May next ensuing the date hereof and forever after be United into One Kingdom by the Name of Great Britain. And that the Ensigns Armorial of the said United Kingdom be such as Her Majesty shall appoint and the Crosses of St Andrew and St George be conjoined in such manner as Her Majesty shall think fit and used in all Flags Banners Standards and Ensigns both at Sea and Land."

24 Miguel Herrero de Miñón, "La Titularidad de los Derechos Históricos Vascos," *Revista de Estudios Políticos,* no. 58 (1987). This author was one of the drafters and reporters on the 1978 Spanish Constitution, and he was the first to interpret Basque historical titles in terms of the right to self-determination.

Miguel Herrero de Miñón, and Ernest Lluch Ernest, "Constitucionalismo Útil," in *Derechos Históricos y Constitucionalismo Útil* (Bilbao: Fundación BBVA, 2000).

Miguel Herrero de Miñón, "Autodeterminación y Derechos Históricos," in *Derechos Históricos y Constitucionalismo Útil* (Bilbao: Fundación BBVA, 2000).

Miguel Herrero de Miñón, *Derechos Históricos y Constitución* (Madrid: Taurus, 2000).

Miguel Herrero de Miñón, *El Valor de la Constitución* (Barcelona: Crítica. 2003).

Herrero de Miñón, Miguel. 2003. "España y Vasconia: presente y futuro (consideraciones en torno al Plan Ibarretxe," in Jornadas de Estudio sobre la Propuesta Política para la convivencia del Lehendakari Ibarretxe. Oñati: IVAP.

25 Eduardo Nieto Arizmendiarrieta, "Reflexiones Sobre el Concepto de Derechos Históricos," *Revista Vasca de Administración Pública* 54 (1999): 142-43.

26 Nevertheless, the 1707 Union Treaty stands that the Union is "forever."

27 In this case very clearly in breach of the Spanish Constitution, specifically, Article 151.2. In the same sense, it implied a breach against the provisions recognizing a right to negotiate this text through Article 137 of the Spanish Parliament Statutory Regulation.
28 See the proposal approved by the Basque Parliament (PSBC).
29 More specifically, in the principle on the right to negotiate a possible different status for Quebec recognized by the Canadian Supreme Court (Decision of 8-20-1998). See arts. 12 and 13 PSBC, with a very particular approach to self-determination based upon the principles stated by the Canadian Supreme Court in 1998 (the right to a bilateral negotiation on the Basque political status).
30 Inter alia at Neil MacCormick, *Questioning Sovereignty: Law, State, and Nation in the European Commonwealth* (Oxford: Oxford University Press, 2002).
31 Inter alia in Michael Keating, *The Independence of Scotland* (Oxford: Oxford University Press, 2009).
32 See the interesting comparative approach made by Jon Arrieta, 2009, between the Spanish 1707 and the British one, in "El 1707 español y el británico," in Conciliar la diversidad. Pasado y presente de la vertebración de España, Arrieta and Astigarraga eds, University of the Basque Country, 28.
33 See Ezeizabarrena, Xabier. 2003. *Los Derechos Históricos de Euskadi y Navarra ante el Derecho Comunitario. Donostia-San Sebastián: Sociedad de Estudios Vascos*, together with the interesting foreword to the book by Miguel Herrero de Miñón.
34 The constitution protects and respects the historical rights of the "foral" territories. The general updating process of this regime shall be enacted, when appropriate, within the framework of the constitution and the Acts of Autonomy. The four foral territories quoted, within the context of this chapter, were defined by the Spanish Constitutional Court as Alava, Gipuzkoa, Navarra, and Bizkaia.
35 See their works, Herrero de Miñón, *Derechos Históricos y* Constitución, and Ramon Fernández, *Los Derechos Históricos de los territorios forales* (Madrid: Civitas, 1985).
36 See Herrero de Miñón. *Derechos Históricos y* Constitución. and Xabier Ezeizabarrena, *La Ciaboga Infinita. Una Visión Política y Jurídica del Conflicto Vasco* (Irun: Alberdania, 2005).
37 Diario de Sesiones del Senado (Spanish Senate), V Legislatura, Comisiones, no. 128, 1994, 62-63, Comisión General de las Comunidades Autónomas (9-26-1994). Alli's speech proved again the peculiar nature of historical rights and the eventual consequences of their breach by the central government. Diario de Sesiones del Senado, V Legislatura, Comisiones, no. 129, 1994, 31, Comisión General de las Comunidades Autónomas, 9-27-1994.
38 Historical rights that would find their limits in human rights (arts. 9, 10, and 11 PSBC); rights that are recognized within the EU context and as a relevant part of their tradition. That is the real will behind the proposal for a new status (PSBC). For Scotland, with the Devolution Act as a clear point of reference.
39 Article 10.2 of the Spanish Constitution: "Las normas relativas a los derechos fundamentales y a las libertades que la Constitución reconoce, se interpretarán de conformidad con la Declaración Universal de Derechos Humanos y los tratados y acuerdos internacionales sobre las mismas materias ratificados por España."
40 Both the Spanish Constitutional Court and similar European domestic bodies are obliged to guarantee European Law, and must request, for example, a preliminary ruling from

the CJEU when they need an interpretative ruling from the European Court (article 234 of the EC Treaty). See also arts. 14, 15, and 16 of the PSBC.

41 It is necessary to distinguish the situations and singularities of the German Länder, Basque Country, or Scotland, for example, and some other cases such as the French départements or the British counties. In the case of Basque historical rights and Scotland demands, at least, three main approaches apply (Article 65 PSBC for the Basque case):
   a) More participation of the Basque and Scottish Parliaments in the EU institutional activities;
   b) Participation of both delegations within the EU Council of Ministers; and
   c) Direct right of standing (locus standi) of both nations in appeals to the CJEU concerning their respective competencies.

42 See Ludger Mees, *El profeta pragmático* (Alberdania, 2006), particularly his constant letters with Manuel de Irujo.

43 See Ezeizabarrena, Xabier. "La Articulación del Federalismo Vasco en la UE y en las Relaciones Internacionales. Euskadi y Navarra ante la UE y las Relaciones Internacionales en la Ley 25/2014, de Tratados y otros Acuerdos Internacionales," Europa de las Regiones y el futuro federal de Europa: Balance y perspectivas de la gobernanza multinivel de la UE, Eurobasque, Dykinson, 2019.

44 Article 5 for the failed Project of European Constitution.

45 Former socialist politician and Spanish minister killed by ETA in 2000 in the city of Barcelona.

46 Herrero de Miñón and Lluch, "Constitucionalismo Útil," 17.

47 Herrero de Miñón, "Autodeterminación y Derechos Históricos," 219-21.

48 Alli, Juan Cruz, "Paz y Fueros. Los Derechos Históricos Como Instrumentos de Pacificación," in *Derechos Históricos y Constitucionalismo Útil* (Bilbao: Fundación BBV, 2000), 329.

49 The Basque Parliament in 2008 enacted an act regulating public consults in this regard, and the consultation organized for the 10-25-2008 was banned by the Spanish Constitutional Court Judgment 103/2008 (STC 103/2008).

# 3

# The Literature of Peripheral Nationalisms:

## Late Nineteenth-Century Western Europe from the Perspective of Political History and Culture

*Francisco Letamendia*

### Protohistory and History of National Minorities in Western Europe[1]

The history of these minorities' problematic relationships with states, when the latter evolved into their state-nation form in the nineteenth century, is an academic topic that has been scarcely covered, and yet which must be in order to examine the specific characteristics of national minorities' literature. It is therefore necessary to briefly review the historical (and, therefore, premodern) evolution of this relationship between minorities and states in Western Europe, as we do here, on the cusp of the nineteenth and twentieth centuries, before specifically addressing their literary production.

### The Literatures of Western European Peripheries from the Perspective of Features of Political Culture

All nationalisms—both of states and national minorities—are identity phenomena, which, in the nineteenth century, made considerable use of political ideologies. I will briefly explain the meaning of these concepts and how they apply to nationalisms discussed here.

Political culture consists of the psychological orientations of individuals and groups toward political entities. This does not include political entities as such (political parties, parliaments, etc.), but, rather, what people believe and feel about them. Political culture is subjective, the invisible fabric that guides individuals and collective agents' political behavior toward political system entities.

How do political culture, identities, and ideologies connect? Political culture provides human orientations toward political situations; identity provides permanence to these orientations; ideologies are the instruments of proselytism and struggle between groups used by identities.

Political identities are always collective: they are born from the perceived difference between us and them, and they are long term, linking the present with the past and projecting it into the future. They can generate open identity fields, with recognition of each others' signs of identity; or closed identity fields, in which stereotypes and hostile projections about the figure of the enemy predominate.

Ideologies have a cognitive aspect, by which the group interprets the social situation; they are always dynamic in nature, being instruments of competition and struggle between groups for them to impose their political objectives. They have emerged as a product of the political mobilization of modernity; therefore, they must be studied in order to understand the conflicts that have taken place since 1789 between state and national minority, nonstate nationalisms. Both of their discourses have been built using political philosophies and theories, religious creeds and other ideologies, whose pieces were amalgamated and became instruments for action.

Political identities and ideologies were born as a result of the great breaks, or cleavages (in Rokkan's view), that took place during modernity and postmodernity:

- The tradition/modernity conflict, which arose after the French Revolution, and the ideologies of liberalism and conservatism.
- The class conflict produced by the Industrial Revolution led, on the working-class side, to the subversive ideologies of the nineteenth century: socialism, anarchism, and communism.
- It is the central-periphery conflict that we are particularly interested in here. Let us start with political identities: the National Revolution, leading to the formation of the nation-state, led to the varied range of national identities, some pro-state, others reactive to it, which instrumentalized very different ideologies.

The nineteenth century (more precisely, the period between 1789 and 1914) led to a double revolution in Europe—the Industrial Revolution and the National Revolution—the result of which was the emergence and consolidation of nation-states. The National Revolution led, for one thing, to the church-state conflict, which, in Catholic societies, particularly involved a struggle to control the education system; in the territorial axis, it created the central-periphery conflict, where specific social groups, different from the central collective—because of their language, religion, or other factors—were discriminated against in the context of the general process of nationalization.

The reaction of the peripheries to the center, far from being an archaic and aberrant process, was mimetic in character, each state copying in the construction of its national society and community through a set of economic, political, and cultural functions, and implemented by all states. The antagonistic reactions of some peripheries—which struggled to be such, and not part of the central state, and in whose territories these functions were carried out—turned these minorities into national minorities during this process. Unable to set up their own society as they lacked the right tools to do so (political parties, for example, did not appear in Western Europe until the twentieth century, with some exceptions such as the Catalans and the Basques), they focused on the construction of the community, where cultural production—and literature in particular—played (and plays) a major role. It is these processes that we will examine in this section.

Let us now talk about states' creations of the national societies and communities, which led to various reactions on their peripheries. State-nation societies were the result of the creation of efficient administrations and unified markets (an objective helped by the Industrial Revolution), the political socialization of the masses through compulsory universal teaching, and its integration via political mechanisms such as universal suffrage. National communities were the work of political culture that fed the loyalty of citizens to the state and generated their sense of being a group belonging to the nation.

However, the construction of nation-state communities discriminated against particular ethnic, linguistic, and religious groups from the start, ones which were different from the dominant group that had historically built the state which almost always prevented their equal access to the cultural and political (not always economic) goods distributed by the state apparatus. These groups could remain passive, which happened in the first half of the century in most cases in the European West (not so in the eastern half, that of the great empires, whose transformation into unified national communities was strongly contested by peripheral national groups, future independent states in the twentieth century, and, some cases, in the twenty-first century). In Western Europe, too, there were groups that reacted in defense of their languages, religions, and cultures, calling for some form of political institutionalization of the territories they inhabited. They were territories different from the center, either because of their religion—a few, such as Ireland—or because of their native language and culture. In the case of Ireland, religious difference was matched by language difference.

This process differentiated three major blocs in Europe. In the eastern or central-eastern bloc of the great empires, the movements of national minorities had been growing since the late eighteenth century based on the ideals of the Enlightenment, which they merged with their national demands. At the same time as the disintegration of the central and eastern empires after World War I, many of these national groups took advantage of their defeat to the European West (and the USA) to form their own states, work that continued after World War II. By contrast, in Central-Western Europe—Germany and Italy, countries heir to the Holy Roman/Germanic Empire, which had both remained anachronistically dispersed during the industrial era—all nationalist energies converged in the second half of the nineteenth century into the triumphant processes of German and Italian state reunification, which made their peripheries inoperative.

Thus, the issue of active national minorities was concentrated in the old European states in the West—the United Kingdom, France, the Kingdom of Spain—and which were unable to silence the demands of their peripheries, but powerful enough to prevent those demands from being met. In fact, it was these nationalist movements that emerged strongly in the second half of the nineteenth century (and some of which have not lost strength today, quite the opposite).

A number of factors led to this convergence. One of them was the formation, to the beat of the Industrial Revolution, of an indigenous bourgeoisie with the will and means to direct these nationalisms and create ad hoc collective instruments (publications, magazines, schools, academies, Floral Games, etc., conducive to autonomous language and culture). The extension of universal suffrage also helped, despite how adulterated it was in some states, for example in the Kingdom of Spain, or perhaps precisely because of that reason, leading to the founding of nationalist political parties. Another important factor was the benevolence shown to them, especially in Catholic countries, by a church engaged with the state in a bitter struggle to retain its traditional monopoly on education. A decisive element, by the early twentieth century, was the patriotic effervescence that the great states injected into their citizens in support of their aggressive colony-sharing projects around the world, and which could not be shared by the elites, victims of minority nationalism, on their small scale, to such jingoism (which eventually led to the hecatomb of World War I). It was, in fact, at the end of the nineteenth century that the first autonomist-nationalist parties were formed in this area of Europe, a process that, due to the weakness of the Kingdom of Spain, appeared first and with special relevance in Catalunya and the Basque Country.

Let us now examine how the relationship between identity and ideology shows itself in such nationalisms. The identity dimension of any national movement consists of the group feeling of belonging and the activity of selecting its signs of identity: territorial factors (which relate the group, ethnic or not, to a specific territory); time factors (which mark the groups' continuity over time); and cultural factors (such as the heritage, among things, of the traditional ethnic language and the group's historical and religious identity). The ideological register, amalgamated with the identity register for practical purposes, leads to the use of philosophies and theories—whether deep or superficial—at the service of the group's national construction objectives.

These minority national identities operate with signs of identity based on an ethnic personality—almost always founded on linguistic or religious differences—formed over long historical periods. The time identity dimension takes shape in all group identity reactions from nationalist movements, nativisms, or utopias when they feel threatened by external factors. The effort to preserve its perception of durability can turn toward the past in a nativist manner, thus producing a "return to roots" (which always modifies ethnic historical memory). Or it can be oriented toward the future, creating the imaginary projection of a "beyond" that brings together the group's aspirations; ethno-national utopias arise from this attitude. (The examples shown to us by history, starting with biblical examples, demonstrate the mythical continuum created during these processes between the historical long and short term.)

The construction of a past based on real or mythical facts—the nativist phase—is the lever needed to channel energies into a desirable future—the utopian phase. This temporary identity sequence is indistinguishable from that carried out by states in the construction of their nation-states. Perhaps the only noteworthy difference is the presence of the tragic heroic in these identity constructions of the past. That is undoubtedly because, in contrast to already consolidated nation-states, their projects are full of failures that are part of their historical memories and must be commemorated—when failure occurred, there had been heroic resistance, they had never surrendered, thus keeping alive the flame of hope for the future.

The Catalan and Scottish examples are well known. Catalunya has turned the desperate resistance of the "Segadors"—who rose in 1659 against the absolutist politics of the Kingdom of Spain—into its national anthem. And in Scotland, William Wallace—"Braveheart," a minor Scottish nobleman who galvanized anti-English resistance, and to who King Edward, after capturing him in 1305, had quartered, disemboweled, and beheaded—is venerated.

In all the cases dealt with, it is necessary to provide an explanation of the historical relations between the center—in other words, the state—and the periphery, or peripheries, that explain the emergence in the latter of mobilizing political movements, which all active nationalisms are. Given the precocity of these processes in Western Europe—which became important before the twentieth century—as well as their current relevance, I will limit synthetic explanation of the genesis of these processes to the Kingdom of Spain.

### National Minorities' Identity and Literature in the Late Nineteenth Century

The cultural manifestations of these European national minorities differed greatly and to the extent to which their languages, traditions, and customs were different. At the same time, during these processes—characterized as in all identity processes by the us-and-them dialectic—their historical relations with the state center have oscillated between forced or simply passive integration, relations based on goodwill, or open, sometimes even armed, conflict. But they also share certain characteristics, which could be summarized as follows:

- The importance of widely preserved historical memory, many of whose stories are, without being false, re-created in depth by community memory. They reflect both successes achieved and tragic events; in other words, the defeats of countries besieged by adversaries endowed of incomparably superior strength, but which did not finish with the community's willpower and ability to resist. This links this literature to romantic historicism, and explains its survival when such stories began, in the mid-nineteenth century, to disappear from European literary production.
- The abundance of accounts of the life, customs, and beliefs of peasants, fishermen, sailors—stories ignored by the state's great literature, but of special interest to minorities because such indigenous social groups have historically been the true keepers of the language, folklore, and traditions of minority peoples. Hence, its importance in these peripheral literatures, as well as their links with European literary *Costumbrismo*. The relevance of these nineteenth-century minority literatures in the *Costumbrista* literary currently has been ignored because they were written in marginalized, long-despised languages.
- The calculated support of the Catholic Church for these minorities—due to its own conflict with the state regarding the monopoly of education—explains the abundance of ecclesiastical or related issues, as well as the fundamentalist feel to many of these initiatives. But we must not forget the quality and modernity of authors such as the Galician poet Rosalía de Castro, with her work being as good as any in Europe at that time. Likewise, cultural movements such as Catalan *Noucentism* in the early twentieth century placed their poetry at the same standard as that of the European modernist poets and symbolists.
- These literatures—aware of the importance of their existence for the awakening of their people—were designated in their countries with

Renaissance-related names such as Renaxenca, Rexurdimento . . . And they were seen, more than as the production of isolated authors, as the creation of an entire community; this was the moment when Floral Games with different denominations were widespread in many of these minorities, and in which literature was produced for the enjoyment and participation—at least symbolically—of the whole community. This connected them, in a sense, to the community nature of medieval literature.

**The Kingdom of Spain**

Hispanic unification carried out by the Catholic monarchs and the Austrian monarchs had been based on religious monolithism; but it had allowed the peculiar characteristics, of the different kingdoms and political authorities throughout the Peninsula, diversity that the Bourbons had attenuated without destroying. In the landscape of nineteenth-century nationalisms, the Spanish example was a model case of a dependent, stunted market; a failure to set up a modern bureaucracy and rhetorical liberalism; and it had been imposed by military force; all of which led to the weak construction of the Spanish national center, and strong peripheral nationalisms, especially the Catalan and Basque nationalisms.

Catalunya

From 1840, the pre-Renaixenca exalted Catalan history and art; Aribau published his "Oda a la patria," and Milá y Fontanals, inspired by the Provencal troubadours, organized the Floral Games of Barcelona in 1859, which brought Valencian and Balearic poets there. Almirall, an active stakeholder in radical Catalanist federalism, created the Republican Committees of Aragon, Catalunya, Valencia, and the Balearic Islands in 1869. His federalism was contested by Mañé y Flaquer and Torras y Bages's conservative regionalism and defense of Catalan tradition. But Catalunya's economic strength made it possible for all Catalan currents to come together. Successive Congresos Catalanistas defended Catalan civil law against Spanish civil law in 1880, and in 1883 drew up the protectionist "Memorial de Greuges," which denounced the threat posed to Catalan interests by the trade treaties with France and England.

Prat de la Riba put together a synthesis of these currents from 1892 onward, developing a program of self-government—the Bases of Manresa—and a nationalist, but not pro-independence ideology—Compendi de la Doctrina Catalanista—and in 1901 he set up the Lliga Regionalista de Cataluña. According to Prat, the great imbalance between the living, dynamic Catalunya and the agricultural, bureaucratic, and inert Spanish state had to be balanced out; the

Catalan market had to spread to the whole of Spain, helping Spain to become a modern imperial power.

Catalan nationalism, therefore, triumphed in the early twentieth century by creating a "national bourgeoisie," managing to unify conservative Catholics of rural origin and liberal urban bourgeois in the objective of Catalanisin society, the standardization of the Catalan language, and the modernization of a Spanish state in which Catalunya could be inserted on a federal basis.

*Catalan Literature: Renaixenca and Noucentisme*

During the first half of the nineteenth century, Romanticism had cultivated unequivocally Catalan themes, although written mostly in Spanish. But by the middle of the century a bourgeois, Catalan-speaking intellectuality of a liberal type had been formed, albeit combative and, in some cases, revolutionary, which led to literature being written in Catalan. Some of the authors, such as Milá and Fontanals, reneged on their liberal past. Between 1840 and 1847, conservative romanticism was still prevalent and included folk features, but authors like Victor Balaguer wanted to make literature an instrument of progress. This movement for renewing Catalan language, literature, and culture was called the Renaixenca: it produced works such as Bonaventura's "La patria," and the Floral Games (Jocs Florals), founded in 1859, which were highly successful. In 1843 the first magazine written entirely in Catalan was published: *Lo verdader catalá.* Jacinto Verdaguer's *Atlantis* was the great epic poem of the period, and it began in 1835 on the reopening of the University of Barcelona, and with the support of authors, some of whom—such as Torras and Bages—were close to the church.

This movement took Catalan culture to the popular media, including rural publications, but it was monopolized by the urban bourgeoisie, and its preference for poetry did not match popular literary production in Catalan, whose authors, Anselmo Clavé and Frederic Soler, regarded it with suspicion. Theater, although not performed as such at the Games until 1865, included the production of the Catalan drama "*Tal farás*" by Vidal and Valenciano; poet Angel Guimerá was also a playwright. The emergence of modernism at the end of the century, with writers such as Joan Maragall, was soon followed by Noucentism, with a distinguished group of authors who combined symbolism with Costumbrismo, as well as with spirited people who set out to transform adverse situations, for example Catherine Albert, known as Victor Català. This movement—twinned with the extraordinary flourishing of the plastic arts, and with Gaudí's architecture as their symbol and flagbearer—stood out among all the periphery literatures.

## Galicia

The Pronunciamiento de Lugo of 1846 led by Faraldo—although himself somewhere between Spanish moderates and liberals—was of clearly national character; the Junta Superior gallega he set up defined Galicia as a "crown colony." The Galician Rexurdimento of the 1860s was led by a triad of excellent poets—Rosalía de Castro, Pondal, and Curros—and a generation of Romantic historians led by Martínez de Murguía, who combined Celtism—considered the essential feature of the Galician nation—with Italian-inspired liberalism.

The Galician republican federalism born in the heat of the Revolution of 1868 was short lived. From 1880 to 1916, the liberal Galicianism of Rosalía and Murguía—led by sectors of the urban, commercial bourgeoisie—was joined by an anti-liberal Galician traditionalism, given support by Carlist and agricultural media. Brañas defined it in his 1889 work *Traditionalism,* in which he defended a decentralized organization of the Spanish state which would repudiate modernity.

But unlike Catalunya, Galician nationalism failed to consolidate itself as a stable political force. Weak industrialization and insufficient urbanization, coupled with the existence of isolated, deeply poor peasantry subject to local landowners, prevented the emergence of a synthetic "national class" to overcome the irreconcilable nature of liberal urban and traditionalist agricultural objectives.

### *Galician Literature: Rexurdimento and Rosalía de Castro*

The Galician Rexurdimento was a return of the Romantic movement that identified with so-called "provincialism," which had promoted Galician interest in literature since the middle of the century. Its intellectual heirs were a group of young people, including Manuel Murguía, Eduardo Portal, and Rosalía de Castro, founded in 1863.

In fact, the real beginning was the publication of Rosalía de Castro's first book, *Cantares Gallegos,* in 1863. This bilingual poet, writing in Spanish and Galician, stood out for the excellence and depth of her poetry, and her fame throughout the state could only be matched by Bécquer. Rosalía was a symbol of the relevance in poetic discourse that women had achieved in the different nationalities in the state during the second half of the nineteenth century. This prominence of women was clear to see in talks and literary salons and, of course, in their work, which is only now being properly taken into consideration after so many years. The work of Galician Rosalía de Castro can be compared with that of Bécquer, moving from being an object of poetry to being a subject in it; it is work of the very highest standard.

Rosalía de Castro's very existence as a writer—she was wife of Galician scholar Manuel Martínez Murguía—in itself pointed out the appearance on the peninsula of a new, middle-class audience in which women played an increasingly important role. In fact, the poetic panorama in the state had no figure, except apart from Bécquer, with enough literary intuition and resources to be able to outshine de Castro. In her work *En las orillas del Sar*, an example of her most personal and intimate poetics, the text has a pessimistic tone in which the color gray predominates. Poetry, love in its various forms, and religion are treated from a perspective of helplessness and desolation. There is no moment of hope that is not immediately blackened by prosaic life. At the center of this bleak panorama, the inexorable feminine gaze that emits its grim judgment:

> Nothing matters to me, black or white butterflies,
> happiness I am told of, nor new misfortunes,
> around my lamp or circling my forehead,
> you cannot keep still.
> The fortunate glass of pleasure is forever
> broken at my feet, and pain fills up and then overflows!
> There is no space for either sorrow or bitterness any more.

Rosalía shows us that perhaps the obligations and miseries that her social role as mother and wife imposed on her meant that her forays into the ideal of beauty and art could not be as spiritually transcendent as those of her male companions. Her writing—which evokes "sweet mothers," "secret tenderness," and the "fear of the occult" of her feminine soul—strips us of the deceit of poetic discourse built by men and based on the imposition of unequal relationships between the privileged and the disinherited, and, in fact, between men and women.

Although nothing was published in Galician between 1863 and 1874, publications in the language increased afterward; the result was the emergence of the first magazine in the language, published from 1876 to 1889. Cultural projects such as the Biblioteca Académica—which published fifty-two works from 1885, including essential books such as *Aires da miña terra* by Manuel Curros Enríquez and *Queixumes dos pinos* by Eduardo Portal—were also carried out. Literary competitions were also promoted, and, in 1886, a contest was held for works written only in Galician.

It was in 1880 that works on political thought were published; for instance, *La proyección política* and *Los precursores* by the Galician Manuel Murguía. Grammar books, dictionaries, and studies of literary criticism and history were also published, both in Spanish and Galician; for instance, *Historia de Galiza*, also by Murguía. The splendid tradition of medieval Galician troubadour poetry was also revisited, as, in 1889, were Alfonso X the Wise's "Cantigas."

In the prose fiction started by Marcial Valleda Núñez, Costumbrismo was imposed as an exaltation of the rural and the folkloric. Only at the end of the century, with Francisco Alvarez de Novoa's work, did urban, bourgeois, psychological narrative begin, precursor to work of the Irmandades da fala authors. The theater was missing over those years.

### Basque Country: The Transformation of the Basque Collective Imagination by Sabino Arana

Self-awareness of ethno-cultural minorities can produce the transformation of premodern symbolic capital into the socio-political capital of modern ethno-national movements. This happened with the nationalist reconstruction of Basque symbolic capital carried out by Sabino Arana at the end of the nineteenth century. This reconstruction was motivated by a double ethnic reaction—against the construction of the Spanish state and against immigration caused by rapid Basque industrialization—and was fueled by the church's ideological arsenal in its conflict with the state.

Basque collective imagination had been born during in the Late Middle Age and the Modern Age. During the thirteenth century, the archbishop of Toledo had claimed noble origin for the Basques, stating them to be descended from Tubal, son of Japheth and grandson of Noah; on the other hand, in the sixteenth century, it had been stated that the Basques had descended from the Cantabrians, an undefeated people never dominated by the Romans or the Arabs. The mythical explanation of the Basques' relationship with the Castilian monarchy—which was used by Sabino Arana to refute it—was based on the Pacto con el Señor. Based on the theory of the Pacto, the "Fuero Nuevo de Vizcaya" of 1526 had established various obligations for the Lord-King of Spain and proclaimed the theoretically voluntary nature of tax (as a donation). Since that century, and in parallel, Basque authors on the Fueros had proclaimed the ancient monotheism of the Basques; in their view, the "New Fuero de Vizcaya" was evidence of the Bizkainos' "purity of blood," linking that with universal nobility to prevent the arrival of outsiders.

Various elements of a nonlegal nature complemented this symbolic capital: among them, the cult of the ancestral house, the genealogical foundation of its nobility, and the inclusion of the Basques in the human universe.

Sabino Arana recovered this symbolic capital as nationalist. The myth of egalitarianism served to praise lost, immemorial Basque democracy and condemn contemporary Bizkaian society—and later Basque society as a whole—for having lost it. In 1893, he described the rural Bizkaia which met in church porches: "Completely free and independent, while harmoniously and fraternally united, they had those small political entities, governed by laws born in their bosom and founded on religion and morality, a perfectly happy existence, without it ever crossing their minds to extend their domains into new lands." The Basque past was mythologized, and all traces of class struggle were removed, the latter being classified as a foreign invention put together by Spaniards and arrogant Bizkaians. Sabino Arana accordingly condemned large-scale capitalists in moral terms: by bringing foreign labor into the country, they were responsible for the introduction of immorality, ungodliness, socialism, and anarchism. His opposition to socialism was also absolute: he saw it as a "maketa" doctrine, which was corrosive to the Basque personality.

The genealogical foundations of the universal nobility of the Basques underwent complete remodeling. Basque-Iberism was explicitly denied: the Basque race—original and unclassifiable among the other races—did not come from mixtures such as the Spanish. The invincibility of the Basque-Cantabrians—although not explicitly—became a longing for the past and a slogan of action for the present, a prism of interpretation for the Carlist wars, and an explanatory factor reducing the complex relations between Spain and the Basque Country to those of conquering country-conquered country. This vision of the Basque Country as a colony gave way to the more modern, progressive aspect of Sabino Arana's work: its clear anti-colonialist sentiment, contrary to the war that the Spanish Army was waging in those years in Morocco.

Traditional peasant society gave rise to the idealization of the rural; the opposition during the Carlist wars between the Carlist countryside and liberal cities reinforced Sabino's taking sides against the urban, and produced the crystallization of the rural as the "essence" of the Basque nation.

Sabino reshaped and disputed the theory of the Pacto señorial ("pact with the lord") in some respects. The total rupture regarding Fueros tradition, and the consequent conversion of pro-Fueros positions into nationalism, took place with the definition of the Fueros. These were the Basque States' "national codes," which had been enacted when they had been independent. Sabino initially claimed the independence of Bizkaia, and only later extended the concept of nation to the Basque Country of the seven territories. Contrary to what the Carlists claimed, being a pro-Fueros amounted to being a Basque nationalist.

Ancient monotheism linked with the influence of religious traditionalism—and most recently of fundamentalism—on Sabino. The Sabinian religious program comprised three points: independence between church and state (priests, who were to retain their political neutrality, could not be affiliated as active members of nationalism), harmony between church and state, and subordination of the state to the precepts of the church. This program was summarized in the motto "We are for the Basque Country, and the Basque Country is for God."

Race was, in Sabino's thought, the concept that encompassed all these characteristics and crystallized the Basque "difference." It was finally an affirmative, symbolic, non-somatic racism, and affirmed the moral excellence of the Basques. The race was the "essential" factor of the nation above the language. For Sabino, Basque was a defensive instrument for protection from the "maketa" invasion, so his nationalism was not expansive and aggressive, nor did he establish a hierarchy of races; without the Basque race there would be no Basque homeland. Affirmative racism was combined with the racism of exclusion toward immigrants. This racism of exclusion, based on the historical memory of "blood cleansing"—however deplorable—was, therefore, distinct from the supremacist, imperialist, and aggressive racisms in vogue during those years around the European powers and at the service of the domination—with consequent aggression—of the world.

### Literature in Basque

Costumbrism, purism, was influenced by the church and was the popular lifeblood of Bertsolarism. Basque literature during the second half of the nineteenth century—which crossed the borders separating Iparralde, the north of the country, from the south, Hegoalde, the two sides being separated by the states' border—converged with the dominant currents in Europe, laying the foundations for the unusual literary production that was to mature during the twentieth century. The poetic movements that set out to develop popular Basque poetry inspired by the prominence of the Bertsolaris were of major significance. In narrative, it was Costumbrista novels that set the tone.

At a time full of wars and incidents, a renaissance inspired by Romanticism took place in both halves of the country. In Iparralde, the rise of poetry owed its impetus to the Floral Games, with a conscious effort to record folklore. The patronage of Prince Louis Lucian Bonaparte prompted the rebirth of Basque language and literature.

After the exhaustion of the Larramendi school, the abolition of the Fueros in 1876 reinspired literature, resulting in abundant verse production. Donostia became the focus of the production of theatrical works, poetry, narrative, and magazines in Basque. Bilbao stood out for two personalities who went beyond the scope of the narrative: Ramón María de Azkue and Sabino Arana.

Novels in Basque were, for much of the nineteenth century, Costumbrista, with all the characteristics of the genre: the theme was almost always agricultural or fishing, highlighting the importance of the Basque language and the Christian faith. The characters did not evolve. The author defined them as good or bad, always commenting on them and the events narrated in the work. Txomin Agirre was the first Basque novelist, with works such as *Auñamendiko lorea,* in 1896, *Kresala,* in 1912, and *Garoa,* which was unfinished. The first was a romantic historicist novel, influenced by the Spanish-language work of Navarro Villoslada, *Amaya y los vascos en el siglo XVII.* The second, written in Bizkaian dialect, told the story of a fishing village; the third, in Gipuzkoan dialect, was set in a farming village. These novels created a pattern followed by many authors.

The theater had its roots in Donostia, although the first school was not set up there but in Ziburu, across the border, where some Donostians fleeing the war set up a school called El Trueno. The best-known members were Marcelino Soroa (1828–1902) and Toribio Altzaga (1861–1941). Soroa wrote musical theater, similar to Zarzuela, in which Basque and Spanish were combined. Altzaga fled with his family as a child to Ziburu, where he finished high school and came into contact with Basque theater. He followed the example of his friend Soroa in his 1890 work "Aterako gera," both being much imitated by Basque authors who came after them.

Philological and anthropological studies were, however, more important than the Basque narrative in the Basque Country. Priest Resurrección Maria de Azkue (1864–1951), president of the Royal Academy of the Basque Language from 1919 until his death, excelled in writing them. In 1888, the year in which he was ordained a priest, he successfully competed for the chair of Basque—promoted by the Provincial Council of Bizkaia—with two illustrious rivals: Sabino Arana and Miguel de Unamuno. His research work on Basque lexicon and grammar and on Basque theater has not become outdated. He worked on the *Euskal Pizkundea,* a Basque grammar book published in 1891, which years later was to be criticized by the author himself as artificial; and on the *Basque-Spanish-French Dictionary,* in Basque, in 1905; and on diverse works from 1914 onward. In 1893, he also wrote *Bein da betiko (Once and for all),* a Costumbrista, satirical novel. The *Cancionero popular vasco* (1918–1921) collected about a thousand pieces from the nearly two thousand that contained his winning work in a competition held by the four Basque provincial governments.

The figure of Sabino Arana (1865–1903), founder of Basque nationalism, goes far beyond his literary production and philological research. The latter had widespread impact throughout the twentieth century, despite being radically corrected in recent decades (but not so much its onomastics, which have endured in Basque personal names). His interest in philology stemmed from his definition of Basque as one of the constituent elements of the Basque homeland. He endorsed Astarloa's spelling model: he had proposed a unified spelling, nevertheless safeguarding the diversity of the dialects of the seven territories of the two halves of the Basque Country.

His vision differed from those of Resurrección Mary of Azkue and Campión, who proposed a unified, literary, standard Basque. Sabino defended his proposal at the 1901 Hendaye Orthographic Congress—of which he was vice chair—advocating a specific dialect for each territory. At the same time, his vision of Basque was radically purist; he set out to replace all loans from Romance languages with neologisms, many of them invented by himself. After his death, the Basque Nationalist Party Commission published a "Basque saints' register," which gave Christian names, which Sabino had said complied with the phonetic laws of Basque. However, most of these new names were his own invention and not adaptations. After the church initially refused to baptize children with them, it had to give in when such names became very popular, their popularity increasing to this day.

**Occitania**

Occitania, the territory of the language d'oc, is a wide linguistic-cultural area in the French state that goes from the Atlantic to the Mediterranean, and from the Central Massif to the Pyrenees, covering the historical regions of ancient Aquitaine (Gascony and Guyenne), Limousin, Auvergne, The Dauphiné, Languedoc, Provence. Lacking a center, or more precisely, based around two centers—the Aquitaine-Atlantic and the Provencal-Mediterranean—Occitania is, therefore, a typical example of an imagined nation (which does not mean that it is insignificant: pressure from the south—recognized as having a glorious historical and literary past—was to be a determining element in French regionalization in 1982).

Provence is the Roman "Province" of Marsilia (Marseille), of the "waters" (Aix-en-Provence), open to all Mediterranean civilizations, bordering with Italy to the east (leading into its valleys), and to the south with Catalunya (of which it currently includes an area, the Roussillon). Aquitaine is the meeting place of the Eusko-Pyrenean ethnic grouping with the Romans and the Gauls; today, the Occitan Gascons and Bearnes share a single department with the Basques of Iparralde: Pyrenees-Atlantiques.

Occitan is a literary language older than the d'oil language or French. The excellence of the poetry of its troubadours (the oldest of whom was Duke William of Aquitaine) made it the main European lyrical language during the eleventh and twelfth centuries. In the thirteenth century, the Kingdom of the Isle de France occupied Occitania using the excuse of the Manichean heresy of the Albigenses; the church set up the Holy Inquisition to support France, and the permanent domination of the French invaders over the refined Occitans was in place. Guyenne was administered by the English (from Bordeaux to Baiona) until recovered by France, this time through negotiations, in the mid-fifteenth century. The memory of the resistance against the invading troops of Simon de Monfort gave birth to epic Occitan literature examples, of which are to be found up to the Modern Age. The echoes of defending an Occitan identity, which were to disrupt centuries of Frankish domination, continued to be heard in Revolutionary and Napoleonic France, which showed boundless hostility to Occitan identity and the very existence of Occitania.

But the explicit affirmation of Occitanism appeared, in parallel with that of Catalanism, in the literary sphere. In 1854, a group of poets led by Frédéric Mistral founded The Félibrige, a literary movement that defended federalism and an Occitan community defined by language, and that shared with clerical bourgeoisie and traditional peasantry nostalgia for the lost order of the rural world.

The members of the Félibrige, however, distanced themselves from social struggles, which took place, in particular, between small winemakers and wholesale wine merchants. When in 1907 it joined the first unionized agricultural proletariat, the very senior Mistral refused to take part in the demonstrations. The "red" members of the Félibriges turned toward republican France.

### *The Occitan Renaissance: Mistral and the Félibrige*

Occitan language and literature, so persecuted by the French revolutionaries, underwent a brilliant renaissance in the second half of the nineteenth century, thanks to the leader of the Félibrige movement and undisputed main stakeholder in Occitanism, Frederic Mistral (1830–1914). After studying at Aix-en-Provence from 1848 to 1852, he became an advocate for the independence of Provence, and above all for the excellence of Provençal, which he defined as "the first literary language of civilized Europe." It was, therefore, above all a movement in favor of Provençal rather that Occitan culture. However, it was the whole of the Occitan territories that was enriched by his contribution, he and poet Joseph Roumanille being the architects of the rebirth of Occitan culture in its entirety.

The Félibrige movement, supported by Alphonse de Lamartine, even welcomed Catalan poets expelled from Spain by Isabel II. Mistral's main work was the novel *Mireia,* published after eight years of writing, in which the author, on Roumanille's advice, opted for simplified spelling rather than the "classic" spelling inherited from the troubadours. The work tells the love of Vincent and the provençal beauty Mireia, a story comparable to that of Romeo and Juliet, which showed the strength of feelings. Charles Gounod composed his opera "Mireille" based on this work in 1863.

Mistral was the author of many other works—*Calendar, Nerte, The Golden Islands, The Forgotten*—which made him one of the most extensive writers in Provençal. In 1904, he was awarded the Nobel Prize along with José Echegaray, with whom he founded the Arlaten museum in Arles, where he died two years later.

The Félibrige movement, having initially been limited to Provençal, soon spread, from 1878, to the whole of Occitania, and even to the Catalan area; but in 1893, the Catalans were excluded, and the sphere of action was restricted to Occitania and Roussillon. The name came from a curiously erroneous popular tradition: in the ancient work *The Revelatinons of Sant Antoni,* the expression "Li sefer, libre de la ley" had been reinterpreted as "the seven troubadours of the law." The nonexistent word "felibre" was wrapped in a halo of prestige and mystery, for it could mean both "book" and "free," which synthesized the spirit of the nineteenth-century movement. (In any case, the Occitan language was to follow two norms: the Mistralian and the classical, thus undergoing a renaissance in the twentieth century outside Provence.)

**Corsica**

A beautiful Mediterranean island closer to Italy than to France, Corsica has a single plain on its eastern coast. Subjugated throughout its history to various different foreign powers (the Papacy, Muslims, the Republic of Pisa from the eleventh century, Genoa until the eighteenth century), the Corsicans, who speak an Italic but non-Italian language, either took refuge in the mountains where they raised livestock or settled in the central area of the island where they developed a subsistence agricultural economy. The occupiers, on the other hand, built their urban centers on the coast.

Competition for scarce resources, especially water, made Corsica—like other Mediterranean societies—ideal for the creation of extended families, and their grouping with dominant families gave rise to clans. Corsican society was therefore divided in all areas into two "partitu" or clans, bitterly opposed to each other, and united inward by their sense of "honor." Any personal affront was to the honor of the clan, and it had to be avenged with "vendettas" that could last for generations, although they were often ritualized to prevent them from ending up in deaths. (However, Corsicans kept their violence to themselves; visitors to the island were treated with the greatest hospitality.) The heads of the clans were the mediators between the political power of the occupiers and the Corsicans.

The revolt of Paoli—an illustrated Corsican—against Genoese domination was used by France to take control of the island from 1768. After initial resistance, the clans, whose chiefs were ennobled by the new invader, accepted the situation, and transferred the divisive French politics that the Revolution led to into their traditional logic. (The Bonapartes—Jacobins as they were—confronted the Paolistas—who were Girondians—and elevated their son Napoleon to the universal glory we all know of. After that, he did not hesitate to subjugate his home island to a state of emergency in order to quell any signs of revolt.)

The clans went from providing land in the nineteenth century to providing state resources such as jobs and subsidies, to which end they took on the form of continental political parties. But they actually remained apolitical, that is, oblivious to any ideological or class conflict, and switched sides depending on the position of the rival clan. At the end of the nineteenth century, Corsica was the poorest territory in the state, its population having fallen from 260,000 inhabitants to 160,000, mainly because of emigration. But the clientelist relationship of the clans with the French center—excellent since the reign of the Corsican Napoleon III—alleviated the consequences of the crisis in the nineteenth century, becoming clients of public administration and the metropolis's trade customs and gaining access to senior positions in the army, the police, and even the French government.

*National Corsican Literature*

The Corsican Revolution of 1729–1763 produced theorists, and national magazines were published. Giulio Malteo Nateli wrote about the "Corsican War," and the correspondence of national leader Pascual Paoli was published, as well as the anonymous "Sentimentí dei nazionale corsi contra l'invasione de lapatria," written in 1771. During the Risorgimento, the Bonapartist Multedo and the republican Borghetti wrote works of a romantic character in Italian, in which they set out to recover the popular heritage "contadineschi" choral works. In 1833 Rennucci composed a "Storia della Corsica de 1789 a 1830." Over the following decades, Merimée aroused interest in Corsican farmers with his *Notes of a Trip in Corsica*; and the German Gregorovius wrote *Corsica* in 1854, a romantic compendium of the history and geography of the island. In 1866, the compilation of anonymous popular poetry *Minutu corsu* was published.

It was from then on that some authors published exclusively in Corsican, for instance, Paolo Mate de la Foata; the Corsican literary magazine *Cirino* published more than forty comedies and comic sketches in Corsican.

The great figure on the cusp between the two centuries was Santu Casanova (1850–1934), considered the Mistral of Corsica, who in Ajaccio founded of the first literary magazine in Corsican, *A Tramuntana,* which proposed the literary unification of Corsican dialects based on the Cismuntan language. His work was the bridge between the old generations of authors in Italian and the new generations of authors in Corsican.

**Brittany**

The Bretons are descendants of the ancient inhabitants of the island of Great Britain; when waves of Germanic tribes—Angles, Saxons, and Jutes—invaded the island in the fifth and sixth centuries, the Britons fled en masse to Armorica, populated until then by peoples who were also of Celtic origin, settling on their lands and turning Armorica into Brittany. They created there a kingdom that survived until 1532, the year which the French king Francis I united the two crowns by the Edict of Nantes, although respecting the customs and administration of the Kingdom of Brittany. In the Modern Age (as in the Basque territories of the South and North), the Contra-Reformation swayed great influence on the country. There were mobilizations in defense of the old customs and contrary to Bourbon centralization—the Bonnets Rouges in 1675; the Marquis de Pontcalleck of 1720—which were repressed with great cruelty.

In 1789, Catholic Brittany distrusted the French Revolution and opposed civil status for the clergy; a new peasant and popular movement was triggered—the Chouans—which was recovered by the exiled nobility (and which was forty years ahead of Carlism). As a result, Brittany lost its unity and was divided into five departments in 1799. During the nineteenth century, Breton society was conservative, cohesive to the doctrine of the church, and the clergy and citizens of high prestige managed to integrate the peasant masses into French national structures at the end of the century. Meanwhile, central power carried out systematic de-Bretonization: the Bretons were the most despised citizens in France, the Breton language was openly oppressed, its use punished at schools, and while some customs do survive, they have been converted into folklore. (Brittany has two languages of its own: Breton, a Celtic language, and Gallo, a Latin language spoken in Upper Brittany.) In the last third of the nineteenth century, a fledgling nationalist movement appeared, mostly literary in character, within the framework of Romanticism;

the Viscount of Hersant de la Villemarqué had compiled a set of popular songs, the Barzaz-Breiz, which was to be the starting point of the rebirth of the Breton language and culture. (But Breton mobilization had to wait for the interwar to reach the sphere of politics.) Between 1870 and 1914, the Bretons received demeaning treatment; this did not prevent them from being sacrificed on the battlefields of World War I, in which 240,000 Breton young men died, one in four soldiers killed in the French Army (while the Breton population is one-eighth of that of France).

*Literature in Breton*

It was Hersant de la Villemarqué's Breton magazine *Barzaz Breiz* that prompted young authors to write in Breton during the second half of the nineteenth century; such was the case of Narcise Quellien, a friend of Renan's and author of the poems "Annaik" and "Breiz," and of Milin, editor of the magazine *Feiz ha Breiz*. Religious literature was also written, encouraged by Biblical traditions, its highpoint being Father Henry's "Sacred Songs." Theater groups also emerged with comedies written in Breton such as Jobig Koat de Montroulez's "The Girl with the Five Men in Love."

**Scotland**

Belonging to this category of large Western peoples such as Quebec or Catalunya, whose mature national structures and abundant population make them perfectly viable as nation-states, was Scotland. The United Kingdom, with a unitary but scarcely differentiated center, has allowed the flourishing and self-regulation of Scottish civil society. Scottish claims for sovereignty over the last century have taken the form of home rule, devolution within the framework of the European Union, and they have gone beyond the framework of nationalist parties.

It occupies the northern third of the island of Great Britain and the northern isles—the Hebrides among them—with a current population of five and a half million inhabitants (10 percent of the whole British population). The linguistic assimilation process carried out by the English triumphed in the Lowlands—home to major Scottish cities such as Edinburgh or Glasgow—and partially failed in the Highlands and Islands, where the Celtic and Gaelic-speaking populations are concentrated (although today there are no more than eighty thousand who speak the language).

In 1603, James I combined the crowns of the kingdoms of Scotland and England; in 1707, London made the Scottish State disappear through the Act of

Union, transferring its parliament to Westminster. The doctrine of the pact has since been part of Scottish political culture. Furthermore, the survival of civil society in Scotland—the church, legal, and teaching systems—was made possible by the uniqueness of the United Kingdom. This, indeed, although unitary, had historically been a weak state, leaving large areas of public life in the hands of self-regulated civilian institutions; the absence of centralization and uniformity prevented the implementation of absolutism in the sixteenth century, and of Jacobinism in the nineteenth century. Education, professional life, and later on, industrial relations were left outside state control.

Therefore, the demise of their Parliament in 1707 did not worry the Scots, who were much more interested in the survival of their laws, which were based on Roman law, contrary to English law, and which is based on common law. Scottish hyper-representation in the London Parliament, which was granted to them to compensate them for the loss of their own institution, also helped, accentuated as a result of the relative decline in their population (Scottish affairs today continue to be addressed at Westminster through specific commissions). In addition, the separate Church of Scotland (the Kirk) played an important role, founded on the doctrine of the Two Kingdoms, in the areas of the regulation of social life and teaching. Until the end of the nineteenth century, there was thus informal home rule in Scotland, with most public administration in the hands of the Kirk or local government. During the Industrial Revolution, the British Empire also offered Welsh and Scottish industrialists and mining owners access to the British and Imperial markets, thus fostering Scotland's loyalty to the Empire.

But the ancestral suspicion of the English had not disappeared. The extension of British competences in Scotland since the late nineteenth century—in 1885 a Secretary of State for Scotland directly dependent on London was created and would be transformed into the Scottish Office after World War I—sparked growing protests.

### *Scotland: The Difficult Survival of Indigenous Languages Confronted with the State Language (English)*

Gaelic literature had a problem common to several of the indigenous language literatures of European national minorities: their inferiority regarding the competence of their work compared with that of peripheral authors who wrote their works in the language of the state. This unequal competition deepened when, in the nineteenth century, nation-state nationalism came into conflict with that of minorities within its territory, which led to the rejection, open or disguised, of its literary production, always suspected of disloyalty toward "the language of the Empire"; the national option thus became the dividing line between them in many cases. Where famous writers emerged in the state language, which happened in Scotland (and also in Galicia and the Basque Country), difficulties facing the works of indigenous authors increased.

This did not prevent peripheral writers, writing in the state language, from reflecting the themes of their country in their works (the quality of which could be excellent); proof of that are the Basque seafood and peasant-themed novels by Pío Baroja, the poetic immersion in the rural Galicia of Valle-Inclán . . . and as for Scotland, the endearing treatment of Scottish history and folklore in Walter Scott's writing. Not to mention bilingual Robert Burns, who wrote in English and Gaelic, unanimously considered the great national poet of Scotland, his poetry being censored in the Victorian Era as subversive. In any case, the reality was that the great Scottish writers who increased in popularity and prestige in nineteenth-century English literature did not worry excessively about their own people. Such was the case, among many others, of Arthur Conan Doyle, creator of Sherlock Holmes; Robert Louis Stevenson, with his creation of Dr. Jekyll and Mr. Hyde, and his superb adventure novel *Treasure Island*; J. M. Barrie, who has charmed generations of children as well as the not so young, with his *Peter Pan.* (The case of Ireland was similar, without independence in the twentieth century substantially changing the basis of the problem.)

In Scotland, in the mid-nineteenth century, there was a renaissance of the literary use of Scottish Gaelic in a process of going back to the origins that affected almost all the arts. A byproduct of the industrialization and urbanization of Scottish society, this did not prevent the continued production of romantic and historical novels such as Walter Scott's, which exalted mythical heroes and Scottish landscapes.

The revitalization of Scottish Gaelic as a literary language had numerous advocates and created quality authors, with Sorley MacLean standing out amongst them. These authors emphasized the linguistic conflict that was taking place in Scotland during these years, highlighting through their characters that the use of Gaelic was becoming increasingly widespread, progressing, however paradoxical it may seem, in step with the increasingly industrialized lifestyle.

**Wales**

On the east of the island of Great Britain, Wales was inhabited at the end of the Stone Age by Celtic Bretons. The Romans began their conquest in 43 CE. The British tribes of pre-Roman times—which occupied the present territory of Wales as well as parts of England and Scotland—then became part of the Roman province of Britain. Several British tribes were organized in post-Roman times into a set of small kingdoms, while converting to Christianity. It was then that British languages and cultures began to separate, with the Welsh being the largest of these groups, which made its independence last until the eleventh century. The early Middle Ages involved struggles first against the English kingdoms, and then against the Normans. Their bellicosity was to continue until the death of the last king of Wales in 1292, when King Edward I of England conquered the principality of Wales and annexed it to England; since then, the heir to the king of England has had the title of Prince of Wales. This did not end Welsh struggles against England; finally, the English took control of the country. King Henry IV, himself of Welsh origin, of Tudor lineage, approved the acts of Wales that fully incorporated the country into the Kingdom of England. Wales thus became part of the kingdom in 1707 and also the United Kingdom, which did not prevent the Welsh from preserving their language and culture, to which the full translation of the Bible into Welsh by William Morgan in 1558 contributed.

In the eighteenth century, two changes greatly affected Wales: the Welsh Methodist renaissance—which shaped a religiously nonconformist country—and the Industrial Revolution, especially dynamic in the coal and iron industries of the southeast of the country. There was a rapid increase in population, and also a de facto divide between the southeastern Welsh—anglicized by the many immigrants—and the rural areas that preserved their traditional idiosyncrasy. The focus of the cultural resurgence was the Eisteddfod, which strengthened many Welsh people's conviction to form a differentiated people.

*The Impact in Wales of the Industrial Revolution*

As in Scotland, the industrial revolution greatly affected Wales, whose southern valleys adjoining England received a significant migratory flow. Many of the newcomers made a great effort to learn the language of the country and integrate into their local communities. This produced a strong demand for all kinds of literature in Welsh language: books, newspapers, magazines, poetry, ballads, sermons, etc. Some well-off immigrants, such as Lady Charlotte Guest, helped enrich indigenous cultural life, and the Eisteddfod tradition multiplied interest in Gaelic literature in all its genres. Poets of the time used Celtic pseudonyms at these traditional festivals, continuing to use them even when they became recognized poets. The novel, however, was late in development; it was Daniel Owen who made it popular after 1885 with *Rhys Lewis* and *Enoch Huws.*

It was in the late nineteenth and early twentieth centuries that Welsh literature began to be used for political purposes. Sander Lewis, leader of Welsh nationalism—who after spending his childhood in Liverpool was imprisoned in Scotland for his protesting—chose theater as a means of national mobilization and awareness. Teacher and writer Kate Roberts followed a similar itinerary.

**Ireland and Contesting the Colonial Past**

The British occupation of the island of Ireland acquired religious connotations in the time of Henry VIII; he was appointed king of Ireland in 1539, four years after the implementation of Anglican Protestantism in his kingdom. In the early seventeenth century, Mary Tudor reinforced the politics of "plantations," settlements of Protestant settlers in the lands of Catholic peasants. After half a century of uprisings, puritanical leader Oliver Cromwell's landing led to the enactment of the Colonization Act, confiscating two-thirds of the land held until then by Irish owners. At the end of that century, Catholic Jacobites, captained by Talbot, rebelled in Ireland against Protestant King William of Orange. James II was defeated by the Orangists on the banks of the River Boyne in Ulster on July 12, 1690. The mythical commemoration of that battle—which symbolizes the imaginary cultural and moral superiority of Protestants, supposedly enlightened and democratic, compared with the Catholics, seen as obscurantist and reactionary—has continued to be the primary symbolic capital of some Unionist currents in Northern Ireland.

For more than a century, until 1829, Catholics, the majority of the Irish population, were excluded from Parliament and subjected to special criminal laws, and the Catholic Church was forbidden, although tolerated. But it was the entire island that was subjected to a British colonial-style mercantilist policy and that promoted an onset of Protestant Irish nationalism (in whose origins had participated, for example, Jonathan Swift, the writer of *Gulliver's Travels*).

At the end of the eighteenth century, the example of the American and French revolutions influenced Ireland, spreading the symbol of European nations flourishing on the Tree of Freedom—which was to be passed on to the Basques later by the bard Iparagirre. Secret societies were formed, from which the United Irish conspiracy association emerged in 1795, and which undertook an insurrection three years later. Leading nationalist leaders, such as Wolfe Tone, were Protestants, but the idea of freedom meant different things to different people. In the north of the island, where the "plantations" had been more intense—and dominated by Presbyterians of Scottish origin—the idea of the Rights of Man was inspired by David Hume and Adam Smith, leaders of the Scottish Enlightenment; in the south, on the other hand, it meant the conveyance of Protestant properties into Catholic hands and the end of the oppression they were being subjected to. However, British troops, similar to Protestants and Catholics in a way, were killing fifty thousand people from a population of four million. The Irish bards, who presented Napoleon as a liberator—although the nationalists vainly awaited his support—sang to the Tree of Liberty in memory of 1798; this theme was to go through Pearse to the current IRA.

Following the uprising, in 1800 the British enacted a Union Act which repealed the Irish Parliament, making the island an agricultural annex to Britain. A Catholic, Gaelic-speaking but counter-revolutionary leader, Daniel O'Connell, opposed this situation, ensuring that the Catholic Emancipation Act was passed in London. Protestants such as Davies and Catholics such as Mitchell collaborated in the insurrectional movement of the Young Irish that grew up around them. The major presence of Protestants in nineteenth-century Irish nationalism is explained by the Protestant monopoly on higher education; while the leaders were mostly Protestant, the mass of followers was composed almost exclusively of disinherited Catholics. But by religion preventing mixed marriages, the existence of two separate cultural groups set up a caste system that was reproduced for centuries. Thus, although Irish nationalism was born anti-sectarian, the dynamics that led the Catholic masses to confront Protestant landholders soon led to sectarianism.

From 1845 to 1849, the Great Famine caused by successive poor harvests aggravated peasant misery and caused one and a half million deaths, with another million Irish people being exiled to the United States, where they entered their own sub-proletariat. (This situation explains why thirty million Americans are currently attributed Irish descent; if you add to this the fact that four of the signatories of the Philadelphia Declaration—the forerunner of American independence—were of Irish origin, it is easy to understand the support that the Irish cause found in that country.)

In the 1850s, an insurgent organization, the Republican Irish Brotherhood, was set up simultaneously in Dublin and New York, and its action groups gave themselves the name "Fenians." This organization, which enjoyed popular support in Ireland in 1867, though not from the clergy, was to unleash a new—and failed—insurrection-followed lynching (such as Birmingham's three "martyrs"). This experience, the first in Western Europe of ethnonational armed struggle, had its antecedent in the eighteenth-century Irish "whiteboysmo"—the movement of the "boys of the parish"—which defended the people against the church and the landowners and demanded the application of "the rights of the English" to the Irish. It was a nonsectarian movement, involving Catholics and Protestants, who communicated through parish-to-parish fires. (But in the nineteenth century, this movement diversified; it acquired a Fenian tone in the South, while it gave rise to Protestant sectarian formations such as the Orange League in Ulster.)

However, and in the wake of the Great Famine, the numbers of day laborers decreased and smallholders increased, while the Catholic Church became national; in the last third of the nineteenth century, there was already a kind of free peasants, Catholics, and democrats who formed the basis of Irish nationalism. Paradoxically, it was a Protestant landowner, Charles Stewart Parnell, who became the leader of this Catholic peasant movement; it is equally significant that he fell out of favor in 1890, having violated traditional Catholic morality because of his adulterous relationship with the wife of one of his lieutenants.

In the last decade of the nineteenth century, new political formations crystallized. In Dublin and Belfast, the labor movement fueled the formation of the Marxist Irish Socialist Republican Party, in whose ranks Connolly served. In 1899, Fenian nationalism inspired the birth of the nationalist Sinn Féin party (in Gaelic, "we alone"), then of a conservative nature. The British liberals, captained by Gladstone, were in favor of restoring Irish self-government in the form of "home rule." This project was opposed by the English conservatives and, above all, the Northern Irish Unionists, who had already grown strong in the nine counties of Ulster. (In this area, there had been intense industrialization focused on steelmaking and shipbuilding and centered on the port of Belfast, very similar to that which at the same time was taking place in the Basque Country.) In 1910, faced with the probable passing of home rule, there was a strong reaction from the Order of Orange, the Ulster Unionist Council was militarized, and its leaders, led by Edward Carson, gathered 450,000 signatures in opposition to the law. This led to the postponement of the entry into force of the home rule approved at Westminster in 1914, which put independence from the UK at the forefront of Ireland's political agenda.

### *Irish Literature in Gaelic Before and After the 1914 Revolution*

The difference in official support, as well as literary impact, between Welsh language authors and those using English, was even greater in Ireland. The second block featured literati as old as William Butler Yeats, Oscar Wilde, George Bernard Shaw (not to mention post-1914 universal literary giants such as James Joyce and Samuel Beckett). At the same time, usually Irish literates in the English language—contrary to the Basque, Galician, and Scottish cases—omitted from their works the themes and the peculiarities of their own country (James Joyce would focus his interest not on Ireland but Dublin, although with a fascinating result).

And yet, despite the decline of Gaelic as a spoken language, throughout the nineteenth century, and especially in its second half, there was a revival of Celtic culture and writing. It began successfully with the publication in 1823 of James Pritchard's *Celtic Grammar*, which paved the way for other prominent Celtists.

Moreover, the national conflict between Protestants and Catholics that led to the nationalist divide between Unionists (pro-British) and Republicans (Irish patriots) was not reproduced (or scarcely reproduced) in the literary field until the 1914 uprising. It was a Protestant cleric, William Reeves, who, when head of the Irish Academy, published his *Memoirs of the Book of Armagnac.*

The Catholic priest Eugene O'Growney promoted for the first literary magazine in Gaelic, *Iris leaghar na Gaeshilge,* published between 1882 and 1909, which ended up being the literary supplement of the first Gaelic newspaper, *Faina an Eire, Dawn.* He published in it the patriotic poem "Mise Eire" ("I am Ireland"); for some time, *Faina an Eire* was the bilingual weekly of the Gaelic League. The definitive impulse for Gaelic was, after the founding of the Conradh na Gaedhilge (the Gaelic League), reinforced in 1900 with the magazine *The Poor Old Woman (An san van vocht),* which was set up by men and women of Ulster interested in the study of Gaelic.

## Notes

1 With regard to the concepts of political culture, identities, and ideologies in connection with the peripheral nationalisms of Western Europe, I have used the summary of various authors' work contained in my following two works:

1. Letamendia, F. (1997). *Juego de espejos. Conflitos nacionales centro-periferia*, Ed. Trotta, especially I. Centro y Periferia 4 (Los nacionalismos periféricos (1): identidad e ideología) (English translation: *Game of Mirrors: Centre-Periphery National Conflicts*), London: Routledge (2019).
2. Letamendia, F. (2013). *El hilo invisible: identidades políticas e ideologías,* Editorial Service of the University of the Basque Country; in particular, chapter I, *El hilo invisible: cultura política, identidades e ieologías*; and chapter 17, *Los nacionalismos.*

I have completed information on the indigenous language literatures of peripheral nationalisms in Western Europe, focusing on the period from the second half of the nineteenth century to 1914, using the following Wikipedia articles: *Literatura en catalán, Literatura en gallego, Literatura en euskera, Félibrige, Literatura en occitano, Literatura en corso, Literatura en bretón, Literatura en gaélico escocés, Literatura de Irlanda.*

# 4

# Independence as a Political Objective in the Basque Country (1789–2019)

*Xabier Irujo*

The National Constituent Assembly of France passed a series of decrees between August 4 and 11, 1789, on the abolition of feudalism, class privileges, and manorial rights that came into force on November 3 of that same year.[1] As a consequence of that decree, the three Basque states—Lapurdi, Zuberoa, and the Kingdom of Navarre—lost their independence and, with it, their exclusive codes of law and their institutions. None of these three states were feudal regimes, and this decree entailed the unilateral and clearly illegal dissolution of the entire legal corpus of the three Basque states of the Northern Basque Country.[2]

As a consequence of this outrage, the state's general of the Kingdom of Navarre met in Donibane Garazi September 19-22 to order the creation of a memorial addressed to the French national assembly. The task fell to the trustee of the kingdom, Étienne de Polverel, who, at the command of the Parliament of Navarre, published said treaty that same year under the title *Tableau de la Constitution du Royaume de Navarre et des Rapports avec la France*.[3] In this document, the Parliament of Navarre made the case that the Navarrese state always had its own laws, institutions, and political independence, both with respect to Castile and with respect to France. In 1789, Navarre—like Lapurdi and Zuberoa and the rest of the Basque territories—had legislative, executive, and judicial powers with full independence and its own territory and customs. Consequently, Navarre was not part of either Castile or France, and the Navarrese were neither Castilian nor French. And the same could be said of Lapurdi and Zuberoa.

In any case, the petitions and protests of the parliaments and representatives of Navarre, Lapurdi, and Zuberoa were ignored and, as a result of the decree of January 12, 1790, the Basque states were included in the new department of the Lower Pyrenees, which also included Bearn.

Faced with the illegitimate dispossession of the Basque states, the people of Lapurdi, Navarra, and Zuberoa demonstrated against the legislation passed by the French assembly. The revolutionary government reacted with vigor. In the context of the War of the Convention (1793-1795), Bertrand de Barère—a member of the public health committee and architect of the La Vendée genocide campaign—stated on January 27, 1794, that the Basque people were a collective of fanatics whose culture and language had to be eradicated (*le fanatisme parle le basque* ).[4] A little less than two months later, the National Convention ordered the mobilization of more than four thousand civilians from various towns in Lapurdi and Navarre. These people, who were forbidden to bring food or warm clothing, marched on foot in reprehensible conditions to various churches in Les Landes where, separated from their families, they lived in extreme situations that led to the death of more than sixteen hundred of them.[5]

These events gave rise to the demand for the restitution of the exclusive institutions of the Basque states and their full sovereignty. In short, it was from the loss of political independence in 1789 that the Basques of Lapurdi, Navarre, and Zuberoa began to claim their independence and the restitution of their old laws or *fueros*.

The French Revolution led to the Napoleonic Wars that ended as they had begun in 1804, with a great slaughter (the Battle of Waterloo on June 18, 1815). But, despite the defeat, some of the principles of French political ideology permeated Spanish society, which adopted one cardinal concept with great ease and excessive enthusiasm: the unity and indivisibility of the Spanish state. In May 1808, Napoleon called an assembly in Baiona with two fundamental aims. On the one hand, following the Jacobin model, passing a constitution for the entire Spanish state. On the other, accepting the abdication of Carlos IV of Castile in favor of his son and heir, Fernando VII, and later naming Napoleon for the throne; the latter went on to transfer it to his brother Joseph Bonaparte. In one day, the crowns of Castile and Navarre had rested on four different heads.

Regarding the constitution for the new state, an assembly called the General Council was organized, meeting in Baiona on June 15, 1808, to discuss and pass the new Spanish constitution. Four days later the Supreme Board of the new government met, and on June 25 representatives from the various territories occupied by Napoleon's troops took part, including representatives from the Basque states of Araba, Bizkaia, Gipuzkoa, and Navarre. Juan Jose Maria Yandiola, representative of the General Councils or Parliament of Bizkaia, stated that it was not legitimate to pass a new constitution for the welfare of the Spanish nation at the expense of the Basque nation. Yandiola, as Polverel had stated before him, believed that Spain needed a constitution, but that Bizkaia—and, in the same way, the other Basque territories—already had their own constitutions—their charters—which had served the people well for several centuries, and without which it could not continue to exist.[6] Luis Gainza and Miguel Escudero were also present at the assembly of Baiona as representatives of the Kingdom of Navarre, and they made the same point that Polverel had in 1789. And the Marquis of Montehermoso—representative of the Brotherhood of Araba—and Jose Maria de Lardizabal—representing Gipuzkoa—also made the same point using the same arguments: the votes of the inhabitants of those states, their wishes, and their demands were to keep their political, administrative, and financial independence.[7]

However, despite the protests of the Basque representatives, the constitution was imposed by Napoleon in order to grant his brother a throne and a crown and, later, when Joseph Bonaparte lost both at the battle of Vitoria in 1812, the historical events of 1808 were repeated at Cadiz in 1812, where the deputies representing the Spanish people passed the Spanish monarchy's constitution without taking into account the protests of the Basque delegates. The first article—"The Spanish nation is the collectivity of the Spaniards of both hemispheres. [Europe and America]"[8]—overthrew at a stroke the legal corpus and the institutions of the four Basque states, whose origin dates back to the year 824 and, by doing so, illegitimately positioned the Basques among the Spaniards. The lack of a valid resolution to the conflict resulting from the foundation of the new political system and dismantling the Basque provincial systems led to two long, bloody wars fought on Basque soil: the First Carlist War or Seven Years' War (1833 -1839) and the Second Carlist War (1872-1876). Political conflict also broke out in Catalunya, which was involved in three Carlist wars and uninterrupted social unrest throughout the nineteenth century.

During the First Carlist War, Agosti Xaho examined the issue of Basque insurrection from a purely political and ideological perspective. He traveled to the Basque Country during the First Carlist War, and then put forward the creation of an independent, federal Basque state in his works, *Voyage en Navarre pendant l'insurrection des basques* (1830-1835) in 1836, and *Paroles d 'un Biscaïen aux liberals de la reine Christine* in 1834, as well as in various articles published in the magazines *L'Ariel, Courrier des Pyrénées* (1844),[9] and *Uskal-Herriko Gaseta* (1848), the latter of which was one of the first newspapers written in Basque. Xaho also believed that the First Carlist War was "a war of extermination against the independence of the Basque people," in the course of which their national independence and their civil liberty were at stake.[10]

Xaho also created some of the first symbols of the Basque independence movement when, in 1836, he published a Basque grammar book dedicated to "Zazpi Uskal-Herrietako Uskaldunei"—"the Basques of the seven territories"—which subsequently gave rise to the motto *Zazpiak Bat*—"Seven in One."[11] The motto *Zazpiak Bat* included the three non-Iberian Basque territories—Lapurdi, Lower Navarre, and Zuberoa—into the Basque brotherhood, as well as the southern Kingdom of Navarre. The underlying cardinal idea was that, although the seven Basque territories that had formed had been states since 1522, they made up a single nation, a political motto that has survived to this day.

In any case, from 1812 onward the Kingdom of Navarre in the south and Araba, Bizkaia, and Gipuzkoa were faced with the same outrage that the Kingdom of Navarre in the north and Lapurdi and Zuberoa had suffered from in 1789: after the passing of the law "of confirmation" of the fueros in October 1839 by the Spanish Parliament, the Basque states were subordinated to the Spanish Constitution of 1837 after seven years of armed conflict during the First Carlist War (1833-1839). Subsequently, the law of August 16, 1841, dismantled the Kingdom of Navarre and made it a province of the Spanish state. Then, as Polverel had done before, the trustee of the kingdom, Angel Sagaseta, officially protested on behalf of the Parliament of the Kingdom of Navarre and published a book—*Fueros fundamentales del Reino de Navarra: y defensa legal de los mismos*—whose first edition of 1840 was censored.[12]

Sagaseta's speech was identical in its principles, scope, and significance to Polverel's from 1789. Sagaseta stated in the name of the Navarrese Parliament that the Kingdom of Navarre was an independent state and, therefore, separate from the kingdoms of Castile and Aragon. Navarre had kept its laws (fueros—charters), its institutions, its own currency and, in fact, its political independence for more than a thousand years since its foundation in 824. Sagaseta added that, after the conquest and division of Navarre between 1512 and 1530, Ferdinand II of Aragon had sworn allegiance to the charters of Navarre, so there was no incorporation of Navarre into Castile and Aragon, but, rather, the kingdom

> remained completely independent of the other kingdoms and as it had existed before with its own jurisdictions, laws, courts, council and all the other signs of complete, independent separation (. . .). That was the true legal status at the death of Fernando III of Navarre, VII of Castile. (. . .) In the course of time, Aragon, Castile and the other kingdoms of Spain were stripped of their respective constitutions; for whatever reasons, the constitutions of Gipuzkoa, Araba, Bizkaia and

> Navarre survived. And is it credible that a liberal, enlightened government will take its extremely ancient constitution away from Navarre? Will it be possible to transform the oldest kingdom on the peninsula into a mere province, thus destroying it as an independent monarchy? The nature of representative government does not allow this; that would be wholly contrary to its essential principles; governments of this type can never ignore justice; they never attack the freedom of other kingdoms, and, if they ever try to be so, that is the result of not being properly educated about their nature and legitimacy; after finding out about them, they leave them unharmed, and respect them.[13]

The answer was two decrees and sending of troops to Basque soil. As a result of the decree of October 29, 1841, Spanish general Baldomero Espartero abolished the right of refusal[14] and the councils, moved customs posts to the coast, and imposed a judicial system controlled by the central government and, as established by the decree of 1844, partially reestablished the charter regime in order to facilitate the modification of the charters in accordance with the provisions of the law of 1839. Sagaseta was exiled and Araba, Bizkaia, Gipuzkoa, and Navarre became provinces of the Spanish state, giving rise to a political vindication that continues to this day, and generating an uninterrupted period of political unrest and revolutions and wars causing death, exile, and prison to an extent that is hard to quantify.

The interpretation of the political nature and independence of the Basque states, which defended themselves using their own institutions both in the context of the French Revolution—Lapurdi, Navarre, and Zuberoa—and in that of the First Carlist War—the four Southern Basque states: Araba, Bizkaia, Navarre, and Zuberoa—is the same one that John Adams made of the Basque political regime in his work *A Defense of the Constitutions of Government of the United States of America* of 1787.[15] In the fourth letter, entitled *Biscay*, Adams wrote that "in a research like this, after those people in Europe who have had the skill, courage, and fortune, to preserve a voice in the government, Biscay, in Spain, ought by no means to be omitted. While their neighbors have long since resigned all their pretensions into the hands of kings and priests, this extraordinary people have preserved their ancient language, genius, laws, government, and manners, without innovation, longer than any other nation of Europe."[16]

The Basque independence movement began in 1789 as a reaction to the liberal French and Spanish constitutionalism and the subsequent foundation of both countries, one consequence of which was the abolition of the Basque states' charters and the institutions, which had been politically independent for a thousand years. The liberal French constitutionalism of 1789 and Spanish of 1812 were also the results of a complex historical process in the political sphere, abrupt and discontinuous, and framed within the context of industrialization. These two characteristics mark the political process started in 1789 and which is still ongoing. On the one hand, the charters, a precedent-based legal corpus, reflected not only the Basque states' laws but also a way of life, the laws being based on custom. When the charters were abolished, the way of organizing Basque society, its way of administering the territory, of managing inheritances and commercial contracts, of administering communal lands and a whole vast sociocultural universe, was suspended, as was their language. So, the sociocultural, economic, and political impact of the elimination of this way of life led to a serious general crisis in Basque culture. On the other hand, the reaction which this political process provoked was massive and forceful as the Basque states had enjoyed a self-governing tradition, including with more than a thousand years of history in the case of the Kingdom of Navarre (824-1841).

After the disintegration of the Basque political system, between 1839 and 1854 there was intense debate between two conflicting positions: constitutionalism and the restoration of the charters. The first response of the Basques to the creation of the new states was to demand the return of the country's charters, laws, and institutions. However, over the years "realist" currents of opinion began to form, initially held by minorities who defended a pact or "agreed arrangement" with the central state in order to recover at least part of the historical rights and the political powers lost in 1839. Which is why the central state began to consider possibilities other than Jacobin centralism, so that the range of ideological possibilities gradually became more complicated as the nineteenth century progressed. Over this period, some attempts at a political agreement took place between the defenders of moderate constitutionalism and the "realist" approach to the charters.

On May 3, 1855, the civil confiscation law was published in the *Madrid Gazette*, which affected public property owned by city and town councils.[17] Public ownership of land had been one of the bases of the Basque political system, which is why the proportion of public land in the Basque territories was higher than 60 percent throughout the Basque states. By means of this law, finance minister Pascual Madoz decreed it to be auctioned, and the funds raised would go to the Madrid finance ministry. This led to the first public call for independence a few days after the confiscation law was published in the *Madrid Gazette*; it appeared in a pamphlet titled *Vascongados*. The only copy that exists today was in a folder labeled *Papeles propios*, belonging to Carlist deputy Manuel Irujo de Tafalla.

The proclamation was very short—around 1,500 words long and printed on two pages—and it contains the four cardinal ideas that had been repeated since Polverel and Sagaseta published their defenses of the charters, laws, and institutions of the Kingdom of Navarre: (1) It is not possible to reach a negotiated agreement with Spain, so it is necessary to break the political ties that unite the Basques to the Spaniards and, by regaining independence, return to being a "separate land"; (2) The Basques do not need anyone to govern their public affairs; (3) The Basques are a nation; and (4) Independence will end decades of political, social, cultural, and economic abuse and the illegal and unjust dismantling of the Basques' institutions and laws.[18]

Betrand de Barère—inspired by the reports by Henri Grégoire and under the political leadership of Maximilien Robespierre, Georges Danton, and Saint-Just—had been one of the promoters of "la terreur linguistique" during the French Revolution. The foundations of the linguistic policy of the French state were laid after the passing between June 1793 and December 1794 of the so-called "autumn decrees," a score of legal texts that seriously affected the survival of the languages spoken in the territory of the republic "because among free people, the language must be one and the same for all."[19] One of the more than twenty-five languages that were spoken in the republic, *Langue d'oïl*, was finally imposed as the state language and was officially classified as *langue française*, a political term that refers to its legal official status, *symbole de l'unité nationale*. The Jacobin party promoted the imposition of the French language to the detriment of all others in all areas of the state administration, the educational system, and the administration of justice.[20] In parallel to the establishment of an official language, both Barère and Grégoire had recommended the destruction of the rest of the languages spoken in the republic, which they disparagingly referred to as *patois*, *jargons*, or *idiomes féodaux*.[21] From that point of view, the use of one language or another was perceived as a political tool; speaking in French made citizens revolutionary and activist, while allowing them to speak in Breton, Catalan, Basque, or Bearnaise meant "leaving them mired in ignorance," and therefore "subjects of the counterrevolution."[22]

Consequently, with this ideology, the French Republic became a militantly monolingual state through the implementation of a free but compulsory public education system where future citizens would learn the language and ideology of their rulers and forget all others. Barère referred to these new schools as "the fields of Mars," while Grégoire preferred to call them "hospitals of the human spirit." In reality, it was the application of the logic and principles of the industrial revolution in the field of politics: the introduction and implantation of administration and public education systems aimed at mass-producing patriotic citizens. In fact, successive Spanish governments after 1839 imitated French language policy and established a monolingual state to the exclusion of the Basque, Catalan, Galician, and many other languages spoken in the state. These events, together with the purely political and institutional demands of the reintroduction of the charters, led to a political-cultural current in the Basque Country known as Euzko Pizkundea ("Basque Cultural Renaissance"), which was at its zenith between 1852 and 1876 but lasted until 1936.

One of the first events of Euzko Pizkundea were the Lore Jokoak ("Floral Games"), literary contests organized in the Northern Basque Country from 1851 by Anton Abadia.[23] These contests were very popular among the Basques. In addition to the literary trend that grew up around them, many of the most representative writers of the time took part; for instance, Joan Batista Elizanburu, Grazian Adema "Zaldubi," Felipe Arrese Beitia, Evaristo Bustintza "Kirikiño," and Pedro Mari Otaño, among many others. In general terms, the themes dealt with in the works of many of these writers included the recovery of the Basque language, which was understood to be the spirit and cornerstone of the country's culture. In all of them, Carlist or pro-charter political principles were combined with principles and ideas related to the need to promote and preserve Basque culture.

One of the most emblematic authors of the time was Joxemari Iparragirre, an enthusiastic Carlist supporter who, during the First Carlist War, had joined the First Gipuzkoa Battalion. He was exiled twice because of his political activism, from Spain in 1839 and from France in 1848. In 1851, he returned to the Basque Country but was imprisoned in Tolosa and then exiled in 1855. There he composed his famous poem, *Nire amak baleki*. Iparragirre was to a great extent the main transmitter of Carlist political symbology, and he was responsible for all Basques adopting a preexisting symbol, the tree of Gernika, as a national symbol (1853) when in 1853 also he composed his famous poem, *Gernikako arbola*; it became and still is the unofficial Basque national anthem.

Between 1879 and 1918, around 115 literary festivals were held in the Basque Country, and those initiatives were echoed in Catalunya from 1859 and in Galicia from 1863.[24] It was from those dates that the Renaixença in Catalunya and the Rexurdimento in Galicia emerged with major cultural programs, plus a clear political agenda and purpose. From 1855 onward, the political demands and pro-independence ideology in Euskadi were centered on the survival of Basque culture.

After more than three decades of political, economic, social, and cultural conflict, and without the government of the Spanish state giving the slightest guarantee for survival of the Basque charter system, in 1872 the Second Carlist War broke out, a conflict that would devastate the country for four years. Consequently, the followers of the Carlist Party's pro-charter and revivalist ideology—most of the Basque population—organized a federal state with four councils or governments for Araba, Bizkaia, Gipuzkoa, and Navarre. A secretariat of state and a war office were set up, as was a ministry of state and justice, and a ministry of education, which promoted the teaching of the Basque language and reopened the University of Oñati. The Carlist state also set up courts of justice and passed a penal code. Coin was minted at Oñati which, together with Lizarra, was the capital of the new Carlist state.[25]

At the end of the war, the president of the council of ministers of the Spanish state, Antonio Cánovas, decreed the abolition of the Basque political system. As stated in the first article of the law of July 21, 1876, the Basques were obliged to carry out "the duties that the political constitution has always imposed on all Spaniards to respond to the call to arms, and to contribute to the expenses of the state in proportion to their assets," which meant that the old Basque states were obliged from that date to contribute to central state public expenses in proportion to their population, paying income, and ordinary and exceptional taxes as set by the Spanish government's state budgets. The fourth article allowed the central government to undertake "all the reforms called for in the old charter regimes, as well as for the welfare of the Basque peoples and for the good government and security of the Nation," while the sixth article established that the Spanish government was "invested by this law with all the extraordinary and discretionary powers that its exact and complete execution requires."[26] In short, the law marked the end of the independence of the Basque states.

At the same time, Canovas prohibited the charter conferences of Araba, Bizkaia, Gipuzkoa, and Navarre, abolished the general councils (parliaments) and governments, and appointed provincial deputies by royal order. The malaise caused by the abolition of the charter laws and the fear of a new insurrection led Canovas to agree to negotiate economic agreements with the Basque administrations in 1878. These agreements were about tax matters, and by them the Basque states Could collect their own taxes and pay an annual income to the state called a quota, the amount of which would be negotiated bilaterally between the four Basque councils or governments and the government of Madrid. In practice, the economic agreements meant accepting independence in fiscal matters, and although in 1893 finance minister Germán Gamazo tried to suppress the provincial fiscal regime in Navarre, the popular rising known as "la Gamazada" made him desist: practically all the people of Navarre took to the streets to claim their historical rights and their fiscal independence.[27]

The abolition of the charters at the end of the Second Carlist War led to the gestation process for the pro-independence program, which was fully formed well into the twentieth century. However, during the long interwar period (1839-1872) a wide range of intermediate positions between the independence movement and centralism—the two extreme positions—also emerged. The prevailing position at the end of the Second Carlist War was that of the liberals, which by means of the law of July 1876 unilaterally imposed the legal measures defended by the most radical constitutionalism of Jacobin origins. However, after several years of a state of war and emergency on Basque soil, the most intransigently centralist positions gave rise to moderate, decentralizing liberalism (charter liberalism) that, together with the fear of a new Carlist insurrection, led to an agreement with the Basque states on tax matters. From these positions it is possible to make out an incipient autonomism, a current of political thought from Catalunya which believed that the resolution of Basque and Catalan political conflicts would have to involve an agreement between them and the state government involving the state authorities accepting a certain degree of decentralization.[28]

Independence in 1876 was still a minority option. The first pro-Basque or Basque nationalist parties emerged at the end of the Second Carlist to defend what had been lost in the war in the political arena; in other words, the full restitution of the charters or the creation of an independent Basque republic. The first party with a marked Basque character was the Asociación Euskara de Navarra, an association set up by Juan Iturralde y Suit in 1877. Some of the most prestigious writers and linguists of the time joined this political and cultural group, including Arturo Campión, Estanislao Aranzadi, Hermilio Oloriz, Serafín Olave, Florencio Ansoleaga, Salvador Etxaide, Esteban Obanos, and Antero Irazoqui. Asociación Euskara's political and social objective was "to preserve and propagate Basque-Navarrese language, literature and history, to study its legislation and try to promote everything that favours the moral and material well-being of the country."[29]

Asociación Euskara was the first organization to use the motto of *Zazpiak Bat,* with the idea that the seven Basque territories made up a single nation, and it was also the first association to organize Basque Floral Games in the Southern Basque Country with the help of Anton Abadia.

In 1886, Sabino Arana Goiri published several articles about the Basque language in the magazines *Euskal Erria* and *Revista de Vizcaya*. Arana made mention of the declining situation of the Basque language in the Spanish state, where only the Castilian language had official status at all levels, to the detriment of Basque, which, the author argued, was the highest characteristic of the

Basque nation: "Basque is, therefore, an essential element of the Euskaldun ('Basque-speaking') nation; without it, its institutions are impossible. The disappearance of Basque would inevitably cause the ruin of the nation, which would die as a leaf dies in autumn when nature deprives it of its nutritive sap."[30] Six years later, Arana wrote his historical and political essay *Bizkaya por su independencia,* which was the basis of his political thought and the foundation of Basque nationalist political ideology.[31] On June 3, 1893, Arana gave a speech at the Larrazabal farmstead, the Begoña neighborhood in Bilbao, to a small group of Basque patriots associated with Ramón de la Sota and attracted by the ideas given by Arana in his work of 1882 and in later writings.

The Larrazabal speech marked the beginning of Sabino Arana's political career and of contemporary political Basque nationalism. Arana began his speech by referring to the Carlist roots of his political ideology which, founded on the principle of the full restoration of the charters, had led to the defense of the right to independence for the Basque nation. The motto of both ideological currents was the same, Religion and Charters; Basque, *Jaungoikua eta Lagizarra* (JEL). Arana went on to explain that if the Carlist Party had defended Carlos de Borbon's rights to the throne, they had not done so because they were monarchists, but, rather, as a means of defending their historical rights, their laws, and their own institutions. "And the motto *Jaungoikua eta Lagizarra* made me see things clearly and got my full attention, and *Jaungoikua eta Lagizarra* was engraved on my heart never to be erased again; and as a guide to all the actions of my life I drew up a private motto whose initials go to the end of the booklet that you know and of all my writings."[32]

In Arana's opinion, Basque nationalism had three fundamental objectives: (1) preserving the Basque language; (2) publishing books and a newspaper on Basque history and politics as well as a Basque grammar book to facilitate the learning, teaching, and spread of the language among the Basques; (3) a synthesis of all these efforts, uniting all the Basques under a single flag, "in order to achieve the necessary strength to shake off the yoke of slavery and worthily and vigorously restore our Homeland."[33] And he ended his speech with "¡Viva la independencia de Bizkaya!"

That same year, 1893, Arana created the *Bizkaitarra* newspaper, and in February 1894, he participated, at the invitation of Asociación Euskara de Navarra member Estanislao Aranzadi, in the acts held place in defense of fiscal self-government, known as Gamazada. Just a few months later, in July, Arana founded *Euskeldun Batzokija* on Correo Street in Bilbao, which would become the headquarters of the new *Partido Nacionalista Vasco/Euzko Alderdi*

*Jeltzalea* (EAJ/PNV), founded secretly on July 31, 1895. Sabino Arana was its first chair, and Ciriaco Llodio was vice chair. Arana designed a Basque national flag known as the *ikurriña* and which was raised for the first time at *Euskeldun Batzokija* in Bilbao that same year, 1894, and which today is the official flag of the Basque Country. Together with the *ikurriña*, the slogans "Euzkotarren aberria Euzkadi da" (Euskadi is the homeland of the Basques) and the aforementioned *Jaungoikua eta Lagizarra* ("God and Charters") were the slogans of the new political party whose members came to be called *Jeltzales*.[34]

The state authorities reacted with violence, the civil governor of Bizkaia fined Euskeldun Batzokija 500 pesetas, and in August 1895, Arana was prosecuted for an alleged crime of provoking rebellion resulting from an article of his published in the *Bizkaitarra* newspaper. The public prosecutor called for a sentence of eleven months in prison and a fine of 125 pesetas, and Arana was sent to Larrinaga prison in Bilbao with an astronomical bail of 50,000 pesetas. Two weeks later, on September 12, Euskeldun Batzokija was closed by executive order of the governor, its 110 partners were prosecuted, and the members of the management were imprisoned with a bail of 5,000 pesetas. Then on October 16, at a meeting of the members of Euskeldun Batzokija held at Manuel Endaia's café, it was decided to hire Navarrese's Daniel Irujo as defense lawyer. Irujo was the son of the aforementioned Carlist deputy Manuel Irujo, author or keeper of the first Basque independence manifesto, and his defense was one of the first public arguments in favor of the independence of the Basque people from a legal perspective.

In Irujo's opinion, in his articles Arana had not defended the Basque Country in becoming part of the domain of another state, but, rather, argued for its independence: the independence of the Basque people. His defense was based on the fact that neither the Spanish constitution of the day, nor any of the previous ones, "of which there had been many," nor the penal code of "civilized nations," allowed punishment of something not classified as a crime qualified by the penal code because of the principle of legal non-retroactivity.[35] In short, defending or proposing the independence of the Basque Country was not a crime, nor could it consequently be understood as a call to rebellion. Having obtained an easy, quick legal victory, the Navarrese lawyer took the opportunity to make a plea in defense of the Basques' right to independence in the courtroom, stating that "Euskadi has the right to live independently. And what people in the world, I ask, can hold as many and as legitimate claims to independence as the Basque people? Open, open the pages of history, and there you will see the pure independence of the Basque people, just as in those very remote times when the tribes that populated the Iberian Peninsula did not make up a nation."[36]

Irujo ended his defense by arguing that anyone who studied the history of the Basque people in detail would understand it as something natural and legitimate, and that the Basques yearn to "restore" their ancient freedoms, their laws, their institutions, and their independence. At the same time, dealing with the prosecution's accusations that Arana was a "separatist," Irujo responded by stating that

> a separatist, a true separatist is the tyrant who usurps a free people their freedom; a nationalist, someone who works for the restoration of his people, who tries to free his people from the slavery to which another stronger people have subjected them. Separatist, in another series of ideas, can be said to be somebody who deprives another of his property; a thief steals; a nationalist is an honest man who defends his own and tries to recover that if it has been lost. Separatism is a crime. Nationalism a virtue. Separatists are the murderers and arsonists who are traitors to Spain, to which they owe everything they are, what they are worth, what they have, what they know, and yet they rise up against her in bloody war. But the Basques who try at all costs to abolish the laws that have killed their independence . . . they are not separatists, they are nationalists. In the same way that the unfortunate Poles are nationalists, they have seen their homeland divided and shared out among the great powers that surround them, and they sigh, naturally, for the reconstitution of their people. As the Irish are nationalists and not separatists, they have managed to form a nationalist party, whose power is felt in the deliberations of the British Parliament. Since they are nationalists and not separatists, the Hungarians, who, having previously seen themselves in a situation analogous to the one in which the Basques find themselves today, have managed, thanks to their efforts, to regain the independence they lost and to reconstitute their kingdom, which is not to be confused with the Empire of Austria, although its King is at the same time Emperor of the Austrians. No; the Basques are not and cannot be separatists; the Basques must be eminently nationalist; and it is highly laudable, in no way punishable, that those who find themselves in the situations Sabino Arana is in work tirelessly to achieve the union of all the Basques, to achieve the formation of a nationalist party that seeks the restoration of their country. Does it constitute, perhaps, a provocation to the rebellion, to try to achieve that union with the mentioned aim? Well, how far off is the example

that Navarre gave when it stood up as one man, vigorously opposing the project of subtraction, of true subtraction, of a centralizing minister who calls himself a liberal has, by contrast, irresistible tendencies towards the most tyrannical despotism?[37]

The court declared Arana not guilty of the crimes of which he had been accused. However, the court case caused some irreparable damage. Although a process such as the preventive custody of the whole executive lasted only a short time, the *Bizkaitarra* newspaper was not published again, the *Euskeldun Batzokija* had to be closed, and Arana's preventive custody was extended until January 1896.[38]

Two years later, Arana wrote and published a pamphlet titled *El Partido Carlista y los Fueros Vasco-Navarros,* and it led to a fierce discussion between Carlists and Nationalists, mainly between Sabino Arana and Eustaquio Etxabe-Sustaeta. The appearance of Basque nationalism on the political scene subtracted a large number of followers from the Carlist Party, mainly among members in favor of full restoration.[39] In fact, the first point of the program of the Basque Nationalist Party was the repeal of the law of October 25, 1839, and the restoration of the historical Basque laws. Etxabe-Sustaeta's followers went on to join the Comunión Tradicionalista Carlista chaired by Victor Pradera, a party that, far from preaching the full restoration of the charters, went on to support the military coup leaders in the insurrection of 1936.

In September 1898, Arana was elected deputy on the council of Bizkaia for the Bilbao district, and two months later he presented his "Project for the constitution of a regional council or higher board of representatives from Araba, Gipuzkoa, Navarre, and Bizkaia" to the Development Commission of the Provincial Council. The state executive continued to put pressure on, and on December 25, Angel Zabala, the leader of the Basque Nationalist Party (EAJ/PNV), was imprisoned for having placed the *ikurriña* on a house under construction. However, EAJ/PNV would soon become the leading political force in Bizkaia and Gipuzkoa. In the May 1899 elections, the first councilors of the party were elected in Bilbao and in other towns in Bizkaia such as Mundaka, Bermeo, and Arteaga. The first issue of *Euzkadi* magazine was published in 1901, and in October of that year the first issue of the weekly *La Patria* was also published.

Faced with the advances of Basque nationalism, the state reacted once again by taking Arana back to the dock. On May 25 1902, Arana tried to send a telegram to the president of the United States, Theodore Roosevelt, congratulating him on his intervention in favor of the independence of Cuba. On May 26,

1902, Arana attempted to send a second telegram to President Roosevelt, in which he congratulated him on granting Cuba its independence: "Roosevelt, Presidente Estados Unidos, Washington. Nombre Partido Nacionalista Vasco, felicito por independencia Cuba Federación nobilísima que presidís que supo librar la esclavitud. Ejemplo magnanimidad y culto justicia y libertad dan vuestros poderosos Estados desconocido historia e inimitable para potencias europeas, particularmente latinas. Si Europa imitara, también Nación Vasca su pueblo -más antiguo que más siglos goza libertad rigiéndose constitución que mereció elogios Estados Unidos, sería libre."[40] The telegram was intercepted by the Spanish authorities, and the public prosecutor requested eight years and one day of imprisonment, believing it to have been a crime of rebellion under article 248 of the penal code of January 1, 1900.

Before being prosecuted, Arana was held in prison, which he entered on May 30, 1902. EAJ/PNV followers sent the president of the council of ministers, Práxedes M. Mateo-Sagasta, a letter signed by nine thousand people requesting the provisional release of Arana, but his reply was that the matter was the exclusive competence of the courts.[41] The trial began on November 7, and on this occasion the defense attorneys were Daniel Irujo and Teodoro Agirre, both fathers of two of the most prominent leaders of Basque nationalism of the twentieth century. One day after the trial began, the court released Sabino Arana without charges. However, the judicial war against Basque nationalism was not limited to taking Sabino Arana before the courts, and on June 18, 1902, the governor of Bizkaia used his executive powers to remove eleven Basque nationalist councilors from Bilbao city council.

Then, on September 30, 1902, Arana appointed Angel Zabala as his substitute at the head of the Basque Nationalist Party, and on November 25, 1903, he died in Sukarrieta at the age of 38.[42]

However, after his death, nationalist ideology, and more specifically pro-independence ideas, gained followers exponentially between 1903 and 1923, providing two decades of consolidation for the independence movement in the Basque Country. At the elections of November 8, 1903, EAJ/PNV obtained a new electoral victory with five councilors on the Bilbao city council, a victory that was seconded in January 1904, by becoming the most voted list with thirteen councilors. However, EAJ/PNV continued to grow, and in 1906 *Aberri* weekly published the party's manifesto with the restoration of the charters and independence as the main political objectives of the new political party. In 1907 Gregorio Ibarretxe, a member of the Basque Nationalist party, was elected mayor of Bilbao, and in 1911 he founded that nationalist Solidaridad de Obreros

Vascos (ELA/STV) in Bilbao. Starting in 1912, the weeklies *Napartarra* in Iruñea and *Arabarra* in Gasteiz were opened, and a year later *Euzkadi* newspaper, the official newspaper of the Basque Nationalist Party, was set up.

In 1906 Ramon Goikoetxea, known as Fray Evangelista de Ibero, published his brochure *Ami Vasco*,[43] considered to be a nationalist catechism or a compendium of Basque nationalist ideology, immediately after Arana's death. Following the pattern of Oloriz's 1894 *Cartilla foral,* the author highlighted the most important points of nationalist ideology in a fifty-six-page pamphlet, including definitions of the concepts of nation, state, nationalism, and homeland. Later, the author interspersed a series of chapters around radical questions of Basque nationalism, such as what Basque nationalism was, what the Basque Nationalist Party was, what needs the Basque nation had, and what the problem of the Basque language in the early twentieth century was. Ibero, like Polverel and Sagaseta before him, understood that the Basque people were a nation and that, therefore, they had the right to establish their own state in order to ensure the future of their culture, customs, and language. Fully pro-independence, the ideology described by Ibero in his booklet was, in a sense, a summary of the work of Sabino Arana, and it was to have considerable influence on the evolution of Basque nationalism throughout the first seven decades of the twentieth century. In fact, the work had two more editions, in the *Euzkadi* newspaper in Bilbao in 1930, and the bilingual edition in Basque and Spanish from *Ekin* publishers in Buenos Aires in 1957.

One event was to strengthen and activate pro-independence discourse just one year later, at the end of the First World War. In a statement before a session of Congress in Washington held on January 8, 1918, President Woodrow Wilson announced his Fourteen Points.[44] In his speech, Wilson addressed what he perceived to be the main causes of the political upheavals that had driven the world to war internationally. He called for the abolition of secret treaties, arms reduction, the promotion of international trade by eliminating economic barriers between nations and by freedom of the seas. Wilson also proposed measures to guarantee world peace, such as the settlement of colonial conflicts in the interest of native peoples, and the observance of the right of self-determination for oppressed minorities protected by a world organization that would provide a system of collective security for all nations.[45]

Wilson's speech was picked up on by the leaders of numerous oppressed nations, from Armenia, Kurdistan, and Palestine in the Middle East to Catalunya, Scotland, and the Basque Country in Western Europe. Jose Luis Villalonga wrote an article in the Bilbao magazine *Hermes*, entitled "The Basque nation and Wilson's principles," in which he stated that the Basque people could and should embrace the principles proclaimed by the American president. Ramón Belaustegigoitia published his work *Las bases de un Gobierno nacional vasco* in Bilbao in 1918,[46] and that same year Toribio Etxebarria, after the debates held at the Casa del Pueblo in Eibar, published a brochure entitled *La Liga de Naciones y el problema vasco.*[47] Etxebarria thus added to the vindication of charter restoration the right of the Basque people to self-determination by stating that the former meant the restitution of the legislative, executive, judicial, and administrative powers of the charter countries, which amounted to their full political sovereignty. And in line with those debates, on November 9, 1918, in a regular meeting of the charter conference, the Carlist deputies Jose M. Garay and Hilario Bilbao proposed charter restoration through the recovery of the general boards (legislative) and the provincial institutions (executive and administrative).

Basque nationalist deputies and senators sent a manifesto in these terms to President Wilson on October 25, 1918: "On the 79th anniversary of the cancellation by the Spanish government of the independence of the Basque people, those signing below, deputies and senators in the Spanish parliaments, on behalf of all the Basques who, aware of their nationality, desire, and work to see it operate freely, salute the President of the United States of America, who, by establishing the foundations for future world peace, has based them on the right of every nationality, large or small, to live as they themselves choose, bases that are accepted by all belligerent states. We hope to see them promptly applied for the best fulfilment of all that justice and individual and collective freedom demand."[48]

In the purely cultural area, between 1918 and 1919, some of the key institutions for the survival of Basque culture emerged: Eusko Ikaskuntza, the Society for Basque Studies, founded in 1918 under the direction of Arturo Campión; Euskaltzaindia, the Academy of the Basque Language, set up in 1919 under the direction of Resurrección Maria Azkue, Luis Elizalde, Julio Urkixo, and Arturo Campión; and years later, the Euskaltzaleak association (1927-1936), led by Jose Aristimuño (Aitzol), Xabier Lizardi, Jokin Zaitegi, and other figures from Basque literature and cultural life from the first third of the twentieth century. All of this was part of the cultural and political current called Euzko Pizkundea, which had emerged in the mid-nineteenth century as a reaction to the situation of marginalization and frank regression that Basque culture and language was going through after the formation of the Spanish and French states.

There was a split in the Basque nationalist program in 1921 with the foundation of Aberri, a party led by Elias Gallastegi, Manu Egileor, and Luis Arana,

Sabino's brother, who vindicated an ideological line marked by his brother, pro-independence and disruptive. In opposition to that policy, the Comunión Nacionalista Vasca, led between 1922 and 1930 by Ignacio Rotaetxe and Ceferino Jemein, and supported by Engracio Aranzadi, Ramón de la Sota, and Luis Eleizalde, among others, advocated identical ideological principles, but at a strategic level it advised taking more realistic and conciliatory positions with respect to the other Basque political parties.[49]

The political crisis at the heart of Basque nationalism was enlarged in 1923 by the dictatorship imposed after the coup of General Miguel Primo de Rivera on September 13. The monarch Alfonso XIII, far from opposing the coup, appointed Primo de Rivera head of the government and president of the military directorate, while acting as head of state himself. Immediately after the coup, nationalist deputies were removed from their positions and Aberri was outlawed.[50] At the same time, General Primo de Rivera, who had been Captain General of Catalunya until 1923, dissolved the Catalan commonwealth by royal decree with the approval of Alfonso XIII on March 20, 1925, and imposed a new provincial statute for the entire state.[51] The *ikastolas*—schools teaching in the Basque language that had been set up during the first two decades of the twentieth century—were closed.

However, despite the suffocating political atmosphere under the dictatorship, the Basque and Catalan independence movements developed between 1923 and 1931, when the dictatorship finally fell. In both cases, pro-independence ideological currents were converging with political options contrary to the dictatorship and the monarchy, which is why the independence movement of the 1930s was now republican. The principles inspired by Wilson's Fourteen Points also helped to link the independence movement with the struggle for the historical and political rights of national minorities, so that the defense of the right to independence or the right to self-determination of peoples, united to the struggle and opposition to the dictatorship, was to position the Basque nationalist parties against the violation of peoples' and individuals' fundamental rights. This democratic line of action was to be accentuated after the events of 1936, General Franco's coup d'état, the subsequent war, and the iron dictatorship of national-Catholic inspiration that lasted until the death of the dictator in 1975.

After almost twenty years apart, in November 1930 Aberri and the Comunión Nacionalista Vasca came together again around the same acronym: EAJ/PNV. At the same time, the nationalist political program saw the creation of a new political party, Eusko Abertzale Ekintza (EAE), or Acción Nacionalista Vasca (EE/ANV). This new Basque nationalist party was located to the left of the Basque Nationalist Party and proclaimed itself to be secular and nondenominational, while at the same time being open to forming an alliance of leftist forces of the Spanish Popular Front. On the other hand, there were other Basque nationalist currents of pro-independence ideology such as Euzko Mendigoxale Batza, founded in 1921, and which in 1932 began to publish the newspaper *Jagi-Jagi*. This political group, which had originally been part of Euzko Gaztedi (EGI)—the youth organization of the Basque Nationalist Party—had split, and its program had focused from the start on the demand for Basque independence. Its most prominent leaders were Trifon Etxebarria "Etarte" and Eli Gallastegi, who signed under many different pseudonyms, including "Gudari."

The fall of the dictatorship of Alfonso XIII, and the subsequent trial in absentia of the monarch, closed an eight-year cycle of political, social, cultural, and economic crisis. The government of the nascent Spanish republic granted Catalunya its statute of autonomy in 1932 but, despite repeated demands from Basque people, the Basque statute projects did not materialize until years later. Immediately after the fall of the dictatorship, the procedures for the drafting and approval of a Basque autonomy statute began. After consulting 427 of the 582 city and town councils throughout the Basque Country, 83 percent of them were in favor of the appointment of a permanent commission of mayors, and the drafting of the statute was entrusted to Eusko Ikaskuntza, the Basque Studies Society, which had been founded in 1918.[52]

The general statute draft for the Basque state was finalized on May 31, 1931. In its terms, an autonomous Basque state would be created within the Spanish state and formed by the territories of Araba, Bizkaia, Gipuzkoa, and Navarre. Thus, according to the first article, "it is declared that the Basque Country, made up of the current provinces of Araba, Gipuzkoa, Navarre and Bizkaia, constitutes a natural and legal entity, with its own political character, and is recognized as such to have right to be constituted and governed by itself as an autonomous state within the entire Spanish state, with which it will live in accordance with the rules of laws of engagement as agreed in this statute."[53] The central government of the state would have jurisdiction in matters such as international relations, criminal and commercial law, currency, communications, and defense. The Basque government would hold the remaining powers, fundamentally all those relating to the legislature and the executive, and all powers in fiscal matters. According to the statute, competence in international relations with the Vatican was also to be the Basque state's requirement. On September 22, 1931, a delegation of 420 Basque mayors traveled to Madrid to deliver the draft statute to the president of the republic, Niceto Alcalá

Zamora.[54] On September 25 and 26, the draft statute was debated in the Spanish Parliament, where it was rejected because it was considered that competence in international relations, including relations with the Vatican, should be exclusive to the central state.[55] Actually, from Madrid, the transfer of powers to a Basque state increasingly dominated by pro-independence forces (Basque nationalists) or forces seeking to return to the past (Carlists) was observed with suspicion.

The rejection of the 1931 statute led to the opening of a new statutory process, led this time by the managers of the four Basque councils, which met in Bilbao on December 15, 1931, and appointed a single management commission for the four territories and with the mission of drafting the new statute of autonomy. The project was concluded in June 1932, and a period of six months began for it to be passed in each of the four Basque territories.[56] The new project did not recognize the Basque territories as a state, and the range of competences with which the new project gave the Basque territories was lesser than that of the 1931 project. At the same time, the Carlist Party and conservative associations and parties viewed the integration of Navarre into the Basque statute with suspicion, which is why the project was finally approved in Araba, Bizkaia, and Gipuzkoa but rejected in Navarre. The uncertain result of the referendum of November 5, 1933, definitively paralyzed the approval process for the draft statute.[57]

It was necessary to wait three more years for a new draft statute of autonomy to be drawn up for the territories of Araba, Bizkaia, and Gipuzkoa. Once approved in the Spanish Parliament, Jose Antonio Agirre, a member of the Basque Nationalist Party, was elected president of the new Basque government on October 7, 1936.[58] But it was too late: with Araba and Navarre in the hands of the coup leaders led by Generals Emilio Mola and Francisco Franco, in practical terms the Basque autonomy lasted from the autumn of 1936 to August 1937 when, after the fall of Bilbao in June, the rebel troops occupied the last strongholds of Basque resistance. After the occupation of the Basque territory, the Basque government went into exile, with its headquarters first in Barcelona (1938), then in Paris (March 1939-May 1940), then in London (June 1940-October 1941), New York (December, 1941-1946), and finally in Paris between 1946 and 1978. During forty years of exile, the Basque government remained active and pursued an international policy that, both ideologically and strategically, was to lay the foundations of the contemporary Basque pro-independence movement.[59]

Based on the 1932 project, the 1936 statute of autonomy was only put into practice in Bizkaia, the only territory controlled by the forces of the government of Euskadi between October 1936 and August 1937. Although the range of powers assigned to the Basques was very limited, the circumstances of the war first and, crucially, the long exile of four decades that followed, made the exercise of Basque political autonomy very wide-reaching in practice, and it went far beyond the agreement on paper. The management and activity of the government of Euskadi, led by Jose A. Agirre between 1936 and 1975, went far beyond the powers stipulated in the 1936 statute. Specifically, after the final defeat of the republican forces in March 1939, the Basque government called a series of meetings at Meudon in April 1939, at which the principle of national unity was adopted as an ideological premise, as a right domestically and a vindication internationally, as a strategic necessity and, economically, as the only possible way to finance the activities of the Basque government in exile. Political and administrative independence was, ultimately, the only way to manage the Basque government in exile and to protect the nearly 200,000 Basque refugees who were outside the Basque Country, including 32,000 minors under the Basque government's responsibility.[60]

With regard to refugees, people in prison and concentration camps, people exiled, persecuted, or simply on the run, collaboration with the government of the republic had been crucial between 1937 and 1939. But since the collapse of the government of the republic in March 1939, the delay or even cancellation of payments due to the Basque government for this purpose made that more difficult and, as a consequence, increased the responsibilities of the Basque government on this critical issue, which led it to reinforce its national approach and take responsibility for the management of this area.[61]

In fact, the self-financing effort of the Basque government in exile was based on, and at the same time was a consequence of, the policy of national unity adopted in Meudon in 1939 as the only means to deal with the political, social, and human responsibility of assisting Basque refugees. The situation of the government of Euskadi in exile became even more difficult when, between May and June 1940, German troops occupied France and the Northern Basque Country. Jose Agirre was in the Dunkirk area at the end of May 1940, but neither he nor his family were rescued by the British forces, and they spent a year and a half on the run while hiding from German security officers in Berlin. The disappearance of Lehendakari Agirre (president) had already been foreseen by the Basque government, so a Basque National Council was immediately set up in London to temporarily stand in for the Basque government until the reappearance of the Lehendakari Agirre.[62] It was Jose I. Lizaso, delegate of the Basque government in London, who put forward, after Agirre's disappearance, the establishment of the National Council of Euzkadi, to be chaired by Manuel

Irujo, son of Daniel Irujo and former minister of justice of the republic; this was unanimously accepted by all Basque delegations abroad.[63]

The National Council of Euzkadi developed a policy of continuity, both ideologically and strategically, with respect to the policies of the Basque government in Paris and based on the government program approved by the representatives there on May 8, 1940: "The Council has not been set up with new policies. It is the continuation those which President Agirre and his councilors set those of us abroad who have been trusted by them to act in collaboration with the democracies, working with them for the benefit of universal interests and, specifically, for the freedom of our country."[64] One of the fundamental points of the Council's policy was the consolidation of the pro-independence movement and communication at an international level. The Basque National Council promoted the negotiation and signing of international agreements with the United Kingdom, Free France, and the United States on strategic and military matters and, at the same time, bilateral international agreements for the protection of refugees were negotiated and signed with governments who had a tradition of receiving Basque migrants such as Argentina, Chile, Venezuela, Uruguay, and Mexico. Political agreements were also negotiated with incipient European and American Christian Democrats groups and, as was to be expected, agreements were also signed with the Generalitat, the Catalan government in exile.

A first agreement on the constitution for an independent Basque state was reached in July 1940 in London. The British government was in a critical situation after the overwhelming and rapid German victory in the French campaign and the advance of Japanese troops in the Far East. The Basque government had supported the Allies against the Axis powers—including General Franco's Spanish dictatorship—strategically and ideologically since September 1 with a public and official declaration. Given these circumstances, the Basque National Council offered the British government the collaboration of no less than two thousand Basque secret agents in occupied territory to collaborate with British intelligence agents. However, collaboration would only take place if a political agreement was previously reached on the independence of the Basque Country, and the thousands of Basque refugees in Europe and America were given the assistance of British officials in those countries. The operations would be financed by the British, but Basque agents would operate under direct Basque command under the orders of the Basque National Council, and Basque would be the units' official language. These Basque agents would operate mainly in occupied Europe, but also in South America, and their objective would be to inform on and break up Axis spy networks.[65] Manuel Irujo negotiated with Winston Churchill through Lord

Boothby, and in less than a month an agreement was reached and signed at the latter's house on July 23 of that year. The agreement was as follows:

> Most secret. Formula
> H. M. Government sympathizes with the cause of the Basque peoples, in their claim for liberty and independence.
> In the event of hostilities breaking out between the British and Spanish Governments, H. M. Government will immediately recognize the Basque National Council as the Provisional Basque Government.
> In the event of a British victory, H. M. Government will undertake to do everything in their power to secure the constitution and security of a Basque State.
> The delimitation of frontiers is a matter for settlement later on.[66]

In May 1941, the Basque National Council in London signed a new agreement, also in matters of strategic services, with the Defence Council of the French Empire led by General Charles DeGaulle. Along the same lines, Irujo prepared a document on November 24, 1941, regarding the ideological and strategic basis for the Basque National Council, under the title "Fundamentos prácticos de la Comunidad Ibérica de Naciones" as the foundations for a declaration of principles of democracy on the Peninsula.[67] Summarized in fourteen points, the text established the ideological and programmatic bases of the Basque independence movement in 1940:

1. Democratic affirmation in a universal, supportive sense for men and peoples.
2. Support for England, Russia, China, and their allies in the current war.
3. Acceptance of the Atlantic Declaration (August 14, 1941).
4. Agreement with the establishment of a federal order in Europe based on coexistence and scaled sovereignties, formulas for economic rapprochement, military defence, and the objective of fair and lasting peace.
5. Research into the Confederation of the West as a viable formula for the European Federation, and to reflect our "Western" character.
6. Franco does not represent the country. Obtaining power to grant such representation for the citizens.
7. Denouncing the system of oppression to which citizens are subjected. There are more prisoners in Spain than in any other country in Europe except for R. and G.
8. Protest against the executions of hostages by Germany.

9. Highlighting the Francoist activities designed to hand over peninsular and colonial territory to Germany for military bases.
10. Exposing the maneuver against Portugal. Democrats will not take advantage of the force being used in that. We aspire to a Community of Nations in which Portugal freely participates, taking its rightful place.
11. Also denouncing the large-scale maneuver which, through the Junta de la Hispanidad, is taking Nazi propaganda in America with imperial aspirations which we do not share, and whose deceptions we must not take advantage of in any way.
12. The Declaration must remain open so that all those who agree with may adhere to it: Nothing exclusive or monopolized.
13. The right of self-determination of peninsular peoples, specifically Catalunya and Euzkadi.
14. Stating as a fundamental belief that the democratic bases that we share will give us a channel through which to examine our differences, reaching an agreement establishing a legal community regime based on the motto of St. Louis: "All human freedoms are solidarity."[68]

In summary, centralism, territorialism, and unitarianism were, in Irujo's opinion, political principles opposed to democratic values and the political rights of peoples, which included, crucially, nations' right to self-determination.[69]

The agreement was validated by the British, although the document would only take effect if there were hostilities between the British and Spanish governments. In that case, Spanish troops could easily occupy Gibraltar, and Allied troops would be forced to land in Cadiz and occupy the whole of the Iberian Peninsula, which would cause innumerable casualties and an inordinate economic cost. Without a doubt, Franco's neutrality was in the interests of the British government. Samuel Hoare, the British ambassador in Madrid, drew up Operación Caballería de San Jorge, a plan to keep Franco neutral and avoid opening a new front during World War II. The plan was simple: a large group of generals close to Franco would be bribed to convince him not to intervene openly in favor of Hitler during the war. As Angel Viñas discovered in the British archives, Generals Varela, Aranda, Orgaz, Kindelan, Galarza, Asensio, and Franco's brother Nicolas, among others, received millions between 1941 and 1943 thanks to the mediation of Juan March, who acted as treasurer and secretary of operations. Viñas estimates that 6.5 million pounds of that time were invested in the business, between 350 and 1,000 million euros in today's money. Taking into account that the number of officers who received those bribes was relatively small and that they took place over a limited period of time, each one of them must have received more than one million euros per year for a period of almost three years. The operation was carried out using astronomical sums, but Franco did not openly support Hitler, nor did he declare war on the United Kingdom, and the amount of money used was less than that of an occupation campaign in the Iberian Peninsula.[70] Another consequence was that the secret formula signed by the Basque National Council in July 1940 was never activated.

After the reappearance of Lehendakari Agirre in Uruguay in October 1941—where he had arrived after escaping from the German intelligence services on December 22, 1944—the representatives of the national councils of Galicia and Catalunya and the Basque government signed the Galeuzca Pact in the Hotel Majestic de México, thus ensuring continuity and underscoring the full force of the agreements signed by the Consell de Catalunya and the National Council of Euzkadi in London four years earlier. Likewise, on October 24 of that year Galeuzca-Uruguay was set up in Montevideo.[71] The Galeuzca declaration of principles was drafted in Buenos Aires, adopted in both Argentina and Uruguay, and based on four basic principles:[72]

1. Galeuzca was committed to the fight for human rights both within the Spanish state and abroad, both in Europe and America. This meant fighting the Franco dictatorship and any other regime not based on the strict recognition of human rights and democratic principles of government. Regarding foreign policy, Galeuzca proclaimed from the beginning its support for the Allied cause and opposition to the Axis and its satellites.
2. Its commitment to democracy involved the defense and promotion of a republican form of government, "a representative democratic regime with universal and direct suffrage, freedom of conscience and religion, freedom of thought and of the press, grassroots justice, guarantees for citizens' rights, to work and to legitimately acquire property, freedom of profession, residence, hiring, and availability of goods in accordance with the particular laws of each state, which may in no case diminish, reduce or adulterate the common minimum established in federal or confederal pacts."[73]
3. In the same way, and as a basic political requirement and essential foundation for all legitimate power, the personality of the different nations and, specifically, the sovereignty of each peninsular nation, should rest on the will freely expressed at the ballot box by the citizens of each one of them, so that Galeuzca recognized as a fundamental, inalienable political principle the right of self-determination of nations, both inside and outside the Iberian Peninsula. This implied a commitment to a confederal state model,

an agreed federation of Iberian or European nations, "to which supernational powers are delegated, such as the coordination of services and forces, shared legislation especially on social issues, collective security, development and application of international law, and the dissemination and generalization of democratic principles of law and justice."[74]

4. Both, internationally and on the Iberian Peninsula, Galeuzca would promote "a policy of collaboration and goodwill, fostering international relations of all kinds, and advocating the foundation of super-state organizations that, with the objective of indissoluble peace, would have the authority and resources necessary to preserve that, punish offenders and ensure the free life of institutions and peoples."[75] In other words, Galeuzca expressed its unconditional support for the work of the nascent United Nations Organization after the Allied victory.

In this area and, as a strategic principle, the signatories of the pact agreed not to negotiate their respective national statutes separately with the republican state but, rather, to agree on them jointly: "Galeuzca establishes that none of the three oppressed nations should accept, separately, a regime of autonomy granted by the Spanish State because only with a total, rational change of the political structure of Spain can our peoples find a guarantee of their own freedom. If circumstances make it advisable to accept autonomy, it must be equal and simultaneous for the nations which are members of the Spanish State."[76]

Lehendakari Agirre assumed and specified these principles in the letter to Galician nationalist leader Alfonso R. Castelao and signed in New York on March 2, 1944: "When I arrived from Europe at the end of 41 that was one of my concerns. I immediately contacted Pi i Sunyer to build strong Basque-Catalan intelligence without delay, and with an express invitation to the Galician organizations. At that time Pi was the only external representative of the Catalan will. I wrote a joint manifesto whose central ideas were: a) The reality of our nationalities and their right to self-determination; b) The creation of a peripheral policy willing to voluntarily form a peninsular political model which Portugal would join when appropriate; c) An invitation to reflection and a pact for Spanish democracy; d) Our total and enthusiastic commitment to the Allies' cause."[77]

The political concept of independence and the basic principles of self-determination, federalism, and human rights developed by some of the Basque nationalist leaders in exile, such as Jose A. Agirre, Manuel Irujo, Francisco Basterretxea, Javier Landaburu, and many others, focused on the idea of a culturally and politically independent Basque Country but which, at the same time, would be socially and economically confederated within Europe. This is how Irujo expressed it in 1941: "We are Basque democrats. As democrats and human members of that universal feeling, we are obliged to support it. As Basque nationals, we are concerned about the free and sovereign personality of the Basque Country. I do not use the word independence because I do not believe in that. There is no independent country. And after the war, independence will be lesser. We all have to be dependent and federated for peace, law and social justice. Our Basque policy is national. In as far as it allows us to achieve that goal, it will have our conscious and continual attention."[78]

After the Second World War, the policy of the Basque government in exile centered on the international isolation of General Franco's dictatorial regime as a means of restoring democracy in the Basque Country and in the rest of the nations in the Spanish state. The main Allied powers accepted the request of the Spanish republican government in exile and the Basque government regarding this issue for two fundamental reasons: the support given by the Spanish state to the Axis during World War II, and the determined support of the Basques, Catalans, and Spanish Republicans to the Allied cause. The military government, headed by General Franco from September 29, 1936[79]—and set up by a coup d'état—planned, organized, directed, and executed the repression on the population between 1936 and 1946 and for a further three decades, and that is why the nascent United Nations Organization declared, through the unanimous resolution of its General Assembly on February 9, 1946, that the Spanish government had been founded with the support of the Axis powers and did not have the minimum conditions required for admission to the UN because of its origins, nature, historical record, and intimate links with the aggressor states.[80] Likewise, during the fifty-ninth session, held on December 12, 1946, the United Nations General Assembly passed Resolution 39 (I), by which a series of sanctions were imposed on the Spanish state:

> Relations of the Members of the United Nations
> with the Spanish State
>
> The peoples of the United Nations, in San Francisco, Potsdam and London have condemned Franco's Spanish regime and decided that, as long as the regime remains, the Spanish state cannot be admitted to the United Nations.
>
> The General Assembly, in its Resolution of February 9, 1946, recommended that the members of the United Nations act in accordance with the letter and spirit of the declarations of San Francisco and Potsdam.

The peoples of the United Nations assure the Spanish people that their sympathy towards them is permanent, and that they will be the subject of a cordial welcome when circumstances allow them to be admitted to the United Nations.

The General Assembly recalls that in May and June 1946, the Security Council carried out an investigation into possible new measures that could be adopted by the United Nations. The Sub-Committee of the Security Council, in charge of the investigation, unanimously concluded that:

(a) In origin, nature, structure, and general conduct, the Franco regime is a fascist regime modeled on and established largely as a result of aid received from Hitler's Nazi Germany and Mussolini's Fascist Italy.

(b) During the long struggle of the United Nations against Hitler and Mussolini, Franco, despite repeated protests from the Allies, granted as much substantial aid as he could to the enemy powers. Firstly, for example, from 1941 to 1945 the Blue Infantry Division, the Spanish Legion of Volunteers and the "Salvador" Air Squadron fought against Soviet Russia on the eastern front. Secondly, in the summer of 1940 Spain seized Tangier in violation of its international status, and as a result the Spanish state maintains a large army in Spanish Morocco as a result of which a large number of Allied troops were immobilized in the north of Africa.

(c) There is incontrovertible documentary evidence that establishes that Franco was a guilty party along with Hitler and Mussolini in the conspiracy to wage war against those countries that in the course of the World War aligned themselves around the United Nations. It was part of the conspiracy that the Spanish state would adopt a position of full belligerence when mutually agreed upon.

The General Assembly, convinced that Franco's fascist government in the Spanish state, which was imposed by force on the Spanish people with the help of the Axis powers and which provided material assistance to the Axis powers during the War, does not represent the Spanish people, and its continued control of the state makes it impossible for Spanish citizens to participate in communion with the peoples of the United Nations in international affairs; recommends that Franco's Spanish government be excluded from international agencies

> established by or in relation to the United Nations, and from participation in conferences or other activities that may be agreed upon by the United Nations or by these agencies until a new, acceptable government is constituted in the Spanish state.
>
> Furthermore, desiring to ensure the participation of all peace-loving peoples, including the Spanish people, in the community of nations, recommends that if, within a reasonable period of time, a government has not been established that derives its authority from the consent of the governed, committed to respecting freedom of expression, religion, and assembly, and with the timely holding of elections in which the Spanish citizens, free from all coercion and intimidation and regardless of their affiliation, may express their will, the Security Council will examine the appropriate measures that must be adopted to remedy the situation; it recommends that all members of the United Nations immediately withdraw from Madrid their ambassadors and plenipotentiary ministers who are accredited there.
>
> The General Assembly further recommends that the member states of the Organization inform the Secretary General at the next session of the Assembly of the measures they have adopted in accordance with this recommendation.[81]

In its origin, nature, structure, and general conduct, the Spanish state had collaborated in the planning, preparation, initiation, and conduct of a war of aggression that entailed the violation of international treaties, agreements, and guarantees, and it had also participated in a shared plan or conspiracy whose objective had been the execution of major atrocities. However, after nine years of international isolation, and under the cover of the Cold War, the Franco dictatorship was finally accepted into the United Nations by Security Council Resolution 109 of December 14, 1955.[82]

The ideological principles of the Basque independence movement had been maturing in exile, and the struggle of the government of the Basque Country, from its headquarters in Paris against the dictatorship, had increased the conceptual scope on which the independence movement was based. Basically, the struggle for the independence of the Basque Country and, by extension, the rights of the Basque people as a nation, and the right to freedom and the other human rights of each one of the Basque citizens, became more and more closely connected. In short, the struggle for the establishment and constitution of a Basque republic in the context of a European federation of free nations was becoming a firm notion in the minds of the main Basque nationalist leaders of the time. The independence doctrine began to have, on the other hand, a basis in some of the major political documents of the time, for instance the principle of self-determination, which was included in the Atlantic Charter of 1941 and in the Dumbarton Oaks Agreement, one of the documents on which the United Nations Charter was based. The principle of self-determination was also embodied in the first article of the Charter of the United Nations, and its inclusion in the Charter marked a milestone in world politics: the universal recognition of self-determination as a right of the principle was a fundamental legal precept for the maintenance of friendly relations and peace between states.

Subsequently, the international agreements of the UN were also to include nations' intrinsic right to self-determination. The *International Covenant on Civil and Political Rights*[83] and the *International Covenant on Economic, Social and Cultural Rights*[84] firmly established in their first article that "all peoples have the right to self-determination. By virtue of that right they freely determine their political status and freely pursue their economic, social and cultural development."[85]

The concept of the right to self-determination included in international agreements implied international recognition—although inapplicable to the Basque case—of the doctrinal principles on which the concept of the right of self-determination of the Basque nation was based, as it had been seen by Jose A. Agirre and Manuel Irujo. Both authors understood the principle of self-determination to be the legal institution that guarantees political life and, therefore, the existence of a nation. Firstly from 1938, and later after his reappearance in 1941, Lehendakari Agirre set up[86] a series of active arts programs aimed at promoting the use of Basque, the normalization of the language, and the maintenance of the signs of identity of Basque culture both in exile and within the Basque Country, mainly from the Northern Basque Country. These initiatives reflected a deep concern for the social, political, and linguistic situation of the Basque language, something continual throughout the Agirre government. Indeed, both he and Irujo understood and defended the Basque people's right to self-determination as the guarantor of the survival of Basque culture confronted by Spanish and French cultural aggression, and political impositions in linguistic or educational matters. In this sense, the survival of the Basque language was always among the first concerns of the Basque government and the Basque national council: "Basque is our fundamental institution. We know that Mr. Lopez Mendizabal in Buenos Aires has set up a school and a professorship. Something else was being done in Argentina on the subject. At Idaho the Basques live their lives in Basque, without paying special attention to the language, nor contributing towards our spirituality. Whatever immediate fortune that may be in store for us, it is necessary, indispensable, obligatory under all senses for us to worry about Basque. To this end, it would be suitable for each Delegation to state what is being done in its area in favor of Basque, what could be undertaken, and the measures that should be adopted. However much effort we put into this endeavor, it will be less than the merit and transcendence of our most valuable national characteristic."[87]

After fifteen years of harsh dictatorship, Ekin was founded, a group of young people whose objective was the political and social training of young Basques in order to regenerate their political ideology, reinforce ideological resistance, and overthrow General Franco's dictatorial regime. Originally, almost all the founding members of this new organization were members or collaborators of EGI, the youth organization of EAJ/PNV, among them Julen Madariaga, José María Benito del Valle, Iñaki Gainzarain, Alfonso Irigoyen, and Gurutz Ansola. On July 31, 1958, St. Ignatius' Day, Ekin was renamed Euskadi ta Askatasuna (ETA) and, after a decade of political activity, in 1968 it carried out its first deadly attack, the execution of Melitón Manzanas, the head of the political-social brigade of the Gipuzkoa Police Department. After several internal splits, and during its fifth assembly in 1967, ETA defined itself as a nondenominational revolutionary movement whose fundamental objective was the liberation of the Basque nation, with two fundamental ideological bases: (1) Politically, the achievement of the political independence of the Basque people with respect to the Spanish and French states, and (2) The implementation of a social model of Marxist orientation in the socio-economic sphere.

After the death of General Franco in November 1975 and the beginning of the long process of transition toward democracy, Basque nationalism was fragmented. In order to unite the left-wing parties and associations around a single political movement, the Koordinadora Abertzale Sozialista (KAS) and ETA made public in Iruñea, on August 30, 1976, its program me of minimums—known as Alternativa KAS—which was supported by Langile Abertzale Iraultzaileen Alderdia (LAIA), Euskal Herriko Alderdi Sozialista (EHAS), and the Langile Abertzale Komiteak (LAK), and Langile Abertzaleen Batzordeak (LAB) trade unions. The program was based on seven main points: (1) The restoration of democratic freedom; (2) Amnesty for political prisoners; (3) Putting in place social measures aimed at improving the living and working conditions of the working class; (4) The withdrawal of state police forces from Basque soil; (5) With regard to the Basque people's right to sovereignty, the recognition of Basque sovereignty and the free exercise of their right to self-determination, which meant granting the Basque people the right to decide their political destiny and, eventually, the creation of an independent Basque state; (6) The immediate and provisional establishment of a statute of autonomy for the territories of Araba, Bizkaia, Gipuzkoa, and Navarre; and (7) The formation of a provisional Basque government.[88]

On January 30, 1978, ETA published a new declaration, reformulating Alternativa KAS in the months prior to the Spanish Parliament passing the new constitution. The new manifesto consisted of five points, arranged according to the following political criteria: (1) General amnesty for political prisoners; (2) Legalization of all political parties, without political censorship, including pro-independence parties; (3) Expulsion of the Civil Guard and other state security forces from the Basque Country; (4) Adopting measures to improve the living and working conditions of the population, mainly of the working class; and (5) Passing a statute of autonomy including the following points:

- Recognition for Basque national sovereignty through the acceptance and legalization of the right of self-determination as a tool for deciding the political future of the Basque people.
- Recognition of Basque as the official language of the Basque Country.
- Establishing a police force to replace the current ones; to be created and directed by the Basque government.
- Control by the Basque government of the armed forces stationed in the Basque Country.
- Providing the Basque people with the necessary powers to equip themselves with the economic, social, and political structures that they consider appropriate for their progress and well-being, as well as for their political future.[89]

In the context of the months prior to the death of General Franco—and, consequently, the end of the four-decades-long dictatorship—the Partido Socialista Obrero Español (PSOE—Spanish Socialist Workers Party) held its thirteenth general congress in exile in the town of Suresnes, in the Paris metropolitan area, October 11-13, 1974. The PSOE, as a constitutionalist party, obviously did not support the independence of the Basque people, but did include "the right to self-determination of the nationalities of Spain" among the central points of its renewed program.[90] Specifically, the socialists at Suresnes concluded that the definitive solution to the problem of the nationalities that make up the Spanish state had to start with full recognition of their right to self-determination, which entailed each nationality's ability to freely determine its relationship with the other peoples that make up the Spanish state. The PSOE also stated its support for the constitution of a federal republic of the nationalities that made up the Spanish state, considering that this state structure would allow full recognition for the peculiarities of each nationality and their self-government while safeguarding the unity of the working class of the diverse peoples that made up the Spanish state. Finally, the PSOE recognized the existence of other differentiated regions that, due to their special characteristics, could establish institutions appropriate to their particular characteristics.[91]

However, the development of realpolitik in the years after the death of the dictator led to the socialist party stepping back in this area, consenting to the draft of a Spanish constitution that recognized the Basques' and Catalans' autonomy—together with that of the other nations in the state—but without granting them the right to self-determination. The debate about the universality of human rights—which began at the United Nations with the magnificent report by Aurelia Critescu in 1981—did not affect the positions of the main Spanish and French parties, which were to continue to be reluctant to recognize the right to self-determination of the peoples within their borders.[92]

Regarding claims to the right to self-determination, one of the main efforts to reach an agreement with the Spanish government on the political situation in the Basque Country was led by president of the Basque Autonomous Community (BAC), Juan José Ibarretxe. He set up a forum for discussion and political debate on September 27, 2002, when in the Basque Parliament he announced the drafting of a new statute of autonomy—from then on, known as the Ibarretxe Plan—and set a deadline for the process of adopting and ratifying the new text by using an open document and a period of public dialogue. The objective of the new autonomy statute was to take a step forward in the resolution of the Basque political conflict by reaching a new agreement for political coexistence between the Basque and Spanish administrations. On October 25, 2003, the draft statute was presented in the Basque Parliament. The *lehendakari* proposed a twelve-month period to present amendments to the government's proposal and, on December 30, 2004, the final draft was presented, discussed, and passed by an absolute majority in the Basque Parliament.

However, Spanish legislation meant that the project had to be approved by Parliament in Madrid. Consequently, on February 1, 2005, the Basque statute project was discussed in the Spanish Parliament. After a very brief discussion, the proposal was rejected by 313 votes against (90.98 percent), 29 in favor (8.4 percent), and two abstentions (0.58 percent).

This result demonstrated the situation of conflict and the lack of mutual understanding around the issue of the historical rights of the Basque people:

The petition approved by the absolute majority of the Basques in the Basque Parliament was rejected in Madrid by 91 percent of the Spanish people as represented in the Spanish Parliament. It was obvious that there was a disconnection.

The main point of the draft statute was the statement that the Basques are a sovereign nation with their own identity and that, therefore, the Basque people have the right to decide their own political future, the right to self-determination. However, the right to self-determination was not included in *Lehendakari* Ibarretxe's proposal in an effort to obtain Spanish approval for the text. The political formula adopted by Ibarretxe was "cosovereignty," by which the Basque and Spanish governments would commit themselves to not changing their political status without prior shared agreement. The draft statute proposed a "state of free association" of the Basque Country with respect to the Spanish state, under which Basque citizens could decide what type of union or level of political autonomy they wanted to establish with the central state.[93]

The draft statute also proposed that the Basque government have direct representation in the European Union in order to protect the basic rights and economic interests of the Basque community in Brussels, as guaranteed to the national minorities of the Dutch, Belgian, and German states. In fact, the text proposed a substantial increase in the current authority of the Basque Autonomous Community (BAC). The new statute would guarantee the exclusive jurisdiction of the BAC in public administration, social affairs, culture, sports (with the creation of a Basque national team such as the Scottish or the Welsh), economy, education, finance, infrastructure, environment, language policy, health, public safety, social security, work, transportation, and housing. Another substantial point of the draft statute was the political recognition of Basque citizenship (as a positive legal concept) and Basque nationality (as a positive cultural concept) for all the inhabitants of the BAC, permitting dual citizenship without any type of reduction to the rights and duties of existing Spanish citizenship. And, in connection with the concept of Basque citizenship, the draft statute tried to provide a solution to the problem of the official relationship with the Chartered Community of Navarre. The draft statute proposed freedom to create official links between the seven historic Basque territories on both sides of the Pyrenees border, between the Spanish and French states. The decisions made by the citizens in each of these regions of the Basque Country would be respected by the Spanish and French governments. Navarre would have—as per the current autonomy statute—the right to join the BAC, thus generating a new Basque autonomous community that would unite the four peninsular Basque territories under a single administration.[94]

*Lehendakari* Ibarretxe's proposal included the essential points for the resolution of the Basque conflict. By not making a call for independence, the Basque administration was trying to create a path to solve the two basic problems facing the Basque conflict in 2005: the lack of a satisfactory political agreement for both sides, and violence. The basis for the proposal was that the lack of political authority of the current Basque Autonomous Community fueled political violence. Adopting a new political framework for coexistence within which both parties felt comfortable enough was undoubtedly the best, and probably the only way to resolve a political conflict that is still unresolved after two long centuries.[95]

As we have said, the proposal was rejected by the Spanish Parliament in February 2005, but it was undoubtedly the model and the origin of the political vindication process in Catalunya, which began in September 2005 with the proposal and passing in the Catalan Parliament of a new Political Statute for Catalunya. Unlike the Basque case, the Catalan statute was approved by the Spanish Parliament, although the content of powers initially granted to the people of Catalunya was drastically reduced. However, after being approved in a referendum in June 2006, the Spanish Constitutional Court declared fourteen of the articles of the statute to be unconstitutional in June 2010. These events gave rise to the Catalan independence movement.

The political approach of Lehendakari Ibarretxe was also reflected in Scotland, which, from 2011, began its own process of demanding Scottish people's historical rights. As Alex Salmond—member of the Scottish National Party and prime minister of Scotland—explained in 2010, independence is not just a political issue, but also a matter of better serving citizens' interests: "The Scottish Government believes that Scotland's future interests would be best served by it assuming all of the responsibilities and rights of a normal European state. Independence would give the Scottish Parliament and Government full responsibility for those matters currently reserved to the United Kingdom Parliament and Government, including key economic and political powers and the right of representation for Scotland in the European Union. Other aspects of an independent Scotland would remain the same. Her Majesty The Queen would remain as Head of State, and the social union with the remainder of the UK would be maintained, with the nations continuing to co-operate on a range of matters."[96]

The political movement promoted by President Ibarretxe also made it possible to reach the Lizarra Garazi Agreement which, years later on October 20, 2011, led to the end of ETA's armed struggle when it announced the definitive end to its activities.

Regarding the Northern Basque Country, after two hundred years of demands, in 2017 certain political power was recognized by a French government for the first time to the Basque territories to the north of the Pyrenees. Indeed, 220 years after the representatives from Lapurdi claimed that, after the loss of their institutions and its independence, at least one Basque department should be created within the French republic, the new entity was created as a commonwealth of Basque municipalities. On January 23, 2017, the 233 representatives of the municipalities that make up the *Communauté d'agglomération Pays Basque* (Basque municipal commonwealth) met for the first time in Baiona and elected the mayor of Baiona, Jean René Etchegaray, as the first president of the entity. The municipal commonwealth will have a budget of around 200 million Euros, and has a permanent commission of sixty-nine representatives and an executive commission of twenty-five representatives. The new entity has competences in matters of economic and sociocultural development and organization, health and social services, municipal policy, territorial coherence, roads and other infrastructures, tourism development, housing, crime prevention, environment, and funeral services.[97]

In 2020, independence became one of the political options with the greatest social support in the Basque Country. As there has not been a like referendum in Scotland, it is difficult to predict what the scale of vote there would be at consultation among the Basques, so the most specific data that we can provide are the electoral results in each of the three constituencies into which the country is currently divided: the Basque Autonomous Community, the Chartered Community of Navarra, and the Northern Basque Country Community.

Regarding the right to self-determination and the initiation of a sovereignty process, the Basque vote is divided into three blocks in the Basque Autonomous Community (BAC). On the one hand, the nationalist bloc is in favor of a self-determination referendum, with both EAJ/PNV and the Bildu coalition supporting pro-independence positions, although within the EAJ/PNV there is a sector that feels comfortable with further development of the current autonomy. The constitutionalist bloc—made up of the Spanish Socialist Workers Party (PSOE), Popular Party (PP), Ciudadanos (Cs), and Vox—opts for a refusal to hold a referendum on self-determination and even for remodeling the regional map with a tendency toward greater centralization. Finally, the left-wing bloc, represented by Podemos, defends the constitution of a federal, republican state, which is why it does not support the Basque independence cause, but does support the holding of a referendum, which has given it connections and made alliances with Basque nationalists possible.

In view of electoral results over the last decade, the independence alternative is the strongest option in the Basque Autonomous Community (with 69.5 percent of the total Basque population), where Bildu and EAJ-PNV get between 61 and 65 percent of the popular vote. In the elections for the local Parliaments in the BAC that were held on May 26, 2019, the Basque nationalist bloc obtained 63 percent of the votes cast, which gave it 64.7 percent of the seats in the Parliaments of Araba, Bizkaia, and Gipuzkoa (a total of ninety-nine seats). The most voted-for party was EAJ/PNV with 39 percent of the votes cast and sixty-two seats; the second force was Bildu with 23.98 percent of the votes cast and thirty-seven seats. The constitutionalist bloc obtained 26.4 percent of the votes cast and 24.8 percent of the seats in the aforementioned Parliaments (thirty-eight in total). Finally, the left-wing bloc obtained 10 percent of the votes cast and 9.1 percent of the seats (fourteen seats). This fact shows political support of 74 percent of the Basque electorate for the exercise of the right of self-determination. The results were similar in the various elections that took place in the spring of 2019. In the municipal elections, the nationalist bloc obtained 75.3 percent of the seats in Basque city and town councils, the constitutionalist bloc obtained 10.5 percent, and the left-wing bloc got 2.6 percent. The last elections for the Spanish Parliament took place in November 2019: the Basque nationalist bloc obtained 55.5 percent of the seats in the BAC, the constitutional bloc got 27.7 percent, and the left-wing bloc obtained 16.7 percent.[98]

In Navarre, which has 20.5 percent of the Basque population, the political arena is more complicated, since the most voted option is not only part of the constitutional sphere but, in fact, the Union of the Navarrese People, a regionalist party, together with the Spanish constitutional forces, mostly PSOE and PP. This regionalist/constitutionalist bloc obtained 62 percent of the seats in the elections to the Parliament of Navarre on May 26, 2019, the Basque nationalist bloc obtained 32 percent, and the left-wing bloc, formed by Podemos and its splinter group Izquierda-Ezkerra, 6 percent. In the municipal elections held that same day, the regionalist/constitutionalist bloc obtained 34.7 percent of the seats, the Basque nationalist bloc 23.9 percent, and the left-wing bloc 1 percent (others, almost 40 percent, were local electoral candidates covering a wide spectrum of the municipal vote in Navarre). In Navarre, therefore, the sovereigntist option is the second force, with popular support of between 25 percent and 32 percent of the vote, mainly in the Basque-speaking areas.[99]

Regarding the Northern Basque Country, which has 10 percent of the Basque population, the option that has achieved most popular support in recent years has been vindicating the association of Basque municipalities, which brought together mass support around the creation of the Basque Country Community (*Communauté d'agglomération Pays Basque*—Euskal Hirigune Elkargoa). This option, which can be described as "decentralizing," has attracted great support among French republican forces and Basque nationalist parties. It is very difficult to specify popular support for the Basque sovereignty option in the Northern Basque Country in 2019, but the Basque nationalist vote is around 10 percent of the full vote, so at present it is a minority option.[100]

The political situation in the Basque Country at present reflects a serious dysfunction between the cultural and sociological reality of Basques and the political-economic status of the country, and that is at the core of the Basque political conflict. One of the key factors in defending independence is the preservation of the Basque language and culture. The Basque Country is a nation divided into three administrative entities as a result of a dismemberment of the cultural reality of the single Basque people, and, given that the collective identity of said people is not politically recognized, the Basque language, which has barely one million speakers, today continues to decline in some areas of the country.

One of the greatest obstacles to the resolution of the Basque political conflict is the lack of democratic political culture. Both the French Republic and the Spanish monarchy are established political democracies, but they lack the full democracy that made political dialogue between the British and Scottish governments possible. The right-wing's ignoring the right to self-determination, and renouncing making and respecting a diagnosis about the political conflict and the birth of the Basque independence movement has been considered by some Basque political opinions to be "political deafness." It also involves ignoring the people's will and, therefore, denying the right to self-determination as a fundamental human right as, in Spanish foreign minister José M. García-Margallos words in 2012, organizing a self-determination referendum is equivalent to staging a coup.

Criminalizing popular opinion and punishing the peaceful vindication of a nation's right to decide does not offer a valid solution to political conflicts, and only delays the solution of the Basque and Catalan political conflicts.

## Bibliography

Agirreazkuenaga, Joseba, "La transición por la "Constitución Vascongada" (1852): De la "Constitución Foral" (1808) al "Estatuto de la autonomía de las regiones de Álava, Guipuzcoa y Vizcaya" (1919)," *I Seminari Catalunya-Euskadi. La Institucionalització política: de les Constitutions històriques als Estatus d'Autonomia (1808-2005)*, Generalitat de Catalunya-Museu d'Historia de Catalunya, Barcelona, 2007, 19-42.

Agirreazkuenaga, Joseba. "Entre Estado y provincia Foral: Proyectos y realidades de la articulación política y jurídica de los territorios forales de Vasconia-Euskal Herria en el Estado Constitucional español, en tiempos de J.Mañé i Flaquer (1823-1901)." In *L'Estat-Nació i el conflict regional: Joan Mañé i Flaquer, un cas paradigmatic, 1823-1901*, 155-196. Barcelona: Publicacions de l'Abbadia de Montserrat, 2004.

Amezaga, Elías. *Biografía sentimental de Sabino Arana.* Tafalla: Txalaparta, 2003.

Azcona, José M. *Zumalacárregui: Estudio crítico de las fuentes históricas de su tiempo.* Madrid: Instituto de estudios políticos, 1946.

Adams, John. *A Defence of the Constitutions of Government of the United States of America.* London: C. Dilly, 1787.

Aguirre, Ángel. *Historia de la antropología Española.* Barcelona: Editorial Boixareu Universitaria, 1992.

Arana, Sabino. *Bizkaya por su independencia.* Bilbao: Tipográfica de Sebastián Amorrortu, 1892.

Belaustegigoitia, Ramón. *Las bases de un Gobierno nacional vasco.* [s.n.], Bilbao: Imp., Lit. y Enc. Viuda e Hijos de Grijelmo, 1918.

*Bases bajo las cuales Navarra y las Provincias Vascongadas seguirán adheridas a la monarquía de Carlos 5º*, Boletín Oficial de Pamplona, No 26, Domingo, 27 de mayo de 1838.

Ben-Ami, Shlomo. *La dictadura de Primo de Rivera, 1923-1930.* Barcelona: Planeta, 1984.

Brea, Antonio. *Campaña del norte de 1873 á 1876.* Barcelona: Administración, 1897.

Campuzano, Francisco, and Andrée Bachoud. *Les nationalismes en Espagne: de l'État libéral à l'État des autonomies (1876-1978).* Montpellier: Université Paul Valéry-Montpellier III, 2002.

Castells, José M. *El estatuto vasco: El estado regional y el proceso estatutario vasco.* Donostia: Luis Haramburu, 1976.

Chaho, J. Augustin. *Escritos sobre la Primera Guerra Carlista.* Zumalakarregi Museoa Ormaiztegi, 2018.

Chueca, Josu. *El nacionalismo vasco en Navarra (1931-1936).* Leioa: Universidad del País Vasco, 1999.

*Congresos del PSOE en el exilio.* Madrid: Editorial Pablo Iglesias, 1981.

*Derechos humanos: Recopilación de instrumentos internacionales.* New York and Geneva: United Nations Publications, 2002.

*Diario de las discusiones y actas de las Cortes*, Cádiz: Imprenta Real, 1811, vol. 8.

*Dumbarton Oaks. Washington Conversations on International Peace and Security Organization. October 7, 1944*, Pillars of Peace No. 4, Book Department. Army Information School, Carlisle Barracks (PA), May 1946.

Egaña, Iñaki. *Diccionario histórico-político de Euskal Herria.* Tafalla: Txalaparta, 1996.

Etxebarria, Toribio. *La Liga de Naciones y el problema vasco.* Eibar: Casa del Pueblo, 1918.

Gallastegi, Cesar et al., *Larramendiren hiztegigintza juridikoa.* Deustu: Deustuko Unibertsitatea, 2007.

Goiogana, Iñaki, Xabier Irujo, and Josu Legarreta. *Un nuevo treinta y uno. Ideología y estrategia del Gobierno de Euzkadi durante la Segunda Guerra Mundial a través de la correspondencia de José Antonio Aguirre y Manuel Irujo.* Bilbao: Fundación Sabino Arana, 2007.

Goyhenetxe, Eukeni. *Historia de Iparralde: Desde los orígenes a nuestros días.* Donostia: Txertoa, 1985.

Granja Sainz, José Luis de la. *El oasis vasco: el nacimiento de Euskadi en la república y la guerra civil.* Spain: Tecnos, 2007.

Henningsen, Charles F. *The Most Striking Events of a Twelvemonth's Campaign with Zumalacarregui in Navarre and the Basque Provinces.* London: J. Murray, 1836.

Iber [Ramón Goikoetxea]. *Ami vasco.* Bilbao: Imprenta de E. Arteche, 1906.

Irujo, Daniel. *Inocencia de un patriota. Notable defensa del fundador del Partido Nacionalista Don Sabino de Arana y Goiri ante el tribunal por el ilustre abogado Don Daniel de Irujo.* Buenos Aires: Irrintzi, 1913.

Irujo, Manuel. *Arana Goiri ante los tribunales.* México: Editorial Vasca, 1953.

Irujo, Xabier, *Doce meses de campaña con Zumalacárregui durante la guerra en Navarra y Provincias Vascongadas.* Ormaiztegi: Zumalakarregi Museoa, 2015.

Irujo, Xabier, *Expelled from the Motherland: The Government of President Jose Antonio Agirre in Exile (1937 - 1960).* Reno: Center for Basque Studies Press, 2012.

Irujo, Xabier, and Pete Cenarrusa. *On Basque Politics: Conversations with Pete Cenarrusa.* Brussels: European Research Institute (EURI), 2012.

Irujo, Xabier, and Alberto Irigoyen. *La Hora Vasca Del Uruguay: Génesis y Desarrollo Del Nacionalismo Vasco en Uruguay, 1825-1960.* Montevideo: Euskal Erria, 2006.

Irujo, Xabier, and Iñigo Urrutia. *Historia jurídica de la lengua vasca (1789-2009).* Bilbao: IVAP-HAEE, 2014.

Journal des décrets de l'Assemblée Nationale, Clouster imprimeur du roi, París, 1789.

Kline, Michael B., and Nancy C. Mellerski. *Issues in the French-Speaking World.* Westport, CT: Greenwood Publishing Group, 2004.

Larronde, Jean-Claude. *El nacionalismo vasco: su origen y su ideología en la obra de Sabino Arana-Goiri.* Donostia: Txertoa, 1977.

"Ley haciendo extensivos á los habitantes de las Provincias Vascongadas los deberes que la Constitución de la Monarquía impone á todos los españoles, y autorizando al Gobierno para reformar el régimen foral de las mismas en los términos que se expresa." *Gaceta de Madrid* 3, no. 207 (1876): 213.

Los Arcos, Javier. *Los fueros y sus defensas: La Gamazada, 1893.* Bilbao: Biblioteca Vascongada, 1897.

Montoliu, Manuel. *La Renaixença i els Jocs Florals. Verdaguer.* Barcelona: Editorial Alpha, 1962.

Oloriz, Hermilio. *Cartilla foral.* Pamplona: Imprenta de Nicolás Marcelino, 1894.

Pablo, Santiago de. *Historia del nacionalismo vasco, 1876-1979.* Gasteiz: Fundación Sancho el Sabio, 1994.

*Pacto Internacional de Derechos Civiles y Políticos.* United Nations G.A. res. 2200A (XXI), 21 U.N. GAOR Supp. (Nº16) at 52, U.N. Doc. A/6316 (1966), 999 U.N.T.S. 171. Entered into force 23 March 1976.

*Pacto Internacional de Derechos Económicos, Sociales y Culturales.* United Nations G.A. res. 2200A (XXI), 21 U.N. GAOR Supp. (Nº16) at 49, U.N. Doc. A/6316 (1966), 993 U.N.T.S. 3. Entered into force 3 January 1976. 1966.

Preston, Paul. *Revolution and War in Spain, 1931-1939.* Madrid: Alliance, 1986.

Preston, Paul, Michael Partridge, and Denis Smyth. *British documents on foreign affairs—reports and papers from the Foreign Office confidential print: From 1945 through 1950*. University Publications of America, 2000.

Proposición no de ley sobre el derecho de autodeterminación del pueblo vasco. Eusko Legebiltzarra/Parlamento Vasco, No. Exp. 11/03/02/01/0138. Boletín Oficial del País Vasco, 22.01.1990/B\IV\134(a) y 26.02.1990/B\IV\134-135(d). Gasteiz, February 15, 1990.

"Recueil de lois et règlemens concerning l'instruction publique, depuis l'edit de Henri IV in 1598 after the journal." *Brunot-Labbe* 1, (1814): 22-26.

*Report on the Right to Self-determination: Historical and Current Development on the Basis of the United Nations Instruments*, United Nations Sub-Commission on Prevention of Discrimination and Protection of Minorities, Doc. E / CN.4 / Sub.2 / 404 / Rev.1. Special Rapporteur, Aurelia Critescu. 1981.

"Resolución 32 (1) de la asamblea general de Naciones Unidas, Sesión 26, febrero 9, 1946." Kelsen, Hans, *The Law of the United Nations: A Critical Analysis of its Fundamental Problems: With Supplement*. New Jersey: The Lawbook Exchange, 2000.

Rodríguez Ranz, José Antonio. *Guipúzcoa y San Sebastián en las elecciones de la II República*. Donostia: Instituto Dr. Camino de Historia Donostiarra, 1994.

Sagarminaga, Fidel. *Reflexiones sobre el sentido político de los Fueros de Vizcaya*. Bilbao: Juan E. Delmas, 1871.

Sagaseta, Ángel. *Fueros fundamentales del Reino de Navarra y defensa legal de los mismos*. Pamplona: Imprenta de Francisco Erasun, 1840.

*Scotland's Future: Draft Referendum (Scotland) Bill Consultation Paper*. Edinburgh: The Scottish Government Riahaltas na h-Alba, 2010.

*Tableau de la Constitution du Royaume de Navarre et des Rapports avec la France*. Paris: J. Ch. Desaint, 1798.

Tamayo, Virginia, and Carlos Tamayo. *Fuentes documentales y normativas del Estatuto de Gernika*. Gasteiz: Diputación foral de Álava, 1981.

Ugalde, Martin. *Historia de Euskadi*. Madrid: Cupsa, 1981.

Viñas, Ángel. *Sobornos: De cómo Churchill y March compraron a los generales de Franco*. Barcelona: Crítica, 2016.

Wilson, Woodrow. *Americanism: Woodrow Wilson's Speeches on the War*. Chicago: Baldwin Syndicate, 1918.

*Woodrow Wilson's Fourteen Points, January 8, 1918. The Atlantic Charter's Eight Points, August 14, 1941. Declaration by the United Nations, January 1, 1942. The Moscow Declaration, October 30, 1943. The Teheran Declaration, December 1, 1943*, Woodrow Wilson Foundation, 1943.

Zabalo, Joseph. *Xaho. El genio de Zuberoa*. Tafalla: Txalaparta, 2004.

## NOTES

1 *Journal des décrets de l'Assemblée Nationale* (Paris: Clouster imprimeur du roi, 1789), 96.

2 The Basque Country—Euskadi or Euskal Herria—is made up of six historical territories: Araba, Bizkaia, Gipuzkoa, Lapurdi, Navarre, and Zuberoa. After the War of 1512-1522, Navarre was divided in two, so that between 1522 and 1789, there were two Kingdoms of Navarre (Lower Navarre in the north, and Navarre in the south). "Iparralde," in Basque,

literally means "the north of the Basque Country: the territories of Lapurdi, Lower Navarre and Zuberoa." In contrast, "Hegoalde" means "the south of the Basque Country: The territories of Araba, Bizkaia, Gipuzkoa and Navarre."

3 *Tableau de la Constitution du Royaume de Navarre et des Rapports avec la France* (Paris: J. Ch. Desaint, 1798).

4 "Recueil de lois et règlemens concernant l'instruction publique, depuis l'edit de Henri IV en 1598 jusqu"à ce jour," *Brunot-Labbe* 1, (1814): 22-26.

5 Eukeni Goyhenetxe, *Historia de Iparralde: Desde los orígenes a nuestros días* (Donostia: Txertoa, 1985), 84.

6 *Actas de la Diputación general de españoles que se juntó en Bayona el 15 de junio de 1808* . . ., Imprenta y fundición de J. A. García, Madrid, 1874, 109.

7 *Actas de la Diputación general de españoles que se juntó en Bayona el 15 de junio de 1808* . . ., Imprenta y fundición de J. A. García, Madrid, 1874, 106-109.

8 *Diario de las discusiones y actas de las Cortes*, Imprenta Real, Cádiz, 1811, vol. 8, 14.

9 In 1848 the magazine was renamed *Ariel Le Républicaine de Vasconie*.

10 J. Augustin Chaho, *Escritos sobre la Primera Guerra Carlista* (Zumalakarregi Museoa Ormaiztegi, 2018), 130.

11 Jospeh Zabalo, *Xaho. El genio de Zuberoa* (Tafalla: Txalaparta, 2004), 69.

12 Ángel Sagaseta, *Fueros fundamentales del Reino de Navarra y defensa legal de los mismos* (Pamplona: Imprenta de Francisco Erasun, 1840).

13 Ángel Sagaseta, *Fueros fundamentales del Reino de Navarra y defensa legal de los mismos* (Pamplona: Imprenta de Francisco Erasun, 1840), 11-13.

14 The right of refusal ("sobrecarta") or "charter vote" was the legal institution by which no law could be passed without the approval of each one of the Parliaments of the Basque states. This rule protected the Basque provincial system, which, in that way, defended itself against possible abuses of power by the executive.

15 John Adams, *A Defence of the Constitutions of Government of the United States of America* (London: C. Dilly, 1787).

16 Adams, John, *A Defence of the Constitutions of Government of the United States of America* (J. Stockdale, London), 1794, 16.

17 Official communiqué of the Ministry of Finance. *Gaceta de Madrid*, no. 879, miércoles mayo 30, Madrid, 1855, 1.

18 *Vascongados;* no date or signature. The proclamation does not have any details about where it had been printed.

19 "Chez un peuple libre, la langue doit être une et la même pour tous," in *Issues in the French-Speaking World*, ed. Michael B. Kline and Nancy C. Mellerski (Westport, CT: Greenwood Publishing Group, 2004), 70.

20 Xabier Irujo and Iñigo Urrutia, *Historia jurídica de la lengua vasca (1789-2009)* (Bilbao: IVAP-HAEE, 2014), 133.

21 *Gazette Nationale ou Le Moniteur Universel*, No. 129, nonidi, 9 pluviose, l'an 2e (Mardi 28 janvier 1794, vieux style), martes, enero 28, 1794, 3a serie, vol. 6, 5-8.

22 Irujo and Urrutia, *Historia jurídica de la lengua vasca (1789-2009)*, 146-147.

23 Cesar Gallastegi et al., *Larramendiren hiztegigintza juridikoa* (Deustu: Deustuko Unibertsitatea, 2007), 34-35.

24 Manuel Montoliu, *La Renaixença i els Jocs Florals. Verdaguer* (Editorial Alpha, Barcelona, 1962), 21 and 73. In 1859 a group of Catalan intellectuals suggested to the mayor of Barcelona, Josep Santamaría, that they organize some *Jocs florals*, and Antoni Bofarull published the first nineteenth-century novel in Catalan, *L'orfeneta de Menargues o Catalunya agonitzant*, in 1862.

25 Antonio Brea, *Campaña del norte de 1873 á 1876* (Barcelona: Administración, 1897), 489-502.

26 Law extending the duties that the Constitution of the Monarchy imposes on all Spaniards to the inhabitants of the Basque Provinces and authorizing the government to reform the charter regime of the same in the terms expressed, *Madrid Gazette*, no. 207, martes, julio 21, 1876, vol. 3, 213.

27 Javier Los Arcos, *Los fueros y sus defensas: La Gamazada, 1893* (Bilbao: Biblioteca Vascongada, 1897), 10-172.

28 Joseba Agirreazkuenaga, "Entre Estado y provincia Foral: Proyectos y realidades de la articulación política y jurídica de los territorios forales de Vasconia-Euskal Herria en el Estado Constitucional español, en tiempos de J.Mañé i Flaquer (1823-1901)," in *L'Estat-Nació i el conflict regional: Joan Mañé i Flaquer, un cas paradigmatic, 1823-1901* (Barcelona: Publicacions de l'Abbadia de Montserrat, 2004), 155-196.

29 Ángel Aguirre, *Historia de la antropología Española* (Barcelona: Editorial Boixareu Universitaria, 1992), 165.

30 Martin Ugalde, *Historia de Euskadi* (Madrid: Cupsa, 1981), 397.

31 Sabino Arana, *Bizkaya por su independencia* (Bilbao: Tipográfica de Sebastián Amorrortu, 1892).

32 Jean-Claude Larronde, *El nacionalismo vasco: su origen y su ideología en la obra de Sabino Arana-Goiri* (Donostia: Txertoa, 1977), 65.

33 Larronde, *El nacionalismo vasco: su origen y su ideología en la obra de Sabino Arana-Goiri*, 65.

34 Followers of the motto "Jaungoikoa eta Legizarra," whose initials are JEL.

35 Daniel Irujo, *Inocencia de un patriota. Notable defensa del fundador del Partido Nacionalista Don Sabino de Arana y Goiriante el tribunal por el ilustre abogado Don Daniel de Irujo* (Buenos Aires: Irrintzi, 1913), 13.

36 Irujo, *Inocencia de un patriota. Notable defensa del fundador del Partido Nacionalista Don Sabino de Arana y Goiriante el tribunal por el ilustre abogado Don Daniel de Irujo*, 20.

37 Irujo, *Inocencia de un patriota. Notable defensa del fundador del Partido Nacionalista Don Sabino de Arana y Goiri ante el tribunal por el ilustre abogado Don Daniel de Irujo*, 26-27.

38 Manuel Irujo, *Arana Goiri ante los tribunals* (México: Editorial Vasca, 1953), 21-22.

39 José M. Azcona, *Zumalacárregui: Estudio crítico de las fuentes históricas de su tiempo* (Madrid: Instituto de estudios políticos, 1946), 293, 464.

40 Irujo, *Arana Goiri ante los tribunales*, 41.

41 Irujo, *Arana Goiri ante los tribunales*, 22.

42 Elías Amezaga, *Biografía sentimental de Sabino Arana* (Tafalla: Txalaparta, 2003), 306.

43 Iber [Ramón Goikoetxea], *Ami vasco*, Imprenta de E. Arteche, Bilbao, 1906.

44 *Woodrow Wilson's Fourteen Points, January 8, 1918. The Atlantic Charter's Eight Points, August 14, 1941. Declaration by the United Nations, January 1, 1942. The Moscow*

*Declaration, October 30, 1943. The Teheran Declaration, December 1, 1943*, Woodrow Wilson Foundation, 1943.

45 Woodrow Wilson, *Americanism: Woodrow Wilson's Speeches on the War* (Chicago: Baldwin Syndicate, 1918), 97-98.

46 Ramón Belaustegigoitia, *Las bases de un Gobierno nacional vasco*, [s.n.], Bilbao, 1918.

47 Toribio Etxebarria, *La Liga de Naciones y el problema vasco* (Eibar: Casa del Pueblo, 1918).

48 Alexander Ugalde, *La Acción Exterior Del Nacionalismo Vasco, 1890-1939: Historia, Pensamiento y Relaciones Internacionales*, Instituto Vasco de Administración Pública = Herri-Arduralaritzaren Euskal Erakundea, Oñati, 1996, 261.

49 José L. de la Granja Sainz, *El oasis vasco: El nacimiento de Euskadi en la república y la guerra civil* (Tecnos, 2007), 194-198.

50 Santiago de Pablo, *Historia del nacionalismo vasco, 1876-1979* (Gasteiz: Fundación Sancho el Sabio 1994), 13.

51 Shlomo Ben-Ami, *La dictadura de Primo de Rivera, 1923-1930* (Barcelona: Planeta, 1984), 134.

52 Paul Preston, *Revolución y guerra en España, 1931-1939* (Madrid: Alianza, 1986), 166.

53 *Estatuto General del Estado Vasco. Aprobado en la Magna Asamblea de Municipios Vascos, celebrada en Estella (Lizarra) el día 14 de junio de 1931*, Imprenta de E. Verdes Achirica, Bilbao, 1931. In Estornés, Idoia, *La Construcción de una nacionalidad vasca: el autonomismo de Eusko-Ikaskuntza (1918-1931)*, Eusko Ikaskuntza, Donostia, 1988, 285.

54 José Antonio Rodríguez Ranz, *Guipúzcoa y San Sebastián en las elecciones de la II República* (Donostia: Instituto Dr. Camino de Historia Donostiarra, 1994), 162.

55 Josu Chueca, *El nacionalismo vasco en Navarra (1931-1936)* (Leioa: Universidad del País Vasco, 1999), 359.

56 José M. Castells, *El estatuto vasco: El estado regional y el proceso estatutario vasco* (Donostia: Luis Haramburu, 1976), 60.

57 Ugalde, *Historia de Euskadi*, 518-519.

58 Virginia Tamayo et al., *Fuentes documentales y normativas del Estatuto de Gernika* (Gasteiz: Diputación foral de Álava, 1981), 832.

59 Xabier Irujo, *Expelled from the Motherland: The Government of President Jose Antonio Agirre in Exile (1937 - 1960)* (Reno: Center for Basque Studies Press, 2012), 213-225.

60 Irujo, *Expelled from the Motherland: The Government of President Jose Antonio Agirre in Exile (1937 - 1960)*, 67-100.

61 Meudon Agreement (Meudon, August 23, 1939), in a letter from Doroteo Ziaurritz to Manuel Irujo, Meudon, August 23, 1939.

62 Letter from José Ignacio Lizaso to Ramón Sota, London, March 12, 1941.

63 Letter from José Ignacio Lizaso to José Antonio Aguirre, London, October 24, 1942.

64 Letter from José Ignacio Lizaso to Ramón Sota, London, March 12, 1941.

65 Irujo, *Expelled from the Motherland: The Government of President Jose Antonio Agirre in Exile (1937–1960)*, 154-156.

66 Letter from José Ignacio Lizaso to Ramón Sota, London, July 9, 1941. See also, letter from Jose Ignacio Lizaso to Commander P. Carey of the Naval Intelligence Division (NID) of the British Admiralty, London, July 30, 1940.

67 Irujo, *Expelled from the Motherland: The Government of President Jose Antonio Agirre in Exile (1937–1960)*, 150-154.
68 Iñaki Goiogana et al., *Un nuevo treinta y uno. Ideología y estrategia del Gobierno de Euzkadi durante la Segunda Guerra Mundial a través de la correspondencia de José Antonio Aguirre y Manuel Irujo* (Bilbao: Fundación Sabino Arana, 2007), 76-77.
69 Rejoinder from Mr. Irujo, in, VVAA, *La Comunidad Ibérica de Naciones*, 119, EKIN, Buenos Aires, 1945.
70 Ángel Viñas, *Bribes: De cómo Churchill y March compraron a los generales de Franco* (Barcelona: Crítica, 2016), 452-487.
71 Letter from Bingen Ametzaga to Joxe Mari Lasarte, Montevideo, October 25, 1944.
72 Goiogana, *Un nuevo treinta y uno. Ideología y estrategia del Gobierno de Euzkadi durante la Segunda Guerra Mundial a través de la correspondencia de José Antonio Aguirre y Manuel Irujo*, 64-67.
73 Galeuzca Agreement, Montevideo, May 9, 1941.
74 Galeuzca Agreement, Montevideo, May 9, 1941.
75 Galeuzca Agreement, Montevideo, May 9, 1941.
76 Galeuzca Agreement, Montevideo, May 9, 1941.
77 Letter from José Antonio Aguirre to Alfonso R. Castelao, New York, March 2, 1944.
78 Letter from Manuel Irujo to Francisco Belausteguigoitia, London, September 16, 1941.
79 The first of October is usually seen as the beginning of General Franco's government, since on that date he took possession of the position that he would not leave until his death in November 1975.
80 Resolution 32 (1) of the United Nations General Assembly, Session 26, February 9, 1946. Hans Kelson, *The Law of the United Nations: A Critical Analysis of its Fundamental Problems: With Supplement* (New Jersey: The Lawbook Exchange, 2000), 77.
81 Paul Preston et al., *British documents on foreign affairs—reports and papers from the Foreign Office confidential print: From 1945 through 1950* (University Publications of America, 2000), 330.
82 109 (1955). "Resolution of 14 December 1955 [S / 3509]. The Security Council, Bearing in mind General Assembly resolution 918 (X) of 8 December 1955 on the admission of new Members to the United Nations, Having considered separately the applications for membership of Albania, Jordan, Ireland, Portugal, Hungary, Italy, Austria, Romania, Bulgaria, Finland, Ceylon, Nepal, Libya, Cambodia, Laos and Spain, Recommends to the General Assembly the admission of the above-named countries to the United Nations." Adopted at the 705th meeting by eight votes to none, with three abstentions (Belgium, China, United States of America).
83 *International Covenant on Civil and Political Rights* . United Nations G.A. res. 2200A (XXI), 21 U.N. GAOR Supp. (Nº16) at 52, U.N. Doc. A/6316 (1966), 999 U.N.T.S. 171. Entered into force 23 March 1976. 12-16-1966.
84 *International Covenant on Economic, Social and Cultural Rights.* United Nations G.A. res. 2200A (XXI), 21 U.N. GAOR Supp. (Nº16) at 49, U.N. Doc. A/6316 (1966), 993 U.N.T.S. 3. Entered into force 3 January 1976. 1966. Part I. Article 1. 1.
85 *Human rights: Compilation of international instruments*, United Nations Publications, New York and Geneva, 2002, vol. 1, part 1, 19.

86 After disappearing during the battle of Dunkirk, in order to escape from the German security forces that were pursuing him, *Lehendakari* Agirre went to Berlin, where he lived under a false identity until he was finally able to leave for Sweden and, from there, take a ship bound for Brazil, where it arrived in October 1941.

87 Program of the Basque Country National Council (London, July 15, 1940) in a letter from Manuel Irujo to Ramon Sota, London, July 15, 1940.

88 Iñaki Egaña, *Diccionario histórico-político de Euskal Herria* (Tafalla: Txalaparta, 1996), 37.

89 Egaña, *Diccionario histórico-político de Euskal Herria*, 37-38.

90 Francisco Campuzano et al., *Les nationalismes en Espagne: de l'État libéral à l'État des autonomies (1876-1978)* (Montpellier: Université Paul Valéry-Montpellier III, 2002), 155.

91 *Congresos del PSOE en el exilio* (Madrid: Editorial Pablo Iglesias, 1981), 223.

92 *Report on the Right to Self-determination: Historical and Current Development on the Basis of the United Nations Instruments*, United Nations Sub-Commission on Prevention of Discrimination and Protection of Minorities, Doc. E / CN.4 / Sub.2 / 404 / Rev.1. Special Rapporteur, Aurelia Critescu, 1981.

93 Xabier Irujo et al., *On Basque Politics: Conversations with Pete Cenarrusa* (Brussels: European Research Institute (EURI), 2012), 405-407.

94 "Propuesta soberanista del 'Lehendakari.' Principales puntos del 'Plan Ibarretxe,' El Mundo," martes, febrero 1, 2005, 1.

95 Irujo, *On Basque Politics: Conversations with Pete Cenarrusa*, 405-408.

96 *Scotland's Future: Draft Referendum (Scotland) Bill Consultation Paper*, The Scottish Government—Riahaltas na h-Alba, Edinburgh, 2010, 5.

97 https://www.communaute-paysbasque.fr/eu/.

98 The electoral results in the BAC can be seen at https://www.euskadi.eus/elecciones/.

99 The electoral results in the CAN can be seen at https://www.navarra.es/home_es/Navarra/Instituciones/Elecciones+2019/.

100 For the results in the Northern Basque Country, see Irujo, *On Basque Politics: Conversations with Pete Cenarrusa*, 322-326.

# 5

# Context and Political Innovations of the So-Called Ibarretxe Plan (2001-2005)

*Igor Filibi*

## Beginnings and Evolution of the State of Autonomies

The Spanish transition to democracy was marked by a double question. Firstly, recovering the democratic system after years of dictatorship; and secondly, addressing the national plurality of the state and achieving a common framework in which different nations could live together in harmony. The negotiated nature of the transition, which in turn prevented a true break with the Francoist system, imposed numerous limits upon what the new constitution could establish. These limits determined aspects such as the electoral system, the definition of the Senate, and the extraordinary conditions necessary to reform the constitution in the future. These determinants also affected the definition of the state of autonomies, preventing the creation of a plurinational state and even of a truly federal state.

In fact, the most that the old regime was prepared to accept was a slight political decentralization, with some symbolic features defined in brief, and consequently ambiguous, fashion, making it possible to continue with the transition process in anticipation of a future in which these aspects could be controlled or even reversed.

In the ranks of Basque nationalism, there were basically two approaches to the transition. There was a pragmatic nationalism, led by the PNV (Basque Nationalist Party), which rejected ETA's violence and opted to save the process, although the constitution did not satisfy the minimum requirements of Basque self-government. The PNV, despite these shortcomings, which prevented it from supporting the constitution, sought to ensure the shift to a democratic system by advocating abstention (and not the vote against). The leaders of the party repeated on numerous occasions that they were hopeful that under a democratic constitution it would be possible in the future to address the Basque question in improved circumstances. But there was also another sector of nationalism, led by Herri Batasuna and that supported ETA's violence, which openly rejected the transition process and voted against the 1978 Constitution, since without acceptance of the right to self-determination and a referendum on secession, democracy did not meet the minimum necessary requirements.

Thus, the Spanish transition process was based on two pacts, one complete and another incomplete. On the one hand, there was a major, complete agreement with regard to the need to construct a democratic system, in spite of the difficulties involved in doing so without a radical break with the dictatorship. On the other hand, it was not possible to reach an agreement with regard to recognition and political accommodation of the nations that existed within the state. In this case, the most that was achieved, thanks to the desire of all those involved to ensure the transition to democracy, was an incomplete agreement, which established minimum conditions that made it possible to continue forward, without closing the model and leaving some elements open to development in different directions. These ambiguous elements, so often criticized by constitutional experts,[1] proved to be indispensable in order to reach a political agreement in relation to the political system.[2] Thus, when one refers to the consensus of the Transition, this should be restricted to the former aspect, recalling that it did not affect the second.

This incomplete agreement was based on a series of constructive ambiguities, such as the role and scope of historical rights, or the Basque Country's economic agreement and Navarra's Economic Agreement. Thus, in relation to historical rights, it is natural that where some see a simple nostalgic concession to history, without great legal significance, others see a full legal basis that preexisted the constitution itself. Thus, for instance, Miguel Herrero Rodríguez de Miñón, one of the "Fathers of the Constitution," said that historical rights represented "the origin of the Basque Country's power," establishing "the non-derogability of autonomy as the expression of self-determination itself and not as a creation born of the Constitution." For this reason, note Expósito and Franco, "it is not possible to determine an exact concept, unanimously accepted by legal doctrine," and Caño Moreno recalls that the different definitions have been "influenced by their author's political orientations." For his part, "Corcuera Atienza believes that the imprecision of the term makes it possible" even "to assert the contents of the very claims for the total reintegration of the ancient Charters."[3]

In fact, the constitutional agreement was—precisely—to make both interpretations possible. Which is why, when the Constitutional Court assumes the capacity to develop with precision and detail provisions that the legislature wished to remain ambiguous, and attempts to close routes that should have been left open, the constitutional spirit and the political climate that made the agreement possible are being violated.

Immediately after the adoption of the statute of autonomy of the Basque Country in 1979, a process began that was marked by the attempts by the Basque institutions to develop statutory provisions and attain the maximum possible degree of self-government, while the state institutions strove to constrain and limit this process. After an attempted coup d'état in February 1981, on July 30, 1982, the Organic Law of Harmonisation of the Autonomous Process was passed, agreed between the two main Spanish parties, UCD and PSOE. This pact formalized the need to limit the scope of the autonomy of the recently created communities, and in particular of the Basque and Catalan nationalities. On October 28 of that year, in a context of crisis, general elections were held in Spain, and the Socialist Party (PSOE) entered government with an overwhelming absolute majority.

Mario Zubiaga[4] identifies in the autonomous process an initial phase of institutionalization (1978–87) and a second phase (1988–98) in which "the management of the resulting model, although it facilitated a notable level of self-government, gradually revealed its original limitations." The author points out that "the prevalence of the idea of 'concession' rather than that of 'pact' permitted a restrictive interpretation of autonomy on the part of the state, blocking the way not only to a legitimate extension of Basque self-government, but also to mere statutory compliance."

In Corcuera's opinion,[5] "the major commitment of the 1990s was that of initiating the process of homogenizing the distribution of competences between the Communities," and the end of this period "appeared to signal the end of a phase characterized by the debate between symmetry and asymmetry, and the beginning of another in which the priority was to consolidate cooperation and participation, defining instruments and redefining institutions to reinforce the State of Autonomies."

For this reason, in 2004, it could be said, by way of assessment of the first twenty-five years of the constitution, that "despite its limitations, the state of Autonomies establishes the bases to address the issue of decentralization, but is far from resolving the accommodation of plurinationality."[6] At a time when the new Basque and Catalan statutes were being drafted, the author identifies three main problems in the design and functioning of the state of:

> the confusion between decentralization and plurinationality; the absence of any clear, stable rules of play that prevent the functioning of the political system from depending upon electoral circumstances; and the lack of guaranteed legal protection before the Constitutional Court vis-à-vis the content of self-government. All this represents a certain adulteration of the spirit with which the 1978 constitution was drafted, and a certain failure, in democratic terms, of the accommodation of the state's internal national pluralism.[7]

## The European and Global Context

### New Developments in Self-Determination: Shared Sovereignty

The old empires had been built upon the evident diversity of peoples, cultures, languages, and identities. They were political entities that articulated a complex patchwork of highly diverse authorities and institutions. Upon conclusion of the First World War, in 1918, the principle of self-determination, also termed the principle of nationalities following US president Woodrow Wilson's Fourteen Point Speech, was applied to the territory of the defeated Ottoman and Austro-Hungarian Empires.

After the Second World War, the two superpowers (USA and USSR) agreed upon the generalization of the right to self-determination. The process of decolonization promoted by the United Nations contributed to the fact that between 1945 and 1975 the number of states in the world tripled.

The end of the Cold War in 1989-91, following the implosion of the Soviet Union, heralded another period marked by the principle of self-determination. Firstly, finalizing the self-determination of the German people was invoked by the 1949 Basic Law of Bonn with its reunification in 1990. Secondly, with the dismembering of the Soviet Union and the emergence of new states, a peaceful process was encouraged and recognized by the international community. Thirdly, a parallel process took place in the Balkans, which also saw the creation of new states, although in this case it occurred after a series of regional wars. Fourthly, there were new forms of self-determination, such as the creation of the European Union, a political entity of a supranational nature. Fifthly, there were other attempts that did not succeed, such as in the former Soviet territory, but in political entities that were not republics and which were not allowed to exercise the right to self-determination (Tuva, Chechenia), or in the form of local wars between the new post-Soviet states (Nagorno Karabaj, Osetia, Transdniestr, etc.).[8]

If one compares a map of 1914 Europe with the present day, two prevailing trends are apparent. On the one hand, there has been substantial fragmentation, with the disappearance of empires and the emergence of a host of national states. On the other hand, there is no denying a powerful trend toward the economic and political unification of the continent, particularly since the creation of the European Union in 1992. These two trends, seemingly contradictory, form part of the process of political reorganization of an increasingly peripheral Europe.[9] The scale of the Union is greater than that of the old empires, but its constituent units are smaller. This appears to indicate that Europe needs to increase its size, especially in view of the growth of the superpowers (USA, USSR), but that numerous nations demand a place on the negotiating tables prior to acceptance of the process of political integration. Integration involves a complete reformulation of sovereignty, and the small European nations were prepared to accept a limitation of their sovereignty, but not to be politically diluted or to abandon their national identity.

This appears to be the sign of the times—not only in Europe—when one sees how Quebec wanted a referendum on secession, only to be in a better position to negotiate its accommodation within the Canadian federation, or when the Scottish National Party launched its slogan of "Independence in Europe," which involved recovering its sovereignty from the United Kingdom before sharing it within the European Union. The same process has taken place with numerous nations that, having won back their sovereignty from the Soviet Union, opted to share it within the EU.

Of course, the European reality is framed within an increasingly interdependent and globalized world context. "A new politics of nationalism has emerged," stated Keating some years ago, and now "claims to self-determination are reformulated and placed in the context of the emerging transnational order."[10] Thus, sharing sovereignty is a central concept in today's world, and not only in the obvious case of the European Union, it is also a more generalized trend that is transforming nation-states, as has been seen in Sri Lanka, New Caledonia, the Nordic countries, Northern Ireland, Gibraltar, etc.[11]

## Toward a Regional Dimension of the European Union

In December 2001, barely days before the introduction of the euro, the European Council of Laeken adopted the Declaration on the Future of Europe and convened a European convention that was to present proposals for the reform of the European Union. The inaugural session of the convention was held on February 28, 2002, and its work finished on July 18, 2003, when the president of the convention, Valéry Giscard d'Estaing, submitted the final draft of the treaty that established a constitution for Europe.

From the outset, there was pressure from different regions, the Committee of the Regions, and the European Parliament to address the role of regions and local entities within the EU. The final draft of the Treaty establishing a Constitution for Europe:

> included various provisions in favour of the regional dimension, notably: a) recognition of the promotion of "territorial cohesion" and respect for "cultural and linguistic diversity" as objectives of the EU (Art. I-3 paragraph 3); b) respect for "regional and local self-government" (Art. I-5 paragraph 1); c) affirmation of the principle of attribution, by virtue of which the Union acts within the limits of the competences conferred upon it by Member States in the Treaty (Art. I-11 paragraphs 1 and 2); d) clarification of the different categories of competences (Art. I-12); e) corroboration that the representation of a Member State on the Council may be exercised by a regional minister (Art. I-23 paragraph 2); f) specification that the objective of "territorial cohesion" seeks to reduce the differences between levels of development of different regions and the backwardness of the less-favoured regions (Art. III-220); and, finally, g) the extension of the principle of subsidiarity to "regional and local level" and the opening of regional parliaments to the possibility of participating in political control *ex ante* of the application of this principle via an innovative "early warning system" (Art. I-11, Protocol on the Application of the Principles of Subsidiarity and Proportionality and the Protocol on the Role of National Parliaments).[12]

Thus, in the EU, the way was paved toward a "regional conception of European construction,"[13] thanks to various documents, prominent among which are the European Parliament Lamassoure and Napolitano Reports,[14] which are reflected, though in diluted form, in the Draft Constitutional Treaty drawn up by the European Convention.[15]

This European trend influenced countries like France. Thus, in spite of the reservations and misgivings expressed by many French political parties and much public opinion, on May 7, 1999, the French government signed the European Charter for Regional or Minority Languages, opening a period of flexibilization and openness toward the regional factor that materialized in the Matignon Process (2000-2002) and in the drafting of the Statute of Corsica. While the European Convention was completing its work, on March 28, 2003, a constitutional reform was adopted in France that modified various elements in relation to regions. Article 1 stated that "the organisation is decentralised," and Article 72 included the regions among the territorial collectives and recognized their "right to experimentation," which "makes it possible to progress more quickly towards territorial collectives with greater will and capacity to assume new competences." This article facilitated, for instance, during the period 2003-2006, the Alsatian experiment of administration of European funds.[16]

Very influential in the Basque case were the Good Friday Agreements signed in Belfast on April 10, 1998, which brought an end to the IRA violence. One of their most important points was the fact that Ireland's self-determination was recognized in certain cases and subject to democratic majorities. Without any doubt, however, one of their main innovations was a concept of shared sovereignty that was inspired by the Nordic Council and the European Union.

### The Basque and Spanish Context

The Northern Ireland Agreement was welcomed with delight and hope in the Basque Country, shaking up the political landscape. Since on April 10, 1998, the agreement was signed, and in May it was ratified via referendum in Northern Ireland and in the Republic of Ireland, then on September 12 the four nationalist Basque parties, along with five other political forces, eight trade unions, and twenty-two organizations signed the Agreement of Lizarra in order to pursue a process of dialogue and negotiation that would bring an end to ETA's terrorist activities.

The consequences of this action were immediate. On September 16, ETA declared a complete, indefinite ceasefire, and on November 3, the Spanish prime minister, José María Aznar—who had replaced Felipe González in 1996—announced that he had authorized contacts with the "Basque Liberation Movement." During the negotiations, the Popular Party government made the significant gesture of transferring 135 ETA inmates to prisons near the Basque Country.

However, in spite of these promising movements, on November 28, 1999, ETA broke the truce, which had lasted fourteen months and sixteen days. The main Spanish political parties felt they had been betrayed, and they insisted that nothing political could be negotiated with ETA, forgetting the obvious precedent of Northern Ireland. The Basque nationalist parties also felt betrayed by the attitude of the Spanish government, which they accused of having missed a historic opportunity to resolve the Basque conflict. Part of Basque nationalism also felt betrayed by ETA, which had broken the truce unilaterally, seriously compromising those that committed to the process.

Ultimately, that attempt was thwarted and, beyond the responsibilities of each of the actors involved, the main consequence was drastic deterioration of the political climate, in both the Basque Country and the Spanish state. Relations between the two were poisoned, and any dialogue between the Spanish and the nationalist Basque parties proved impossible. In the same way that in 1998 the nationalist Basque parties were able to reach a consensus that materialized in the Lizarra Agreement, now it was the Spanish constitutionalist parties that formed a common front to challenge Basque nationalism. The new strategy did not distinguish between ETA, the nationalism that supported ETA (Herri Batasuna), and the nationalism traditionally referred to as institutional (PNV, EA).

ETA reacted with a wave of increasingly cruel fatal attacks, continuing the trend initiated with the killing of Miguel Ángel Blanco (July 13, 1997). Thus, on January 21, 2000, ETA murdered an army lieutenant colonel, on February 22 the secretary general of the Socialist Party of the Basque Country and his bodyguard, on May 7 a journalist, in May and June two Popular Party councilors, in July an ex-civil governor, in August a businessman . . .

In the middle of this chain of terrorist attacks, on April 26, 2000, José María Aznar won the general elections and was sworn in as prime minister of Spain with an absolute majority. On November 21 of that year, ETA killed Ernest Lluch in Barcelona. He had been a prominent leader of the Catalan Socialist Party but had retired from political life in 1986 and taught at the university. Lluch had always been known for his openness to the plurinationality of the state and was an intellectual committed to peace in the Basque Country. His murder was seen as a turning point that shook Catalan society. A million people demonstrated against ETA in Barcelona.

On December 8, 2000, the Popular Party and the Socialist Party signed the Agreement for Freedom and Against Terrorism. In this agreement, it was stated that "ETA's return to terrorist violence" evidenced "the failure of the strategy promoted by the PNV and EA, which abandoned the Ajuria Enea Agreement in order to put a political price on an end to the violence, in concert with ETA and Euskal Herritarrok (EH). The price to be paid was the imposition of self-determination to achieve the independence of the Basque Country." This document reflected what leaders of both parties had been saying for months, and which some judges would subsequently condense into the phrase "all [Basque nationalism] is ETA."

From that point onward, the state intensified a campaign of total war on Basque nationalism, criminalizing every manifestation of Basque nationalism, with the support of the mainstream media, a judicial harassment, and a new political discourse that attacked the very existence of the idea of the Basque nation.[17] The symmetrical strategy employed by ETA and the state led to an unprecedented degree of polarization of Basque society.

On May 13, 2001, early elections were held in the Basque Country. The self-designated constitutionalist parties polarized the electoral debate, demanding a vote for the constitution; in other words, for Spain, or a vote for ETA. There was no room whatsoever for any kind of Basque nationalist strategy. The discourse emanating from the state was that constitutionalism was in fact a majority sentiment in the Basque Country, but that the blackmail and fear generated by terrorism intimidated the population and thus created an apparent Basque nationalist majority. Spain was mobilized as never before, with the national parties traveling to the Basque Country on a daily basis to support constitutionalism in elections that were described as "constituent" for the future of the Basque Country.

The population responded to their respective leaders' calls and voted en masse, resulting in a historical 79.97 percent turnout. This figure provided clear evidence of the total mobilization of Basque society, as neither before nor since had or has there been a similar turnout (see table 1). The significance of this figure is underscored by the fact that in the first democratic elections, in 1977, in which the representatives who drafted the 1978 Constitution were elected, there was a 76.93 percent turnout (Source: Basque government).

Table 1: Turnout in Elections to the Basque Parliament

| Year | Turnout |
|---|---|
| 2016 | 60.20 % |
| 2012 | 63.96 % |
| 2009 | 64.68 % |
| 2005 | 68.00 % |
| 2001 | **79.97 %** |
| 1998 | 69.99 % |
| 1994 | 59.69 % |
| 1990 | 60.99 % |
| 1986 | 69.62 % |
| 1984 | 68.49 % |
| 1980 | 59.76 % |

Source: Prepared by the author, Basque government (https://www.euskadi.eus/resultados-electorales/)

The results of the "constituent" Basque elections of 2001 were crystal clear. The coalition formed by the two nationalist Basque parties, PNV and EA, obtained an overwhelming majority with their 604,222 votes and thirty-three of the seventy-five seats. The second most-voted party was the PP, with 326,933 votes and nineteen seats, followed by the Socialist Party with 253,195 votes and thirteen seats, and the EH coalition, with 143,139 votes and seven seats. A long way behind was Ezker Batua, with its 78,862 votes and three seats.

In any case, as was explained earlier, what was at stake in these elections was not everyday administration, but the model of country. What was being decided was, for some, whether the Basque Country was a nation, and whether the Spanish Constitution, interpreted as it had been by successive Spanish governments, fulfilled the aspirations of the Basque people, who wished to decide upon their future themselves. For others, on the contrary, it was a question of whether the Basque people fully supported the constitution, understood it as a guarantee of freedoms and against the violence of ETA, as well as understandings regarding that the model of state claimed that Spain was a nation and that the Basque Country was merely a region thereof.

For this reason, the simple result obtained by the nationalist coalition does not give the true result of the vote, for it was necessary to add up the votes of both blocks. Alien to this logic were the three votes obtained by Ezker Batua, which favored a transversal policy that transcended the two opposing blocs. The Basque nationalist bloc, very divided internally, boasted forty seats courtesy of its 52.84 percent of the vote. The constitutionalist bloc had thirty-two seats and 41 percent of the votes. These figures, endorsed by the highest turnout in the history of the Basque people, left no room for doubt. The Basque Country was a nation, and the parties that defended this claim represented a clear majority of Basque society. The Basque citizens rewarded the peaceful project and unity presented by the PNV and EA, which obtained six more seats than in the previous elections (in which they had participated individually), and, in turn, punished Batasuna (now with the electoral coalition EH), which lost seven seats in comparison with 1998.

With this significant electoral legitimacy, the Basque government, led by *Lehendakari* (President of the Basque government) Juan José Ibarretxe, prepared to implement its electoral manifesto, which consisted in supporting the end of violence, overcoming confrontation between blocs, and making it possible for the Basque people democratically and peacefully to choose its political future.

In parallel fashion, on June 29, 2002, the Organic Law on Political Parties entered into force, allowing for the illegalization of parties that offered protection and political support for terrorism. On August 4, ETA detonated a car bomb at the Santa Pola Civil Guard barracks, killing two people and injuring thirty-four. The Batasuna leadership refused to condemn the attack and the government-initiated proceedings to illegalize this political party. On August 26, a National Court judge ordered the precautionary suspension of all Batasuna's activities. The illegalization of this nationalist party led to major changes in the Basque electoral map in future elections.

While the lehendakari continued with the drafting and parliamentary processing of his proposal, the Proposal for a Political Statute, in Spain, the political landscape underwent substantial modification in 2003. In November there were elections in Catalunya, and during the main campaign event, PSOE Secretary-General José Luis Rodríguez promised the Catalan people, whose representatives were drafting a new statute of autonomy, that he would accept the text in the terms approved in the Catalan Parliament if it enjoyed wide support. Although *Convergencia i Unió* won the elections, on December 14, the Tinell Agreement was signed, via which the *Partido Socialista de Cataluña* agreed to form a left-wing government with *Esquerra Republicana* and *Initiative for Catalunya Verds (ICV).*

In this new political climate, in Navarra, the electoral coalition Nafarroa Bai (Aralar, EA, Batzarre, PNV, and independents) obtained the best results of a pro-Basque formation, with 18 percent of the votes. And at the end of the year, on December 30, the Basque Majority approved the Proposal for a Political Statute for the Basque Country, thanks to the thirty-six votes of the coalition government (PNV-EA + EB) and three votes of EH, in a maneuver intended to show the latter's discrepancies vis-à-vis the text, but to facilitate its adoption. The proposal to reform the statute was then sent to Madrid for its negotiation in the Spanish Parliament.

On March 14, 2004, the Socialist Party triumphed in the general elections in Spain, in a context marked by an Islamist terrorist attack in Madrid and Prime Minister Aznar's mendacious attempt to attribute the attack to ETA. The new Socialist prime minister attended the investiture with a considerably more open discourse regarding the national plurality of the state—the so-called "plural Spain"—and an ambitious agenda of territorial reforms.[18, 19]

Amid a climate of great tension, with a Popular Party licking its wounds after the unexpected electoral defeat and exercising a fierce opposition, on February 1, 2005, the Lower House, following a single discussion session, voted by an overwhelming majority to reject the proposal for reform of the statute of the Basque Country.

### The Proposal for a New Political Statute

The Proposal for a Political Statute of the Community of the Basque Country comprises a preface, a preliminary heading, six additional headings, and two provisions (one transitory and one final).

In the Preface, the Basque people is identified within the context of the peoples of Europe and described as comprising seven territories, grouped within three political communities within two states. The second paragraph declares that:

> The Basque People have the right to decide their own future, as determined by absolute majority of the Basque Parliament on February 15, 1990, and in accordance with the right to self-determination of all peoples, recognised at an international level in the International Agreement of Civil and Political Rights and in the International Agreement of Economic, Social and Cultural Rights.

It is then stated that the exercise of this right is based on a respect for the right of the citizens of the different legal-political areas (Autonomous Basque Community, Autonomous Community of Navarra, and Basque territories in France) to be consulted in order to decide their own future. The text goes on to state that this right should be exercised via a new pact materialized in a new model of relations with the Spanish State.

The Preliminary Heading delimits the territory of the Community of the Basque Country (Art. 2), establishes the symbols (Art. 3), recognizes Basque nationality, which is added to Basque citizenship (Art. 4), and refers to the rights of Basque people resident abroad, and their descendants (Art. 5). It also presents a legal framework to establish different types of relations with the Autonomous Community of Navarra (Art. 6) and with the Basque territories in France (Art. 7). This part is completed with the values of self-government and various articles in relation to rights and freedoms (Arts. 9-11).

Heading I refers to the regime of political relations with the Spanish state and its guarantees. The first chapter develops the status of free association, while the second refers to the system of guarantees of self-government, and the third establishes the modification and modernization of the Political Statute.

The very title and structure of this section of the statute illustrate the fact that one of the main objectives of the document, along with increased self-government, was protection thereof, i.e., safeguarding it from possible unilateral modifications by the central state.

**Status of Free Association**

The status of free association is described as a "singular regime of political relations with the Spanish State," based on "respect and mutual recognition." And a similar formula is added to that of the Statute of Gernika (1979), in reference to the fact that "acceptance of this regime of free association does not constitute any waiver of the historical rights of the Basque people, which can be updated at any time in accordance with their own democratic will" (Art. 12).

It is also established that Basque institutions will have the power to manage and regulate the holding of democratic consultations in the Basque Country via referendum: a) within the bounds of their authority; b) on relations they may wish to have with other Territories and Basque Communities; c) with regard to relations with the Spanish State and its Autonomous Communities, and d) and relations at a European and international level (Art. 13.1).

It is worth highlighting Art. 13.3, which states that, "When, in the democratic exercise of free decision, Basque citizens should manifest in a referendum proposed for this purpose, their clear and unequivocal wish, upheld by an absolute majority of votes declared to be valid, to make complete or substantial changes in the format and regime of political relations with the Spanish State, as well as their relations with Europe and the international community, regulated in this Statute, the Institutions of the Basque Community and the State, shall consider themselves obligated to guarantee the negotiation process in order to establish the new political conditions that will allow the materialization of the democratic will of Basque society by common agreement" (Art. 13.3).

Apparent here is the direct influence of the stance adopted by the Canadian Supreme Court regarding this question in the case of Quebec. This article presents significant aspects that should be mentioned. Firstly, there is insistence upon the democratic nature of a referendum and the fact that this act should be channeled via a consultation focused on this point. Secondly, the wish expressed by means of this referendum should be "clear and unequivocal," albeit requirements in terms of participation or votes in favor are not established. Thirdly, that political will, endorsed by the result of the consultation, places an obligation upon all parties involved to open a process of negotiation. However, fourthly, the obligation to negotiate is a mandate that makes it necessary for both parties to reach a final agreement that must be acceptable to both the Basque institutions and the state.

Apparent here is a renunciation on the part of Basque nationalism, which is the majority belief in Basque society and the Parliament, to follow any kind of unilateral process. This, in a context marked by the violence of ETA, represents a clear stance against violence and a renunciation of the use of revolutionary or unilateral routes. In this sense, one can see a clear commitment to build bridges between the different national sensibilities present in the Basque Country, upon the minority who identified themselves as Spanish, a right to veto any significant change in the political status of the Basque community or in its relations with the Spanish state.

If this chapter is interpreted bearing in mind the document as a whole, it is clear that the new statute seeks: (a) a negotiated agreement that creates a political community with a high degree of self-government; (b) with its competences shielded against unilateral interpretations by the central state in those institutions where Basque nationalism is in the minority, offering in turn the agreement to renounce any unilateral act in the Basque territory by way of a guarantee for the Spanish national minority. This is a game of reciprocal guarantees, allowing for a framework of coexistence that can create new conditions of trust between the parties, so as to generate a climate of loyalty to common institutions by dint of having been agreed upon by all those involved. This balance of reciprocal guarantees is based on a new conception of sovereignty, which must be democratic, and within a concept of self-limitation of power.

As opposed to sovereignty as an absolute and hierarchical power, Lehendakari Ibarretxe, in his speech of presentation of the project in the Lower House, declared that "The Basque Country is not a subordinate part of the Spanish state. I want to state this quite clearly here as the representative of the Basque Parliament. The Spanish state will be a common project only if we, as the parties that comprise it, so wish. If that is our decision."

The Basque proposal implies that sovereignty, a concept that emerged centuries ago in a very different context, must evolve and transform in order to adapt to a democratic system. Democracy cannot be shackled by undemocratic factors, of a structural nature, that limit or pervert popular will. Thus, those that govern a democratic state cannot ignore a political will, equally democratic but different to the majority-held will in the state, which in turn is majority in a specific territory within the state.

In these conditions, original Basque nationalism demanded a classic referendum on self-determination, with a clear question to decide upon the secession of that territory and the creation of an independent state. The document under analysis here, however, proposes something radically different: Majority democratic will within the state, perfectly legitimate, should control itself, limit itself, with regard to a territory in which national identity, culture, and political will are substantially different from that majority state will. Meanwhile, Basque nationalism, as a majority in the Basque territory, cannot ignore the existence of a substantial part of the population that, despite being a minority, is extremely significant and shares the majority-held will within the state as a whole. Once again, in symmetrical fashion, this political, democratic, and majority will in its territorial sphere should control itself and cannot seek to implement all the measures to which national movements aspired in other times, when the sole objective was independence and the creation of their own state.

**Guarantees of Self-Government**

Article 14 establishes the principles of political relations with the state: reciprocal institutional loyalty, cooperation, and balance of powers. It then establishes that unilateral measures on the part of the state, such as Article 155 of the Constitution, which contemplates the limitation or suspension of autonomy, shall not be universal in their application, adding that neither "will it be possible universally to issue coercive measures of obligatory compliance for Basque Country."

The next two articles create two mechanisms of cooperation and resolution of conflicts. Article 15 establishes a Basque Country—State Bilateral Commission, formed by an equal number of representatives appointed by the government of the state and by the Basque government, which "will deal in general with the institutional relations of intergovernmental co-operation."

Article 16 addresses possible conflicts between the Basque Country and the state, creating a new Special Court of the Constitution Court, which will be set up within the Basque Country–State Court of Conflict, made up of six magistrates, half of whom will be appointed by the full session of the Court, at the proposal of the Senate, and half by the Basque Parliament.

This article constitutes one of the statute's main innovations, by focusing on the functioning of the Constitutional Court as supreme interpreter of the Constitution and arbiter between state powers and institutions. The conflict over the scope and development of Basque autonomy had converted this organ, in the opinion of the Basque government and of the nationalist Basque parties, into one of the main problems in the application and development of the autonomic process.

The Spanish Constitutional Court is known to group together very diverse functions, as is established by Article 161 of the Constitution: (a) appeals against alleged unconstitutionality of laws and regulations having the force of law; (b) appeals for protection against violation of the rights and liberties contained in Article 53.2 of the Constitution; (c) conflicts of jurisdiction between the state and the Autonomous Communities or among the Autonomous Communities themselves; d) other matters assigned to it by the Constitution or by organic laws.

It is worth mentioning that the court exercises all its functions with the same members, appointed with the same criteria (Art. 159). However, as can be seen, judging the violation of fundamental rights and freedoms, which can be regarded as a technical interpretation of these rights in the light of a specific case, is not the same as resolving a conflict between two administrations—which often have to cooperate between themselves since their powers overlap—and which should incorporate a space of legal and inter-institutional dialogue. In the former case, this is an extremely technical question, while in the latter, judgment of the case inevitably involves considerations that could be described as political and institutional. In the case of a conflict between administrations, the dialogue and negotiation should be part of the resolution process, and when the conflict transcends this avenue of cooperation and must be addressed legally, given the nature of the subject matter, it seems fair that both parties should have the same capacity to present their legal arguments and reasoning, and that the system should grant them equal representation on the decision-making organ.

The Spanish Constitution, by favoring with its method of appointment of magistrates the central institutions of the state, is not defending the common or general interest of the state, but is favoring the predominance of some organs—the central ones—over others—the autonomous ones. This is in spite of the fact that the latter are equally constitutional and are to no lesser degree the administrators of the common or general interest of their respective Autonomous Community.

This becomes more apparent when one realizes that the method of appointment of the members of the Constitutional Court (Art. 159.1), beyond the names of the different institutions, has meant in practice that the members of the Constitutional Court have been agreed upon and shared between the two main Spanish political parties: Popular Party (PP) and Spanish Socialist Workers' Party (PSOE). In any case, the PSOE has agreed to assign one of its candidates to one of the Basque or Catalan nationalist parties. But this was a political concession made by these two parties, as the system made it impossible for a political party that was not very important at a state level, even if it enjoyed a clear majority in one of the "nationalities" of the state, to opt for a position on the Constitutional Court.[20]

In terms of legitimacy, this system posed some problems because these two political parties, which have succeeded in achieving large majorities in the state as a whole, nevertheless had very much minority representations in the Basque and Catalan regions.

This systematic imbalance, in favor of central government in its relations with the nationalities and regions, appears on various occasions in the constitution. Among others, two can be highlighted. Firstly, in the aforementioned composition and appointment of the members of the Constitutional Court. Secondly, in the privileged treatment granted to central government when it presents a constitutional challenge against the provisions and resolutions adopted by the bodies of the Autonomous Communities. In this case, when the central government contests actions taken by the Autonomous Communities, this "shall bring about the suspension of the contested provisions or resolutions," in preventive fashion, a suspension that the court must ratify or lift within a period of not more than five months.

Seeing this, it is obvious that the constitution does not place every constitutional body on equal footing, conferring upon central government decisions an air and presumption of superiority the reasons for which are not explained. This inequality expresses a constant sense of prevention, and almost fear, in relation to the autonomous dimension of the state, which implies nonacceptance of the implications of the political decentralization of the state. This could, doubtless, be explained from a perspective of political sociology, but with great difficulty upon the basis of legal reasoning. For what happens if a central government employs this powerful tool and issues a constitutional challenge against an autonomous law, as part of a political dispute or following an election tactic? What happens if ultimately the arguments employed by the state's central body are shown to be flawed? How is it possible to mitigate the damage done to the general interests of that autonomous community by the suspension of a law that must have been completely legal and operative since its official publication? The assumption that the central government's arguments will generally prove superior to those employed by the autonomous communities grants a disproportionate and unfair advantage to the former.

This diagnosis is what led the Basque Parliament to include in the new statute some mechanisms that would balance the scales, incorporating, among the principles, regulating relations with the state the balance of powers (Art. 14). Thus, a new procedure of negative conflict of jurisdiction is established, in which the Basque government is the actor and the central government is the executing authority (Art. 16.3), and the objective is to eliminate the automatic suspension of provisions and resolutions contested by central government (Art. 16.5).

The next four headings of the statute detail the legislative, executive, and judicial powers of the Basque Community (Heading II); political and institutional relations within the Basque Community (Heading III); the exercise of public power (Heading IV); and a paragraph devoted the sphere of the economy, finances, and the treasury (Heading V).

Heading VI was groundbreaking, as it developed political relations between the Basque Community and the European and international arena; in other words, the Basque Country's foreign policy, broken down into three dimensions: relations with Europe, foreign relations, and development cooperation.

Relations with Europe focus on diverse aspects regarding the accommodation of Basque self-government within the framework of the European Union (Art. 65), seeking to prevent the transfer of competences toward community level resulting in the loss of control of these areas, as well as a mention of cross-border and interregional cooperation (Art. 66).

The section on foreign relations incorporates into the statute existing practice, consolidated in the wake of the new constitutional doctrine established by Ruling 165/1994, in May, which included both relations with Basque centers overseas and the Basque government's official delegations in various countries. Prior control was also established over international treaties signed by the Spanish state that could alter or restrict the powers set out in the statute (Art. 68).

The third chapter of Heading VI includes one single article (Art. 69), indicating cooperation for development as the Community's own policy of solidarity and, by attributing it this maximum significance, making this policy a central dimension of Basque foreign policy.

Finally, the last two provisions are not mere functional appendices of the entry into force of the new statute and substitution and derogation of the old one, for they include a significant novelty. The transitory provision establishes a maximum of six months in which to agree upon the conditions for transfer of pertinent competences from the central state to the Basque Community, seeking legally to shield a process that, in the case of the 1979 statute, was never completed, owing to political objections and was deliberate on the part of successive Spanish governments. Thus, from the beginning until the transitory provision, the statute demonstrates, with a wide range of mechanisms, the will not only to increase self-government, but also to shield the latter against potential subsequent interpretations by central state institutions with a view to limiting its scope or preventing all of its measures from being deployed.

## Final Considerations

To conclude this brief analysis of the Proposal for a Political Statute, I shall first identify its sources of inspiration and then offer a final assessment of the document.

The Proposal for a Political Statute indicated in its own text two bases or sources: the right of peoples to self-determination, internationally recognized by International Covenants on Civil and Political Rights; and the declaration by the Basque Parliament adopted by absolute majority on February 15, 1990.

Xabier Ezeizabarrena[21] noted that the reform proposal is materially and formally based on two elements: historical rights and the case of Quebec. López Basaguren[22] also underscored the influence of the case of Québec, though he added that, in his opinion, this was a distorted interpretation of the doctrine established by the Canadian Supreme Court in 1998.

Josu de Miguel[23] added as a further element of inspiration the concept of associated state proposed by the United Nations in its regulation of self-determination in its Resolution 1541.

As was seen earlier, to these sources of inspiration should be added the Good Friday Agreement in Northern Ireland. However, beyond the influence of specific cases, this document should be framed within the global context, and above all the European Union, in which there is a general trend toward formulae of shared sovereignty.

To assess the impact of the document, examination of the abundant literature it generated reveals that a vast majority of Spanish authors argue that the Project for a Political Statute emerged "as a consequence of the drift of Basque nationalism towards more radical positions and its gradual and continuous loss of electoral support." According to these analyses, "the proposal itself does not introduce new elements into the nationalist ideological corpus," as it simply "reproduces and concretizes some of the more or less recurrent demands of Sabinian ideology" [in reference to the founder of Basque nationalism, Sabino Arana]; conceding only that the originality "lies in its quest to become a fully valid legal instrument."[24]

In any case, it is not a minor innovation, as this is the first time in Spanish constitutionalism that the right to self-determination has been presented through government channels, ceasing to be a strictly partisan claim.[25] Galeote also observes that, "beyond the question of its legitimacy or illegitimacy, it is obvious that its 'officialization' by the Basque Government," raises the question of "the incapacity of the state of the autonomies to integrate historical nationalities."

Something that literature does acknowledge is that this is "an unprecedented proposal in the Spanish autonomous landscape," "is the first of the statutory reforms that can be described as *'new generation'* since it bears no resemblance to the existing statutory text."[26] Furthermore, this proposal breaks with the previous tradition, when reforms in the area of territorial organization of the state were promoted by the state via *"major pacts"* between the main parties, since it was now the autonomous territories themselves that assumed the leadership of the reforms from "a situation of parity (of '*like to like*') with the state itself."[27]

This new trend surprised and upset both the institutions of the state and its intellectuals. The Socialist government aligned itself with the Popular Party in its refusal even to discuss the Basque text, since in its election manifesto it proposed a reform of the state of autonomies. Thus, the notion that the Basque people itself should initiate the process of institutional reform was not accepted. Moreover, when the government requested the Council of State's opinion "with regard to a series of constitutional reforms that affected the territorial dimension of the state," "this consultative body took advantage of a seemingly innocuous question—the inclusion in the Constitution of the term 'Autonomous Communities' " to develop "a genuine proposal of constitutional politics, by recommending the closure of the *model of state*, characterized since its beginnings (. . .) as an open model."[28]

There were also complaints within the academic world. In the opinion of a reputed constitutionalist, "Ibarretxe's proposal is not a secessionist text; but it certainly lays the foundations for secession to take place. One could say then that the text presented is an instrument of severance with the constitutional and statutory order, although formally it might derive from the latter."[29] Other authors insist that, as well as secession, what was sought was "the construction of a political system that excludes the non-nationalist half of the population."[30]

In general, Spanish legal doctrine was extremely critical of the Proposal for a Political Statute, questioning both its legitimacy and its legality. However, although opposition to the proposal's content is perfectly legitimate in any democracy, Iñaki Lasagabaster notes that, "If an autonomous parliamentary assembly drafts and adopts a proposal for statutory reform, that proposal cannot end with simple rejection by an absolute majority in the Spanish Parliament." Such an abrupt action would represent a lack of consideration for a decision taken by the highest representative body of the Autonomous Community. Moreover, it should be remembered that proposing a reform of the statute is one of the Basque Parliament's main competences. And neither should it be forgotten that rejection of the project eliminated the possibility of negotiating the content with the Spanish Parliament, where the majority is very different from that of the Basque Parliament. For all these reasons, concludes this author, "The behavior of the majority political forces of the state evidences limited democratic culture. As does the way in which this question has been interpreted by the Constitutional Court."[31]

Considering it far from being a rupturist document, Ezeizabarrena recalls that the Basque Nationalist Party called for abstention in the 1978 constitutional referendum, while in this proposal the reform of the statute advocates acceptance and ratification of the core of that legislation. He concludes by observing that "this is, without a doubt, a clear commitment to voluntary integration" within the state, which, "however, appears to be of little significance to central government," since the latter repeatedly hindered its processing in the Basque Parliament with various obstacles and appeals.[32]

In conclusion, it might be said that the Proposal for a Political Statute attempted to innovate, altering in significant aspects the previous strategy, with a de facto renunciation of independence as the sole possible objective of self-determination. In this way, it was positioned within the contemporary parameters of shared sovereignty, on a different path to unionism or simple secession, thus adopting a post-sovereign approach.[33]

Another author who underscored the innovative nature of the text was one of the fathers of the Spanish Constitution, Miguel Herrero de Miñón, who recalled that even before the Transition, Spanish constitutionalists "strove in vain to pigeonhole the claims of their nationalist colleagues within the classic concepts of the General Theory of the State." For this reason, "Perhaps the difficulty lay and now lies in the fact that reality must create its own categories rather than adapt to the categories created by other realities. This was what Jellinek recommended and the reason why he constructed the category of fragments of state."[34] In this sense, there is no doubt that Lehendakari Ibarretxe's proposal, irrespective of its merits and shortcomings, constituted a novel contribution to the debate on the political articulation of the Basque Country.

## Bibliography

Albertí Rovira, Enoch. "Las regiones en el debate sobre la nueva arquitectura institucional de la Unión Europea." *Investigaciones Regionales*, no. 2 (2003): 175-196.

Ares Castro-Conde, Cristina. "La dimensión regional de la UE y el proceso de debate sobre el futuro de Europa." *Revista de Estudios Regionales*, no. 81 (2008): 149-170.

Ares Castro-Conde, Cristina. "La regionalización à la française: El alcance del derecho a la experimentación." *Revista de Estudios Políticos*, no. 143 (2009): 31-55.

Bengoetxea, Joxerramon. "Las regiones constitucionales autónomas: Un estatus especial en la UE." *Iura Vasconiae*, no. 7 (2010): 479-507.

Corcuera, Francisco Javier. *Radicalidad y moderación en el nacionalismo vasco*. Madrid: Alianza, 2006.

Expósito Suárez, Israel, Franco Escobar, and Susana Eva. "Historia de las reivindicaciones nacionalistas vascas hasta el Plan Ibarretxe." *Anales de la Facultad de Derecho*, no. 21 (2004): 7-44.

Ezeizabarrena, Xabier. "La propuesta de reforma del Estatuto de Euskadi: una apuesta por la soberanía compartida." *Iura Vasconiae: revista de derecho histórico y autonómico de Vasconia*, no. 3 (2006): 393-462.

Filibi, Igor (2007), "The influence of the European integration in the Basque conflict: sharing sovereignty as a post-national solution?" Paper presented at the Sixth Pan-European Conference, European Consortium for Political Research, Standing Group on International Relations (Torino, September 12-15, 2007).

Filibi, Igor. "Federalismo y regionalismo en Europa: ¿hacia qué camino político camina la UE?" *Cuadernos Europeos de Deusto*, no. 60 (2019): 125-156.

Galeote, Géraldine. "El estatus de libre asociación: ¿Hacia un modelo original para el País Vasco?" *Pandora: revue d'etudes hispaniques*, no. 3 (2003): 247-256.

Herrero de Miñón, Miguel. "La singularidad vasca en la actualidad." *Iura Vasconiae*, no. 12 (2015): 425-437.

Keating, Michael. *Plurinational Democracy: Stateless Nations in a Post-Sovereign Era*. Oxford: Oxford University Press, 2001.

Keating, Michael, and Zoe Bray. "Renegotiating sovereignty: Basque nationalism and the rise and fall of the Ibarretxe Plan." *Ethnopolitics* 5, no. 4 (2006): 347-364.

Lasagabaster Herrarte, Iñaki. "La propuesta de reforma del Estatuto de Autonomía del País Vasco: del Parlamento Vasco al Congreso de los Diputados. El final de un ciclo (2000-2004)." *Iura Vasconiae*, no. 12 (2015): 217-253.

López Basaguren, Alberto. "Sobre los fundamentos del Plan Ibarretxe: El derecho de autodeterminación y el ejemplo de Québec." In *Breve guía para orientarse en el laberinto vasco*, 41-48. Bilbao: Fundación para la Libertad, 2008.

Miguel Bárcena, Josu de. "Variaciones contemporáneas del derecho de autodeterminación: El derecho a decidir y la propuesta de reforma del Estatuto de autonomía del País Vasco." *Anuario da Facultade de Dereito da Universidade da Coruña*, no. 10 (2006): 261-278.

Requejo, Ferrán. "El Estado de las autonomías, un cuarto de siglo después." *Pasajes: Revista de Pensamiento Contemporáneo*, no. 13 (2004): 21-24.

Solozábal, Juan José. "Reflexiones constitucionales sobre la propuesta de modificación estatutaria de Ibarretxe." *Revista Española de Derecho Constitucional*, no. 73 (2005): 255-280.

Trujillo Fernández, Gumersindo. "Homogeneidad y asimetría en el estado autonómico: contribución a la determinación de los límites constitucionales de la forma territorial del Estado." *Documentación Administrativa*, no. 232-233 (1993): 101-120.

Urjewicz, Charles. "Tipología de los conflictos postsoviéticos." *Anuario Internacional CIDOB 07/1995* (1995): 451-455.

Vírgala, Eduardo. "La reforma territorial en Euskadi: los Planes Ibarretxe I (2003) y II (2007)." *Cuadernos Constitucionales de la Cátedra Fadrique Furió Ceriol*, no. 54/55 (2006): 159-187.

Vivancos Comes, Mariano. "El socialismo vasco: entre el estatuto de Gernika y la alternativa soberanista." *Cuadernos Constitucionales de la Cátedra Fadrique Furió Ceriol*, no. 66 (2009): 15-57.

Vivancos Comes, Mariano. *La propuesta de Nuevo Estatuto Político de la Comunidad de Euskadi. Análisis de un Estatuto de "segunda generación."* Universidad de Valencia: Tesis Doctoral, 2010.

Zubiaga, Mario (2002). *Hacia una consulta soberanista*. Manu Robles-Arangiz Institutua, Documento no. 4.

## Notes

1 Gumersindo Trujillo Fernández, "Homogeneidad y asimetría en el estado autonómico: contribución a la determinación de los límites constitucionales de la forma territorial del Estado," *Documentación Administrativa*, no. 232-233 (1993): 101-120.

2 Israel Expósito Suárez et al., "Historia de las reivindicaciones nacionalistas vascas hasta el Plan Ibarretxe," *Anales de la Facultad de Derecho*, no. 21 (2004): 23.

3 Suárez et al., "Historia de las reivindicaciones nacionalistas vascas hasta el Plan Ibarretxe," 17, 32.

4 Zubiaga, Mario (2002). *Hacia una consulta soberanista*. Manu Robles-Arangiz Institutua, Documento no. 4: 5.

5 Francisco Javier Corcuera, *Radicalidad y moderación en el nacionalismo vasco* (Madrid: Alianza, 2006), 4.

6 Ferrán Requejo, "El Estado de las autonomías, un cuarto de siglo después," *Pasajes: Revista de Pensamiento Contemporáneo*, no. 13 (2004): 21.

7 Requejo, "El Estado de las autonomías, un cuarto de siglo después," 24.

8 Charles Urjewicz, "Tipología de los conflictos postsoviéticos." *Anuario Internacional CIDOB 07/1995* (1995): 451-455.

9 Igor Filibi, "Federalismo y regionalismo en Europa: ¿hacia qué camino político camina la UE?" *Cuadernos Europeos de Deusto*, no. 60 (2019): 125-156.

10 Michael Keating, *Plurinational Democracy: Stateless Nations in a Post-Sovereign Era* (Oxford: Oxford University Press, 2001), 17.

11 Filibi, Igor (2007), "The influence of the European integration in the Basque conflict: sharing sovereignty as a post-national solution?" Paper presented at the Sixth Pan-European Conference, European Consortium for Political Research, Standing Group on International Relations (Torino, September 12-15, 2007).

12 Cristina Ares Castro-Conde,"La dimensión regional de la UE y el proceso de debate sobre el futuro de Europa," *Revista de Estudios Regionales*, no. 81 (2008): 150.

13 Enoch Albertí Rovira, "Las regiones en el debate sobre la nueva arquitectura institucional de la Unión Europea," *Investigaciones Regionales*, no. 2 (2003): 194.

14 Ares Castro-Conde, "La dimensión regional de la UE y el proceso de debate sobre el futuro de Europa," 152.

15 Joxerramon Bengoetxea, "Las regiones constitucionales autónomas: Un estatus especial en la UE," *Iura Vasconiae*, no. 7 (2010): 479-507.

16 Cristina Ares Castro-Conde, "La regionalización à la française: El alcance del derecho a la experimentación," *Revista de Estudios Políticos*, no. 143 (2009): 34.

17 Iñaki Lasagabaster Herrarte, "La propuesta de reforma del Estatuto de Autonomía del País Vasco: del Parlamento Vasco al Congreso de los Diputados. El final de un ciclo (2000-2004)," *Iura Vasconiae*, no. 12 (2015): 221-222.

18 Mariano Vivancos Comes, *La propuesta de Nuevo Estatuto Político de la Comunidad de Euskadi. Análisis de un Estatuto de "segunda generación"* (Universidad de Valencia: Tesis Doctoral, 2010), 615.

19 Mariano Vivancos Comes, "El socialismo vasco: entre el estatuto de Gernika y la alternativa soberanista.," *Cuadernos Constitucionales de la Cátedra Fadrique Furió Ceriol*, no. 66 (2009): 18.

20 This is the sense in which one should interpret the words that the Lehendakari dedicated to the PSOE and PP leaders in his speech presenting the reform proposal in the Lower House: "the future of self-government in the Basque Country is not going to be decided in meetings by you, Mr Rodríguez Zapatero, or by you, Mr Rajoy, you are not going to shape the will of the Basques. (. . .) we, the Basques that live and work in the Basque Country, shall decide upon our future."

21 Xabier Ezeizabarrena, "La propuesta de reforma del Estatuto de Euskadi: una apuesta por la soberanía compartida," *Iura Vasconiae: revista de derecho histórico y autonómico de Vasconia*, no. 3 (2006): 393-462.

22 Alberto López Basaguren, "Sobre los fundamentos del Plan Ibarretxe: El derecho de autodeterminación y el ejemplo de Québec," in *Breve guía para orientarse en el laberinto vasco* (Fundación para la Libertad, 2008), 46.

23 Josu de Miguel Bárcena, "Variaciones contemporáneas del derecho de autodeterminación: El derecho a decidir y la propuesta de reforma del Estatuto de autonomía del País Vasco," *Anuario da Facultade de Dereito da Universidade da Coruña*, no. 10 (2006): 270.

24 Vivancos Comes, La propuesta de Nuevo Estatuto Político de la Comunidad de Euskadi. Análisis de un Estatuto de "segunda generación," 616-18.

25 Géraldine Galeote, "El estatus de libre asociación: ¿Hacia un modelo original para el País Vasco?" *Pandora: revue d'etudes hispaniques*, no. 3 (2003): 254.

26 Vivancos Comes, La propuesta de Nuevo Estatuto Político de la Comunidad de Euskadi. Análisis de un Estatuto de "segunda generación," 615.

27 Vivancos Comes, La propuesta de Nuevo Estatuto Político de la Comunidad de Euskadi. Análisis de un Estatuto de "segunda generación," 616.

28 Vivancos Comes, "El socialismo vasco: entre el estatuto de Gernika y la alternativa soberanista," 21.

29 Juan José Solozábal, "Reflexiones constitucionales sobre la propuesta de modificación estatutaria de Ibarretxe," *Revista Española de Derecho Constitucional*, no. 73 (2005): 261.

30 Eduardo Vírgala, "La reforma territorial en Euskadi: los Planes Ibarretxe I (2003) y II (2007)," Cuadernos Constitucionales de la Cátedra Fadrique Furió Ceriol, no. 54/55 (2006): 161.

31 Lasagabaster Herrarte, "La propuesta de reforma del Estatuto de Autonomía del País Vasco: del Parlamento Vasco al Congreso de los Diputados. El final de un ciclo (2000-2004)," 240.

32 Ezeizabarrena, "La propuesta de reforma del Estatuto de Euskadi: una apuesta por la soberanía compartida," 393-462.

33 Michael Keating et al., "Renegotiating sovereignty: Basque nationalism and the rise and fall of the Ibarretxe Plan," *Ethnopolitics* 5, no. 4 (2006): 347-364.

34 Miguel Herrero de Miñón, "La singularidad vasca en la actualidad," *Iura Vasconiae*, no. 12 (2015): 435.

# 6

# The Basque Dream of Independence

## Ideology and Organizations of the Basque Independence Movement

*Iñigo Bullain*

### Introduction to the Basque Question

Some years ago, while on vacation in New York City, we were asked on a bus tour where we came from. After most travelers answered with the names of various US states, our son Lander said we were from the Basque Country, adding, aware by the puzzled looks of the trip companions, that it was a non-official country (NOC) in Europe. If given the chance for a short explanation, we could have said that the Basque people is an old nation historically located in southwestern Europe, between the Garone and the Ebro Rivers, around the Pyrenees and the Gulf of Biscay.[1] Its non-officialness stamps from not having a state, its territory being long divided between Spain and France. Yet the mystery about the origins of the Basque language, which is neither related to the Indo-European or to the Uraltic Ursprachen, and that brought to the land personalities like Humboldt or the Prince Louis-Lucien Bonaparte, still persists.

Hundreds of years of Spanish and French rule have not succeeded in eliminating the consciousness of being a people or the will to resist policies of centralization and homogenization. If history has proven to be a cemetery for many peoples, the Basque Country can be understood as the land of a social group with a will to last. But it was only in the nineteenth century that a nationalist and independence movement got organized and took a contemporary root in quest for a united Basque Country, a demand that came at odds with the fact that separation among the Basque people is old. As long ago as 1200 the territories of Biscay, Gipuzkoa, Araba, and La Rioja were separated from Navarre and incorporated to the Crown of Castile, while Navarre, the core of Basqueness, maintained herself as a sovereign state until 1512, when it was conquered by the troops of the Duke of Alba.[2] As for the northern provinces of Lapurdi/Labord and Zuberoa/

Soule, they were a domain of England for several centuries before they became part of France. The exception was the continuity of the Kingdom of Navarre, north of the Pyrenees, as an independent state until 1620, its capital moved from Pamplona to Pau, the main city of Bearn.[3] Nowadays in political terms, Euskadi, constituted as the union of Araba, Bizkaia, and Gipuzkoa, enjoys since 1979 a limited autonomy according to the Spanish Constitution and its statute of autonomy, while Navarre, separately, also has its own autonomy.

Though legitimation of power is based today on legal-rational thought according to constitutional terms, it should not be forgotten that coercive power is more frequently the constituent source of political power.[4] In fact, a succession of conquest brought the suppression of the Basque institutions and laws of self-government (Fueros).[5] In the Northern Basque provinces in southwest France, where 300,000 people live, administrative powers for several matters were only recovered in 2017.[6] Likewise, the conquest of Navarre, its division and partial annexation to the Crown of Castile and later to France, was not made according to democratic decisions adopted by legitimate national institutions, but through acts of force made by a foreign use of violence. Thus, for the Basque independence movement, Spanish and French legality are illicit, and therefore, in democratic terms, only the free determination of the Basque people will be the rightful way to solve the so-called Basque question.

In this chapter, the historical approach to the Basque independence movement will outline three periods of around forty years, each during which the Basque independence movement has been developing both ideologically and through different organizations. In my view, a first period extends from Aryanism to the suppression of the Basque republic. It begins with the foundation in 1895 of the Basque Nationalist Party (BNP) erected by Sabino Arana in Bilbao, and it ends in 1937 with the suppression by Franco troops of the Republic of Euzkadi after having developed into a more social and open movement supported by new organizations. The second period is marked by exile, the ferocious repression of Franco's dictatorship, and the emergence of ETA and the Basque National Liberation Movement (BNLM). This period extends until 1979, when Basque autonomy was recovered under Spanish democracy. The third period has been long shaped by ETA's violence and lasts until 2011 when a complete and definitive ceasefire was declared. It records the pulse between the BNP and the so-called *ezker abertzalea,* or patriotic left, both having tried to command the nationalist movement according to different strategies. During those years, while the BNP tried to consolidate autonomy under Spanish law, the BNLM fought against it in the name of independence and (revolutionary) socialism.

The history of the Basque Country, which is told by different and opposed narratives, is both old and complex, recorded by the Romans as far back as two thousand years ago.[7] Besides, the Basque Country doesn't have an official narrative, and in the official history of Spain and France its position is often ignored or misplaced. In addition, the historical dominance of Navarre,[8] both politically and demographically, shifted to Bilbao and Biscay in the second half of the nineteenth century, a change that had big consequences for the modern political institutionalization of the Basque Country.

In globalized times, to avoid assimilation—being only 5 percent of the population of Spain and less than 1 percent of France[9] —represents a big challenge. Only three million Basques live among a population of one hundred million under Franco-Spanish rule. Therefore, as the poet sang: ". . . being divided and after centuries of serfdom the tasks for our country are huge . . ."[10]

## Origins of the Basque Independence Movement

The contemporary Basque Independence Movement (BIM) came into light at the end of the nineteenth century, as a reaction to the suppression of the "foral" regime of the Basque provinces and Navarre by the Madrid government.[11] Previously, the Basques living in France (Iparralde, or the North in Basque terms) had been dispossessed in 1789 of their institutions by the French Revolution.[12] Before that, Navarre had also been suppressed as an independent state and divided by Spain and France.[13]

During many centuries under foral self-rule, Basque institutions had been entitled to govern its territory and its people. Basque institutions determined who had access to the land and who could take residence in the territory. Basque laws decided how to organize institutions, elections, or local and territorial government as well as the right to the administration of justice. Basque territories were exempted territories, outside of Castile's fiscal rule, and Basque people were not subject to military duties. There was a constitutional protection of Basque laws[14] by the Castilian Supreme Court, the Chancilleria of Valladolid, a special chamber that considered demands affecting "Biscay's questions," and there were not Basque representatives in the Castilian Parliament, as both Navarre and the Basque provinces had their own Cortes and Juntas, while the Castilian Crown had a delegate "corregidor" in the provinces or "virrey" in the Kingdom of Navarre.

This system of self-rule that functioned for centuries was contested when Spain tried to become a constitutional state inspired by the French model. The proposals made by the so-called liberals that had promoted the Cadiz

Constitution (1812) wanted to get rid of Basque "particularities." In their view, under the banner of citizenship and equality, Spanish rule was to be one for all and imposed from Madrid. Likewise, autonomy was neither granted nor foreseen to the territories of the Spanish empire at the other side of the Atlantic. For centuries Basques had been devoted subjects of the Castilian Crown and had actively participated as sailors, soldiers, priests, civil servants, and merchants in the running of the Empire, and Basque elites had been close associates in the administration of the monarchy. As high secretaries or royal confessors, they had lobbied in defense of Basque liberties and self-rule.[15] But in the name of the Spanish nation, without the consent of Basque institutions, Spanish constitutionalism wanted to put an end to the pact, or *foedus*, that had sustained in various forms the foral regime since 1200 or since 1512 in Navarre.

Thus, for many, Basques liberalism was perceived as both a threat to Basque liberties and a menace to religion. The question of who was to succeed Fernando VII, either his liberal daughter or his absolutist brother, gave path to a bitter war that lasted from 1833 to 1839, and the issue of royal legitimacy was entangled in the Basque Country with the defense of self-rule under the foral system, bringing together the three provinces and Navarre (*laurak bat*). Soon, except in the capital cities, the Basque Country became a stronghold of what later was called Carlism, after the name of the pretender, Carlos VII. Years of war concluded with a compromise to respect the Fueros in conformity with the Spanish Constitution in the so-called "Abrazo de Vergara." The extent of such compatibility was the subject of different interpretations and prolonged discussion, followed by a period of decades when different legalities, foral and Spanish, interchanged periodically.

Though Navarre accepted in 1841 a severe reduction of self-government in a law later called "Paccionada," it was never signed by the Navarre institutions, Cortes or Diputacion, but by Madrid-appointed representatives of the new "province." That law had transformed the Kingdom of Navarre into a Spanish province, leaving only some administrative and fiscal autonomy, and as the three (other) Basque provinces refused to sign such a deal, a diplomatic confrontation between Basque institutions and the Spanish governments followed over two generations. Sometimes foral government was installed, sometimes was substituted by Spanish legality and institutions.

In the early 1870s, another war erupted after the first Spanish republic had been established. Again, the Basque Country, the three provinces, and Navarre—as well as Catalunya—were the epicenter of the conflict (1872-1876), and once again Madrid won the war. But this time after defeat, a law based on the "right of war," as Canovas del Castillo brutally recognized at the Cortes in

Madrid, suppressed the foral regime for the three provinces. This decision came from a man who had secured the restoration of the Bourbons to the Spanish throne and who had fostered a bigoted bipartidism between conservatives, led by himself, and liberals led by Sagasta. Based on caciquism, the system was a mockery of democracy that during the twentieth century degenerated into a military-backed dictatorship.

For years the aim of most personalities and political forces in the Basque Country was to reconcile Spain with the old Basque liberties. Yet a man, Sabino Arana, came up with a different and new approach: the demand for Basque independence. Basque nationalism and within its Basque independentism were in addition the result of a century during which Spain lost its Empire, first in America (1810-1820) and later its remains in the Caribbean and the Philippines (1898). For the Basque people both outcomes were big losses. Not only Spain had destroyed Basque liberties, but Spain itself had lost its "grandeur" and attraction as an empire where Basque elites had gained powerful positions and richness. Thus, as Spain developed into a peninsular centralist nation, foralism, as a particular way to be part of the Spanish project, transformed into Basque nationalism. If Spanish nationalism was a threat to Basqueness, then Basque nationalism would in turn become a threat to Spain. If liberal Spain imposed homogeneity to all Spaniards, making it impossible for Basques to be Spaniards in their traditional and particular way, and if in Spain all were to be the same, then the Basques would remark their differences and promote separation.

Nationalism was conceived as a movement and an instrument for the political and social transformation of the Basque Country that gradually was to become the dominant force in Basque politics.[16] The party that first aimed at independence for Biscay soon expanded to other Basque territories,[17] and the Arana brothers matched the goal of independence with the so-called "*Zazpiak Bat,*" or the territory of the seven provinces, four under Spanish rule and three in the French republic where at the time, and still today, the Basque language is spoken. Other territories where Basque had been spoken were not considered as part of the Basque Country. Hence, this vision of the nation being based on language disconsidered other historical perspectives that understood the state unit of the Kingdom of Navarre as the center for political demands.

For some historians, like Ortueta or Urzainqui, the State of Navarre was the constitutional dimension of the Basque nation,[18] close but not to be equaled and assimilated with the territory of the Basque language. As we will see, the different interpretations about the question of the political significance of Navarre, and the consideration of the Basque people in its relation to the

Basque language, had important consequences in the future.[19] In addition to the "euskaldunak," those who possess the Basque language, other people of Basque origin who had become wascon in the north of the Pyrenees or Romanize in southside Navarre, Rioja, or Castile[20] could also be historically counted as well as Basque people. That means that beyond what is today called Euskal Herria, the country of the Basque language, the Basque Country could be understood as a wider space than the Seven Provinces, including the territories mentioned by Krutwig in his famous book *Vasconia.*[21]

Arana, who was not a historian, presented the seven provinces as if they had been independent territories that had freely decided to made accords of allegiance with subsequent states: Navarre, Castile, Spain, or France in exchange of due respect to self-rule. According to Arana, as these agreements had not been respected by the abolitory laws of 1839 and 1878, the territories were to be considered free to become independent again, but this time forming a united Basque republic according to the language map that prince Bonaparte had published in London in 1863.[22] It was also in Iparralde where the French Basque nobleman Abadie[23] had first financed a revival of Basque culture under the concept of the *Zazpiak Bat,* or Seven is One,[24] and it was a northerner or iparretarra too, Agustine Chaho, the first who contemporaneously encouraged Basque independence.[25]

Arana gave race and religion a paramount consideration. He developed the "JEL" acronym that today is still part of the name of the party: "Jaungoikoa and Lagizarra," or God and the old law, meaning the Fueros. Arana came politically from a traditionalist past, later to be dissociated from carlism and to embrace integrism, a radical Catholic stand for politics. He promoted a new name for the Basque Country, Euzkadi, a neologism in substitution for the traditional name of Euskal Herria. He understood Euzkadi as a political project consecrated to God. He coined a political definition: "Euzkotarren Aberria Euzkadi da" or Euzkadi is the nation of the Basques, adding that Euzkadi was dedicated to God: "Gu Euzkadirentzat eta Euzkadi Jaungoikoarentzat" or "We for Euzkadi and Euzkadi for God." Arana contemplated the Spanish liberal state as a danger to Catholicism, and the increasing number of workers coming from Spain, that had settled in Bilbao and its surroundings as a source for denationalization and socialist promotion of atheism. Arana spoke in tough terms against those foreign workers who came from Spain, nicknaming them "maketos," and in order to prevent "pollution," to become a member of the Batzoki, or Basque Society that he first founded, and later to affiliate to the party, it was required to have Basque names. Thus, the quest of "apellidism"[26] made it necessary to consider the surnames of the previous generations going back to the grandparents.[27]

Arana combined language to map the territory and blood in order to recognize membership to the nation. His interpretation of the *Zazpiak Bat* being independent territories is a fantasy without historical record,[28] and his defense of a Basque race, obviously, erroneous. His ideas were first ignored and later contested as racist, but the apple-to-blood clearness echoed an important criterion in the Basque and Spanish society that, since the end of the sixteenth century, had promoted "old cristians" to the top of the society, relegating converts from Judaism and Muslim origins to second-class subjects. To secure a privileged position in a society based in ethnic division and social testaments, the Basque elite promoted theories of originalism as far as to consider Basque people descendants from Jaffe, who had settled in the Basque Country after the universal deluge, where Basques had stayed independent without mixing with Romans, Visigoths, or Arabs. These kinds of fantasies well looked at in the Spanish court were successful enough as to procure the Basque people to be considered of noble origin. The so-called "hidalguía universal," or universal gentryness, made Basques first-rank citizens, with access to the highest employment in the court and state administration. Thus, farmers or Basque fishermen share privileges and ranked with the Spanish aristocracy.

But aranism was not politically successful until a prominent naval capitalist (Sota) and his group of "euskalerriacos" joined the party. It was then that the BNP started to have a real chance of taking part in politics and to gain representation at local and provincial levels as Arana himself managed to do. Its success came along with a leaning toward demanding autonomy inside Spain and therefore abandoning independence as a political goal.

### Nationalism Without Arana

This trend toward "españolismo," apparently adopted by Sabino in his last days, was contested inside the nationalist movement, and later on tensions gave rise to a fracture. Around 1914 the party inertly divided into factions named "Comunion" and "Aberri." The latter being more radical or pro-independentist, and the former being more pragmatic or favoring autonomy, a balance that has been a characteristic of the party ever since.[29] Sabino Arana had died in 1903, years before the inner split. His political activity lasted only ten years, since the "Declaration of Larrazabal"[30] when he was 28, until his death at the age of 38. Both sides declared firm allegiance to the doctrines of the "Master." Arana's brother Luis, always a loyal independentist, was a leading figure of Aberri, a party line named after the weekly publication of *Juventud Vasca* or *Basque Youth*, that in 1921 recovered the traditional name of PNV after separating from Comunion. Anyway, after reunification in 1930, he still was a reference of the BNP, though his clashes with the direction of the party were numerous.

The dictatorship of Primo de Rivera that was established in 1923 deemed both Comunion and PNV illegal, and political activities had to be developed under the cover of cultural and sports associations. One of those was the EMB (Euzko Mendigoizaleen Batza), a group that favored trekking in the mountains. The beautiful landscape of the Basque Country, where slopes and mountains gather as a soft continuation of the Pyrenees near the sea, was a suitable environment for the Basque youth to assemble in freedom, far from the eye of the Spanish authorities. The mountaineers gave birth to a publication, *Jagi-Jagi*, which became a stronghold of the independence movement within Basque nationalism.[31] Its leader, Eli Gallastegi, was for many years an important figure who renovated aranism in "aggiornamento" with the times. Through his articles in *Jagi-Jagi*, Gallastegi showed empathy toward the social struggle that developed along the years with the broadening of industrial and urban capitalism. In 1922 he fostered Emakume Abertzale Batza, or the Union of Basque Patriot Women, inspired in Cumann namBan. Gallastegui, who had to go into exile, founded in Mexico "Patria Vasca," which published five numbers and a sixth last number in 1932, this time back in Bilbao. In 1934 he left the PNV and opposed any participation in the war, going again into exile first to Ireland and later to settling in Iparralde until his death in 1974.

This more social and open approach of Basque nationalism showed by Gallastegui was to be one of the landmarks of a new party founded in November 1930, named Acción Nacionalista Vasca (ANV), or Basque Nationalist Action (BNA), which would ally with the Spanish republicans and the left, departing from the traditional confessionalism of Basque nationalism with which the BNP was always deeply involved.[32] BNA was not a split of Comunion or BNP but a new organization fostered by dissidents who didn't participate in the reunification process of Bergara (11/16/1930). BNA defended the right to self-government and recognized the sovereignty of the Basque people and its right to choose its future freely, which included the founding of an independent state. BNA coined "Aberri ta Azkatasuna," or Homeland and Liberty, as its motto, respected the Spanish legality, and promoted unitarism in the Basque Country, evolving from the center left to a socialist (non-Marxist) party. In June 1936, it was refounded as an independence party of the left. It edited a periodical named *Euzko Lurra* and later *Acción Vasca.* The BNA was open to collaboration with forces that recognized the distinct Basque political personality, but its erratic electoral stand during the Spanish II republic made BNA an extra parliamentary force in Madrid. Yet, they held local representation in numerous towns of the Basque Country, becoming a member of the Basque government and, after the war had erupted, even the Spanish government. Its laicism and leftish profile made ANV a kind of a forerunner of the Basque left, which would decades later shape links to ETA and the Basque National Liberation Movement (BNLM).

At the beginning of the 1930s, the Spanish II republic was proclaimed the BNP, already reunited, and assumed the task of joining forces to obtain autonomy within the Spanish republic, but this goal proved to be full of difficulties. While Catalunya managed to form an autonomous government in 1931,[33] the Basques had to wait until 1936 to have one.[34] This road to Basque autonomy was long and windy. First the BNP favored associating itself with the traditionalists, but this joint venture failed,[35] and in the process Navarre distanced itself from the other three provinces.[36] The process for autonomy had to start again, and this time local authorities were replaced by provincial delegates nominated by the central government where republican forces had a majority, whereas nationalists and traditionalists dominated local institutions. After a new text was made among nationalist, socialists, and republicans, a referendum was called in 1932 for the three provinces. Although an extended majority of 80 percent of the voters expressed favoring it, the Spanish Parliament, which after new elections in 1933 had changed, now favoring the right, stopped the process, considering that a sufficient majority had not been obtained in one of the provinces.[37]

So, it was not until after a new Spanish election held in 1936 that put socialists and republicans back in government that those new negotiations for autonomy started. This time, it was conducted by Jose Antonio Aguirre, who was to be the head of the Basque government, and Indalecio Prieto, a member of PSOE and minister in the Spanish government who had made his political career in Bilbao. When the Civil War started in July 1936, negotiations accelerated. Though the insurgents had partly taken control of the Basque Country and the whole of Navarre,[38] the republicans and socialists, seeking the support of Basque nationalism, agreed to support autonomy. Therefore, a new text, which was very different from the one voted on in 1932, obtained a majority in the Spanish Parliament, precisely in the last seance it held in Madrid in October 1936. The autonomy granted was much reduced and represented much less than the foral self-government had delivered, but the war permitted the Basque government to act as a quasi-independent government and the Republic of Euzkadi to perform as a semi-sovereign state.

The Basque government, a national coalition of different parties, commanded an army of eighty thousand *gudariak* or Basque soldiers,[39] procured passports and coined money, ran an administration without almost any supervision from Madrid, and was widely detached from the limits imposed by the statute of autonomy. The Basque Republic of Euzkadi proved to the Basque people that a Basque state was possible even during extreme circumstances. It has probably been the most important achievement of Basque nationalism and the main inspiration to independentism so far. The existence of Euskadi as a quasi-independent state from 1936 to 1937 recalls the experience of the Baltic republics, when the long-dreamed Cantabrian republic was finally made real.

### Exile, Franquism, and ETA.

Franco's dictatorship put an end to the legal development of the Basque nationalist movement that, in forty years, had achieved, as far as commanding, a quasi-independent republic. Franco's army occupied the remains of the Republic of Euzkadi after a savage war moved against civilians, as towns like Durango, Otxandio, Mungia, or Gernika were targeted and destroyed by air raids.[40] The next forty years to come were marked by persecution, exile, and violence. If, during its first forty years of existence, the Basque independence movement had to develop under the close surveillance of Spanish law, and Basque nationalism was prohibited temporarily during that period, during Franco's forty years of harsh dictatorship, repression against the Basque language and Basque culture brought the Basque nation almost to collapse.

The Basque government, led by the charismatic lehendakari, Jose Antonio Agirre, and an entourage by big personalities like Javier de Landaburu, Manuel de Irujo, Telesforo Monzón, Jose Maria Lasarte, Heliodoro de la Torre, Ramón Aldasoro, Santiago Aznar, Juan Gracia, Alfredo de Espinosa, Juan de los Toyos, Juan Astigarribia, Gonzalo Nardiz, and Jesus Maria Leizaola, who later took the lehendakaritza after Agirre's death in 1960, was confident in exile that with the end of World War II the Allies would turn against Franco's regime. Aguirre toured intensively through South America, where he was welcomed both by the Basque diaspora and republican governments as a head of state. Later he taught courses at Columbia University and settled in New York City. After World War II, the Basque government was established in Paris, he closely associated with the process of European integration that would develop in the late 1940s and early 1950s.[41] Therefore, it turned out to be a big disappointment when the US recognized and helped Franco continue its cruel dictatorship, as symbolized by the "Pacto de Madrid" between Franco and the US on September 26, 1953. After that, both in the Basque Country and among Basque political forces in exile, a period of despair followed.[42]

Working in Latin America, several personalities had maintained the flag and the national fire alive through different publications, like *Irrintxi* or *Radio Euzkadi* (Venezuela), *Sabindarra* (Argentina), or *Euskadi* (México). People like Martin Ugalde, Matxari, Joseba Rezola, Pello Irujo, Justo Garate, and many others, were active in the resistance and sometimes even critical with the Basque government.[43] But it was at the end of the 1950s that a new organization was created among a group of students from Bilbao and San Sebastian, first developed as a cultural ring of young nationalists who were increasingly discontent with the strategy and passivity of the BNP's old guard. This organization in the 1960s would develop as a national liberation movement inspired in groups like the IRA or the FLN argelien, animated by the success of the Cuban revolution or the Vietnamese struggle for independence. They named themselves ETA (Euzkadi ta Azkatasuna) or Basque Country and Freedom. ETA put aside the xenophobic and religious trends of aranism and, instead of foralism or autonomy, aimed for independence and socialism, fostering Basque as the national language and the reunification of the seven provinces. From the late 1960s until Franco's death, ETA commanded the opposition to the dictatorship,[44] its revolutionary personality being perceived as radical nationalism.[45] ETA developed a revolutionary strategy to fight the dictatorship and later continued the fight against the Spanish democracy through an organization named Basque National Liberation Movement (BNLM), which had certain similarities with the one run by the IRA and Sinn Fein. During the last fifteen years of Franco's dictatorship, ETA contested the civic strategy of the BNP with a military and civilian front,[46] and the quest between the two groups still persists today, both competing for power and accusing each other of failing the Basque people.[47]

## Autonomy and Violence

After the end of Franco's dictatorship and during a third period of forty years, ETA's violence continued, this time against the Spanish democracy and opposing Basque autonomy. Through the so-called strategy of "action-reaction-action," ETA managed to receive a constant flow of militants due to the frequently undiscriminated repression practiced against the Basque population. To get support and legitimation, ETA presented herself as the utmost advocate of Basque independence. In the referendum to vote on the Spanish Constitution in December 1978, only a very few Basques expressed a vote in favor.[48] In ETA's view, that meant that the Spanish state had to be forced to negotiate a different status for the Basque Country. Instead, the BNP, after a majority of the Basque people voted in 1979 in favor of a statute of autonomy, conformed with autonomy and tried to consolidate self-rule.

ETA considered negotiation as a tool for continuing the struggle and the struggle as a tool for negotiating with the Spanish state. Several attempts: Argel in the 1980s; Lizarra-Garazi in the 1990s; or Loiola in the decade of 2000 concluded upon nothing but the reactivation of terror. Though ETA had changed the interlocutor—the Spanish state, BNP, and PSOE—its failure to reach a sustainable agreement favored both a debilitation of the organization heavily weakened by a more intense police and judicial cooperation at the international level and the progressive detachment of the part of the Basque society that had sympathized with the use of violence as a political means.

In 2011, ETA declared a complete ceasefire and started a process of disarmament that concluded in 2018. After fifty years, the record of violent activity overreached more than one thousand deaths, with over eight hundred caused by ETA, and two hundred caused by Spanish police and paramilitaries against militants and the civil population. Moreover, thousands were wounded, especially among the Spanish military and policemen, as well as civilians passing by. Over four thousand Basques denounced being victims of torture, and later were registered according to an international protocol implemented by the Basque authorities, mainly at the hands of the Spanish Civil Guard and national police. ETA committed over three thousand attacks, more than one every week during a period of forty years, and thousands of Basque entrepreneurs were regularly extorted.

ETA despised the autonomous institutions that included only three provinces, accusing the Basque police of being collaborators and agents of cipayism.[49] In exchange, the BNP, which has run the Basque government ever since it was (re)established in 1979, with the exception of the years 2009-2012, agreed with the policy of dispersion that was enforced to hold Basque prisoners in widespread reclusion across Spain. For many years, the elected representatives of the BNLM only attended the Basque Parliament sporadically, and a stalemate between ETA and the Spanish police lasted for decades. In the 1990s, ETA targeted politicians and journalists as a way to "socialize pain." After several attempts to negotiate a political solution failed, the political wing of the BNLM forced an end to the armed struggle. Previously in 2001, an inner split in the BNLM gave rise to a new party, Aralar, which was opposed to violence. ETA had already lost most of the support and was considered destructive to the Basque cause and its future, even for a majority of

Basque nationalists. In 2011, ETA formally accepted the end of terrorism and proceeded under international supervision to destroy arms and ammunition, without receiving any concessions in return from the Spanish government that have since maintained a rigorous and dubious, if not unlawful, treatment of the militants held in the Spanish prisons.

During these years, Basque institutions under the leadership of the BNP have consolidated a certain degree of autonomy in many fields. This, especially, because Euskadi and Navarre depend on their own fiscal resources, unlike other autonomous communities that depend on the money transfers from Madrid. Since 1841 in Navarre, and since 1878 in the three Basque foral provinces, there has been a particular system of fiscal autonomy, temporarily suppressed in Biscay and Gipuzkoa by Franco, and again established in 1981. This system of fiscal autonomy is based on the Concierto or Convenio Economico, and it allows the foral territories to have more power to develop autonomous policies.

Nevertheless, both the BNLM and the BNP have frequently denounced the limits of autonomy. While the BNP has focused on getting the completion of the statute of autonomy approved in 1979, considering it a departing point of Basque sovereignty, for the Spanish point of view the so-called Statute of Gernika was a final point of destination for Basque self-government. The Spanish governments refused to transfer powers and, acting with the complicity of the Spanish judiciary, have systematically reduced the scope of the powers of the Basque Parliament, enacting invasive Spanish laws that the Spanish Constitutional Court has usually backed. The effect of the European integration process has also played in favor of the central government, the autonomous communities only having very few powers to participate in the EU affairs, while central governments monopolize representation in the European institutions to recover internally divided powers.

For years the BNLM discourse on Spanish democracy has been very critical, proclaiming it was a mere adaptation of Franquism. Paradoxically, facts like the huge corruption involving the monarchy and the Spanish political parties, the connections between big money and corporations with the media, or the extreme nationalist profile of Spanish police and justice, which were not cleaned from their Franquist past but were allowed to have a continuity, have emerged after ETA put an end to revolutionary violence. In any event, because of this and previous experiences of violence, which go as far as the War of the Convention (1793-1795), it can be said that the Basque society is a severely traumatized society that still lives in a hangover of violence.

### The Future of the Independence Movement

The Basque independence movement, unlike recently in Catalunya, has never gained control or become a majority within Basque nationalism. Furthermore, there is not a clear horizon to secure self-government in the European Union. The Basque Independence Movement (BIM) has reached the twenty-first century amid the crossing of three centuries along a very difficult path, surrounded by huge repression, unlawfulness, and exile, as well as violence and the watching eye of Spain and France. As the threat of assimilation advanced, the wish to evade, free from Spanish or French dispossession, increased too.

The Basque independence movement has always faced big obstacles, and the last it's yet to overcome is the shadow and memory of ETA's violence. The so-called armed struggle or terrorism has deeply divided the Basque society and its political forces. It will take a long time to cure the pain inflicted by the revolutionary violence, though the memories of police abuse have also been long and painful. But probably the main obstacle that independentism has to face is the secular division of the Basque people, both to the north and south of the Pyrenees, and between Euskadi and Navarre in the Iberian Peninsula, or among the political forces or between natives and newcomers.

The defeat of ETA hasn't weakened Basque independentism electorally.[50] Nevertheless, neither independentism in the Basque Country or in Catalunya has succeeded in obtaining a clear majority for independence. At the same time, Spanish nationalism hasn't succeeded in obtaining a majority in the Basque Country or Catalunya in supporting the project of the Spanish nation. This situation has developed into a political blockage. Only in the so-called Spanish Spain, the territories historically subjected to Castile, has there been a solid national majority. But unless this Spanish majority recognizes the existence of others, not as solid majorities in the Basque Country and Catalunya, the blockage will continue and will be a source of perennial tensions and instability. Yet, the non-existence of a solid and homogeneous national majority in the Basque Country or in Catalunya goes in parallel to the existence within these territories of powerful social, political, and cultural minorities in defense of the Basque, Catalan, and the Spanish nations.

In a society dominated by a massive consumption of media information, clearly dominated by Spanishness, symbols like the Spanish flag or the Spanish national anthem haven't achieved majority support in the Basque Country and in Catalunya, but a massive rejection. Banal and trivial nationalism could prevail, but the absence of shared political objectives or the lack of consensus in relation to sovereignty and the legitimation of power reflect a serious and lasting political conflict. During forty years of Spanish post-Franquist democracy, Spanish nationalism has imposed the Spanish nation as the only sovereign nation, while who is part of the Spanish nation or a member of the Spanish people are questions previously decided by Spanish law. While Spanish constitutional patriotism has portrayed itself as civic and virtuous, it has considered concurrent peripheral nationalisms as discriminatory, ethnical, authoritarian, and oppressive. In my view, there have been a lot of publicity efforts by Spanish unionism to pretend that national supremacism represents universal enlightenment. Unfortunately for Spanish nationalism, the past shows that intolerance, authoritarianism, and fanaticism are overwhelmingly present throughout Spain's history, from the Catholic kings to Franco's dictatorship and beyond.[51]

Elections have also proven that the party system in Spain and the party systems in Euskadi, Navarre, and Catalunya are not the same. While in "Spanish Spain" the Spanish political parties are the only ones that secure a clear majority of the votes and parliamentary representation, in Euskadi Basque parties hold over two-thirds of the seats in the autonomous Parliament in Vitoria-Gasteiz. Similarly in Pamplona, a combination of the local unionist navarrist party and the Basque parties hold a clear majority, and in the Parliament in Barcelona, Catalan and independence parties have a massive majority of the seats. Hence, in these three Parliaments, Spanish parties are a minority, and as a consequence of such representation disparity, it's clear that the Basque and Catalan demoi are and will never be well represented in the Spanish Parliament. Therefore, in Spain the territorial question also represents a structural democratic deficit that seriously affects political representation, as it happens too between the Scottish and the Parliament in London, where very different minorities are represented.

Though other organizations have promoted the ideas of independence such as BNP or BNA before, and Eusko Alkartasuna[52] or Aralar later, for more than forty years, ETA, and the BNLM that it promoted, have been the trademarks of Basque independentism. The combination of politics and violence shaped the last years of Franco's dictatorship as well as the first thirty years of the Spanish democracy and the Basque autonomy that came after. Though the approach of the BNP to gain more autonomy inside Spain, dismissing demands for independence, has been the current tone during the past decade, it is only with the end of ETA that a new period has started where Catalan independentism has gained protagonism, and Scotland has substituted the Irish reference.

The future of the territorial distribution of power in Spain is undefined. Some have proposed that Spain should accept itself as a nation of nations; hence, that a formal recognition of the Basque Country and Catalunya as political nations should be agreed upon, therefore considering Spain as a plurinational state. Others talk of a plural Spain that logically should become a federal state, a position currently defended among the "progressive" forces of PSOE and Podemos that, since the end of 2019, are sharing the government in Madrid. Other Spanish parties of the right and the ultra-right defend the status quo or even a recentralization of powers. So far, the national recognition of the Basque Country and Catalunya has been viewed only by regarding them as cultural nations or nationalities, the term used in Article 2 of the Spanish Constitution. But the proposals for a federation are vague and usually favor symmetric federation, while an asymmetrical federation would be preferable for most Basques and Catalans. Usually, the proposals for a federation do not contemplate the previous consent of the federative unities and simply contemplate turning the existing autonomous communities into federal units. Yet, Spanish autonomies were conceived to maintain the Basque Country and Catalunya surrounded by a majority of Spanish/Castilian-based communities, as bulls are surrounded by *mansos* in the *encierro* to conduct them more easily to the desired destiny. Only by the singularity of the fiscal autonomy granted by the Concierto/Convenio Económico have diverse party systems and languages made a real difference. This singularity has induced some to propose a Concierto Político for the Basque Country as a way to extend the scope of self-government to other areas.

Having a weak demography and an important flux of new emigrants to the Basque Country is a relevant question, and it is uncertain if these new Basques will become "euskaldun" or Basque speakers. Demography data shows that one in four of the children born in the Basque Country are from a mother born abroad. If the BIM will have a chance to succeed in the future, it will be because the goal of Basque independence has become attractive for many with foreigner origins. Though it is not certain that the nation-state will be the political unit of the future, it is plainly clear that Basque people will have to share its future with many newcomers from Latin America or the north of Africa. If the BIM wants to succeed, it will have to give all, both natives and newcomers, a sense of a common future, a shared vision of a Basque Republic within the European Union.

To gain support, the BIM will have to explain why autonomy within Spain is not the right or best answer, why it will be better to dissent from the autonomous practice the PNV represents, or dissent from a transition to a federal state as the PSOE has proposed. In that particular sense, the precedent of how the foral system worked in a composed monarchy could be of high interest for a better understanding of what might be a future federal or confederal asymmetrical system.[53]

Another relevant question will be the answer related to the internationalization of human affairs, as the invisibility of nations without a state proves more and more evident. As the recognition of national identity is usually linked to citizenship, and states like Spain or France pretend to be mononationals, the existence of other people, language, or nations without a state of their own are obscured in the international arena. In this context, the right to a self-decided national identity is a demand that the BIM could propose, opposing the echoing of the Westphalian world where what was settled for religion later turned to nationality: "cuius regio eius natio," so to say.

The Catalan experience and the Scottish way for independence are being closely followed, and the outcome of both nations will undoubtedly have an impact in the BIM strategy. Obviously, the reaction of the EU to an inside enlargement will have a very important effect, because member states are afraid of the contagious effect that an independent Scotland could have in other autonomous nations of the EU. Most EU states were configured as undemocratically suppressing national minorities, and therefore it won't be easy for the BIM and other independence movements to get support in geopolitical terms. So far, the EU has not given a "third way" to nations like Scotland, Catalunya, Flanders, the Basque Country, or Corsica; that is, offering a special status to those nations in which in their autonomous Parliaments have a majority that seeks to have a guarantee of self-rule inside the European framework. This lack of participatory and representative status in the EU brings in autonomous nations to more easily to seek independence in order to obtain visibility and influence.

The strategy of combining politics and military power, bullets and ballots, similar to other groups seeking national liberation, did not succeed like in Ireland's granting of a referendum, but the defeat of ETA and the lack of a political negotiation have not resulted either in the end of independentism nor of Basque nationalism, as Spanish unionism had wished. The recent change of strategy by the BNLM, from violent opposition to pragmatic politics, giving support to the 2020 Spanish budget as if it were a kind of a leftist BNP, could represent the shaping of a new period that in my view, formally already started in 2011.

For the Basque independence movement's renouncing of the revolutionary trail with the declaration of definitive ceasefire by ETA, a new period started in 2011. But after forty years of ETA and the preceding forty years of Franquism, the hangover of violence is very strong, and the birth of a new situation is developing very slowly. An organization like *Gure esku dago*, inspired in the Catalan movement of promoting civic independence, has not gained momentum in the Basque Country, and the limits of the Spanish democracy, as exposed in dealing with the Catalan question, are obvious. The so-called coalition of Article 155 (PP, C's, PSOE, Vox) went as far as to suspend autonomy in 2017, and the Spanish judiciary has limited the powers of the Catalan Parliament to discuss issues, approve proposals, or elect candidates to the presidency of the Generalitat, among other restrictions.

The new majority shaped to outpost the Popular Party in 2018, which was confirmed through the Spanish elections a year later, has been able to establish a progressive coalition government—in Spanish political terms—between PSOE and Podemos with the support of Basque and Catalan sovereignist parties. If this convergence were to last, perhaps a new political status could be negotiated for the Basque Country and Catalunya. But if opposition to change persists within the "Spanish Spain," and taking into account that the procedure to reform the constitution grants "de facto" veto power to the Spanish right, a scenario of increasing political instability is likely to be expected. The Spanish state is accumulating serious difficulties concerning its head of state, the military, and the judiciary, all deeply affected by corruption, coup intentions, and ultra-national views. It is hard to imagine how long a situation of extended provisionality could last, or what could be the outcome of the national conflicts that affect the Basque Country, Catalunya, and Spain. In any event, perseverance and endurance will be needed because as the adage says: "Izan direlako gara eta garelako izango dira," or "Because they were, we are, and because we are, they will be."

## Bibliography

Agirreazkuenaga, Joseba. *The Making of the Basque Question: Experiencing Self-Government (1793-1877).* Reno: Center for Basque Studies, University of Nevada, 2011.

Aristi, Pako. *Independentziaren Paperak.* Donostia: Erein, 2012.

Ariznabarreta, Joseba. *Pueblo y Poder. Cuadernos para la reconstrucción de la razón.* Zarautz: Itxaropena, 2007.

Arrieta, Jon. *La diadema del Rey. Vizcaya, Navarra, Aragón y Cerdeña en la Monarquía de España (siglos XVI-XVIII).* Leioa: Universidad del País Vasco, 2017.

Bullain, Iñigo. *Revolucionarismo Patriótico. El Movimiento de Liberación Nacional Vasco: Origen, Ideología, Estrategia y Organización.* Madrid: Tecnos, 2011.

Bullain, Iñigo. "A Basque (and Catalan) Republic within a Federal Context: Reflections on New Scenarios in the Crisis of the Autonomous State." In *The Ways of Federalism in Western Countries and the Horizons of Territorial Autonomy in Spain,* edited by Alberto López Basaguren and Leire Escajedo San Epifanio, 781-809. Berlin/Heidelberg: Springer Verlag, 2013.

Bullain, Iñigo. "Naciones Autónomas Europeas." In *Europa de las regiones y el futuro Federal de Europa. Consejo Vasco del Movimiento Europeo, EuroBasque,* 411- 429. Madrid: Dykinson, 2019.

Chacón Delgado, Pedro Jose. *Nobleza con Libertad. Biografía de la Derecha Vasca.* Bilbao: Atxular Atea, 2015.

Fernández Sebastián, Javier. *La génesis del fuerismo. Prensa e ideas políticas en la crisis del Antiguo Régimen (País Vasco 1750-1840).* Madrid: Siglo XXI, 1998.

Fernández Soldevilla, Gaizka. "De Aberri a ETA, pasando por Venezuela." Rupturas y continuidades en el nacionalismo vasco radical (1921-1977). *Bulletin d'Histoire Contemporaine de l'Espagne*, no. 51 (2017): 219-264.

Gallastegi Uriarte, Eli. *Por la libertad vasca.* Tafalla: Txalaparta, 1993.

Ibarra, Pedro. *Memoria del antifranquismo en el País Vasco. Por qué lo hicimos (1966-1976).* Iruña: Pamiela, 2017.

Igartua, Iván et Zabaltza, Xabier. *Euskararen historia laburra/A Brief History of the Basque Language.* Donostia: Etxepare Institutua, 2012.

Irujo, Xabier. "El Gobierno de Jose Antonio Agirre en el exilio (1936-1960)." *Iura Vasconie,* no. 9 (2012): 375-430.

Irujo, Xabier. *Gernika, 1937: The Market Day Massacre.* Reno: Center for Basque Studies, University of Nevada, 2015.

Jimenez González, Aitor. "Enemigos del Estado: Las guerras legales de España contra obreros e independentistas." Misión Jurídica. Revista de Derecho y Ciencias Sociales. Bogota, no. 15 (2018): 181-203.

Jimeno Jurio, and Jose Maria. *Nabarra jamás dijo no al estatuto vasco.* Txalaparta: Tafalla, 1997.

Kamen, Henry. *Imagining Spain. Historical Myth & National Identity.* New Haven and London: Yale University Press, 2008.

Krutwig, Federico. (bajo el pseudónimo de Fernando Sarrailh de Ihartza). *Vasconia. Estudio dialéctico de una nacionalidad.* Buenos Aires: Norbait, 1962.

Landart, Daniel. *Enbataren Zirimolan.* Donostia: Elkar, 2013.

Lizarralde, Imanol. *Teoria Francesa y estrategia del MLNV (1967-2015).* Aranalde: Lasarte-Oria, 2016.

Letamendia, Francisco. *Historia del nacionalismo vasco y de ETA.* Barcelona: R&B, 1994.

López Adan, Emilio. *El nacionalismo vasco en el exilio (1937-1960).* Donostia: Txertoa, 1977.

Lorenzo, Jose María. *Gudari, una pasión útil. Vida y obra de Eli Gallastegi (1892-1974).* Tafalla: Txalaparta, 1992.

Nuñez Seixas, Xosé M. Suspiros de España. *El nacionalismo español entre 1808-2018.* Barcelona: Crítica, 2018.

Ortueta, Anacleto. *Sancho El Mayor, Rey de los Vascos.* Iruña: Mintzoa, 2002.

Ortueta, Anacleto. *Nabarra, Estado político de Vasconia. Compendio de su perspectiva histórica y política. Edición de Gaizka Aranguren.* Iruña: Pamiela y Nabarralde, 2002.

Pablo, Santiago de; Ludger Mees, et Jose Antonio Rodruiguez Sanz. *El Péndulo Patriótico. Historia del Partido Nacionalista Vasco.* Barcelona: Crítica, 1999.

Preston, Paul. *A People Betrayed: A History of Corruption, Political Incompetence and Social Division in Modern Spain.* London: W. Collins, 2020.

Renobales, Eduardo. *ANV, El otro nacionalismo. Historia de Acción Nacionalista Vasca/Eusko Abertzale Ekintza.* Tafalla: Txalaparta, 2007.

Renobales, Eduardo. *Jagi-Jagi: Historia del Independentismo Vasco.* Bilbao: Ahastuak, 2010.

Resina, Joan Ramon. *The Ghost in the Constitution: Historical Memory and Denial in Spanish Society.* Liverpool, UK: Liverpool University Press, 2017.

Rubio, Coro et Pablo, Santiago de (coords). *Los liberales. Fuerismo y liberalismo en el País Vasco (1808-1876).* Vitoria/Gasteiz: Fundación Sancho el Sabio, 2002.
Ugalde, Alex. *La acción exterior del nacionalismo vasco (1890-1936). Historia, pensamiento y relaciones internacionales.* Oñati: IVAP, 1996.
Ugalde, Alex. *EuroBasque (1947-2018). La contribución vasca al federalismo europeo.* Vitoria-Gasteiz: EuroBasque, 2019.
Ugalde, Martin. *Lezo Urreiztieta (1907-1981).* Donostia: Elkar, 1990.
Urteaga, Eguzki. "La política de ordenación y desarrollo del País Vasco norte." *Revista Vasca de Administración Pública*, no. 117 (2020), 293-338.
Urzainqui, Tomás. *La Navarra Marítima.* Iruña: Pamiela, 1999.
Torrealdai, Joan Mari. *El libro negro del euskara.* Donostia: Ttarttalo, 1998.
Zabaltza, Xabier. *Mater Vasconia. Fueros, lenguas y discursos nacionales en los países vascos.* Donostia: Hiria, 2005.

## NOTES

1 Prehistoric remains in Atapuerca and Lascaux, which represent what was the utmost western extension of the Kingdom of Pamplona and the north oriental axis of the Duchy of Wascony, are dated as some of the oldest human sites in Europe.

2 It was then that the court settled in Pau, where Navarre as an independent state existed until 1620 when French troops conquered it. At the time, France had a population of over twenty million, Spain around ten million, and Navarre had only a few hundred thousand citizens.

3 From 1623 onward, the general-states of Navarre met in Donapaleu/Saint-Palais where coins were striked too.

4 The following dates represent crucial episodes of violence: 1200; 1512; 1839; and 1978; and the Navarre rebellions in 1521; 1632; 1654; and 1665.

5 Fueros are a set of norms and institutions recollected in other legal codes, like in Labourd, Soule, Aragon, Bearn, Foix, and other territories across the Pyrenees that share a common heritage. The Kingdom of Navarre, which lasted as a political entity for almost a thousand years (IX-XIX centuries), was the only realm in Europe that had not a barbaric/german origin but an autochtonous one.

6 The rural population of Iparralde has long been subject to perennial emigration, mainly to South America and Paris, though some headed to the western US too. In the latest decades, the conurban area of the Basque Côte, BAM, has attracted thousands of pensioners coming from around the Hexagone. Due to the fact that the French republic never granted autonomy and has not yet given any official status to the language, Basque is in rapid decline. On the political new status of the Basque provinces in France, see Eguzki Urteaga, "La política de ordenación y desarrollo del País Vasco norte," *Revista Vasca de Administración Pública*, no. 117 (2020), 293-338.

7 News about the Basque Country was first given by the Romans in the first century BC, when they conquered Aquitany and later Hispania. After the Roman Empire collapsed in the West during the fifth century, Basque people fiercely opposed the barbarian invasions of visigoths and franks. Around the year 600 AD, a Duchy of Wascony (wasc/Basque, as

it was pronounced at the time) emerged around the Pyrenees. It was later inherited by the kings of England until the fifteenth century when it passed onto the kings of France.

8 From 824 until 1620, Navarre was, in diverse shapes across centuries, a european independent state that maintained self-government even further, in time: until the eighteenth century in France, and until the nineteenth century under Spanish rule.

9 About three million people currently live in the seven Basque territories, where about 750,000 people speak or understand Basque. However, many more Basque descendants have populated mostly Argentina, as well as America, Chile, and Mexico. The so-called Basque diaspora is scattered all along the Americas, and even the US, where Basque communities have grown mainly in Idaho, Nevada, and California.

10 . . . "hainbeste mendetako gure morrontzak baditu mila tankera eta, zuhur aukeratzen ez badugu, bertan galduko gera" . . . "gure herriko lanak handi dire, astun dire, zatiturik gaudenontzat . . . ." Xabier Lete and Lourdes Iriondo. "Itsasoan urak handi dire," music and lyrics by Julen Lekuona.

11 The abolishment of the Fueros occurred during the nineteenth century.

12 Previously, the Kingdom of Navarre had remained independent from the French Crown until 1620, when the French Army under Louis XIII incorporated "the wonder of the world" in Shakespearean terms, to France. The laws of the land, the fueros of Bearn and Navarre, as well as the Basque institutions of Labourd were maintained until 1789, when in the name "egalité," Paris' rule was imposed.

13 The Edict of the Union by Louis II of Navarre (XIII of France), enacted in 1620, was repealed as an act of treason against the laws, liberties, and rights of the kingdom by the Parliament of Navarre. At the formal ceremony of incorporation of Navarre, to the kingdoms of Castille and Leon and Granada made in Burgos on the July 7,1515, there was not a single representative of the kingdom of Navarre. Therefore, "ex injuria jus non oritur" (from an illicit act source: no right). According to the American legal doctrine of Stimson-Welles, there is no international recognition of acquisitions by force.

14 Derecho de sobrecarta in Navarre, and Pase foral in the provinces.

15 For many centuries, Basques living under the Fueros professed a local patriotism that ran in parallel to their loyalty to the Crown. They felt somewhat Spanish, whatever that was supposed to be, as far as their Basqueness was recognized. The so-called foralism was the institutional organization of Basque self-rule maintained by the territories from 1200 to 1876 in the so-called Basque provinces and from 1512 onward until 1841 in Navarre.

16 Before the BNP was formally founded on July 31, 1895, Saint Ignatius of Loyola's day according to the Roman Catholic calendar, the Arana brothers had already founded the "Euskaldun Batzokije," or Basque Society in Bilbao, and later the BBB or Biskaiko Buru Batzar or Biscay Head Congress. After the PSOE, founded a few years before the PNV, the BNP is the second-oldest party active in Spanish politics.

17 One of its first publications was called *Bizkaitarra*, which was also how the supporters of the party were called afterward, independence being firstly proposed for the territory of Biscay. As a reaction to the loss of the Fueros, different associations were founded in Pamplona and San Sebastian. Their aim focused on promoting Basque culture while demanding the restitution of the foral system. In Bilbao, another association that was founded in 1898, called "Euskalerriacos," which was led by Sota, would eventually merge

with the movement that Sabino Arana founded. Due to Bilbao being the new Fenicia, the city would take the political lead, too, shadowing the association Euskara (1878-1883) founded in Pamplona/Iruña as well as the Euskal Herria review (1880-1918) based in San Sebastian/Donostia.

18 As a colonized people, the struggle to maintain an independent spirit has never been easy. As the king of Navarre, Jean d'Albrech, said: "Navarre is a fly between two monkies," that is, a disturbance for France and Spain, who would end up destroying the kingdom, dividing its territory, and annexing its people.

19 Regarding the Basque language, Arana developed a particular linguistic register, purifying Basque from words of Latin origin. This cleansing and the simultaneous invention of thousands of neologisms turned his writing incomprehensible. He deviated from the literary language that Joanes Leiçarraga printed in the fifteenth century, and who had achieved to integrate with Basque the same European thesaurus as other languages had done regarding Latin and Greek.

20 Though identified as Castilian, the Romanized Basques in the peninsula developed a different dialect; the so-called navarre-riojan dialect that is recorded in the monastery of San Millán de la Cogolla.

21 Federico Krutwig was a Basque intellectual who, while in exile, wrote a book titled *Vasconia*. The book had a big impact on the nationalist movement and gave Basque independentism a new and modern look. The novelesque life of Federeico Krutwig was the subject of a short novel by Manu Erzila, *Obligazio Bat* (Donostia: Hiria Liburuak, 2006).

22 The prince Louis Lucien Bonaparte was the nephew of General Bonaparte. He became a respected linguist who traveled through the Basque Country doing research about the language. He created the first map of the Basque language according to dialects, first published in London in 1863.

23 From Zuberoa, a territory which is to the northeast of the Pyrenees, Abbadie constructed a castle and an astronomical observatory that still stands today, close to Hendaye.

24 Due to the continuous repression of the language in Spain and France, the first Basque newspapers were founded in San Francisco, CA, and Buenos Aires.

25 Xabier Zabaltza, *Mater Vasconia. Fueros, lenguas y discursos nacionales en los países vascos,* (Donostia: Hiria, 2005).

26 He created a neologism, "abizenak," referring to the names of the ancestors but associating Basqueness to names—"apellidos." Arana disregarded the idea that current Basque names were a product of the fifteenth century, or that until the nineteenth century any person could register under a chosen name.

27 The norms that were established for people to become members of the first Batzoki or Society, founded in Bilbao, are very illustrative of this. A selection of the articles of the statutes of the "Euskaldun Batzokija" are reproduced in Zabaltza, *Mater Vasconia. Fueros, lenguas y discursos nacionales en los países vascos,* 539-545.

28 Ortueta pronounced himself against Labayru's assertion that Bizcaya had a political personality in the eleventh century. Ortueta also underscores the consequences of treason in 1076 of Iñigo Lopez, a tenant of Navarre who defected to Castile. In page 45, Ortueta reproduces the acknowledgement of Menendez Pidal regarding the vasconic dissidence against visigots. The Basque provinces pivoted during 1076-1200 between Navarre and Castile, and

during 1076-1134 Aragon and Navarre established a joint sovereignty. Tudela was conquered in 1114 by Alfonso el Batallador. According to Ortueta, the Navarrese monarchs didn't share the Spanish national sentiment and heritage related to the Visigoths. Moreover, the upper Ebro valley did not have Toledo or Madrid as the center. Castile first dismembered and later annihilated the Basque state, and finally suppressed the fueros. The Navarre dynasties were Arista; Jimena; Champagne; Evreux, Foix; and Borbon. And the prominent families in the provinces were Vela, Jimenez, Guevara, Haro, Onaz, Gamboa, and later in Navarre, Agramont, and Beaumont. At the end of the seventeenth century, the population of both Biskay and Gipuzkoa was about 80,000; 60,000 in Alava; and around 200,000 in Navarre. Krutwig recalls that Rioja was given to Castile in 1177, and that Bureba, Alto Ebro,Villarcayo, Medina, Cuatro Villas, Castro, and Santoña were part of Navarre.

29 This has been developed by Santiago de Pablo and Ludger Mees in *El Péndulo Patriótico: Historia del Partido Nacionalista Vasco (1895-2005)*. Barcelona: Critica, 2005.

30 Vid., Luis de Guezala, "Desde un balcón en Larrazabal," in Deia November 11, 2020.

31 The name Jagi-Jagi was taken from a patriotic song that began calling for the Basque people to get up, written in the peculiar Basque language coined by Arana:

> *¡Jagi, jagi, euzkotarrak, lasterr dator eguna!, Sorrkaldetik agiri da, argi gozo-biguna. Bere aurrian bilddurrtuta igesi dua illuna. ¡Jagi, jagi, euzkotarrak, lasterr datorr eguna!*
>
> *Sorrkaldetik agiri da JEL-eguzki ederra. Bere argijak berotuko dausku geure bijotza. ¡Jagi, jagi, euzkotarrak, eta batzau gattezan! Arrtu danok izkillubaketa aurrera goyazan.*
>
> *Geure Aberri-areyua gustijak il daiguzan.*

32 An antecedent in terms of political laicism was the foundation in 1909 of the Partido Republicano Nacionalista Vasco by Francisco Ulacia in Bilbao.

33 The so-called Pacto de San Sebastian, where Catalan, socialist, and republican forces met and reached a compromise to fight for the republic and autonomy, was held in the Basque city of San Sebastian in 1930. Basque nationalism was not invited, considered not to be in the same line of revolutionary change as well as being too close to the Catholic Church and tradition.

34 Galeusca was first created in 1923 and renovated in 1933.

35 Traditionalism viewed autonomy as a way to protect the population from the republic and laicism. However, Basque nationalism would later prove that it was not a pro-monarchy force, but a force favoring the republic.

36 The details of what happened in the assembly that met in the Gayarre theater in Iruña/Pamplona to ratify the text showed that the favorable majority was turned into opposition due to tricks. Jimeno Jurio, *Nabarra jamás dijo no al estatuto vasco* (Txalaparta: Tafalla, 1997).

37 In Araba, only 45 percent of the census voted in favor.

38 Though a frontline never existed, in Navarre the fascist repression killed over 3,000 people out of a population of 300,000. That is about the same number of victims created in Chile after the coup by Pinochet, but within a much bigger population of about ten million.

39 There were seventy-nine Basque battalions under the unified military command of "Euzko Gudarostea," as listed in 26-04-37: seven had no affiliation, one STV, one Republican, two Jagi-Jagi, seven CNT, five I.R., four ANV, eleven socialists, twenty-five PNV, and seventeen comunists (nine JSU and eight P).

40 About the destruction of Guernica, see Xabier Irujo, *Gernika, 1937: The Market Day Massacre* (Reno: Center for Basque Studies—University of Nevada Press, 2015).

41 Alex Ugalde, *EuroBasque (1947-2018). La contribución vasca al federalismo europeo* (Vitoria-Gasteiz: EuroBasque, 2019).

42 Within the Basque government in exile, there were several confrontations. The first affected a socialist counselor, Santiago Aznar, who was expelled from the PSOE, as he was deemed a "deviacionist" due to the fact that he recognized the national character of the Basque government, while for Prieto and PSOE the Basque government was simply part of the republican legality. In 1949, the PCE was expelled from the Basque government as a consequence of the Cold War. Leizaola, who had taken the place of Aguirre, expelled ANV in 1979.

43 The contrast between the proposal made by Manuel de Irujo in London, for a Consejo Nacional de Euskadi in 1941, and the adherence of the BNP to the strategy of a common Spanish opposition as portrayed during the congress held in Munich in 1962, is quite telling. This orientation went in opposition to the Patriotic Front issued by the Manifest of Baiona 1944, or the Pact of Baiona 1945 that was joined: Pnv, Anv; Stv (founded in 1911).

44 In 1970, the dictatorship judged sixteen members of ETA in the notorious "Proceso de Burgos," which gave ETA and the Basque conflict international attention and support.

45 Iñigo Bullain, *Revolucionarismo Patriótico. El Movimiento de Liberación Nacional Vasco: Origen, Ideología, Estrategia y Organización* (Madrid: Tecnos, 2011).

46 In 1969, half of all the political prisoners in Spain were members of ETA.

47 Personality and divisions in the political life have been chronic, like in BNA between Nardiz and Solagaistua; or the number of splits and new parties in the Basque left like: ESB; ESI; EE/EuE; EA/Hamaika; and HB/Aralar.

48 In Navarre, only 50 percent of the census voted in favor of the Spanish Constitution. In Gipuzkoa 28 percent and in Biscay just 30 percent ratified the text.

49 Fifteen ertzain or Basque policemen were murdered by ETA.

50 During the Second Spanish Republic, three groups had an equivalent electoral force in the Basque Country. More or less one-third of the vote went to the traditional and monarchist parties; one-third to socialist and republicans; and one-third to Basque nationalists. Today, it is two-thirds for Basque nationalism while the Spanish parties all around get less than one-third of the representation in the Basque Parliament. The results of the elections in 2020 distributed seventy-five seats in the Basque Parliament as follows: BNP:31; EH-BILDU:21; PSE:10; PODEMOS:6; PP+CIU:6; VOX:1.

51 Vid. Nuñez Seixas, Xosé M. *Suspiros de España.* El nacionalismo español entre 1808-2018. Barcelona: Crítica, 2018.

52 Eusko Alkartasuna was founded in 1986, splitting from the BNP under the leadership of Carlos Garaikoetxea, the first elected lehendakari after 1979. Aralar, a split of the patriotic left opposed to violence, was founded in 2001; Alternatiba, in 2009, was created as a split from the Spanish United Left in the Basque Country, and Sortu appeared in 2012, representing the continuity of the former Herri Batasuna, the main political wing of the Basque National Liberation Movement.

53 Jon Arrieta, *La diadema del Rey. Vizcaya, Navarra, Aragón y Cerdeña en la Monarquía de España (siglos XVI-XVIII)* (Leioa: Universidad del País Vasco, 2017).

# 7

# Catalan Nationalism and the Catalan Independence Movement Under the Franco Dictatorship and the Restoration of Democracy (1939-2003)

*Carles Santacana*

In broad strokes, this chapter lays out the evolution of Catalan nationalism and the independence movement (a minority strand in Catalan nationalism that openly advocates for the independence of Catalunya) over the course of two starkly different periods, the dictatorship of General Franco and the constitutional regime of 1978, which instituted a parliamentary monarchy in Spain and recognized the right to political autonomy for the nationalities and regions within the Spanish state. As explained in other texts in this volume, the Catalan nationalist movement (both in its cultural and civic aspects and in its political dimension) achieved hegemony in Catalunya during the Second Spanish Republic (1931-1936), not only in the political-institutional arena but also in the social sphere.[1] In the political-institutional arena, the Republic recognized the right to autonomy within the state, granting Catalunya its own Parliament, and accepting the existence of a specific Catalan party system that was distinct from its Spanish counterpart. In the social sphere, a plethora of cultural, civic, and sporting associations came to adhere, more or less explicitly, to the tenets of Catalan nationalism. The fact is that, despite the various problems that arose in the actual management of autonomy and despite the suspension of autonomy itself between October 1934 and February 1936, the practical incorporation of Catalan nationalism within Catalunya's political institutions was seen as inseparable from the consolidation of the Republic. Against this, the rebels who rose up against the Republic in July 1936 and triggered the Spanish Civil War (1936-1939) sought to bring down the Republican democracy and end the autonomy of both Catalunya and the Basque Country. For this reason, the occupation of Catalan territory by General Franco's army had special connotations. The rebels were relentless in their insistence on the reintegration of Catalunya in Spain, branding all strands of Catalan nationalism as "separatist." The state that emerged out of the military victory was an iron-fisted dictatorship[2] led by General Franco, which grounded its power primarily on military success and a ferocious crackdown against every sector that had stood in opposition to the coup. The state was transformed into a one-party dictatorship and the sole party was the Falange Española Tradicionalista (popularly known as the Falange), which was broadly comparable to the fascisms of the period, but with its own unique feature, which was the central role played by the Catholic Church. As it was formulated under Francoism,[3] Spanish identity had a number of underlying elements: firstly, it had a military mindset, which identified the army with the nation; secondly, it relied on the discourse of the Falange, which denied social classes and any other element that might call into question Spanish national unity. It was also strongly Catholic, assimilating state and religion and treating Catholicism as an inherent aspect of being Spanish. Beyond that, the regime presumed to claim leadership of the Hispano-American community, which enabled it to put the Spanish language at the core of that community's identity, which was then spreading across Latin America. The radicalization of the Spanish Civil War gave heightened impetus to such a radical unitarian discourse, which acquired control of all the levers needed after military victory to turn it into a dictatorial state policy.

This policy rapidly took concrete form in relation to Catalunya: Catalunya's statute of autonomy was abolished in 1938, even before the end of the Spanish Civil War, resulting in the disappearance of its autonomous government (known as the Generalitat), its Parliament, and the institutions that had been created. As in the rest of Spain, political parties were disbanded and outlawed. The word "Catalunya" disappeared completely from the names of libraries, shops, and cultural and sporting associations. The official rhetoric insisted on referring to Catalunya's four provinces individually at the expense of the concept of Catalunya itself. The repression, carried out by the Franco dictatorship throughout Spain against any individuals and organizations that were democratic, socialist, communist, or anarchist, was expanded in Catalunya to encompass Catalan nationalists too, even if they were Catholic and/or conservative.[4] The aim of the regime was to wipe the slate clean, eradicating a Catalan nationalism that it regarded as the source of all ills. A few days after Franco's troops marched into Barcelona, a former conservative Catalan nationalist member of Parliament, Fernando Valls Taberner, wrote an article in *La Vanguardia,* the leading daily newspaper in Barcelona. Entitled *La falsa ruta* (The Wrong Path), his article stated that Catalan society had taken the "wrong path" because it had been led astray by Catalan nationalism. According to Valls Taberner, Catalan nationalism had opened the floodgates to the social revolution that had struck in the early days of the Civil War. He argued that Catalan nationalism had falsified the true history of Catalunya to the point that it made the populace of Catalunya believe that it was a nation. If the problem had to do with the construction of a false identity, the leading culprits obviously had to be the writers and intellectuals[5] who had fabricated such a false discourse. The persecution carried out by the Francoist dictatorship, therefore, was not confined to politicians, but also extended to Catalan nationalist intellectuals and cultural figures, who were held to be the main perpetrators of misleading the people and making them believe that what was only a local identity was, in reality, a national character.

In this climate of rooting out and destroying whatever remained of Catalan nationalism, the Second World War (1939-1945) broke out, undercutting the positions of Republican exiles in France, such as Lluís Companys, president of the Generalitat, who was detained by the Gestapo, handed over to Spanish authorities, and executed by firing squad in Barcelona on October 15, 1940. The slaying of Companys made a stark political point: he had been the democratically elected president of Catalunya's autonomous government. After the end of the Second World War, the Francoist government was in a very weak position, fearful that the Allied victory would lead to its downfall. As a consequence, the regime felt compelled to make gestures toward change, specifically by diminishing and concealing the role of the one-party Falange, whose roots were fascist, in order to give greater prominence to the Catholic component of the dictatorship. At the same time, the regime wanted to show a less radical policy toward Spain's non-Castilian cultures, allowing some expressions of those cultures, so long as they were archaic and traditional in nature and there was no possible interpretation that might link them to Catalan nationalist demands. The result was the promotion of a Catalan identity that was parochial and stuck in the past, expressed primarily through folkloric dances and activities, most especially the *sardana*, a popular dance that the Catalan nationalists considered to be a "national dance" and that the Francoist authorities permitted as a symbol of a rural Catalunya and an example of its distinct regional character. From the Catalan nationalists' perspective, it was a clear case of distorting a portion of their cultural heritage, which was depicted as an archaic regional contribution of Catalunya to the superior whole of a unified Spain. Meanwhile, permission was granted to publish some books in Catalan, but only ones written in an archaic language that predated its official codification, which had taken place under the government of the Mancomunitat, an earlier twentieth-century effort to bring together the four provinces of Catalunya into a single commonwealth. In this way, everything related to Catalan culture was identified as an antiquarian curiosity,[6] of no consequence in matters of importance.

Against this backdrop, Catalan nationalism had very little scope for action. In the early years, the onus fell largely on those who had gone into exile, where they sought to maintain their cohesion as a community through cultural activities, such as journals and magazines, book publishing, and the annual celebration of a Catalan literary contest known as the Jocs Florals. In political terms, defeat in the Civil War represented not only a complete break with the upward rise of Catalan nationalism over the preceding thirty years, but also an enormous internal crisis. On one hand, the social revolution and religious persecution unleashed in the summer of 1936 prompted conservative Catalan nationalist sectors to abandon their previous affiliation and align with Franco. On the other hand, after the Civil War, the reproaches fired back and forth among the losers were unsurprisingly constant. Nobody wanted to shoulder responsibility for the defeat; in the Catalan case, the conflicts also stemmed from the tense relationship that had arisen between the governments of the Republic and of Catalunya when the former moved to Barcelona in late 1937 in the middle of the war and went about constraining the Catalan government's ability to act.

This all had consequences for the political life of Catalan nationalism in exile. On one hand, the exiles strove to maintain the institution of the Generalitat, which succeeded in reconstituting a short-lived government between 1945 and 1948. Primarily, however, the Generalitat managed to persist through the figure of its presidents, Josep Irla (1940-1954)[7] and Josep Tarradellas (1954-1980).[8] The main force to champion the Generalitat was Esquerra Republicana (the Republican Left party or ERC), which worked to defend the status quo created under the Republic. Hopes for the restoration of the Generalitat in Catalunya were bound up with the efforts undertaken by the institutions of the Republic in exile,[9] which ultimately proved fruitless. However, not all Catalan nationalists in exile were in agreement on the need to defend the status quo under the Republic. Some argued that defeat in the Civil War had nullified the Catalan nationalist commitment to the Republic and its versions of autonomy. A split opened between Republican loyalists and other sectors that called for the establishment of new aims. During the Second World War, a body called the Consell Nacional de Catalunya (National Council of Catalunya) was founded in London. According to the National Council of Catalunya, the period of Republican autonomy was over. Instead, it now aspired to obtain the right to self-determination for Catalunya once Franco's dictatorship had disappeared. Its most distinguished representative was Carles Pi i Sunyer,[10] who had served as mayor of Barcelona for ERC. There was also a core group of representatives who were clearly pro-independence, led by the anthropologist Josep M. Batista i Roca. However, they exerted very limited influence. As a consequence, no organized pro-independence group of any importance ever developed in exile, beyond the activism of a few public figures and poorly structured groups. In addition, the consolidation of the Francoist dictatorship, which secured international recognition in the 1950s, dealt a heavy blow to all the exiles, who found themselves increasingly remote from the dynamics back home. A number of younger exiles took the decision to return to Spain. At the same time, an explicitly pro-independence political party emerged in Catalunya. Called the Front Nacional de Catalunya (National Front of Catalunya or FNC) (1940),[11] it was a clandestine group made up of former members of ERC and Estat Català (literally, Catalan State). The new FNC adopted a pro-independence flag known as the Estelada, which featured the usual four red bars against a gold background appearing in the standard *Senyera* flag of Catalunya but added a white star against a blue triangle to the left, and the party embarked on a significant program of resistance activism, including the sabotage of official events and the raising of Catalan flags.

### Rebuilding Catalan Nationalism in the 1950s and '60s

While the consolidation of the Francoist dictatorship proceeded domestically, thanks to repression and, internationally, thanks to its Cold War role as a barrier against communism, this does not mean that the regime exerted any real control over Catalan society. In the mid-1950s, the Francoist authorities complained of the poor political integration of Catalunya's economic elites, who did not want to play a political role and took little part in any statewide public office. Certainly, most members of the Catalan bourgeoisie were indebted to the dictatorship for the recovery of their businesses (which had been collectivized by workers during the Civil War) and for its dismantling of the labor movement. At the same time, however, they refused to get involved politically.

On the other hand, Catalan nationalism did succeed in sustaining a certain level of activity, whether underground or lawfully through activities that outwardly appeared to be exclusively cultural in nature. In both cases, the commitment of sectors of the Catholic Church proved crucial by promoting or giving cover to the activities.[12] In the slow grind of its resurgence, Catalan nationalism not only had to overcome the conditions imposed by the dictatorship, but it also needed to digest the trauma of the Civil War itself. Catalan society had been divided by the conflict, making the trauma internal as well. This raised questions about Catalan society and its most profound characteristics. Two books helped in the process. One was written by the philosopher Josep Ferrater Mora. Entitled *Les formes de la vida catalana* (*The Character of Catalan Life*), it was published in Chile in 1944 and in Catalunya in 1955. The other was written by the historian Jaume Vicens Vives, entitled *Noticia de Cataluña* (*News of Catalunya*) (1954). While the effects of the two books were very much limited to intellectual coteries, they represented the first reflections to be published at home by intellectuals with little or no track record prior to the Civil War. As mentioned earlier, the Francoist authorities had noted the distance between the regime and local elites, and decided to take action: in 1957, Pere Gual Villalbí, the foremost leader of the Catalan employers' association, was appointed minister without portfolio, and even more importantly, Josep Maria de Porcioles,[13] a highly active notary, was appointed mayor of Barcelona, injecting a notable dynamism into the municipal government and becoming de facto the most important local official in Catalunya. In addition, the regime organized an extended tour by General Franco to Catalunya in 1960 as part of a campaign called "Operation Catalunya," which attached great importance to three "concessions" that the government planned to make to the Catalans as a sign of goodwill: the transfer of the military fortress of Montjuïc Castle to the city of Barcelona, the approval of a special regime for the municipal government of Barcelona (which would also apply to its counterpart in Madrid), and a compilation of Catalan civil law, whose value was more symbolic than real. In connection with Operation Catalunya, a concert was held in May 1960 featuring the choir of the Orfeó Català, a choral society of great importance in the world of cultural Catalan nationalism, and which had been banned from performing from 1939 to 1945. Several government ministers were in attendance. The authorities had forbidden the singing of the Orfeó Català's anthem, *El cant de la senyera* (in English, *The Song of the Senyera [Flag]*), but Catalan nationalist activists in the audience sang the anthem anyway.[14] Several arrests ensued, including the Catalan nationalist activist Jordi Pujol, who was held to be the instigator. Plainly, the outcome of these events demonstrated that the operations of the Francoist regime did not enjoy a welcome reception in the early 1960s, not by Catalan nationalists who were Catholic and even less so by their Marxist counterparts regrouping among the young intellectuals of the communist PSUC.[15] Far from its official triumphalist discourse, therefore, the dictatorship had concerns about the underground resurgence of Catalan nationalism.

The Francoist authorities were well aware that they had failed in achieving their goal of eradicating Catalan nationalist culture, and they engaged in secret debates over which strategy to pursue, but without arriving at any real results.[16]

The cultural resurgence[17] of Catalan nationalism (and its political resurgence)[18] also brought something new to the table that would have political consequences as well. Since the Catalan Renaissance of the nineteenth century, the importance of the language in Catalan nationalism's shaping of identity had gone into the building of relationships among the territories where Catalan was spoken: Catalunya, Valencia, and the Balearic Islands in Spain, and a small area known as Northern Catalunya, which had been ceded to France in 1659. The appeal to a common language, with its dialectal variants, was constant, but there was no success in coming up with a name to identify the entire Catalan-speaking domain. Even more importantly, the cultural movement's shift toward making political demands differed in time and intensity in each territory, so that any political action was entirely piecemeal. As a result, Catalan nationalism culturally asserted a common language and culture, but politically focused its actions solely on the former Principality of Catalunya. Despite its enormous limitations and its minority character, the cultural resurgence of the 1960s put this issue on the table. Particularly influential was the Valencian intellectual Joan Fuster,[19] who published two books in 1962: *Nosaltres els valencians* [*We, the Valencians*] and *Qüestió de noms* [*Matter of Names*]. In these two works, Fuster reflected on Valencian history and identity, which he understood in the context of what he dubbed the Països Catalans, or the Catalan-speaking territories. In the second of his two works, he made a forceful defense of this name, arguing that it combined an affirmation of the cultural unity of the entire linguistic domain with the diversity of each territory. Fuster's proposal was an immediate hit in Catalan nationalist circles and led to many new undertakings, such as *Serra d'Or*[20] (a publication sponsored by Montserrat Abbey that drew on the involvement of all anti-Francoist cultural sectors); the Catalan encyclopedia *Gran Enciclopèdia Catalana,* which began appearing in 1969 and used Fuster's territorial designation; and even the later Congrés de Cultura Catalana (Congress of Catalan Culture), which operated in 1975-1977.

Another important element in the reconstruction of Catalan nationalist culture was the role played by internal migration from poorer Spanish regions. In the 1960s, the migrants arrived in large numbers to settle in an economically more prosperous Catalunya, giving rise to a debate that boiled down in reality to what it meant to be a Catalan citizen. The question was a straightforward one: who is Catalan? Clearly, the debate was theoretical in nature, since from a legal perspective there was only one nationality, the Spanish nationality. Migration to Catalunya from the poorer regions of Spain proved to be a fundamental issue,[21] one that had already been significant in the 1920s. During the Second Spanish Republic, however, the debate had revolved largely around the relationship between migration and anarchism. Now, in the '60s, the issue was not the same, among other reasons because the crackdowns of the Francoist regime had rooted out anarchism. However, the demographic impact of the waves of migrants was very significant: over a million people joined a preexisting population that did not even reach four million. In addition, the newcomers were concentrated in a number of very specific spots, where their sheer size posed objective difficulties to engaging in interactions with the autochthonous population. The newcomers were also coming into a society about which they knew nothing except the official version put out by Francoism, which failed to explain the history and also outlawed the Catalan language in the public sphere, where it was absent from institutions, schools, and the media, being limited instead to the private sphere and to very narrow cultural circles. These issues made it necessary to rethink who was Catalan. The proposal that afforded the greatest sociopolitical functionality was the one put forward by the writer Paco Candel in his book *Els altres catalans* (*The Other Catalans*) (1964). Candel, who belonged to a family that had migrated to Catalunya in 1927, wrote his book based on personal experience, reporting on the harshness of life in Barcelona's suburbs and urging the full social integration of these sectors into Catalan society. In Candel's view, such an integration started with the newcomers being accepted as Catalans regardless of their place of origin or their general lack of knowledge of the Catalan language. The title of Candel's book turned into a sort of political slogan. The underlying concern, which made it necessary to rethink the Catalunya emerging at the time, was chiefly the danger of social division, against which the greater part of Catalan nationalism wanted to oppose the image of single people made up of natives and immigrants alike. Candel called on native-born Catalans to facilitate integration, though in reality, they had no instruments with which to do so, only the voluntarism of a number of associations with a limited ability to act.

In addition, the resurgence of Catalan nationalism in the 1960s can be discerned with striking clarity in the modernization of its cultural offerings. Even though the only television broadcaster and practically all the radio stations put out an archetype of Spanishness that only permitted a folkloric Catalan identity, cultural Catalan nationalism came up with formulas to overcome these limitations. Foremost among them was the musical movement known as the Nova Cançó

(New Song), which heralded the emergence of young singers who performed in Catalan and drew on modern forms for their cultural product, taking inspiration from the French chanson and US folk music. As a consequence, cultural expression in Catalan became innovative and appealing for the younger generations.

### The New Marxist Pro-Independence Groups

Unsurprisingly, the development of the pro-independence movement could not remain unaffected by the cultural recovery and renewed associationism of the 1960s or by the inevitable generational change taking place. The pro-independence movements in exile never achieved sufficient cohesion and gradually diminished as their instigators died. Back home, the National Front of Catalunya (FNC) held onto its historical pro-independence positions but did not attain a predominant role among the opposition. The '60s were a decade of decolonization, which unfolded in the context of the Cold War. As is widely known, the anticolonial struggle was often carried out by socialist movements, which developed a doctrine of liberation from twofold oppression: national and social. This sort of discourse attracted significant sectors among the younger generations, including Catalan pro-independence groups. In this context, the youth members of the FNC, who were organized into the Bloc Escolar Nacionalista (Nationalist Student Bloc or BEN), took up the new Marxist ideological paradigm, which was a far cry from the tenets of the FNC itself. Their ideological dispute and generational change were instrumental to the paradigm shift within the BEN, which ultimately led in 1969 to the departure of practically all of the youth members of the FNC, who formed a new political party, the Partit Socialista d'Alliberament Nacional dels Països Catalans (Socialist Party of National Liberation of the Catalan-Speaking Territories or PSAN).[22] As the name makes very explicit, the PSAN was a communist party with communist symbols, and it echoed the calls for national liberation in vogue at the time. In addition, it identified its national scope of action as the entire Països Catalans, or Catalan-speaking territories. The PSAN's break with the presuppositions of the FNC was complete, running the gamut from ideological identification to national scope of action, though it was very peaceful in practice. The PSAN even went so far as to make changes at the level of symbols, when a young party member, Pep Ribas, designed a new version of the pro-independence flag, the Estelada. In place of the white star in a blue triangle, Ribas substituted a five-pointed red star in a gold triangle to convey the party's communist affiliation. Thus, young people seized control of the pro-independence movement by adopting an international frame of reference and taking inspiration from struggles in a remote Third World, with constant references to Cuba, Algeria, and Vietnam.

Josep Ferrer, the ideologue behind the foundation of the PSAN, drew a sharp distinction between old and new nationalisms.[23] After raising the issues of class alienation and national alienation, Ferrer concluded that the Catalan-speaking territories embodied one of the new nationalisms, even though it had once been one of the old nationalisms. The key distinction was that in the old nationalisms the demands of the working classes were exploited and directed by the bourgeoisie, whose ideological baggage harked back to the liberal revolutions in France and the United States. By contrast, the new nationalism of the working classes had an anticapitalist and socialist outlook and related aims, because it drew on the Soviet revolution and especially on anticolonial nationalism.

At the same time, sub-state nationalisms underwent a resurgence in Western Europe in the wake of May 1968. In a few regions of France (Occitania, Brittany, Corsica), the resurgence was small, while in the United Kingdom, Scottish and Welsh demands played some role. Truly international attention, however, was captured only by Northern Ireland, which became a major touchstone for other irredentist movements. Without exception, all the new movements prominently featured the younger generations, who were inspired by the epic spirit of the anticolonial struggles and experienced them very much in relation to the ideological clash of the Cold War.

This explains the growing admiration for national liberation movements and their interpretation as anti-imperialist, a reading that was fueled by theories of internal colonialism. The Occitan scholar Robèrt Lafont set out to apply this paradigm in his book *La révolution régionaliste* (*The Regionalist Revolution*) (1967), which was quickly translated into Catalan in 1968. While the book is primarily known for Lafont's interpretation of internal colonialism and underdevelopment, it is important now to highlight that it also developed a new concept, namely a Europe of peoples, which would be used again repeatedly by Catalan nationalism, whether pro-autonomy or pro-independence. Lafont was followed closely by resistance-focused Catalan nationalists. For example, his book *Sur la France* (*On France*) (1968) was rapidly translated into Catalan and given a new title *Per una teoria de la nació* (*Toward a Theory of the Nation*) (1969). The book's foreword, which was banned, nonetheless appeared in *Nous Horitzons* (*New Horizons*), the underground cultural magazine of the PSUC. Oddly enough, Lafont's *Décoloniser en France* (*Decolonizing France*) (1971) did not get translated, probably because its analysis of French Occitania could not be extrapolated to the Catalan case.

The new Marxist pro-independence stance of the PSAN took hold slowly (though significantly in the world of culture), starting in Catalunya and spreading soon to Valencia and the Balearic Islands, ultimately making the party's expanded national scope of action a reality. In spite of its clearly pro-independence aim, the PSAN did take part in the Assemblea de Catalunya (Assembly of Catalunya) (1971), which was a cross-party platform that also drew on the participation of supporters of autonomy and federalism, while the party also began in 1972 to organize itself along various "battlefronts." In 1974, the PSAN splintered and the Provisional PSAN came into being, modeling its name on the IRA in Ireland. In short, the shift in paradigm was absolute and succeeded in revitalizing and rejuvenating the pro-independence movement, but with only a very limited degree of social impact.

## Catalan Nationalism and the Pro-Independence Movement in Spain's Transition to Democracy

In the final years of the Francoist dictatorship, Catalunya witnessed intense mobilization in the labor movement, the neighborhood association movement, and the cultural and political opposition, which to a large extent all included the political autonomy of Catalunya among their demands. This broad array of oppositional forces pushed toward a unified program of democratization with the creation in 1971 of the previously mentioned Assemblea de Catalunya (Assembly of Catalunya),[24] which included every anti-Francoist sector. The group's program called for civil liberties, amnesty for political prisoners and exiles, restoration of the statute of autonomy that had been in place during the Republic, and coordination of the anti-Francoist struggle with all the other peoples of Spain. Thus, the demand for autonomy became a shared objective among the anti-Francoist forces as a whole, but it must be also be stressed, that autonomy was understood simply as a first step toward the exercise of the right to self-determination. While it is true that only a minority was behind the organized pro-independence movement, the establishment of self-determination as an ultimate possibility indicates that the demand for autonomy was not necessarily viewed as a limit on the future. Clearly, when the dictator Franco died in 1975, Francoism had failed to achieve its aim of eradicating Catalan nationalism. Cultural offerings in the fields of publishing, theater, and movements like the Nova Cançó had each played a key role, even though they faced major challenges, were forced to use unofficial channels, and enjoyed no promotion in the major media outlets, especially television. Despite these difficulties, however, they proved crucial. Not only did Catalan nationalism not disappear, it also sought to connect itself to the global concerns and trends of the 1960s. On the political side, the call for political autonomy for Catalunya was the least common denominator among the anti-Francoist opposition.[25]

Franco's death precipitated events. The politicians of the dictatorship had no capacity to sustain a political regime that was internationally isolated (the few remaining European dictatorships had fallen in Greece in 1973 and in Portugal in 1974). Moreover, the regime faced strong internal opposition, especially in Catalunya, the Basque Country, and the more industrial areas of Spain. The Francoists tried to slow down the advance toward democracy, which appeared to be the only realistic option in Europe. The transition from dictatorship to democracy was a sum of countervailing weaknesses: the dictatorship was unable to go on, yet at the same time the opposition had not been unable to bring Franco down. The entire political dynamic revolved around changing the Spanish political-institutional system, which would have to include some solution that responded to the demands for autonomy emanating from the Basque Country and Catalunya; in particular, foreign correspondents reported on the maturity and pluralism of the anti-Francoist opposition in Catalunya, which differed from other territories insofar as it included non-Marxist sectors.[26] From Franco's death in November 1975 to the first elections of the new period in June 1977, the situation was very confusing. Juan Carlos I, the new king, sought to make a gesture of rapprochement by visiting Catalunya on his first official trip, while at the same time setting in motion a governmental committee to study a potential institutional recognition of Catalunya, similar to that of the Mancomunitat of 1914. For their part, the opposition forces mounted protests in support of freedom and autonomy in the teeth of continued police persecution. On September 11, 1976, the celebration held to commemorate Catalunya's national day, which is known as the Diada, showed the sheer scale of Catalan nationalist demands. Even though the event received authorization only at the last minute and it was not allowed to be held in Barcelona, a hundred thousand people came out to observe a Diada that had been prohibited for nearly forty years. The demands of the protest were unanimous: together with calls for freedom and democracy, the assembled multitudes also sought the restoration of the autonomy that had been lost at the end of the Civil War and the return of the president of the Generalitat in exile, the old republican Josep Tarradellas. The years of 1976 and 1977 saw intense social and political activity among groups emerging out of the ranks of anti-Francoism. Foremost among them was the Marxa per la Llibertat (March for Freedom),[27] which traveled the length and breadth of the Catalan-speaking territories for three months in the summer of 1976, calling for amnesty and self-determination, despite the prohibition of the Spanish government. Another group was the previously mentioned Congrés de Cultura Catalana (Congress of Catalan Culture),[28] which was not an ordinary congress or conference, but a cultural program that included scientific sessions with debates on the future in every field of endeavor from literature to the economy. In 1976 and 1977, it also held hundreds of events to disseminate the history that had been outlawed under Francoism, and it ran campaigns to demand official status for the Catalan language and the protection of natural heritage. All of these activities, together with the public reappearance of President Tarradellas on his return from exile, lent a great intensity to the dynamics in Catalunya, with the anti-Francoist sectors taking on an enormous public role. At that stage in the transition to democracy, the Spanish and Catalan dynamics differed sharply. Catalunya was a society that had been heavily shaped by anti-Francoism, but its real role was very much subsidiary because the balance of power was not the same in Spain, where anti-Francoism was much weaker. The anti-Franco Catalan nationalist forces who took an active part in the democratic transformation of the Spanish state did so in exchange for the recognition of their right to political autonomy, which logically left no political space for a pro-independence project.

In June 1977, Spain held its first general elections since Franco's death, but with significant restrictions still in place: the republican and pro-independence parties remained outlawed and there continued to be political prisoners. In the case of Catalunya, this meant that the Republican Left of Catalunya (ERC), the leading Catalan party in the period of the Second Spanish Republic, could not run under its own name, but only in a coalition cobbled together at the last minute. Despite the circumstances, the results revealed a number of interesting things. Elsewhere in Spain, victory went to the Unión de Centro Democrático (Union of the Democratic Center), a coalition headed by Prime Minister Adolfo Suárez and made up mostly of politicians who had served under the dictatorship. By contrast, the victory in Catalunya went to the socialist slate, and the parties calling for autonomy won nearly 80 percent of all votes cast.[29] The Esquerra de Catalunya (Left of Catalunya) coalition, which contained pro-independence groups, garnered only 3 percent of the votes, while the CUPs (Candidatura d'Unitat Popular), which included the PSAN, did not even reach 1 percent. While the foregoing results reflect what happened in the lower house of the Spanish Parliament, the results were different in the Senate, where the pacifist activist Lluís Maria Xirinachs[30] won election on a clear platform to break with Spain. In any event, the 80 percent achieved by the Catalan socialists in the lower house forced the Spanish government to restore the Generalitat and permit the return of Josep Tarradellas, which proved to be the sole act of rupture in the Spanish transition, given that it recognized a president who had been elected in exile under Republican law. The symbolic power of restoring the

Generalitat was hugely important; it served to consolidate the pro-autonomy approach and sideline other options.

In this context, the pro-independence movement was only able to occupy a minority space. A telling example took place on the Diada of 1977, one month prior to the restoration of the Generalitat. On Catalania's national day, a million people marched in the streets of Barcelona calling for a statute of autonomy and the return of the exiled president. In the morning, however, the pro-independence groups assembled thirty thousand people at the iconic Fossar de les Moreres, a memorial square in Barcelona alongside the basilica of Santa Maria del Mar, where the activist Jordi Carbonell[31] uttered a phrase that has since become emblematic: "Que la prudència no ens faci traïdors" ("May prudence not make us traitors"). The gathering at the Fossar de les Moreres was important because it showed that the pro-independence movement, even though a minority, retained some ability to rally people. In addition, the event enshrined the actual physical site of the gathering as a place of memory for the pro-independence movement and gave it a special meaning as the burial place of ordinary citizens who had been the last defenders of Catalan institutions in the War of the Spanish Succession in 1714. Carbonell's aim was thereby to recast the groups' Marxist-inspired program of national and class liberation in a historical key.

The transition to parliamentary democracy reached a legal milestone in December 1978 with the approval of the Spanish Constitution, which proclaimed the indissolubility of the Spanish nation, the existence of a single political subject—the Spanish people—and, lastly, the impossibility of Catalunya or the Basque Country ever exercising self-determination. The Spanish Constitution also established a system of regional autonomy, which was extended to all territories. As a result, any political demands from the autonomous regions were diluted through a one-size-fits-all treatment that became known as "café para todos" ("coffee for everyone"). The leading Catalan forces had played a significant role in the negotiations over the drafting of the constitution, which garnered the support of the vast majority of Catalan voters (90.5 percent voted in favor of the constitution, with a turnout of 68.1 percent). Only two voices spoke up in opposition: Heribert Barrera, a member of the lower house from the Republican Left of Catalunya, and Senator Lluís Maria Xirinacs. Barrera and Xirinacs unsuccessfully fought for the inclusion of the right to self-determination. After the approval of the constitution, Catalan parliamentarians drafted a new statute of autonomy, which also won ratification by referendum (88.1 percent voted in favor, with a turnout of 59.6 percent). This prepared the way for the first elections to the Parliament of Catalunya in March 1980. The resulting winner was the nationalist coalition Convergència i Unió (Convergence and Unity or CiU), and the coalition's leader Jordi Pujol became president of the Generalitat.

## From the Construction of an Autonomous Region to the Emergence of an Institutional Pro-Independence Movement (1980-2003)

At the time, the Catalan pro-independence movement was definitely a marginal political force. However, independence was a stated goal of the youth wing of Convergència Democràtica (Democratic Convergence or CDC), which was Jordi Pujol's party, and its ERC youth counterpart. From the approval of the statute of autonomy in 1979, Catalunya's politics, as well as the politics of Catalan nationalism, focused on the construction of an autonomous region.[32] The road was not exactly a smooth one, given the constant conflicts that broke out with the central government over matters such as the start-up of a Catalan public television broadcaster and various disagreements that arose over the interpretation of the statute of autonomy. With CDC as the senior partner, the CiU coalition settled in as the stable central force in the process of constructing the autonomous region, governing Catalunya from 1980 to 2003 under the continued leadership of Jordi Pujol,[33] while the largest opposition party, the Partit dels Socialistes de Catalunya (Socialists' Party of Catalunya or PSC-PSOE), held onto local power, especially in the Barcelona municipal government, which it controlled continuously from 1979 to 2011.

Against this backdrop, the pro-independence movement faced many challenges to become a major political agent, including its own limitations. For example, ERC was formally in favor of a federalist solution and self-determination, even as PSAN and other even smaller groups were explicitly pro-independence. ERC lacked a clear definition of its ideology and typically appeared to represent a purist, romantic nationalism far removed from the transactional nature of institutional politics. Most of ERC's leaders were seasoned old hands, and their points of reference predated the Civil War. In the 1980s, they acted primarily as a useful support for CiU. On the other hand, the groups that were explicitly pro-independence went through continual fragmentation. In the first elections to the Parliament of Catalunya in 1980, the pro-independence groups split into two candidacies: Nacionalistes d'Esquerra (Left Nationalists), which also included independents; and Bloc d'Esquerra d'Alliberament Nacional (Left Bloc for National Liberation), which enjoyed the support of Herri Batasuna, the far-left Basque nationalist coalition. For these sectors, the Basque nationalist left was a key point of reference at the time. Perhaps in imitation, the armed group Terra Lliure (Free Land) also operated at the time, while political schisms and realignments transpired one after the other, including the creation in 1984 of the Moviment de Defensa de la Terra (Movement for Defense of the Land). Broadly, this was a politics typical of minority cells,[34] with the sole exception of the Left Nationalists,[35] who tried to overcome the dynamic but proved unsuccessful in their attempt.

On the other hand, Spanish nationalism embarked on a phase of modernization in the 1980s and 1990s, seeking to update its discourse and shed its Francoist rhetoric. It used Spain's accession to the European Economic Community in 1986 as an element of internal prestige. In some sense, the Spanish nationalism that informed both the governing Partido Socialista Obrero Español (Spanish Socialist Workers' Party or PSOE) and the main opposition party, the conservative Partido Popular (People's Party or PP), took the view that once autonomy had been granted to Spain's nationalities and regions, the historical disputes would be well and truly over, subsumed into the modernization of the Spanish nation. The key was that constitutional recognition of autonomy did not, under any circumstances, amount to a recognition of the plurinationality of the Spanish state. In this respect, a sharp line was drawn and maintained between the Spanish nation and any assertion of a Catalan, Basque, or Galician nation, and the distinction cropped up repeatedly in numerous and especially sensitive conflicts, such as the linguistic normalization of the Catalan language and the recognition (even if only theoretically) of the right to self-determination.

These circumstances account for why, even though a majority of Catalan nationalists were insistent in their choice to build a government, their strategy was not inconsistent with the mobilization that occurred in some sectors of civil society. In this vein, it is necessary to mention the role of a cluster of associations that created a movement known as the Crida a la Solidaritat en defensa de la llengua, la cultura i la nació catalana (Call for Solidarity in Defense of the Catalan Language, Culture, and Nation) (1981), which organized numerous events in defense of the Catalan language, filled FC Barcelona's soccer stadium with ninety thousand attendees, and even chartered a train to Strasbourg to ensure that their demands would be heard in Europe. At the same time, there was an effort to update the nationalist discourse in publications like *Debat Nacionalista* (*Nationalist Debate*) and *Jornades de reflexió sobre el nacionalisme català a la fi del segle XX* (*Days of Reflection on Catalan Nationalism at the End of the Twentieth Century*), which carried on for several issues. In all of these platforms, openly pro-independence sectors had a significant presence, but their political aim was not made openly public in a civic platform until the founding of the Convenció per a la Independència Nacional (Convention for National Independence), which held its first gathering in 1987 under the motto "Catalunya, estat" ("Catalunya, state").

The fall of the Berlin Wall and the collapse of the Soviet Union once again put the question of nationalities on the table internationally. Statehood for the Baltic countries (Lithuania, Estonia, and Latvia) had an enormous impact on Catalan nationalism, which diminished later when violence erupted in the former Yugoslavia. However, the way in which the Baltic States gained independence was very appealing, and it spurred the Parliament of Catalunya to pass a declaration on the right to self-determination in December 1989. The declaration was a proposal of ERC that garnered the support of CiU and Iniciativa per Catalunya (Initiative for Catalunya), a political party made up of former communists. In reality, the declaration was a generic statement on the national rights of Catalunya, which its supporters did not wish to see relinquished.

In the evolution of an explicitly pro-independence force with electoral impact and institutional presence, it is necessary to train the spotlight on ERC,[36] the long-standing left-wing republican party that had governed Catalunya during the Second Spanish Republic but had been marginal during the transition to democracy. As noted earlier, ERC was critical of the Spanish Constitution and broke with the political consensus of the time. Though ERC did not declare that it was explicitly pro-independence, its chief criticism of the Spanish Constitution was that it recognized only the sovereignty of the Spanish people, thereby denying the sovereignty of the Catalan people. ERC did call for Catalan sovereignty, but its proposal was federalist in nature. As indicated before, there were pro-independence groups at the same time who had even less weight electorally and whose political culture was remote from that of the old republicans. Their fundamental differences were both ideological and generational. ERC leaders were fiercely anti-communist, and their nationalism was rooted in the 1930s. The pro-independence groups were largely young students and intellectuals with Marxist political training. Their languages and points of reference were starkly different: ERC spoke of Catalunya and made occasional references to the Balearic Islands and Valencia, but it did not adopt the entirety of the Catalan-speaking territories as its national scope of action, which was a crucial aspect for the pro-independence Marxists. ERC reached a high point in 1980, when it won roughly 10 percent of the votes and gained the speakership of the Parliament of Catalunya. However, ERC's more-or-less explicit support for the conservative Catalan nationalism of CiU and Jordi Pujol plunged the party into a crisis that became a turning point in its fortunes.

Young leaders in the Marxist pro-independence ranks joined the old party. A prominent example was Josep Lluís Carod-Rovira. The entry of this group triggered a major shift: ERC became an explicitly pro-independence party, and in the next date with the ballot box, the municipal elections of 1987, the party's election slogan was "Ara, els ajuntaments per la independencia" ("Now, town halls for independence"). ERC's slate of candidates also included a well-known activist, Àngel Colom, who had led a civic organization mentioned earlier, the Crida a la Solidaritat (Call for Solidarity). In addition, the party expanded its national scope of action to the Catalan-speaking territories as a whole, and it set up organizations in Valencia, the Balearic Islands, and Northern Catalunya (in the French Roussillon), sparking notable conflicts with nationalist groups in those territories. While ERC had only a token presence outside Catalunya, the significance was clear. For the Catalan parliamentary elections of 1992, ERC's slogan was succinct and direct: "Cap a la independència" ("Toward independence"). The theoretical underpinnings of the new project, which included specific demands, such as an economic agreement like one enjoyed by the Basque Country, were spelled out in the first volume of ideological content sponsored by the party (*República catalana*, Llibres de l'Índex, 1992). The book's content is crucial to understanding the new foundations of the revitalized pro-independence movement. These new foundations were at once pragmatic and utopian: pragmatic because they endeavored to start from Catalan society as it really was, taking into consideration the impact of the consumer society, mass immigration, and the growing weight of the Spanish state in Catalan society; and utopian in the sense that they put forward a proposal for a Catalan republic that would strengthen the notion of citizenship and give momentum to its own cultural and communication space, setting in motion a federal arrangement for the entirety of the Catalan-speaking territories. The most innovative aspect was an effort to come up with a solution to the national integration of inhabitants of immigrant origin that would eschew any direct identification between language and nationality. In addition, the new ERC was able to claim responsibility for disbanding the small, armed group Terra Lliure (Free Land), heightening the credibility of its peaceful pro-independence project.

ERC's generational renewal and the overhaul of its discourse, which was now clearly pro-independence and more distant from CiU, resulted in improved election results (from a low point of 4.1 percent in 1988 to 7.9 percent in 1992, 9.5 percent in 1996, and 8.7 percent in 1999). Nevertheless, ERC went through a difficult period when an odd split occurred in its leadership, and Àngel Colom and Pilar Rahola left to found the short-lived Partit per la Independència (Party for Independence) (1996). Overcoming this temporary setback in the elections of 1999, ERC took advantage of the fact that agreements struck between the governing PP in Madrid and the ruling CiU in Barcelona were weakening the Catalan coalition. ERC tempered its discourse and bolstered its support, chiefly by proposing the creation of a new statute of autonomy to overcome the limitations of the one approved by referendum in 1979. Notably, the statute of 1979 was celebrating its twentieth anniversary in 1999. Thus, it was time to take stock, and the only parties to call for reform were ERC and Iniciativa per Catalunya (the former communists and greens).[37] In this climate of stocktaking, one matter that grew in importance was the issue of taxation.[38] With this key proposal in its platform, ERC stood again in the Catalan parliamentary elections of 2003 and secured a previously unimaginable result (winning 16 percent of the votes and becoming the third most-voted party), which enabled it to tip the parliamentary scales, in favor of a new three-party coalition government with the socialists and former communists that was fully committed to drafting a new statute of autonomy. This marked the first time that a pro-independence party formed part of the government of the Generalitat and possessed the ability to achieve its primary short-term objective: a new statute of autonomy. ERC had reached the end of a long road that had led from the margins of politics to a capacity to exert an impact on institutions, thus marking the beginning of a new phase in Catalan politics and the drive for independence.

## Bibliography


Alquézar, Ramon. *Esquerra Republicana de Catalunya. 70 anys d'història. 1931-2001.* Barcelona: Columna, 2002.

Aracil, Rafael and Antoni Segura. *Memòria de la transició a Espanya i Catalunya.* Barcelona: Edicions de la Universitat de Barcelona, 2000.

Archilés, Ferran. *Una singularitat amarga. Joan Fuster I el relat de la identitat valenciana.* Catarroja: Afers, 2012.

Batista, Antoni, and Josep Playà. *La gran conspiració. Crònica de l'Assemblea de Catalunya.* Barcelona: Empúries, 1991.

Balcells, Albert. *Catalan Nationalism: Past and Present.* London: Macmillan, 1996.

Bassa, David, Carles Castellanos, and Raimon Soler. *L'independentisme català (1979-1994).* Barcelona: Llibres de l'Índex, 1995.

Benet, Josep. *L'intent franquista de genocidi cultural contra Catalunya.* Barcelona: Publicacions de l'Abadia de Montserrat, 1995.

*Busquets i Grabulosa, Lluís. Xirinacs. El profetisme radical i noviolent.* Barcelona: Balasch editor, 2017.

Cabana, Franeesc et. al. *Catalunya i Espanya. Una relació económica i fiscal a revisar.* Barcelona: Proa, 1998.

Calvet, Josep, and Oriol Luján. *Poble català, posa't a caminar. 40 anys de la Marxa de la Llibertat.* Barcelona: Angle Editorial, 2016.

Canals, Enric. *Pujol Catalunya. El consell de guerra a Jordi Pujol.* Barcelona: Pòrtic, 2013.

Carbonell, Jordi. *Entre l'amor i la lluita. Memòries.* Barcelona: Proa, 2010.

Colomer, Josep Maria. *La idea de nació en el pensament polític a Catalunya (1939-1979).* Barcelona: L'Avenç, 1984.

Crexell, Joan. *Els fets del Palau i el consell de guerra a Jordi Pujol.* Barcelona: La Magrana, 1982.

Culla, Joan B. *El pal de paller. Convergència Democràtica de Catalunya (1974-2000).* Barcelona: Pòrtic, 2001.

Culla, Joan B. *Esquerra Republicana de Catalunya, 1931-2012. Una història política.* Barcelona: Edicions La Capana, 2013.

Díaz i Esculies, Daniel. *El Front Nacional de Catalunya (1939-1947).* Barcelona: La Magrana, 1983.

Domingo, Andreu. *Catalunya al mirall de la immigració. Demografia i identitat nacional.* Barcelona: L'Avenç, 2014.

Dowling, Andrew. *Catalunya Since the Spanish Civil War. Reconstructing the Nation.* Eastbourne: Sussex Academic Press, 2012.

Dowling, Andrew. "Political Cultures, Ruptures, and Continuity in Catalunya under the Franco Regime." In *Funcions del passat en la cultura catalana contemporània. Institucionalització, representacions i identitat,* edited by Josep-Anton Fernández and Jaume Subirana, 221-239. Lleida: Punctum, 2015.

Ferré, Carme. *Intel·lectualitat i cultura resistents. Serra d'Or (1959-1977).* Cabrera de Mar: Galerada, 2000.

Fuster, Jaume. *El Congrés de Cultura Catalana. Què és i què ha estat?* Barcelona: Laia, 1978.

Guillamet, Jaume. *El desafiament català. Un relat internacional de la transició.* Barcelona: L'Avenç, 2014.

Juliá, Santos. *Historias de las dos Españas.* Madrid: Taurus, 2004.

Lladonosa, Mariona. *Nosaltres els catalans. Del catalanisme catòlic al pujolisme.* Barcelona: Publicacions de l'Abadia de Montserrat, 2019.

Lo Cascio, Paola. *Nacionalisme i autogovern. Catalunya 1980-2003.* Catarroja: Afers, 2008.

Marín, Martí. *Josep Maria de Porcioles. Catalanisme, clientelisme i franquisme.* Barcelona: Base, 2005.

Molinero, Carme, and Pere Ysàs. *Els anys del PSUC. El partit de l'antifranquisme (1956-1981).* Barcelona: L'Avenç, 2010.

Morales, Mercè. *La Generalitat de Josep Irla i l'exili polític català.* Barcelona: Base, 2008.

Núñez Seixas, Xosé M. "Nuevos y viejos nacionalistas: la cuestión territorial en el tardofranquismo." *Ayer* 68, (2007): 68-73.

Pi i Sunyer, Carles. *Memòries de l'exili. El Consell Nacional de Catalunya, 1940-1945.* Barcelona: Curial, 1978.

Piñol, Josep Maria. *El nacionalcatolicisme a Catalunya i la resistència (1926-1966).* Barcelona: Edicions 62, 1993.

Poblet, Francesc. *Nacionalistes d'Esquerra (1979-1984).* Barcelona: Fundació Josep Irla, 2004.

Riquer, Borja de. *La dictadura de Franco.* Madrid: Marcial Pons, 2010.

Rubiralta, Fermí. *Orígens i desenvolupament del PSAN (1969-1974)*. Barcelona: La Magrana, 1988.

Sabaté, Flocel. *Historical Analysis of the Catalan Identity*. Bern: Peter Lang, 2015.

Sánchez Cervelló, Josep. *La Segunda República en el exilio (1939-1977)*. Barcelona: Planeta, 2011.

Santacana, Carles. *El franquisme i els catalans. Els informes del Consejo Nacional del Movimiento (1962-1971)*. Catarroja: Afers, 2000.

Santacana, Carles. "Una lectura franquista de la cultura catalana als anys quaranta." In *Entre el malson i l'oblit. L'impacte del franquisme en la cultura a Catalunya i les Balears (1936-1960)*, edited by Carles Santacana, 56-61. Catarroja: Afers, 2013.

Santacana, Carles. "Pensar Cataluña desde el franquismo," In *Naciones y estado. La cuestión española*, edited by Ferran Archilés and Ismael Saz, 171-188. València: Publicacions de la Universitat de València, 2014.

Santacana, Carles. *Josep Tarradellas. L'Exili 2 (1954-1977)*. Barcelona: Dau, 2015.

Saz, Ismael. *España contra España. Los nacionalismos franquistas*. Madrid: Marcial Pons, 2003.

Termes, Josep, and Jordi Casassas. *El nacionalisme com a ideología. Materials de treball i estudi*. Barcelona: CETC/Proa, 1995.

Tubella, Imma, and Eduard Vinyamata. *Les nacions de l'Europa capitalista*. Barcelona: La Magrana, 1977.

"Vint anys de l'Estatut d'Autonomia de Catalunya," In Ideas. Revista de Temes Contemporanis 4 (1999).

## NOTES

1 For an overview, see the corresponding chapters in Albert Balcells, *Catalan Nationalism: Past and Present* (London: Palgrave Macmillan, 1996).

2 For a general view, see Borja de Riquer, *La dictadura de Franco* (Madrid: Marcial Pons, 2010).

3 The nationalism put into practice by Franco's dictatorship contained fascist elements and elements of National Catholicism. For a fundamental examination, see Ismael Saz, *España contra España. Los nacionalismos franquistas* (Madrid: Marcial Pons, 2003). Another work, which focuses on the world of intellectuals, is also useful: Santos Juliá, *Historias de las dos Españas* (Madrid, Taurus, 2004).

4 For a stocktaking of the different forms of persecution directed against Catalan nationalism, see Josep Benet, *L'intent franquista de genocidi cultural contra Catalunya* (Barcelona: Publicacions de l'Abadia de Montserrat, 1995).

5 This line of reasoning can be followed in Carles Santacana, "Pensar Cataluña desde el franquismo," in *Naciones y estado. La cuestión española*, ed. Ferran Archilés and Ismael Saz (València: Publicacions de la Universitat de València, 2014), 171-188.

6 A clear example of this distortion occurred in 1945 on the centenary of the Catalan poet Jacint Verdaguer, who was commemorated very differently by the Franco regime, the Catalan nationalist resistance in Spain, and the exiles abroad. See Carles Santacana, "Una lectura franquista de la cultura catalana als anys quaranta," in *Entre el mason i l'oblit. L'impacte del franquisme en la cultura a Catalunya i les Balears (1936-1960)*, ed. Carles Santacana (Catarroja: Afers, 2013), 56-61.

7 On Irla's actions in those years, see Mercè Morales, *La Generalitat de Josep Irla i l'exili polític català* (Barcelona: Base, 2008).

8 See Carles Santacana, *Josep Tarradellas. L'Exili 2 (1954-1977)* (Barcelona: Dau, 2015).

9 See Josep Sánchez Cervelló, *La Segunda República en el exilio (1939-1977)* (Barcelona: Planeta, 2011).

10 See Carles Pi i Sunyer, *Memòries de l'exili. El Consell Nacional de Catalunya, 1940-1945* (Barcelona: Curial, 1978).

11 See Daniel Díaz Esculies, *El Front Nacional de Catalunya (1939-1947)* (Barcelona: La Magrana, 1983).

12 For a focused look at progressive Catholicism, see Josep M. Piñol, *El nacionalcatolicisme a Catalunya i la resistència (1926-1966)* (Barcelona: Edicions 62, 1993). For a more in-depth examination of the convergence between Catholicism and militant Catalan nationalism, see Mariona Lladonosa, *Nosaltres els catalans. Del catalanisme catòlic al pujolisme* (Barcelona: Publicacions de l'Abadia de Montserrat, 2019).

13 For a portrait of Porcioles as mayor, see Martí Marín, *Josep Maria Porcioles. Catalanisme, clientelisme i franquisme* (Barcelona: Base, 2005).

14 See Joan Crexell, *Els fets del Palau I el consell de guerra a Jordi Pujol* (Barcelona: La Magrana, 1982). Also, Enric Canals, *Pujol Catalunya. El consell de guerra a Jordi Pujol* (Barcelona: Pòrtic, 2013).

15 The role of the PSUC was very important in the reconstruction of left-wing Catalan nationalism in the 1960s and in the popular unity platforms of the anti-Francoist opposition. See Carme Molinero et al., *Els anys del PSUC. El partit de l'antifranquisme (1956-1981)* (Barcelona: L'Avenç, 2010).

16 Their chief action was to set up a secret committee of the National Council of the Movement, a body that was part of the one-party Falange. See Carles Santacana, *El franquisme i els catalans. Els informes del Consejo Nacional del Movimiento (1962-1971)* (Catarroja: Afers, 2000).

17 For a broad view of the resurgence over a longer period of time, see Andrew Dowling, *Catalunya Since the Spanish Civil War: Reconstructing the Nation* (Eastbourne: Sussex Academic Press, 2012). This seminal work covers the entire chronology of the present paper.

18 For a general view of the overhaul of approaches within the various ideological strands of Catalan nationalism, see Josep Maria Colomer, *La idea de nació en el pensament polític a Catalunya (1939-1979)* (Barcelona: L'Avenç, 1984).

19 The literature on Joan Fuster is vast. One of the most thought-provoking works is by Ferran Archilés, *Una singularitat amarga. Joan Fuster i el relat de la identitat valenciana* (Catarroja: Afers, 2012).

20 For a look at the crucial role played by this publication in the shaping of a Catalan nationalist and anti-Francoist culture, see Carme Ferré, *Intel·lectualitat i cultura resistents. Serra d'Or (1959-1977)* (Cabrera de Mar: Galerada, 2000).

21 For an overview of the debates on immigration within Catalan society, see Andreu Domingo, *Catalunya al mirall de la immigració. Demografia i identitat nacional* (Barcelona: L'Avenç, 2014).

22 For more on the PSAN, see Fermí Rubiralta, *Orígens i desenvolupament del PSAN (1969-1974)* (Barcelona: La Magrana, 1988). Also of interest is a comparative look at the

phenomenon of the new nationalisms. See Xosé M. Núñez Seixas, "Nuevos y viejos nacionalistas: la cuestión territorial en el tardofranquismo," *Ayer* 68, (2007), 68-73.

23 Ferrer, in his model of new nationalisms, linked the Catalan case to the other examples in Europe. See his foreword in Imma Tubella et al., *Les nacions de l'Europa capitalista* (Barcelona: La Magrana, 1977), 18-23.

24 See Antoni Batista et al., *La gran conspiració. Crònica de l'Assemblea de Catalunya* (Barcelona: Empúries, 1991).

25 For an analysis of the continuities and breaks in the political culture of Catalan nationalism between 1939 and 1975, see Andrew Dowling, "Political Cultures, Ruptures, and Continuity in Catalunya under the Franco Regime," in *Funcions del passat en la cultura catalana contemporània. Institucionalització, representacions i identitat,* ed. Josep-Anton Fernández and Jaume Subirana (Lleida: Punctum, 2015), 221-239.

26 The impetus of anti-Francoism in Catalunya during the transition to democracy is well reflected in the reports of foreign correspondents collected in Jaume Guillamet, *El desafiament català. Un relat internacional de la transició* (Barcelona: L'Avenç, 2014).

27 See Josep Calvet et al., *Poble català, posa't a caminar. 40 anys de la Marxa de la Llibertat* (Barcelona: Angle editorial, 2016).

28 Jaume Fuster, *El Congrés de Cultura Catalana. Qué és i què ha estat?* (Barcelona: Laia, 1978).

29 For a full breakdown of the results, together with a timeline and supporting materials, see Rafael Aracil et al., *Memòria de la transició a Espanya i Catalunya* (Barcelona: Edicions Universitat de Barcelona, 2000).

30 Xirinacs was also a prominent figure in the protests against the dictatorship and played a critical role during the transition to democracy. He exerted a strong influence on the pro-independence movement at a number of moments. See Lluís Busquets i Gabrulosa. *Xirinacs. El profetisme radical i noviolent* (Barcelona: Balasch editor, 2017).

31 For an examination of the long career of this intellectual and his significance in the anti-Francoist opposition and the pro-independence movement, see Jordi Carbonell, *Entre l'amor i la lluita. Memòries* (Barcelona, Proa, 2010).

32 This issue is covered by an extensive literature. As a starting point, see Paola Lo Cascio, *Nacionalisme i autogovern. Catalunya 1980-2003* (Catarroja: Afers, 2008).

33 Jordi Pujol exercised hyper-leadership, successfully uniting diverse sectors that ranged from a pro-independence minority to moderate Catalan nationalists, in order to meet the goal of becoming the central force in the country. Beyond the published biographies of Pujol, the evolution of this political space is addressed in Joan B. Culla, *El pal de paller. Convergència Democràtica de Catalunya (1974-2000)* (Barcelona: Pòrtic, 2001).

34 See David Bassa, Carles Benítez, Carles Castellanos, Raimon Soler, *L'independentisme català (1979-1994)*, (Barcelona: Llibres de l'Índex, 1995).

35 See Francesc Poblet, *Nacionalistes d'Esquerra (1979-1984)* (Barcelona: Fundació Josep Irla, 2004).

36 See Joan B. Culla, *Esquerra Republicana de Catalunya, 1931-2012. Una història política* (Barcelona: Pòrtic, 2013). Also, Ramon Alquézar. *Esquerra Republicana de Catalunya. 70 anys d'història. 1931-2001* (Barcelona: Columna, 2002). For a more in-depth look specifically at generational and political change, see Carles Santacana, "El pensament

nacionalista d'ERC," in *El nacionalisme com a ideologia. Materials de treball i estudi,* ed. Josep Termes y Jordi Casassas (Barcelona: CETC/Proa, 1995), 143-155.

37 For the different positions of the political parties, see "Vint anys de l'Estatut d'Autonomia de Catalunya," Idees. Revista de Temes Contemporanis, 4 (1999).

38 The issue of taxation was raised by a host of economists reflecting a range of ideological leanings (CiU, PSC, ERC), including future members of the Catalan government. See *Catalunya i Espanya. Una relació económica i fiscal a revisar* (Barcelona: Proa, 1998).

# 8

# The Politicization of Catalanism and the Birth of the Catalan Independence Movement (1880-1939)

*Giovanni C. Cattini and Daniel Roig*

Outside Catalunya and the various lands with Catalan culture, little is known about the history or social significance that Catalanism has had in the construction of contemporary Catalunya. This factor is no small matter because Catalanism has been the cornerstone from which Catalan civil society has mostly expressed itself. Of course, in its beginnings, the persistence of Catalan particularism among the popular classes and the vindication of their own language, which is also as a language of culture, was of vital importance for its further expansion. Especially from 1833, with the publication of *Oda a la Patria* by Barcelona writer Bonaventura Carles Aribau: it is a poem with high symbolic content that, while illustrating the diglossia already existing among the Catalan ruling classes, with the adoption of Spanish as a preeminent language, also meant the emergence of a new cultural and literary movement in Catalunya, the *Renaixença*.

After that, a whole scope of intellectuals and writers became part of this background stream. And although in its origins it was a rather culturally elitist movement, developing at the same time as Romanticism and nostalgic about the old glories and exploits of the medieval Catalan past, soon the awareness of a culture and differentiated identity, with clear national connotations, permeated the whole of Catalan society.

This culturalist line with language as the central axis continued to set the tone throughout the nineteenth century. More importantly, its consolidation and social expansion were essential for Catalanism to end up moving to the political arena during the last third of the 1800s. There is no doubt that when it took off, the revolutionary political experience that had been taking place since the late 1860s also played an important role. This especially occurred after the intense period of high political voltage that marked the first attempt, in 1873, to implement a democratic, federal republic in Spain. However, with a few exceptions, under no circumstances did these political expressions yet imply the vindication of full national independence. That does not deny, however, that since then, political Catalanism as a whole has been based on a minimum common denominator: distrust of a state of a centripetal nature, which does not respect regional and historical singularities, and wary—if not hostile—of the economic interests of the region and of Catalan elites, the latter being more prone to an industrializing model than to the agriculture-based structure typical of most of the rest of the state.

In this way the "Catalan problem," or the "Catalan question," as it came to be called—following the mark left by the Cuban conflict—soon ended up manifesting some of the main flaws of the Spanish nationalization process: its territorial articulation and the adoption of a model of cultural uniformity based on the Castilian pattern. In this perspective, the political responses that Catalanism gave were not, in fact, very different from those that were to arise within so many other European national minorities—grafts within multinational states and empires—with tensions of different kinds, and which, at the same time, were also to bring their claims to the arena of the nascent mass politics.

So, while some of these aspects would merit some further clarification, this text is inevitably much more modest in scope. However, it offers more than just an approach to the beginnings of the process of politicization, which was a major feature of Catalanism in the late nineteenth century. It also provides a succinct analysis of how the evolution toward nationalist and pro-independence positions took place, and how those same positions also had notably different nuances and tones throughout the first third of the twentieth century. In fact, while some of these points have already been the subject of great interest in Catalan historiography for decades—with a certain contribution from Spanish, and to a very lesser extent French, historiography—the issue, however, has not had as much impact in other historiographic areas. There are still major gaps in English and for English speakers on the subject. All of which is very much in contrast with the vastly increasing number of studies on the history of political Catalanism and Catalan independence that have appeared over the last two decades in both Catalan and Spanish, and which have increasingly provided a much broader, completer view of Catalanism as a social and political phenomenon.

## The Bourbon Restoration in Catalunya and the Shaping of the Catalan Political Movement (1874-1901)

After the *Sexenio democrático* ("six years of democracy"—1868–1874), and the ephemeral first Republic (1873–1874), a coup brought the Bourbons back to the throne in the shape of Alfonso XII. The new Restoration regime led to the prominence of two new political parties: the liberals, led by Práxedes Sagasta and represented in Catalunya by the mayor of Barcelona, Francesc Rius y Taulet, and writer Víctor Balaguer; and the conservatives, led by Antonio Cánovas del Castillo, whose Catalan associates were politician Manuel Duran y Bas and writer Joan Mañé Flaquer. Initially, the Catalan bourgeoisie had supported the restoration of the monarchy, but it soon disagreed with the tariff policies imposed by the Madrid governments, which led to the bankruptcy of Catalan companies, not strong enough to compete with English or French goods. Added to this was the desire to promote a campaign of legal uniformity that threatened the continuity of Catalan civil law; it was a factor that would lead to the politicization of a movement that, until now, had merely claimed linguistic and cultural singularities.

In this context, three large political "families" could be defined as Catalanists: first, the sector that came from the federalists, whose point of reference was Valentí Almirall, founder in 1879 of *the Diari Català*, the first journal in the Catalan language; second, Catalans linked to the *Renaixensa* and whose inspiration were playwright Angel Guimer and writer Pere Aldavert; and, third, the so-called "vigatà" sector headed by the Reverend Jaume Collell, who structured a Catalan Catholic regionalism around the weekly *La Veu de Catalunya*, supported by a large sector of the Catalan Church.[1]

The coexistence of these different spirits was not easy. However, the first unitary milestones of the Catalan movement were the organization of two Catalan congresses (1880 and 1882-1883) and the foundation of the Catalan Centre (1882), a Catalan entity that ended up promoting the well-known *Memorial de Greuges*. This text, presented to King Alfonso XII in 1885, was one of the first political actions of Catalanism: it defended decentralization of the state, protectionist economic policy, and the recognition of the cultural, linguistic, and legal particularities of the region. In addition, the mobilizations against free trade led, in July 1886, to public delivery of the first openly independence speech, by left-wing Republican Josep Narcís Roca y Farreras, at a public meeting rejecting economic agreements with Britain planned by Sagasta's government.

However, during the early 1880s, the great protagonist and dynamist of Catalan discourse and practice was undoubtedly Valentí Almirall (1841-1904), a former federalist republican who had been very active since the *Sexenio democrático*. According to his lights, the solution for Catalunya's place in Spain was regional autonomy, feasible in either a republican or a monarchical regime. To this end, Almirall tried to get the Centre Català to take part in the elections. But its failure in the 1886 legislative elections was the beginning of its decline:

the following year, almost 40 percent of the members split to create the Lliga de Catalunya, a name with clear Irish resonances. La Lliga had the support of the rather radical sector, linked to the magazine *Renaixensa,* and also of various different entrepreneurs and industrialists. But above all, it was supported by the university students at the Centre Escolar Català such as Enric Prat de la Riba, Francesc Cambó, Josep Puig i Cadafalch, and Lluís Duran Ventosa.

The Universal Exhibition of Barcelona of 1888 was held at this time. The involvement of Barcelona's leading groups in the organization responded to a wide range of reasons, ranging from the desire to impose Barcelona and Catalunya as the economic capital of the whole backward state, to the desire to make internationally visible the birth of a thriving metropolitan center. In this context, the arrival of the Queen Regent in Barcelona to inaugurate the Universal Exhibition was used by la Lliga to organize an act of vindication in the name of defending the moral and material interests of Catalunya. In that way, the Lliga gave the sovereign Maria Cristina of Habsburg Lorraine its *Missatge a la Reina Regent,* very similar to the claims presented in the *Memorial de Greuges.*

At the same time in the late 1880s, the main stimulus for the Catalan movement was discussion on interpretations of the Civil Code in reaction to the threats facing the various different foral rights in Spain. This new attempt at political standardization stirred Catalan society up, and it quickly mobilized with a wave of demonstrations in defense of Catalan law that spread all over Catalunya, and which eventually prompted José Canalejas, the new minister of justice, to review the controversial articles.[2]

This moment of patriotic effervescence had its zenith in the foundation of the Catalanist Union (UC) in 1891. At its first public assembly, held on March 25, 26, and 27, 1892, a new political program was released: *Bases per a la Constitució Regional catalana,* better known as *Bases de Manresa.* In reality, the document was not a constitution, but rather an instrument for spreading the Catalan creed. The first Base was legislated on the reach of central power, while the other sixteen referred to regional power. Thus, while the text lacked doctrine, any real possibility, or politics, it did demonstrate the vitality of a vindicative movement that, over the years, was to become one of the main actors in Catalan political life.

Be that as it may, with the Spanish-American War and the loss of the last colonies in 1898 (Cuba, Puerto Rico, and the Philippines), two essential events for the subsequent definition of the Catalan political framework took place: the vindication of the economic agreement; and the *Tancament de Caixes* ("box closure") movement, which was to erupt when the economic agreement not only did not take place but, to the contrary, in 1899, the minister of finance's budgets increased tax pressure. Faced with popular irritation over these events, Prat de la Riba understood the evolution of the times and the need to move away from the more dogmatic UC positions, contrary to taking part in elections. This paradigm shift was the one that allowed the electoral success of the Catalan candidacy of 1901, the basis for the foundation of the Regionalist Lliga.[3]

### The First Steps of Catalanism in Institutions (1901-1914)

The electoral triumph of 1901 showed that Catalanism had managed to connect with a small part of Barcelona's electorate and some prominent representatives of employers in industry. Soon after, la Lliga would also win some seats in the Barcelona city council. However, this presence was still very small and always lesser than Unión Republicana's, led by Alejandro Lerroux: a journalist and politician of Andalusian origin, pro-Spanish, known for his demagogic style, and able to maintain considerable support in popular neighborhoods of the city. In the rest of Catalunya, monarchical Caciquism still held sway, although gradually it would lose force to the growing Lliga and other alternatives of republican nature.

And another remarkable political phenomenon was the emergence of a wide range of associations of different kinds, many of them sympathetic to UC, but which were clearly already pro-independence. Their influence would be seen in the medium term, even if initially most of them had no more than a few dozen members. Meanwhile, during the first years of the century, their contribution was to provide radical Catalanism with symbolism and a particular collective imagination about the Catalan issue. But also, they provided the need to provide Catalan nationalism with a much more combative version to counteract the moderate, institutional vocation of the Lliga Regionalista.

In this sense, and even taking into account its heterogeneity, the Catalan movement had a few common denominators in its use of the history of medieval splendors as an origin, and the loss of freedoms in 1714 as justification for their claims.[4] That led to one of the national symbols becoming the commemoration of September 11—the day of the fall of Barcelona to the Bourbon troops of Felipe V—and against which the authorities became accustomed to reacting with varying degrees of force, depending on the intensity of the political context in which the "Diada" was held. In 1901, for example, young radicals who laid laurel wreaths at the foot of the statue of Rafael Casanova—one of the national heroes from 1714—were arrested. It was in the wake of those arrests that the first association for Catalan pro-independence prisoners, *La Reixa*, was formed to help all those arrested *"per actes realitzats fent manifestació d'amor a la pàtria catalana."*[5] At this same period, and in addition to that anniversary, the "Cant del Segadors" became the national anthem, and the *Senyera* the national flag, thanks to an extensive network of choral and Athenaeum associations that acted as a circuit for the transmission of Catalan ideas and symbols.[6]

In the political sphere, in November 1905 there were some events of great importance: some three hundred officers of the Barcelona garrison stormed the workshops and the offices of the satirical magazine *Cu-Cut!* and *La Veu de Catalunya,* which was associated with the Lliga. The military claimed to have responded to the affront of a humorous vignette that had ridiculed them. Undoubtedly, the events created a wave of outrage and a protest by Catalan deputies in the Spanish Parliament, which responded by condemning Catalanists and passing a Special Jurisdictions Act that placed crimes against the homeland and its symbols under military jurisdiction. Faced with this measure, Catalan deputies and prominent Republicans, such as the former president of the first Spanish Republic Nicolás Salmerón, ended up abandoning the chamber in protest. It was at this juncture that a new electoral coalition appeared in which all Catalan formations joined except that of the Lerroux republicans: "Solidaritat Catalana" (1906). Its success was seen in the elections of April 1907 when the Catalan coalition took forty-one of the forty-four seats at stake in Catalunya, with almost 70 percent of the electoral census (male) having participated.

At this time, Prat de la Riba was elected president of the Provincial Council of Barcelona. Thanks to Solidaritat, Catalanism had come into contact with the masses, had an electoral success, and controlled an institution with provincial competences. Prat de la Riba also had a vision of state (at the regional level, since at no time was he to promote political secession), with an ambitious program and a clear idea on which areas of preferential action were needed. His best supports were the Youth Section of the Lliga Regionalista, which acted as a channel to prepare the young people from the best-educated middle classes; as well as so-called *noucentisme,* an intellectual movement promoted by the Catalan writer and philosopher Eugeni d'Ors, who suggested responding to the crisis of classical liberalism with determined participation in public affairs and even in politics.[7]

Finally, this climate of euphoria was broken between 1908 and 1909 by both internal and external divergences. On the one hand, the crisis of the solidarity movement again laid clear the tensions between conservative and progressive Catalanists. On the other hand, a second, much more serious fact was to have catastrophic effects on Catalan life in general: in July 1909, growing social protest against the mobilization of reservists to be sent to Morocco exploded in five days of extreme violence, with hundreds of barricades and some eighty religious buildings burned. The revolt—called "separatist" by some media and different politicians of Madrid—ended up being suppressed by the army, leaving almost a hundred dead, dozens wounded, and different shootings—among others, that of the Mason teacher and philo-anarchist (philosophical anarchist) Francesc Ferrer i Guardia—in addition to declaring more than a hundred republican and lay centers and entities subversive.[8]

Finally, in the political sphere, the effects of a tragic week were also decisive. The Lliga Regionalista suffered a significant electoral setback because of its collusion with the repression. Workers eventually founded the National Labour Confederation (1910) with anarcho-syndicalist ideology. Part of republicanism would continue political organization around Lerroux for a time. In turn, left-wing Catalanists set up a new platform, the Republican Nationalist Federal Union (UFNR), which had some electoral success in 1910-1911. A success, in short, that would not only be limited to the political sphere: republican culture also continued to be expressed through a growing network of casinos, centers, and Athenaeums, which combined politics (nonelectoral), leisure, education, and consumer cooperatives.

### Toward the Constitution of Catalan Self-government: The Commonwealth of Catalunya (1914-1923)

From July 1911 to December 1913, Catalan and Spanish politics were dominated by negotiations for a law which would allow provincial delegations to collaborate. They led to a decree that allowed the creation of provincial commonwealths, resulting in the creation, in April 1914, of the Commonwealth of Catalunya, the only one in the whole of the Spanish state.

In this sense, it is significant that the struggle to achieve this regional body was capitalized by the Regionalist Lliga, which from 1912 became the hegemonic electoral force in Catalunya. The spectacular new rise of regionalism frightened UFNR Catalanist republicanism, which wanted to counter it by forming an electoral pact with Lerrouxism (Pact of Sant Gervasi, 1914). But by having a spectacular failure, Republican Catalanism went into a phase of organizational fragmentation that, in fact, was not to overcome until the early 1930s. Even so, in just eleven years and with modest strength, political Catalanism had already managed to become the first force in Catalunya and had the capacity to determine the political agenda, as was to be shown by the work of the Commonwealth of Catalunya.

In this area, the most spectacular events took place in the arts. The Catalan language, for example, received strong institutional support, thanks to which bodies such as the Institut d'Estudis Catalans—founded in 1907 and the only academy of sciences that did not correspond to a state recognized by the International Union of Academies—was able to work in standardizing modern Catalan under the guidance of philologist Pompeu Fabra. But the Commonwealth also stood out in the educational and technical sphere, giving impetus to a whole network of popular libraries and a whole series of schools and agencies, such as the School of Civil Servants, the School of Teachers, the Monument Conservation and Cataloguing Service, the Geological Map Service, and the Health Studies Service, among many others. It also promoted agricultural cooperation through the School of Agriculture, as well as created a network of secondary roads and railways to help link the country together, and installed telephones in all Catalan towns.[9]

Apart from this government action, at the outbreak of the Great War the new situation brought another factor to Catalan particularity. During this period, industrial activity was extraordinarily boosted, which led to major immigration to the Barcelona area, and which definitely consolidated its leadership with respect to the whole of Catalunya: Barcelona went from 533,000 inhabitants in 1900 to one million in 1930, with considerable acceleration from 1914. This extraordinary increase in economic activity, especially involving exports to countries at war—mainly to France—produced considerable accumulations of wealth. But it also led to scarcities and increased the prices of basic goods, further widening the distance between social classes. The new rich proliferated, while the working and middle classes went through hardship and growing difficulties, a factor that led to a notable increase in trade union membership. The CNT which was to have its epicenter in Catalunya, grew from fifteen thousand members in 1915 to seventy-four thousand in 1918, and grew still more dramatically over the following year.[10]

This tension also showed in the political and ideological sphere—not only because of the passions that war brought up between supporters on one side or the other, and with very few people declaring themselves to be neutral—but also because of the new social and political tensions that made the crisis of the Restoration regime clear to see. So, while central politics responded to all this by closing Parliament, in Catalunya—with mostly pro-Allies' public opinion—this disparity of criteria ended up positioning the main Catalan party, the Lliga Regionalista, against the economic policy of the state, especially from the end of 1915.

It was at this juncture of political radicalization that the Lliga's main leader, Francesc Cambó, initiated a double strategy: on one hand, weaving complicity with other peripheral territories of the state; and on the other, finding the political alliances needed to force constitutional reform. This challenge on the part of the main Catalan leaders took place by holding an Assembly of Parliamentarians, meeting in Barcelona on July 19, 1917, with the aim of speaking about a new territorial division, among other issues. But its short-lived existence, because of the police break-in that same day, ended up creating a climate of Catalan turmoil once more. However, it was more than this that put the government in a difficult situation. A month earlier, in June, an underlying conflict within the army had also broken out in Barcelona. In fact, it was a corporate mobilization because of the living conditions of local officers, but in that context of turmoil it became a matter of state. Much more complex was the third crisis of that summer, when on August 13 the two main trade unions in Spain, the UGT and the CNT, declared a revolutionary strike, resulting in some eighty people being killed during the army's repression. This did not prevent the Lliga Regionalista, frightened by those events, from ending up initiating direct collaboration with the government, especially when in early November two members of the Lliga—Joan Ventosa i Calvell and Felip Rodés—were named as ministers, generating a dangerous split inside the Lliga.[11]

In fact, in August 1917, Catalanism had to deal with the untimely death of Prat de la Riba after the main political reference for independence—Donec Martí i Julia (1861-1917)—had died two months earlier. As president of the Commonwealth, he was replaced by another Catalanist, architect Josep Puig i Cadafalch. His presidency was one of continuity, something of merit in itself taking into account the constant boycott by the central government, as well as one of the most complex moments in Catalunya in the first third of the 1900s. This was the situation which arose at the end of the Great War, when the extraordinary stimulus it had created in Catalunya was suddenly truncated, bringing class struggle to the highest levels, with the Russian Revolution as a backdrop, and laying bare the inability of the political system to run an area like Catalunya, which during the previous years had changed radically.[12]

This radicalism in the atmosphere also affected the Commonwealth, exacerbated by the continual difficulties with the central government. In response, the School of Civil Servants was mobilized, advising on the draft for an autonomous regime—in line with Irish home rule—which was endorsed by the Catalan municipalities. The project was presented in Madrid in November 1918, but the violent response of official politics and the capital's media ended up leading to the withdrawal of Catalan parliamentarians and, again, a strong popular reaction in Catalunya. The Commonwealth did not wait to respond and consisted of a draft statute, proclaiming its readiness to implement it. The text was endorsed by 1,046 of the 1,072 Catalan townhalls (representatives of 99 percent of the total population), and ratified by the Commonwealth Assembly in January 1919, amid a context of violent clashes between radical Catalanists and pro-Spanish groups. However, the Spanish Parliament agreed once more in its discussion of the Catalan text, and categorically denied the possibility of a popular referendum in Catalunya.

A few days later, the situation was further complicated by the outbreak of the worst labor dispute in the twentieth century in Catalunya; a minor issue in the company Riegos y Fuerzas del Estado, better known as *la Canadenca*—being a subsidiary of a Canadian company—ended up paralyzing the whole of Barcelona and the surrounding areas with a mass, unprecedented strike. Although the government tried to mediate between the employer and the CNT, it could not prevent a wave of extreme violence from taking hold of the city from spring 1919.

It was in this context that the first explicitly independent political party—the Nationalist Democratic Federation (FDN)—was to suddenly appear at the beginning of 1919: a republican organization, led by a former colonel of Quixotian tints, Francesc Macià (1859–1933), who had left the army following the *Cu-Cut!* events of 1905. In the FDN, different groups of radical Catalanists came together: from old followers of Martí i Juli and left-wing republicanism from the lower middle- class, to young workers on the road to proletarianization. Although its electoral results were meager—only Macià was able to retake his seat—the mere existence of the FDN put an end to the traditional apolitical nature of Catalan separatism. In fact, its appearance was not only due to the enthusiasm aroused at that time by the Wilsonian proclamations about the right of self-determination, but also by a process of internal coming of age. However, that did not mean giving up the armed option, as was to be seen years later. Nor did it mean failing to exploit some of the most combative myths of independence, starting with the thousands of Catalan volunteers enlisted in the French Foreign Legion during the Great War, sponsored by another old Catalan independence militant, Dr. Joan Solé i Pla (1874-1950).[13] More importantly, from these same circles there were also unsuccessful attempts to send President Wilson a memorandum about Catalunya's national claims, taking advantage of his presence in Paris in early 1919.

Apart from the FDN, over time, other sectors of Catalanism—openly opposed to the Lliaga's moderation and government collaborationism—ended up radicalizing their positions about national issues. The split was to be led by younger members of the Lliga, together with former UFNR militants and republican intellectuals such as Antoni Rovira i Virgili, ending up forming a new political party in June 1922, Acció Catalana (AC). Its good results in the last elections before the dictatorship, in addition to its leaders' prestige as intellectuals, seemed to augur a successful future for it. At the same time, during that same summer of 1922, Macià transformed the FDN into a new organization, Estat Català. The following year, another group of liberal and intellectual professionals, such as Gabriel Alomar, Rafael Campalans, and Manuel Serra i Moret, founded the first socialist party in political Catalanism, the Unió Socialista de Catalunya (USC). It was in this context that General Primo de Rivera led his coup on September 13, 1923.

## Catalanism under the Dictatorship of Primo de Rivera (1923-1930)

As captain general of Catalunya, Miguel Primo de Rivera promised the bourgeoisie and local personalities that his coup would be transient, aiming to preserve public order, cleanse politics of the corruptions of Caciquism, and be respectful of the administrative decentralization of the country. Once installed in Madrid, Primo de Rivera removed all doubts. On September 18, 1923, the dictator passed a "Royal Decree against Separatism," expressly drawn up to deal with Catalan nationalism, and he initiated systematic persecution against the presence of Catalan, or any of its manifestations and symbols in education, in the public sphere, or in official institutions and bodies. At the same time, in January 1924, Alfons Sala of the Unión Monárquica was appointed president of the Commonwealth in place of Puig i Cadafalch, a step before its final closure in 1925. It was a factor that led to much of the Catalan ruling class that was sympathetic to the Lliga Regionalista becoming quickly disenchanted with the dictator. At the same time, some Castilian intellectuals associated with the magazine *La Gaceta Literaria* signed a manifesto of support for Catalan culture and language in March 1924.

On the other hand, after years of social conflict, the CNT had been greatly weakened. In March 1923, the main centrist leader, Salvador Seguí, *Noi del Sucre*, had been assassinated, and Primo de Rivera's coup faced no notable opposition from the labor movement. In fact, the union was declared illegal in May 1924, and its publication *Solidaridad Obrera* was banned. Nor were the diverse Catalan associations spared repressive action. In total, some 150 entities were closed throughout Catalunya, as were twenty regional newspapers, and in June 1925 even the Barcelona football club's ground was closed under the pretext that there had been hissing against the Spanish national anthem.[14]

Faced with this repressive spiral, a few Catalan leaders, such as Francesc Macià, went into exile, and people from the AC founded a secret radical group, the Societat d'Estudis Militars, which in fact did very little. However, radical nationalism was reactivated during this period with manifestos, plans of action (such as the failed Garraf Plot against the king in May 1925) and, especially, the aborted attempt to invade Catalunya from Prats de Molló—in French Catalunya—organized by Macià in November 1926, with the intention of making the Catalan peoples' right to national sovereignty a reality.[15] Despite the failure, the subsequent trial in Paris in January 1927 gave visibility to the Catalan claim and great notoriety to Macià, who from then on promoted a large fundraising and aid campaign for the proclamation of a Catalan Republic, especially among the Catalan communities in Argentina and Cuba.

### The Republic, Achieving Catalan Autonomy, and the Civil War (1931-1939)

The dictatorship fell in January 1930, being replaced by a somewhat more permissive military regime led by General Dámaso Berenguer, and which would soon become known as the *dictablanda*. In this new framework, the various Catalan political parties began to regroup. Of the previous forces, the Lliga Regionalista had been the one most weakened by the dictatorship. AC, after some internal problems, managed to reorganize its political sphere by the new Partit Catalanista Republicà (PRC), which journalists believed was destined for political hegemony. On the left, Estat Català—represented internally by the future Republican mayor of Barcelona, Jaume Aiguader (1882-1943), together with the social democratic group centered on the weekly *L'Opinió* and other Republican nuclei—founded the Intel·ligència d'Esquerres platform, alma mater of the pro-amnesty mobilizations for social and political prisoners, and of the demand for democratic elections. Further to the left, a new political space had been forged, driven by young independence militants: firstly, with the founding of the Partit Comunista Català in 1928; and from 1930, after its merger with Joaquim Maurin's Federació Comunista Catalana-Balear, with the creation of the Bloc Obrer Camperol, a heterodox Marxist party was to have a remarkable capacity for influence within the Catalan left.[16]

In addition to organic evolution, in March 1930 there was another significant event: the journey of Spanish intellectuals to Catalunya at the invitation of Catalans in gratitude for the support they had given them during the years of the dictatorship. This understanding facilitated Catalan presence in the so-called Pact of Donostia, which was held in this Basque city in August 1930, and which involved the participation of different Spanish republican forces.

Although there was no written record of the meeting, in Donostia the strategy to end the monarchy and proclaim the republic was finally drawn up, and commitment was agreed for future constituent parliaments to automatically accept the status of autonomy freely drafted by Catalan representatives. The agreement was also signed, in October 1930, by PSOE and UGT.

Finally, with Admiral Aznar replacing Berenguer, the municipal elections of April 12, 1931, were held, the first since 1923. La Lliga chose to shore up the monarchy, but its failure was remarkable. The PRC stood by itself with a Catalan program, which was not radical in political or social terms. The other Catalan republican groups took advantage of the unifying prestige of Macià—newly returned from exile—to create a new political formation: Esquerra Republicana de Catalunya (ERC), which was radical in the political and national spheres and, as was said at the time, had an approach to society typical of the most advanced countries. ERC was the main winner of the election: it picked up the aspirations for change ranging from the middle class to sectors of the working class. But, above all, the new Esquerra was able to connect with the age range which had joined the census since 1923, and which had not previously voted.

Be that as it may, the main Catalan characteristic on that April 14 was its rapid development and the double republican proclamation: first one without definition, the Spanish one issued by Lluís Companys; and then that of Macià, who would proclaim the Catalan Republic as *"estat integrant de la Federació Ibérica"* (a member state of the Iberian Federation). This last act caused alarm in the provisional government of the republic, which on April 17 had sent a commission of three ministers to convince Macià to turn back, assume the presidency of an interim Generalitat, and accept the importance of the constituent period over any other consideration.

For many prestigious pro-independence activists, this "withdrawl" of support for the Catalan Republic was a complete betrayal by the old pro-independence leader. Its most immediate consequence was the fragmentation of the political sphere that, until then, had remained loyal to Macià. So, while the bulk of the militants followed in his steps, coexistence with other ERC political groups was not always easy. In fact, even before April 14, what was to be one of the leading anti-Macià pro-independence organizations had been founded: Nosaltres Sols! (the Catalan translation of the Irish *Sinn Fein)*. It was set up in early 1931 by a militant much younger than Macia, Daniel Cardona i Civit (1890-1943), in favor of an insurrectional route to achieve independence.

In this context and following what had agreed with the government of the Republic, the Generalitat launched the draft of its statute: on August 2, the so-called *Estatut de Núria* was approved in a plebiscite with 75 percent participation and 99.45 percent votes in favor, although women were not entitled to vote. With all this support, the debate on the statute began in May 1932, influenced by the new Spanish Constitution, which defined Spain as an "integral state compatible with the autonomy of municipalities and regions."[17] But again the atmosphere in Madrid was hostile toward Catalunya, and there was another boycott against Catalan products as there had been in early 1919, and that led to demonstrations against teaching in Catalan and statements made by intellectuals such as Miguel de Unamuno and Ortega y Gasset against political autonomy. Eventually the statute was passed, notably cut on September 9, 1932, among other factors due to the alarm created by General Sanjurjo's coup d'état in early August.

However, it should not be forgotten that this constituent process also shook up politics in Catalunya. By the end of 1931, some Catholic but strongly Catalan sectors had created the first Christian Democratic party in Catalunya, the Unió Democràtica de Catalunya. And the fragmentation of the former Macià supporters from Estat Català had divided into two groups: on the right, the conservative-oriented Partit Nationalist Català (PNC), while on the left Estat Català-Partit Proletari (EC-PP), with Marxist tendencies.[18] La Lliga also ended up restructured and adapted to the new republican legal situation and was renamed Lliga Catalana in early 1933. While at ERC, even though it had easily won the first legislative elections to the Catalan Parliament in November 1932, internal tensions soon erupted between the L'Opinió and Estat Català groups. Firstly, it occurred in January 1933, with a government crisis that involved the departure of Generalitat councilors associated with L'Opinió. And then the latter group left because of its discomfort with the more-or-less violent action of the so-called *escamots*—shock forces of paramilitary aesthetics that, already at that time, were accused of wanting to imitate fascism.[19] Finally, as a result of this confrontation, the L'Opinió group was expelled in September 1933. The following month, the most visible figure in the group, Joan Lluhí i Vallesc, together with other leaders such as Josep Tarradellas, founded the Partit Nacionalista Republicà d'Esquerra (PNRE).

However, it was after this internal crisis that Macià suddenly died on Christmas Day, 1933. His successor was Lluís Companys, a member of the most republican and leftist faction of ERC, and from the start his presidency was beset with difficulties; not only because of the electoral upset that had taken place after the Spanish legislative elections in November, but with the victory of a right-wing coalition hostile to the republican regime, the Confederación Española de Derechas Autónomas (CEDA), led by José María Gil Robles. But above all, it was because the new correlation of forces augured a U-turn from the reformism of the first two republican years. In fact, it was in this context that the conflict between the *rabassaires* (tenant peasants of vineyards) and owners, which had affected the Catalan countryside for years, broke out again because of the latters' desire to end the traditional *rabassa morta* contract, which lasted until the vines died. Consequently, the Catalan Parliament passed a law on cultivation contracts to resolve the conflict, but it was taken to the Constitutional Court in the spring of 1934 by a coalition of agriculturalists and employers led by the Lliga Catalan; the court found in the latter's favor.

This judicial setback undoubtedly stirred things up, especially from June, when various Catalan nationalist parties and organizations began to prepare for a possible insurrection. Furthermore, in early October, three CEDA ministers joined the Lerroux government, a gesture that was seen by the vast majority of republican forces as a serious threat against the republic's very existence. Faced with this affront, and pressured by different radical nationalist groups, Companys proclaimed the co-federal "Catalan State of the Spanish Federal Republic" on October 6, 1934. But the proclamation—unlike future events in Asturias—was quickly neutralized by the army.[20]

As a result of those events, the government in Madrid proceeded to the practical suspension of political autonomy, replacing the Generalitat with a governor-general of Catalunya. President Companys and his government, local authorities, and hundreds of people were imprisoned or expelled from public office. And many others went underground or straight into exile. However, the situation was soon to change again: by the end of 1935, some cases of corruption linked to Prime Minister Lerroux and his party came to light and that led to the call for early elections by February 16; they were to be held in the midst of great social and political polarization. The victory of the left and republican forces in both Catalunya and the state as a whole led to the release from prison by October 6 of those retaliated against, and consequently to the return of Companies to govern from the Generalitat.

So, for a few months, and despite increasing tension, it seemed that ERC had regained the social and political vitality that had made Catalan life from 1931-1932 stand out. The PNRE was reinstated in the party, a factor that was to contribute to the partial subordination of the hegemony that most nationalist sectors had until October 1934. And in fact, this shifted toward more federalizing positions and culminated in the split in May 1936 of the pro-independence current of CKD—headed by former health adviser Josep Dencs—to found a new political party that recovered the old historical acronyms of Estat Català (EC), and which the PNC and NS would soon join. However, part of the old Macià guard—such as indestructible culture adviser Ventura Gassol—remained in the ERC. But that did not prevent the party from suffering a new departure two months later, when part of the youth branch, which had not joined EC now and left CKD to join the new Partido Socialista Unificado de Catalunya (PSUC), was founded in July 1936 as the result of the combination of USC, pro-independence people from EC-PP, the small Catalan delegation of the PSOE, and the tiny Communist Partit of Catalunya, with Stalinist tendencies.

Of course, the start of the Civil War and the start of the social revolution created an exceptional situation that made life very difficult for republican and democratic positions (and of course for conservatives), the areas in which Catalanism were most strongly rooted.[21] In turn, the radical Catalanism represented by EC would eventually break up again in late 1936 because of profound ideological and strategic differences. Many of its militants were to die at the front, while many others continued their work from exile. In fact, the very progress of the war made it increasingly difficult to live together in the rearguard: in May 1937, violent clashes in Barcelona led to the expulsion of dissident communists from the Partido Obrero de Unificación Marxista (POUM) and anarchist groups from the country's institutional life. And this also changed the powers that the government of Catalunya had acquired since the outbreak of war. From then on, the government in Madrid, led by socialist Juan Negrín, quickly lessened Catalan self-government until its definitive suppression with the occupation of Catalunya by General Franco's troops in January 1939.[22] Finally, Lluís Companys, still president but now in exile in France, was arrested by the Gestapo in August of the following year, handed over to the Franco authorities, and executed by a firing squad in the early morning of October 15, 1940, in Barcelona while shouting *"Per Catalunya."*

## Conclusions

Although Catalanism was a popular phenomenon in its origins and covered all layers of society from the first half of the nineteenth century, it would not be until the last third of the 1800s that the first political proposals actually appeared. This process culminated in 1892 with the draft of the first political text of constitutional character, the so-called *Bases de Manresa*. However, it was not until 1901, with the foundation of the Lliga Regionalista, that political Catalanism consolidated itself as a force led by politicians such as Prat de la Riba and Francesc Cambó. Other Catalan political formations, of republican and leftist nature, or directly pro-independence, also contributed to this expansion.

In turn, some unique milestones, such as the great electoral success of Solidaritat Catalana in 1907, paved the way for the first experiences of self-government during the contemporary period, the Commonwealth of Catalunya, which was unable to complete its political autonomy, especially after the failure of the campaign for home rule that the Lliga championed between 1918 and 1919.

Following Primo de Rivera's coup d'etat in 1923, repression against any expression of Catalanism, both culturally and politically, came quickly. It was in that context that a new figure would emerge, Francesc Macià, leader of the pro-independence organization Estat Català, and so, at the end of the dictatorship, he was able to bring together around him different republican and philo-socialist sectors, leading to the foundation of Esquerra Republicana de Catalunya in early 1931. Its great election victory that same April made it the hegemonic party throughout the republican period. And although on the change of regime Macià tried to force a Catalan Republic, both the recovery of the Generalitat and the achievement of autonomy marked a clear turning point with regard to the previous period. Thus, only the events of October—after the failed declaration of the (co)federal Catalan State by the new President Companys, such as the outbreak of the Civil War and subsequent repression from 1939—removed Catalan self-government, and along with that the entire process of nationalization was carried out until then by the now-political Catalanism.

## NOTES

1 Angel Smith, *The Origins of Catalan Nationalism, 1770-1898* (Basingstoke: Palgrave Macmillan, 2014).

2 Daniele Conversi, *The Basques, the Catalans and Spain: Alternative Routes to Nationalist Mobilization* (Reno: University of Nevada Press, 2000).

3 Giovanni C. Cattini, "The Advent and Politiciation of Distinct Catalan Identitities (1860-1898)" in *Historical Analysis of the Catalan Identity*, ed. Flocel Sabaté (Berna: Peter Lang, 2015), 269-300.

4 Alland, Alexander Jr., and Sonia Alland, *Catalunya, One Nation, Two States: An Ethnographic Study of Nonviolent Resistance to Assimilation* (New York: Palgrave Macmillan, 2006).

5 Pere Anguera, *L'Onze de Setembre. Història de la Diada (1886-1938)* (Barcelona: PAM, 2008).

6 Giovanni C. Cattini, "Myths and Symbols in the Political Culture of Catalan Nationalism (1880-1914)," in *Nations and Nationalism*, no. 21.3 (2015), 445-460; Josep Ramon Llobera, *Foundations of National Identity: From Catalunya to Europe* (New York: Berghahn Books, 2004).

7 Jordi Casassas, *La voluntat i la quimera. El noucentisme català entre la Renaixença i el marxisme* (Barcelona: Ed. 62, 2017).

8 Josep Maria Pons-Altés, "Barcelona and the Tragic Week of 1909: A crazed mob or citizens in revolt?," in *International Journal of Iberian Studies*, no. 29.1 (2016), 3-19.

9 Jordi Casassas, "What Made Catalunya Unique (1901-1939)," in *Historical Analysis of the Catalan Identity*, ed. Flocel Sabaté (Berna, Peter Lang, 2015), 301-328.

10 Chris Ealham, *Class, Culture, and Conflict in Barcelona, 1898-1937* (London: Routledge, 2005).

11 Francisco Romero Salvadó and Angel Smith (eds.), *The Agony of Spanish Liberalism: From Revolution to Dictatorship 1913-23* (Basingstoke: Palgrave Macmillan, 2010).

12 Daniel Roig i Sanz, "1917. El impacto de la Revolución rusa en España y Cataluña," in *Y el mundo cambió de base: una mirada histórica a la Revolución rusa*, ed. Andreu Mayayo, José Manuel Rúa (Barcelona: Yulca, 2017).

13 Joan Esculies and Daniel Martínez Fiol, *12,000! Els catalans a la Primera Guerra Mundial* (Barcelona: Ara Llibres, 2014).

14 Josep Maria Roig Rosich, *La Dictadura de Primo de Rivera a Catalunya: un assaig de repressió cultural* (Barcelona: PAM, 1992).

15 Giovanni C. Cattini, *El gran complot: quí va trair Macià?: la trama italiana* (Barcelona: Ara Llibres, 2009).

16 Albert Balcells, *Catalan Nationalism: Past and Present* (London: MacMillan, 1996).

17 Sandie Holguín, *Creating Spaniards: Culture and National Identity in Republican Spain* (Madison: University of Wisconsin Press, 2002).

18 Fermí Rubiralta, *Una història de l'independentisme polític català* (Lleida: Pagès, 2004).

19 Enric Ucelay-Da Cal, *The Shadow of a Doubt: Fascist and Communist Alternatives in Catalan Separatism, 1919-1939* (Barcelona: Institut de Cisncies Polítiques i Socials, 2002); Daniel Roig i Sanz. "Catalanisme radical, nacionalisme integral i feixisme a la Catalunya dels anys trenta: historiografia, teoria i estat de la qüestió," en *Segle XX: revista catalana d'història*, n. 9 (2016), 51-82.

20 Manel López Esteve, *Els fets of October 6, 1934* (Barcelona: Base, 2013).

21 Paul Preston, *The Spanish Civil War: Reaction, Revolution, and Revenge* (New York: W. W. Norton & Co., 2007).

22 Andrew Dowling, *Catalunya since the Spanish Civil War: Reconstructing the Nation* (Portland: Sussex Academic Press, 2013).

# 9

# The Catalan Independence Process Until the Referendum of October 1, 2017

*Antoni Segura i Mas*

In today's world, the globalization process—which "is not an ideology, but, rather, an objective process of structuring the whole economy, societies, institutions, cultures"—and a reaffirmation of identities coexist. They are not mutually exclusive; there is a systemic relationship between them. Therefore, in the global, interdependent world, old identities that were believed to have been surpassed or are reaffirmed as new ones—whether of a religious, national, ethnic, territorial, gender, ecological nature—reappear. The contradiction is only apparent, then, to the extent that the old nation-states are incapable of managing globalization, revive identities that are "a reconstruction of the meaning of people's lives at the moment in which until now had been a form of aggregation, of organization" and the state stops performing its function effectively and becomes one more agent "of globalization and not of a particular community, and the reaction is the alternative construction of the meaning (of life) based on identity" (Castells, 2004).

Identity construction can also be negative when it is the result of the "fear of the other"—migratory flows are another effect of globalization—and leads to racist populist movements. We have seen this in Europe and in the United States over recent years, where, under the claim of exclusive patriotism, neo-fascist movements are gaining force. On the other hand, to the extent that the European Union is formulated as the Europe of the States—and not that of the peoples or nations—there is a seizure of politics by citizens who believe that another Europe and another type of globalization are possible. And this is apparent in movements such as 15M, as in national demands in Scotland or Catalunya, as, outside of the European context, in the failed Arab "revolts for dignity" of 2001 (with the exception of Tunisia). In a few words and recalling the slogan of the American Revolution in the second half of the eighteenth century: "No taxation without representation." In short, globalization allows "secessionist movements" to achieve global supply and affect international relations (Muro and Woertz, 2018). They are also the expression of citizens' political empowerment, the "right to decide." Consensus policies are therefore needed for the challenges of this systemic relationship between globalization and identities (Connolly, 2013, on Catalunya, Flanders, and Scotland).

Finally, there are three types of collective identities connected with the historical movement and the circumstances that surround a community: legitimizing identity, which is "built from the institutions and in particular from the state" (United States, France); resistance identity, which appears "when human groups feel either culturally rejected or socially or politically marginalized, and react by building, using historical material, forms of self-identification that allow them to resist their otherwise assimilation into a system in which their situation would be structurally subordinate" (indigenous movements in Latin America, Catalunya during the dictatorship); identity-projects which "are articulated based on self-identification, always with cultural, historical, territorial materials. And, even if it is always based on these materials, there is a project to build a community." The latter is an identity with a future rather than a past. This is Catalunya's situation (Castells, 2003, 2004; Segura, 2013).

Catalunya is a historical nation in the extreme northeast of the Iberian Peninsula, with a surface area of 32,108 km$^2$ (like the state of Maryland), and with a population of 7,543,825 inhabitants on January 1, 2018 (Idescat). It has its own culture and language—Catalan—and appeared as a differentiated political entity when Charlemagne created the Hispanic March to stop Muslim advance, based on the Pyrenean counties, and with their own domain and administration. In the tenth century, Guifré el Pilós was the last count named by the Franks, and he established a lineage for his counties, which was not subject to allegiance to the Frankish kings.

Two centuries later, as Catalan cellist Pau Casals recalled at the headquarters of the United Nations when collecting the Medal of Peace in 1971, the Pau i Treva de Déu movement—promoted as a response from the church and the peasants to the violence of the feudal nobles—was the embryo of the Corts Generals Catalanes, over which the monarch presided and which brought together the military, the nobility, the church, and the urban bourgeoisie to legislate and set taxes. Dating from the thirteenth century, it is one of the oldest parliaments in the world. The institutions were completed by the Generalitat—the permanent delegation of the General Court—and the Consell de Cent—the governing body of the city of Barcelona made up of five councilors and one hundred prominent men (urban patricians, craftsmen, merchants).

The General Court's system of negotiated sovereignty was very advanced for the time and obliged the monarch to agree on certain decisions with the estates, especially with the city bourgeoisie that financed royal projects. The Catalan institutions remained in force until the War of Succession (1702-1714), when the Austracist defeat and the capitulation of Barcelona on September 11, 1714—remembered as National Day—entailed the loss of those institutions for the first time. They were to be reinstated during the Second Republic with the Republican Generalitat, a parliament, and the 1932 statute of autonomy. But Franco's victory during the Civil War—the Abraham Lincoln Brigade took part in defense of the Republic—meant the loss of these institutions once more. As Antoni Rovira i Virgili (1999) wrote in 1940, the Franco dictatorship wanted to end "the spirit, the idea, the culture, the strength, and the life of Catalunya. They want to destroy not only the political edifice, but, even more so, the national soul. The coup is against Catalunya as a nation, against Catalan civilization."

Throughout history, the citizens of Catalunya have persevered to reinstate those institutions and achieve the full self-government. However, for centuries Catalunya has been a land of transit, a Mediterranean emporium, a battlefield, and a place of refuge, four characteristics that have forged a mestizo, integrating identity, tolerant and cosmopolitan at the same time. For this reason, Catalanism does not claim to have ethnic roots; rather, the best thing that defines the *fet català* is the language, the culture, the mood, the way of being, the pacts made between different people, its Mediterranean and European vocation, the will to be and the defense of freedoms and institutions. In short, a project identity. And that is how it has been from the beginning, because it is not the major bourgeoisie of the manufacturing companies, or that of the business, that keeps the pulse of recovery going; on the contrary, it is the popular classes and popular Catalanism that keep the flame of vindication alive.

At the same time, since the second half of the nineteenth century, associative life has had a strength and consistency that is not to be found in other places: movements linked to the working class (trade unions), in civil society and popular culture (athenaeums), and republican-inspired political parties, federal and Catalanist. Thus, between the Renaissance and the Second Republic, the strength of the civil society of associative movements was forged to the beat of social struggles and national demand. And in times of difficulties or uncertain political changes—democratic transition, today—a cohesive civil society and strong associative movements always reappear. And this is how, despite repression and secrecy, aspirations for self-government and social change survived the Franco regime. The struggle for individual and national freedom became inseparable, and values were shared by the entire opposition—political and union movements, neighborhood and student movements, and all types of cultural associations—and exemplified by the creation of l'Assemblea de Catalunya in 1971.

Two years after the death of the dictator, the results of the first democratic elections—June 15, 1977—endorsed the "Catalan singularity" or Catalan rupture (Mayayo, 2002) because, contrary to what happened in the rest of the state (with the exception of the Basque Country), in Catalunya the victory of the left and of Catalanism was unquestionable. So while in the state as a whole, the "Official Party" of Prime Minister Adolfo Suárez (a former minister of the movement who had led the transition from the Franco regime's legality) won, the Unión del Centro Democrático (UCD) winning 34.4 percent of votes; in Catalunya, victory fell to the Catalan version of the Spanish Socialist Workers' Party (PSOE), the Partit dels Socialistes de Catalunya (PSC), with 28.6 percent of the votes, followed by the Catalan communists—the Partit Socialista Unificat de Catalunya (PSUC)—with 18.1 percent of the vote, and then the Pacte Democràtic per Catalunya (PDC), a coalition of sovereignist parties, and the Republican Left Party of Catalunya (ERC) created in 1931, with 16.9 percent and 4.7 percent of the vote, respectively. The UCD only received 5.7 percent of the vote. Three-quarters of the votes were for Catalan parties and more than half for left-wing ones.

**Elections to the Spanish Parliament. June 1977.**

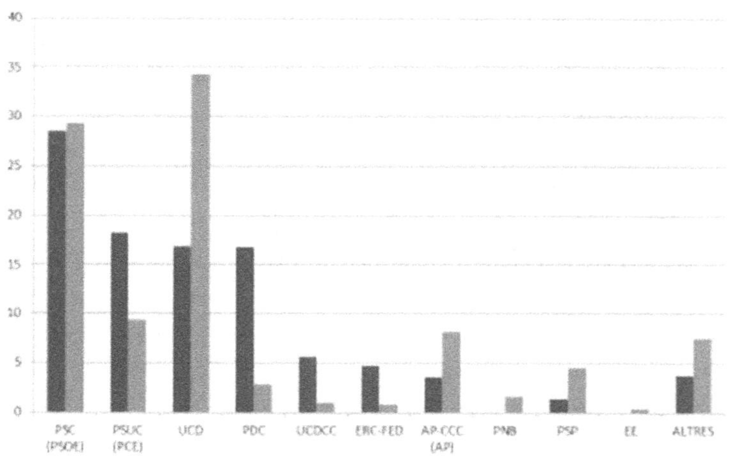

Shortly afterward, the 1977 Diada marked a milestone in the history of Catalunya. Without riots, without confrontations, but with forcefulness, about a million Catalans of diverse origins showed that the democratic transition could not be considered to have finished without reinstating the Generalitat and the statute. On September 29, the Spanish government provisionally reestablished the Generalitat, and on October 23, President Josep Tarradellas returned from exile to preside over it. That meant the recognition of the institution and of historical continuity, the reinstatement of historical continuity. The reinstatement of the Generalitat connected with republican legality, and it became the only fact of the Spanish Transition that linked with the legality annihilated by the coup d'état of July 18, 1936, and the defeat of 1939.

Two years later (on October 25, 1979), the statute of autonomy of Catalunya was approved in a referendum, with 57 percent participation and 88 percent favorable votes. Compared with the 1932 statute, it involved more powers, but without concessions of high symbolic and political importance in matters such as justice and security. In short, more powers with finalist transfers, but less political power and, by the will of the Catalan parliamentarians, without an economic agreement. In other words, without the possibility of collecting taxes, and therefore depending on finance from the central government.

Very soon it was seen that financial dependence could drown the institution, and hopes placed in the statute were broken by the generalization of the autonomic process that homogenized and equalized all the Autonomous Communities downward, thus diluting Catalan and Basque aspirations for strong self-government. However, the majority Spanish parties believed that it had gone too far and proceeded to re-centralize with the *Ley Orgánica de Harmonización del Proceso Autonómico* (LOAPA) in 1982. For Catalan and Basque nationalists, that was a posthumous victory for the failed coup attempt on February 23, 1981, carried out by sectors of the army nostalgic for Francoism and which refused to accept the State of Autonomous Communities—and particularly the differential characters of Catalunya and Euskadi—because they considered that it undermined the unity of Spain. In sum, a unique historical opportunity was lost in recognizing the national and current plurality of the Spanish State, which is an enviable heritage wealth, and not a problem.

In the first regional elections (March 1980), CiU won power, and that was followed by twenty-three years of governments led by Jordi Pujol, who managed the regional powers with the will to provide the country with the basic instruments for its economic, territorial, and social development, and understanding Catalunya as a great community that brings together all those who live and work in the country. At the same time, CiU contributed to the stability of Spanish governments (1977, 1979, 1993, and 1996), noting, however, that the will to regenerate Spain had become an impossible undertaking.

The State of the Autonomous Communities and the LOAPA were designed to deactivate demands for self-government from historical nationalisms (Catalunya, Euskadi, and Galicia) and to homogenize/equalize the level of all Spanish citizens, regardless of where they were residing. As the case of Catalunya reveals, a quarter of a century later, these objectives have not been met.

On the one hand, the demands for self-government and more powers have not diminished; to the contrary Catalan/nationalist options continue to be the majority (89 percent of the seats).

Parliament of Catalunya. Catalan and nationalist party seats, 1980-2003

| Year | CiU | ERC | PSC | ICV | CiU+ERC+ PSC+ICV | % of total seats | PP | Cs | Others* |
|---|---|---|---|---|---|---|---|---|---|
| 1980 | 43 | 14 | 33 | 25 | 115 | 85.2 | - | - | 20 |
| 1984 | 72 | 5 | 41 | 6 | 124 | 91.9 | 11 | - | - |
| 1988 | 69 | 6 | 42 | 9 | 126 | 93.3 | 6 | - | 3 |
| 1992 | 70 | 11 | 40 | 7 | 128 | 94.8 | 7 | - | - |
| 1995 | 60 | 13 | 34 | 11 | 118 | 87.4 | 17 | - | - |
| 1999 | 56 | 12 | 52 | 3 | 113 | 83.7 | 12 | - | - |
| 2003 | 46 | 23 | 42 | 9 | 120 | 88.9 | 15 | - | - |
| 2006 | 48 | 21 | 37 | 12 | 118 | 87.4 | 14 | 3 | - |
| Average (percentages) | | | | | | 89.1 | | | |

CiU: Convergence i Unió ERC: Republican Esquerra de Catalunya PP: Partit Popular
PSC: Partit dels Socialistes de Catalunya ICV: Initiative for Catalunya Verds Cs: Ciudadanos
(*): 1980, Partido Socialista de Andalucía; 1988, Centre Democràtic i Social.

Source: Parliament of Catalunya

On the other hand, all Catalanist forces agreed that the Generalitat's finance system was insufficient and that, at the same time, between 1986 and 2009, Catalunya (the group of citizens of Catalunya) suffered each year, on average, a fiscal deficit equivalent to 8 percent of its GDP (Loscos work group, 2005, 2009; Resultados, 2012). Thus in 2005, Catalunya, with a per capita income of 18.8 percent above the Spanish median, showed a fiscal deficit of 8.7 percent of GDP, a situation only comparable to that of the state of New Jersey which, with a per capita income 18.3 percent higher than the United States median, has a fiscal deficit of 8.8 percent of GDP. In short, Catalunya is worse off than

New York State (18.6 percent above the median, a fiscal deficit of 4.0 percent) and Massachusetts (17.9 percent and 3.9 percent) in the United States, the State of Western Australia (7.7 percent and 3.9 percent), the province of Alberta in Canada (45.0 percent and 3.2 percent), the State of Baja California in Mexico (14 percent and 6.5 percent), and the territory of Flanders in Belgium with an income below the median (99 percent) and a fiscal deficit of 4.4 percent of GDP. Of course, the situation in the autonomous community of the Balearic Islands was even worse, with a per capita income 12.1 percent above the median and a fiscal deficit of 14.2 percent of GDP in 2005 (Vilalta, 2012).

Despite these major contributions from Catalunya and other Autonomous Communities, the compensation fund did not manage to reduce the differences in purchasing power—or the standard of living—between the communities. The failure of the State of Autonomies is evident (Segura, 2007 and 2006).

At the beginning of the twenty-first century, the end-of-cycle feeling was accentuated, and in the November 2003 elections, CiU was once again the force with the most seats (forty-six), but with the sum of PSC, ERC, and ICV giving an absolute majority of seventy-four seats. On December 14, 2003, these three political forces signed the *El acuerdo para un gobierno catalanista y de izquierdas en la Generalitat de Catalunya,* which was to be presided over by Pasqual Maragall, and whose main objective was to be drawing up a new statute to put an end to the fiscal deficit, respecting the principle ordinality—after contributing to solidarity funds, Catalunya was below communities that were the net recipients of these funds—and self-government further developed.

The situation was unsustainable and fueled disaffection toward Spain and in favor of the independence movement, since many citizens saw no other way to turn around the abusive drain of funds than the foundation of their own state. The new statute that Maragall put forward as president of the Generalitat was the last attempt by Catalan socialism to remain in Spain.

On September 30, 2005, the Parliament of Catalunya approved the text of the new statute with a majority of 120 deputies (89 percent of the total). In Spain, the PP in opposition took advantage of the statute to launch a campaign against the PSOE government and accuse the statutory text of "breaking Spain up." The conservative party campaigned to collect signatures against the statute and to boycott Catalan products, fueling anti-Catalan phobia in the rest of the state. Some socialist leaders, such as the presidents of Andalusia and Extremadura, also saw the statute as a threat against the interests of their communities.

On November 2, 2005, the statute was admitted for process in the Spanish Parliament. Then it went through the sieve of the Constitutional Commission at the Congress of Deputies. The anti-Catalan campaign of the PP intensified, and on January 21, 2006, José Luis Rodríguez Zapatero—prime minister of the Spanish government—and Artur Mas—head of CiU and leader of the opposition in Catalunya—made an agreement, while ERC rejected it. On February 18, 2006, the Platform for the Right to Decide (PDD) and civil society organizations demonstrated in Barcelona under the slogan "*Som una Nació i tenim el Dret a Decide*" (We are a nation, and we have the right to decide), demanding that the Congress of Deputies approve the statutory text without making any alterations to it.

On March 30, the Spanish Parliament approved the statute with 189 votes from the PSOE, IU/ICV, and the Catalan nationalists (except ERC), Basques, Galicians, and Canary Islands parliamentarians. The referendum was held on June 18, with 49 percent turnout and 73 percent favorable votes. The low turnout denoted fatigue and disenchantment with the final text approved by the Spanish Parliament, greatly amended with respect to the one that had been passed in the parliament of Catalunya. ERC left the government, Maragallnd decided not to stand for reelection and brought forward the elections to November 1, 2006. On July 31, the PP made an appeal to the Constitutional Court against the new Statute of Catalunya, and this was later supported by the ombudsman and the governments of Murcia, La Rioja, Aragon, Valencia, and the Balearic Islands.

**Graphic 6. Participation of Catalonia to the income and expenditure of the central public sector (% of total autonomous communities)**

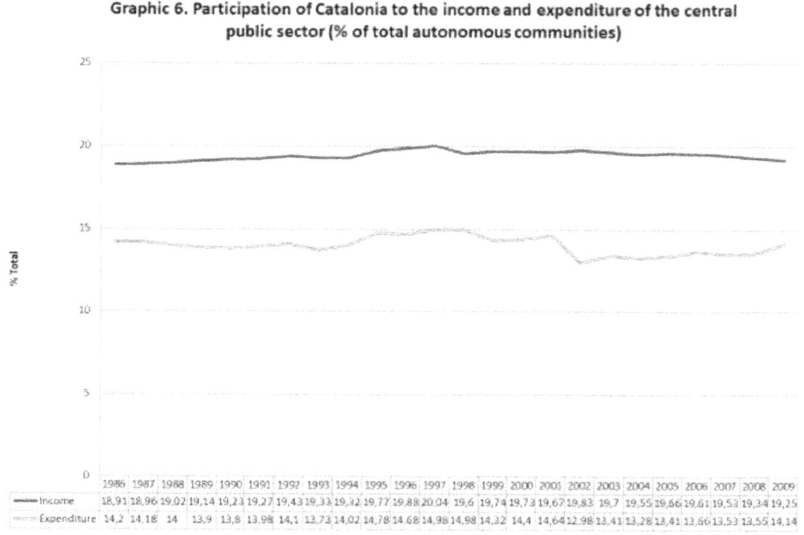


| | 1986 | 1987 | 1988 | 1989 | 1990 | 1991 | 1992 | 1993 | 1994 | 1995 | 1996 | 1997 | 1998 | 1999 | 2000 | 2001 | 2002 | 2003 | 2004 | 2005 | 2006 | 2007 | 2008 | 2009 |
|---|---|---|---|---|---|---|---|---|---|---|---|---|---|---|---|---|---|---|---|---|---|---|---|---|
| Income | 18,91 | 18,96 | 19,02 | 19,14 | 19,23 | 19,27 | 19,43 | 19,33 | 19,32 | 19,77 | 19,88 | 20,04 | 19,6 | 19,74 | 19,73 | 19,67 | 19,83 | 19,7 | 19,55 | 19,66 | 19,61 | 19,53 | 19,34 | 19,25 |
| Expenditure | 14,2 | 14,18 | 14 | 13,9 | 13,8 | 13,98 | 14,1 | 13,73 | 14,02 | 14,78 | 14,68 | 14,98 | 14,98 | 14,32 | 14,4 | 14,64 | 12,98 | 13,41 | 13,28 | 13,41 | 13,66 | 13,53 | 13,55 | 14,14 |

Source: Generalitat de Catalunya, *Resultats de la balança fiscal de Catalunya amb el sector públic central 2006-2009* (Barcelona, Generalitat de Catalunya: 2012).

The elections led to a second tripartite chaired by José Montilla (PSC). The new government had to face the economic crisis that followed the bankruptcy of Lehman Brothers in 2008; the deterioration of Catalunya-Spain relations as a result of the negotiations on the new financing; and the contradictions caused by the formation of a new tripartite that was not accepted by part of the ERC rank and file. On November 7, 2007, President Montilla delivered a conference in Madrid in which he warned of growing disaffection in Catalunya.

Disaffection grew, fueled by difficulties to specify a new finance model since Catalunya was suffering from excessive fiscal drainage; due to the effects of the economic crisis (unemployment went from 6.5 percent in 2007 to 17 percent in 2010); and the PP's Catalan-phobic campaign. Furthermore, as can be seen in the graphs, there was an additional offense in that the Catalan contribution to the state public sector corresponded to its GDP, but the state public sector in Catalunya did not. And, furthermore, the percentage of state investments in Catalunya between 2000 and 2010 was well below those at state level: from a minimum of 4 percent in 2009 to a 30 percent difference in 2000 (median 10.8 percent).

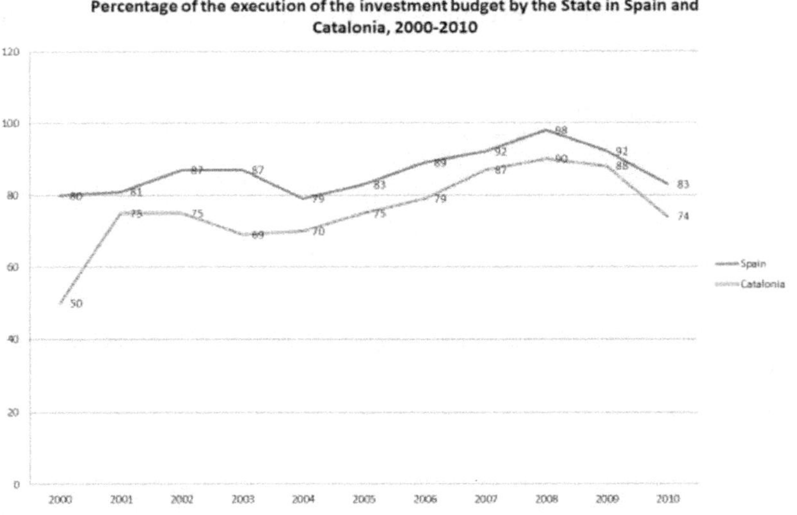


Source: Germà Bel, *Anatomia d'un desengany*, Barcelona, Destino, 2013: 216.

The low level of investment had an impact on the maintenance and renovation of infrastructures at a time when economic growth prior to the crisis, fueled by the real estate bubble, had caused a 20 percent increase in the population, from 6,207,533 inhabitants in 1999 to 7,475,420 in 2010. And civil society began to activate. On December 1, 2007, the PDD called a demonstration under the slogan "*La Nación Catalana diu prou! Tenim the dret de decidir sobre les nostres infraestructures*" (The Catalan nation says enough! We have the right to decide on our infrastructures.). It was supported by almost 150 organizations, unions, and parties. The PSC did not support it and aligned with the PP and Cs. The demonstration was the first step in a broad civil society movement that led to the consultation campaign and the constitution of the Assemblea Nacional Catalana (ANC) on March 10, 2010.

The consultations began in Arenys de Munt on September 13, 2009, promoted by the Associació de Municipis per la Independència (AMI). Until April 2010, eight series of consultations were held, covering 554 municipalities in which 4,674,252 people live, almost two-thirds of the population of Catalunya. 884,504 people voted, with an average participation of 18.9 percent and 811,447 favorable votes (91.7 percent).

On November 26, 2009, twelve Catalan newspapers published a joint editorial ("*La dignitat de Catalunya*") in which they expressed their concern about the delay of the TC in passing judgment on the statute, and reminded their readers that "the Catalans pay their taxes (without Fuero privileges); they contribute with their work to transfer income to the poorest parts of Spain; they face economic internationalization without the large benefits of being the capital of the State; they speak a language with a greater demographic margin than that of various official languages in the European Union, a language that, instead of being loved, is often subjected to obsessive scrutiny by official Spanish nationalism . . . These days, Catalans think, above all, of their dignity."

On June 28, 2010, the TC published its sentence. It was a heavyweight charge against the statute, not so much from a legal point of view as a political one. Article 97 of "the Consell de Justícia de Catalunya" was declared unconstitutional, thirteen articles partially unconstitutional, and twenty-four articles and three additional provisions were reinterpreted. The sentence broke the 1978 constitutional pact since, according to Article 151 of the Spanish Constitution, the last procedure for the approval of a statute is ratification in a citizens' referendum, not the TC. The answer was unanimous: Òmnium Cultural and several associations called a demonstration for July 10 under the slogan "*Som una Nació. Nosaltres decidim*" (We are a nation. We decide). The demonstration brought together hundreds of thousands of people in Barcelona and was led by President Montilla and the Catalan government. It was a transversal, plural, collective reaction with dignity and purpose. For many Catalans, the statutory route no longer had any way forward, and on July 10, 2010, they broke with Spain emotionally and politically.

CiU decided that the statutory phase had concluded and committed to the right to decide and Catalunya's own finance model. Meanwhile, the forces of the tripartite, worn out by the failure of the statutory process and by the economic crisis, had no chance of success in the coming electoral contest. CiU won with 38.5 percent of the vote and sixty-two parliamentarians and, with the support of the PP, formed a government, approved budgets, and began a legislature marked by the second recession of the Catalan economy (fourth quarter of 2001 to first quarter of 2013; unemployment rose to 20.4 percent, and in Spain it reached 22.6 percent), which Artur Mas's government intended to combat with a policy of austerity, thus in line with Mariano Rajoy's new PP government.

Results of elections to the Parliament of Catalunya in votes (%) and seats, 2010-2017

| | 2010 | | 2012 | | 2015 | | 2017 | |
|---|---|---|---|---|---|---|---|---|
| Candidacies | Votes | Seats | Votes | Seats | Votes | Seats | Votes | Seats |
| CiU | 38.5 | 62 | 30.7 | 50 | - | - | - | - |
| PSC | 18.3 | 28 | 14.4 | 20 | 12.7 | 16 | 13.8 | 17 |
| PP | 12.3 | 18 | 13.0 | 19 | 8.5 | 11 | 4.2 | 4 |
| ICV-EUiA | 7.4 | 10 | 9.9 | 13 | - | - | - | - |
| ERC | 7.0 | 10 | 13.7 | 21 | - | - | 21.3 | 32 |
| YES[1] | 3.3 | 4 | - | - | - | - | - | |
| Cs | 3.4 | 3 | 7.6 | 9 | 17.9 | 25 | 25.3 | 36 |
| CUP | - | - | 3.5 | 3 | 8.2 | 10 | 4.4 | 4 |
| JxSí[2] | - | - | - | - | 39.6 | 62 | - | - |
| CSQEP[3] | - | - | - | - | 8.9 | 11 | 7.5 | 8 |
| JxC[4] | - | - | - | - | - | - | 21.6 | 34 |

(1) Solidaritat Catalana per la Independència.
(2) Junts pel Sí.
(3) Catalunya Sí que es pot. In 2017, Catalunya En Comú Podem (CECP) was founded.
(4) Junts per Catalunya, the candidates supported by Carles Puigdemont from exile.

Source: Parliament and Generalitat of Catalunya

On September 11, 2012, with the motto "*Catalunya, nou Estat d'Europa*" (Catalunya, new State in Europe), the most multitudinous Diada that had ever taken place was held in Barcelona. It was the answer to the malaise created by the austerity policies, the economic situation of the Generalitat, the scandalous compensation of unscrupulous senior executives, evictions, unemployment, the lack of social policies, cases of corruption. . . . Shortly after, Rajoy's refusal of the fiscal pact during his meeting with Mas closed the door to any negotiation. The TC's 2010 ruling and Rajoy's refusal to review the finance model was the origin of the current political conflict (Muro, 2018; Segura, 2013; Tormos, Muñoz, Hierro, 2015)

On September 27, the Catalan Parliament approved resolution 724/IX with eighty-four votes in favor (CiU, ERC, ICV, SI, socialist deputies Joan Laporta and Ernest Maragall), which "solemnly proclaims . . . the inalienable and imprescriptible right of Catalunya to self-determination as a democratic expression of its sovereignty as a nation and urges the 'Government to hold a consultation . . . in the next legislature.'" The PP and Cs voted against and the PSC abstained. Moreover, the legislature was concluded, and elections were called for November 25 with the commitment to carry out a consultation within the Spanish, European, or international legal framework during the following legislature (in agreement with the PSC in this, as Pere Navarro supported an agreed, legal referendum). All the bridges between the Spanish government and the Generalitat had been burned. They were not to be built again.

The November elections were a shock for the two main Catalan parties, CiU paying for its austerity policies and losing twelve seats (getting fifty), and the PSC paying for the errors of the socialist government in Madrid that had not foreseen the effects of the economic crisis and had just undergone an electoral disaster at the hands of the PP and lost eight (twenty). On the other hand, ERC went from ten to twenty-one, ICV-EUiA from ten to thirteen, and Cs—an anti-Catalan party—from three to nine. The Candidatura d'Unitat Popular (CUP) got three seats.

On January 23, 2013, eighty-five deputies (CiU, ERC, ICV-EUiA, and one from CUP) out of 135 voted in favor of the "Declaration of sovereignty and the right to decide of the people of Catalunya," which obliged the parties to position themselves as Catalanists, and which caused the PSC to implode (five deputies—Àngel Ros, Marina Geli, Joan Ignasi Elena, Rocío Martínez-Sampere, and Núria Ventura—did not vote because they did not want to oppose it, as proposed by the leadership). It was not the first time that the Catalan Parliament had taken an initiative in defense of the sovereignty of the people of Catalunya, with precedents in a bill from 1989, two motions in 2011, and three resolutions in 1998, 2020, and 2012. On March 2, the Rajoy government took the declaration of January 13 to the TC, where it was declared legally invalid. On April 11, the Advisory Council for the National Transition (ACNT) was formed, and its objectives were "to define the structures of a Catalan state, to offer information to citizens so that they can know about first-hand what the advantages and disadvantages may be to an independent Catalunya, and advise the Government during the whole process of sovereignty." It was chaired by Carles Viver and Pi-Sunyer, and was made up of fifteen professionals of academic and media prestige. On June 26, the National Pact for the Right to Decide—promoted by CiU, ERC, ICV-EUiA, and CUP, the four Catalan councils, the Barcelona City Council, trade unions, chambers of commerce, business associations, the Consell Interuniversitari de Catalunya, and more than forty entities among which the ANC, Òmnium, AMI, Institut d'Estudis Catalans (IEC), neighborhood associations, and mothers and fathers of students, etc.—was founded. Its objectives included "creating a space for permanent debate and dialogue on the right to decide," promoting "democratic debate" on the right to decide, and "collecting proposals that emanate from civil society and its agents and institutions."

On July 25, the ACNT released the first report (of a total of eighteen) entitled, "The consultation on the political future of Catalunya." It stated that it was possible to hold a legal, nonbinding referendum without legal effects, through different channels: Articles 92 (referendums regulated and called by the state) and EC Article 150.2 (delegation or transfer of powers); Catalan law 4/2010 on referendums; the Catalan law of popular consultations, not referenda; and the reform of the Spanish Constitution. President Mas sent a letter to Prime Minister Rajoy that same day wherein he raised "the need to address dialogue and negotiation which allow the holding of a consultation with the Catalan people in an agreed manner, in the shortest possible term, in the legal frameworks that we establish." He received no response until September 14, 2013. In it the prime minister of the Spanish government subordinated dialogue to "institutional loyalty and respect for the legal framework" which, in Rajoy's terminology, meant that he did not see the legal-institutional space in which to hold a referendum.

And on September 11, 2013, 1.6 million Catalans had demonstrated in favor of the right to decide, forming a human chain of four hundred kilometers to link the borders of the Autonomous Community from south to north, from Pertús to Alcanar-Vinaroz. It was called the Via Catalana, recalling the chain made in the three Baltic republics in 1989 to claim independence from the USSR. For the first time, the conflict had international resonance, to the extent that the Spanish minister of foreign affairs, José Manuel García Margallo, acknowledged that the chain had been "a successful call, organization, logistics, and communication."

On December 12, Mas announced the calling of the referendum for November 9 (9-N) with a double question: Do you want Catalunya to become a state? If so, do you want this state to be independent? The Spanish government warned that the referendum violated the Spanish Constitution. On January 16, 2014, the Parliament of Catalunya passed the referendum (by eighty-seven votes, 64 percent: CiU, ERC, ICV-EUiA, and Socialist deputies Geli, Elena, and Ventura) requesting the Congress of Deputies authorization to hold a consultative referendum. In March, the TC declared the declaration of January 23, 2013, to be unconstitutional, and in April, the Spanish Parliament rejected the Catalan Parliament's request.

A new massive Diada (1,800,000 people) formed a gigantic V (will, vote, and victory) in Barcelona. The ends were at the end of Diagonal and Gran Via and met in the Plaza de las Glorias Catalanas. Mas called on Rajoy's government to negotiate. In September, the ANC and AMI delivered 750,000 signatures to the Catalan Parliament demanding that independence be declared if the referendum could not be held. On September 19, the Parliament approved the Law on Non-Referendum Popular Consultations and other forms of citizen participation by 106 votes in favor (CiU, ERC, PSC, ICV-EUiA, and CUP), 79 percent of the total. On September 27, Mas signed the decree calling for the 9-N consultation, and two days later Rajoy's government appealed to the TC against the law and against the decree; the TC accepted the appeal, not giving an immediate sentence. Mas then opted for a process of citizen participation, and voting took place on November 9. More than 2.3 million people participated, and the votes in favor of independence exceeded 80 percent. President Mas, Vice President Joana Ortega, and councilors Irene Rigau (education) and Francesc Homs (presidency) were tried for disobedience and prevarication and, in November 2018, sentenced to pay 4.9 million euros for the use of public funds on the consultation forbidden by the TC.

After 9-N, the sovereignist parties and entities believed that it was necessary to call new elections with the explicit objective of holding a referendum on self-determination and proclaiming, if necessary, the independence of Catalunya. On July 20, 2015, a unitary list was presented—Junts pel Sí (JxSí)—that brought together all the pro-independence forces—except CUP—and some pro-independence forces heading the candidacy lists of the electoral districts. In the case of Barcelona, it was Raül Romeva, an ex-ICV MEP, followed by Carme Forcadell (ANC), Muriel Casals (Òmnium), Artur Mas (CDC), Oriol Junqueras (ERC), and Eduardo Reyes (Súmate). The candidate for the presidency of the Generalitat was Artur Mas, while the vice presidency of the government and the presidency of the Parliament were to be for ERC. They announced that, if they obtained a majority, they would activate a declaration by the Parliament to initiate the independence process, which would culminate in constituent elections and a referendum on a Catalan constitution in eighteen months: "The state blocked self-government and the Catalan institutions . . . and we will proceed to the proclamation of independence," also unilaterally. (Raül Romeva)

The Diada of 2015—1.4 million people filled the Avenida de la Meridiana—was the fourth demonstration showing the independence movement's capacity for mass mobilization. This time the usual absences of the PP and Cs were accompanied by those of PSC and Catalunya Sí que es Pot (CSQP), a coalition made up of ICV, EuiA, Podem, and Equo founded in July to take part in the Catalan and Spanish elections. The September 27 elections were presented as a plebiscite. The results, however, did not confirm the expectations of JxSí, which obtained sixty-two seats, and which, along with CUP's ten, made a parliamentary majority. However, in 2012 the sum of CiU and ERC seats separately had been seventy-one (with three for CUP); along the way, two seats had been lost, while the percentage of the pro-independence vote remained the same, 47.9 percent in 2012 and 47.8 percent in 2015. This set up two watertight blocs—except for CSQP, supporters of the referendum but not of unilateralism—where votes might be transferred internally, but not between them. To some extent, it was a failure: the results were enough to govern, but not enough to carry out a unilateral declaration of independence without causing serious social fracture. This is what the CUP implied in the words of Antonio Baños: CUP was committed to the path of civil disobedience and rejected the investiture of someone "identified" with corruption—a reference to Mas—who had taken a step aside and put forward someone he trusted, the mayor of Girona and CDC activist Carles Puigdemont. He was sworn in as president on January 10, 2016.

On January 12, Puigdemont promised loyalty to the people of Catalunya, but not to the king or the constitution or the statute. The next day, the legislature began with the purpose of building state structures within eighteen months. In June, CUP did not support the budget. During the first fortnight of July 2016, CDC was dissolved; since May 2015, it had had fifteen headquarters seized by Barcelona Court nº 30 as a result of the Palau Case (a case of corruption linked to the illegal financing of the party), and undermined by the Jordi Pujol's confession (July 25, 2014), in which he acknowledged that he had received unregulated money abroad for more than three decades in inheritance from his father, and the Partit Demòcrata Europeu Català (PdeCAT) was founded. It was an attempt to disconnect the main leaders from corruption. Shortly after, *Público* newspaper denounced the Spanish Ministry of the Interior's *Operation Catalunya*. When Jorge Fernández Díaz was minister, it had been used for spying on pro-independence politicians, and creating and spreading fake news (this story of a dirty war has been covered by the documentary *Las Cloacas de Interior*, 2017).

Diada was commemorated in five locations. Multitudinous, but smaller: Barcelona, 540,000 protesters; Salt, 135,000; Tarragona, 110,000; Berga, 60,000; Lleida, 30,000. On September 28-29, Puigdemont passed a motion of confidence in which he promised to hold an independence referendum, agreed to or not, with the state by September 2017. In Madrid there was a provisional government because, after the results of December 20, 2015, Rajoy had not run for reelection and Pedro Sánchez had not been able to form an alternative majority. After repeating the elections (June 26, 2016), Rajoy formed a government with the support of Cs.

On October 6, the Catalan Parliament urged the government to call a binding self-determination referendum within a year and to build state structures; the TC annulled the resolution in February 2017. On December 23, the "Pacte Nacional pel Referendum" was formed. In January 2017, President Puigdemont, Vice President Oriol Junqueras, and Foreign Minister Romeva presented the referendum to the European Parliament. In July, the Civil Guard took statements from people connected with the preparation of the referendum.

Finally, after a further refusal by Rajoy to agree on the question and the conditions of the referendum, Puigdemont opted for the unilateral route and, on June 9, 2017, announced that the referendum would be held on October 1, 2017, and that it would be held to answer the following question: "Do you want Catalunya to be an independent state in the form of a republic?" A path of no return had begun, which inevitably led to institutional confrontation. On the one hand, Rajoy had chosen to make the conflict judicial instead of seeking a political solution. On the other hand, Puigdemont had opted for the unilateral route. In July, the ministry of finance decreed a financial intervention in the Generalitat, a measure that it repeated on September 15.

On September 11, a million people demonstrated in Barcelona for Yes in the referendum. On September 6 and 7, in very tense sessions, the Catalan Parliament—with the votes of JxSí and CUP—passed the referendum laws, calling it transitory, in order to avoid the legal gap between the voting and the proclamation of the Catalan Republic. The TC suspended the laws as a precautionary measure, and the Spanish government insisted that the referendum would not take place because it was illegal. The security forces tried to locate ballot boxes and ballots. On September 20, the Civil Guard carried out Operation Anubis with simultaneous searches of several ministries and Generalitat buildings and private homes, which resulted in fourteen arrests.

The police tried to enter the CUP headquarters without a search warrant. In a peaceful and spontaneous way, tens of thousands of people gathered in the Rambla de Catalunya—the Ministry of Economy—and in Caspe street—headquarters of the CUP. As a result of these incidents, on October 16 the president of the ANC, Jordi Sànchez, and of Òmnium Cultural, Jordi Cuixart, were arrested and accused of rebellion. Three ships arrived at the ports of Barcelona and Tarragona to house police reinforcements.

Shortly before October 1 (1-O), Rajoy's government stated that the referendum would not be held because there would be no ballot boxes, no ballot papers, no electoral receivership, no census, no colleges, and no polling stations. But at nine in the morning, there were ballot boxes, ballot papers, polling stations, and more than 2.3 million people—around 43 percent of the electoral census and 92 percent of them in favor of independence—voted despite the brutality of the police and Civil Guard charges. The images went around the world, and the action of the security forces and the Spanish government was condemned by the international press and various international leaders and institutions (United Nations High Commissioner for Human Rights), and there were calls for dialogue (*La Vanguardia,* October 3). There were also signs of solidarity: "We are with you Catalunya" (Paul Mason, *The Guardian*, October 2; for Enric Marin and Joan M. Treserras (2018), October was "the most massive act of peaceful democratic disobedience that has taken place in Europe since the end of the Second World War."

The police violence of 1-O increased social tension in Catalunya and broadened the base of the parties in favor of the right to decide. On October 3, the Mesa por la Democracia—which brought together unions, political parties, and some six hundred entities—called a "strike for the country" to protest the police charges that, according to the Catalan Health Service (2017), had caused 1,066 patients to be treated for contusions (43.9 percent) or polytonusions (38.6 percent) in the health regions of Barcelona city (32 percent), Girona (26 percent), Lleida, Alt Pirineu and Arana (12 percent), and Terres de l'Ebre (11 percent). Catalunya was paralyzed and in Barcelona about 750,000 people demonstrated. In the evening, the televised speech of King Phillip VI provoked outrage. It was entirely in Spanish and addressed to the Spanish, but without a hint of empathy toward the citizens who had been beaten. He stated that "Catalan society is fractured and split" and blamed the Catalan authorities that "have tried to break the unity of Spain and national sovereignty, and it is the right of all Spaniards to democratically decide on their life in common" (Text . . ., 2017). In short, a stubborn defense of "constitutional patriotism" (Spanish nationalism). Puigdemont's speech on the following day was more conciliatory. Protests against the presence of the police and the Civil Guard were growing in some Catalan towns, but there were no violent incidents.

Over the following days, some companies—Banco de Sabadell, CaixaBank, and others—moved their headquarters outside of Catalunya in order not to lose the protection of the European Central Bank if independence were to be declared. The Rajoy government helped them to change headquarters. On October 7, transversal demonstrations in Catalunya and Spain called for dialogue: "*parlem.*" The mayor of Barcelona, Ada Colau, made the same request. On Sunday, October 8, 350,000 people summoned by the Catalan Civil Society (SCC, which includes Cs and PP) demonstrated in Barcelona in favor of the unity of Spain. There were no incidents. Speakers included the former Socialist minister and president of the European Parliament, Josep Borrell.

At seven o'clock that evening, Puigdemont appeared in the Catalan Parliament. Various European leaders—especially Donald Tusk, president of the Council of Europe—were trying to prevent the declaration of independence. The president made public the results of the referendum, assumed responsibility for the ballot and the "Declaration of the representatives of Catalunya" (without legal value) signed by JxSí and CUP, in which, addressing "the people of Catalunya and all peoples of the world," he proclaimed: "we constitute the Catalan Republic, as an independent and sovereign state, of democratic and social right," emphasizing that "the constitution of the Catalan Republic . . . responds to the impediment on the part of the Spanish state to make effective the right to the self-determination of the people," involving "the entry into force of the Transitional and Foundational Law of the Republic," and initiating "the constituent, democratic, citizen-based, transversal, participatory and binding process," affirming "the will to open negotiations with the Spanish state," bringing "to the knowledge of the international community and the authorities of the European Union the constitution of the Catalan Republic and proposed negotiations with the Spanish state," and appealing "to states and international organizations to recognize the Catalan Republic." But, shortly after, he suspended the declaration of independence in order to facilitate dialogue and international mediation and find an agreeable solution. The thirty thousand people concentrated near the Parliament, traveled, in eight seconds, from enthusiasm to disappointment. CUP felt betrayed and said it did not renounce the Republic.

On October 11, Rajoy asked Puigdemont to clarify whether he had proclaimed independence—under threat of applying Article 155 of the Spanish Constitution—and reiterated his refusal to any negotiation that did not conform to the Spanish constitution. Puigdemont responded in two letters (October 16 and 19) in which he was ambiguous about the declaration of independence and insisted on his predisposition to dialogue despite the arrest of Cuixart and Sànchez, which had provoked protests throughout Catalunya. The institutional confrontation had no end in sight. On October 21, Rajoy activated Article 155, which had to be approved by the Senate by an absolute majority, "after a request made to the President of the Autonomous Community was neglected." That led to intervention in the Autonomous Community, the dismissal of the government, the dissolution of the Parliament, and the holding of elections when "institutional normality has been restored."

On October 26, a plenary session of the Parliament was called to analyze the situation that, once the preliminaries of 155 had been activated, could either retract and call elections or unilaterally declare independence (DUI) and launch the Republic pending international recognition.

In the days before, the tension grew. The CUP and the Referendum Defence Committees (CDR) declared independence had been proclaimed and demanded that the Republic be set in motion. University students who had demonstrated on the morning of the October 26 made the same demand, as did the most mobilized and radicalized sectors on social networks. The Catalan government, ERC, and PDeCAT, as well as a large part of public opinion, were doubtful and divided between the "Fem via cap la República ja!" that Marta Rovira tweeted, and the attempts of some councilors—with Santi Vila as their visible head—for the president to call elections. A last-minute negotiation attempt was also promoted by a group of Catalan businessmen and some leaders of the PSC (Miquel Iceta, José Montilla), with the mediation of Basque president Iñigo Orkullu; their aim was to prevent Rajoy from applying Article 155 if Puigdemont called elections. The latter asked for Article 155 to be stopped, along with the requests from the State Attorney General's Office, the release of Cuixart and Sànchez, and the withdrawal of the reinforcement police and civil guards deployed in Catalunya. This was explained by Margarita Robles, Socialist spokesperson in the Congress of Deputies, when she announced that the PSOE would not support Article 155 if Puigdemont called regional elections.

At midmorning on October 26, Puigdemont had decided to call elections, but Rajoy did not make any commitment, and the session of the Senate began, resulting the following day in the approval of the application of Article 155. Some PDeCAT deputies and mayors threatened to resign, and ERC said it would leave the government if elections were called. At noon, PDeCAT seemed about to break, and in front of the party headquarters in Barcelona cries of "traitors" could be heard. Puigdemont retreated and opted for a DUI. His statement calmed things down. Vila resigned, and the party closed ranks around the president.

On October 27, at 3:20 pm, the parliamentary committee announced that the proposal for a resolution by JxSÍ and the CUP-Crida Constituent, which included the declaration of October 10, had been approved by seventy votes in favor, ten against, and two abstentions (the deputies of the PSC, the PP, and Cs left the room before the vote). In the resolution, the Catalan government was urged to "dictate all the resolutions necessary for the development of the Law of transitional legal foundation for the Republic" and detailed the actions that needed to be carried out to deploy the Republic. Forty minutes later, the Senate approved intervention in the Autonomy of Catalunya.

This time independence has been proclaimed, but with dubious legal effects because it had been done with a motion for a resolution. In Plaça de Sant Jaume (headquarters of the Generalitat), there was a party with thousands of people celebrating the advent of the Republic. In Palau, where the Spanish was still flying next to the Catalan flag, the Catalan government was holding a meeting with concern; it was to be the last. Subsequently, the Catalan government went silent, and did not institutionalize the proclamation (it was not included in the Official Gazette of the Generalitat, nor in the Official Butlletí of the Parliament of Catalunya, nor were the corresponding rights processed). No state recognized the Catalan Republic. On October 28, the Official State Gazette (BOE) published Royal Decree 944/2017, which set in motion the measures provided for (but not developed) in Article 155 of the Spanish Constitution: the Catalan government was terminated, the Catalan Parliament was dissolved, elections were called for December 21 (21-D), and the Generalitat was intervened. At the same time, the judicial action started, and provisional prison was declared for the members of the Catalan government, accused of rebellion, sedition, and embezzlement of funds, while President Puigdemont and four councilors made the conflict international by going into exile. Political and civil society representatives and Catalan police officers were also charged.

And in that context, the 21-D elections took place with a mobilized electorate (both those in favor of the unity of Spain and those in favor of independence). The independence forces revalidated the results of 2015, and again, obtained the social majority a little below 50 percent, while the PP became marginal (4.2 percent of votes).

It was surprising that Rajoy decided to hold elections in Catalunya within the minimum period set by law once Article 155 had been activated. The ease with which pro-independence parties with imprisoned or exiled leaders accepted the elections is also surprising. This is explained by a double weakness.

On the one hand, the Catalan government was able to declare independence, but it was difficult to put that into practice since it did not have the means to do so, nor did it have sufficient social support. Indeed, the C ruling (June 2010) and Rajoy's refusal to negotiate a new finance model (September 2012) led to the rejection of the statutory route and the commitment to the right to decide. And Rajoy's immobility led to an increase in the number of citizens willing to vote for independence from 2010-2012, reaching a ceiling close to 50 percent as reflected in the electoral results. In sum, half of the individuals who wanted a federal state would vote in certain circumstances—recentralization initiated by the PP, or exhaustion of the statutory path—in favor of independence, and now individuals with dual Catalan and Spanish identification began to support independence, until there was a leap toward exclusively Catalan national identification (Prat, 2012; Tormos, Muñoz, Hierro, 2015). As can be seen in the graph below, from 2010-2012, respondents who felt more Catalan than Spanish or only Catalan-increased, exceeded 50 percent of the total between the two options, as did those who believed that Catalunya should be an independent state and those who would vote in favor of independence in a referendum.

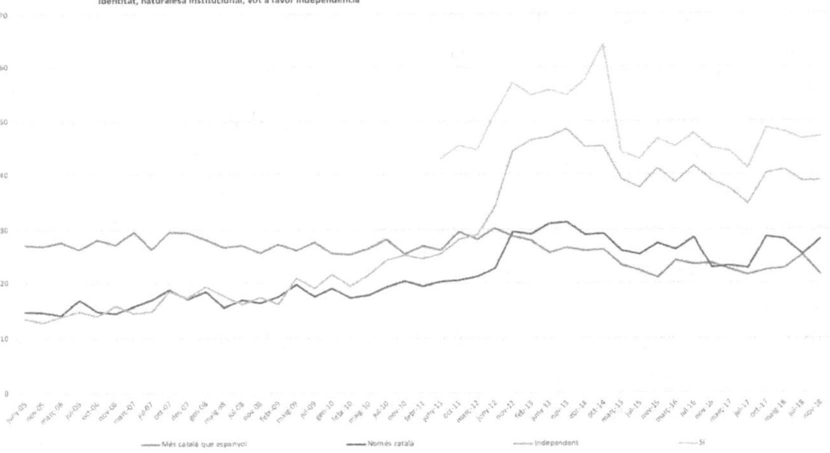


On the other hand, Rajoy's weakness to implement Article 155 in its entirety, as imposing it against the will of the majority of citizens and groups of officials, could lead to a response with unpredictable results. Hence, the decision occurred to launch it and at the same time call elections for 21-D. The pressure from European leaders—who demanded that the conflict be closed quickly in order not to destabilize the EU—was also key.

It is obvious that both the Catalan and Spanish governments made serious mistakes throughout the process. Rajoy's errors were a combination of negligence, lack of initiative, and dialogue that led to immobility: being unable to offer any proposal or alternative to Catalan disaffection and, on the other side, an inability to take politics into the legal arena. Rajoy was unable to understand that he was facing a political problem and underestimated the rise of independence, thinking it would disappear along with the economic crisis. And he was arrogant when he belittled the organizational capacity of Catalan civil society. And on 1-O, he committed the most serious mistake: using the police against citizens who went to vote. This delegitimized his arguments in the eyes of the world and subsequently contributed to the discredit of the Spanish administration of justice by encouraging an investigation based on the accusation of rebellion when the violence had only been used by the forces of public order. Discredit reached insurmountable extremes when the investigating judge had to withdraw the Euro arrest warrant against Puigdemont, given the possibility that the Belgian justice would reject it because of lack of legal basis, just as the German justice had.

For the independence movement, the insufficient critical mass favorable to independence was not sufficiently taken into account: it was a mistake to wait for international recognition; any comparison with what happened in Eastern Europe a quarter of a century earlier ignored the geopolitical context; in 1990-1991, the United States had made every effort to weaken the USSR as much as possible, favoring its implosion; Germany and Austria supported the independence of Slovenia and Croatia. On the contrary, today, after Brexit, the economic crisis, and the electoral rise of Eurosceptism and the extreme right, what the governments in the EU want is to maintain the stability of the states in Europe at any cost, and a Catalunya which had achieved independence by peaceful means and without renouncing the European tradition would have been an undesirable factor of contagion. And it was naive not to sufficiently assess the response capacity of the Spanish state. But the most important mistake was not taking advantage of Rajoy's error by responding to the 1-O vote with unacceptable police action—which was condemned by all (see graphs on p.222)—to force negotiations to hold an agreed referendum. Negotiations that, possibly, would have had international support because, despite the police charges, more than two million citizens demonstrated their willingness to go to the polls. That was enough to demand negotiations, but insufficient to declare independence based on a non-homologated referendum.

Ultimately, the "Catalan problem," like the "Basque problem," when held in front of the mirror of the Spanish right-wing's concept of state, was shown as it really was: either reflected in "Ortega's shared existence" or in José Calvo Sotelo more brutal "Better a red Spain than a broken Spain;" in the current

"Let's go for them," propagated by the political-media-legal-financial-police-academic network; or in the eternal, insoluble "Spanish problem."

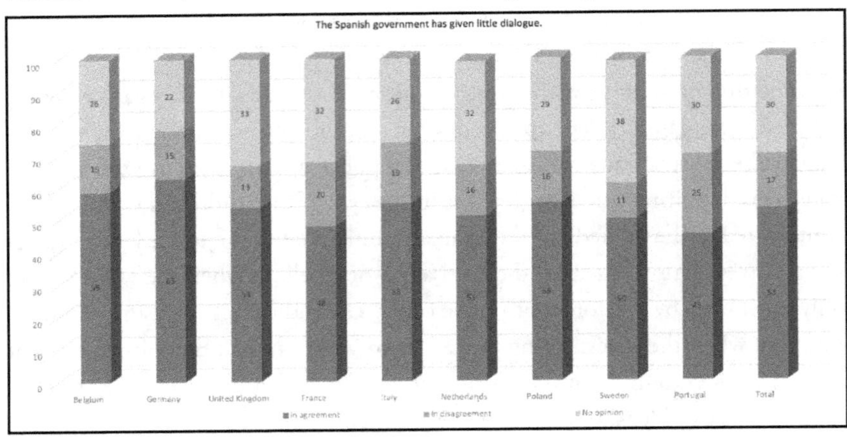


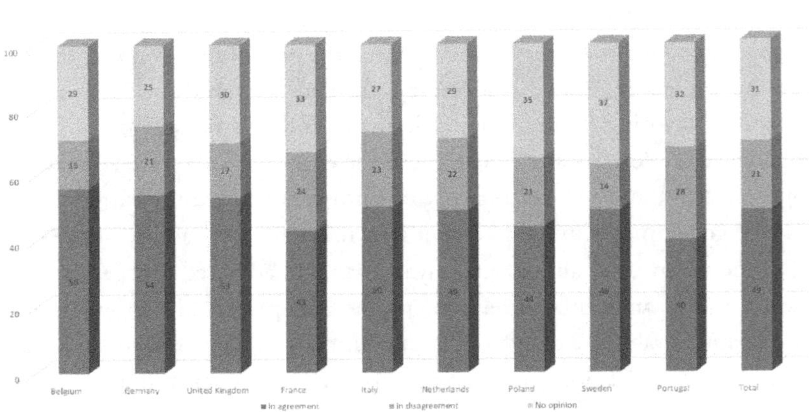


## Bibliography

Castells, Manuel. *L'era de la informació.* Vol. II *El poder de la identitat.* Barcelona: Edicions de la Universitat Oberta de Catalunya, 2003.

Castells, Manuel. "Globalització i identitat. Una perspectiva comparada" *IDEES*, no. 21 (2004): 17-28.

Connolly, Christopher K. "Independence in Europe: Secession, Sovereignty, and the European Union," 24 *Duke Journal of Comparative & International Law*, vol. 24 (2013): 51-105.

Grupo de trabajo para la actualización de la balanza fiscal de Catalunya (designada por la parte catalana de la Comisión Mixta de Valoraciones Administración del Estado-Generalitat de Catalunya) (2005), *La balanza fiscal de Cataluña con la Administración Central.*

Idescat. Generalitat de Catalunya. Institut d'Estadística de Catalunya (IDESCAT): https://www.idescat.cat/?lang=es.

Loscos Fernández, Fco. Javier. "Balanzas fiscales territoriales: perspectiva general y experiencia en España," a Aspectos territoriales del desarrollo: presente y futuro. Spanish Commercial Information (ICE) Revista de Economia. Madrid: Ministry of Industry, Tourism and Commerce. No. 848 (May-June 2009): 89-114.

Marín, Enric, and Joan M. Tresserras. *Obertura republicana. Catalunya, després del nacionalisme.* Barcelona: Pòrtic, 2018.

Mayayo i Artal, Andreu. *La ruptura catalana. Les eleccions del 15-J del 1977.* Catarroja-Barcelona-Palma: editorial afers, 2002.

Muro, Diego. "The Stillbirth of the Catalan Republic." *Current History.* 117:797 (March 2018): 83-88.

Muro, Diego, and Eckart Woertz (Eds.). *Secessions and Counter-secession. An International Relations Perspective.* Barcelona Center for International Affairs (2018): https://www.cidob.org/publicaciones/serie_de_publicacion/monografias/monografias/secession_and_counter_secession_an_international_relations_perspective/(language)/esl-ES.

Prat i Guilanyà, Sebastià. *El suport a la independència de Catalunya. Anàlisi de canvis i tendències en el període 2055-2012.* Monografies. Generalitat of Catalunya: Center d'Estudis d'Opinió (2012).

*Resultats de la balança fiscal de Catalunya amb el sector públic central 2006-2009* (2012). Barcelona: Generalitat de Catalunya. Departament d'Economia i Coneixement. Monografies 14.

Rovira i Virgili, Antoni. *Els darrers dies de la Catalunya republicana. Memòries on l'èxode català.* Barcelona: Proa, 1999 (first edition, Buenos Aires, 1940).

Segura i Mas, Antoni. "Un balance del Estado de las Autonomías en España (1976-2002)," a Rafael Quirosa-Cheyrouze Muñoz (Coord.), *Historia de la Transición en España. Los inicios del proceso democratitzador.* Madrid: Biblioteca Nueva (2007): 331-352.

Segura i Mas, Antoni. "Regional Financing System, Economic Crisis, and the Independence Movement in Catalunya," a Joseba Agirreazkuenaga and Xabier Irujo (edit.), *The Basque Fiscal System Contrasted to Nevada and Catalunya: In the Time of Major Crises.* Reno: Center for Basque Studies, University of Nevada, 2016: 89-101.

Segura, Antoni. *Chronicle of Catalanism. From Autonomy to Independence.* Barcelona: Angle Editorial, 2013.

Tormos, Raül, Jordi Muñoz, and Maria José Hierro. *Identificació Nacional: causa o conseqüència. The Effects of the Debate on Independence in the Catalan Identity.* Papers de Treball. Generalitat of Catalunya: Center d'Estudis d'Opinió, 2015.

Vilalta, Maite (Professor of Public Heritage of the University of Barcelona) (2012). *Balanzas fiscales: Metodología, resultados y elementos para un debate*: http://idpbarcelona.net/balanzas-fiscales-metodologia-resultados-y-elementos-para-un-debate/.

# 10

# Historical and Symbolic References in the Collective Imagination of the Catalan Independence Movement and New Symbols for the Twenty-First Century

*Teresa Abelló and Queralt Solé*

In recent years, Catalunya has appeared in the international press primarily due to matters relating to the claim to independence from the Spanish state. For a variety of reasons beyond the scope of this paper, the idea of independence, long present in Catalan society, has attracted increasing support and become widespread among broad swathes of the population, to the extent that half of all Catalans express a favorable view of it.[1] With support for independence having reached this level, the Catalan people have expressed their desire to hold a referendum on the question. Representative sectors of Catalan civil society, particularly the organizations *Òmnium Cultural*[2] and *Assemblea Nacional Catalana*[3] (Catalan National Assembly), have channeled this societal demand, presenting the case for a referendum before Catalunya's institutions of autonomous government, the *Parlament*,[4] and the government of the *Generalitat*,[5] which has repeatedly unsuccessfully petitioned the Spanish state to authorize a referendum.

Throughout this process, a variety of actions have taken place which have had political and social consequences, though these will not be the focus of this chapter.[6] Certain elements associated with the Catalan independence movement have emerged and become widespread, becoming established symbols. Four stand out: the Catalan national anthem, the Catalan flag, massive public demonstrations that fill public spaces, and ballot boxes. This chapter will focus on these four symbols.

The independence movement is the furthest expression of a movement to reclaim and defend Catalunya's unique identity, whose origins date back to the late nineteenth century. It is what is generically referred to as "Catalanism," a broad movement for national recognition that will be discussed later in this chapter. The independence movement embraces this Catalanist past while presenting clearly defined political objectives. Catalanism has, since its nineteenth-century origins, created a significant body of symbols that have, at times, been controversial due to the broad scope of the movement. Over the years, as the Catalanist movement evolved, it incorporated new symbolic elements that helped define it in the context of different moments in history. It is the sum of all these elements that shapes the identity of the movement. Although some are no longer actively referred to or displayed, the symbols and myths of Catalanism are part of the fabric of the independence movement, and we will need to refer to them to understand the symbology in current use.

### Historical Symbology

Symbols are intrinsic to political territories, nations, and states. Each nation has its own symbols, which serve to unify collective consciousness and show that its members belong to a given community. Symbols such as flags, national holidays, institutions, and rituals have been accepted as the materialization of the nation. Sociologists have emphasized the power of symbols to represent all manner of realities, including social realities and collective aspirations, and have concluded that all peoples, countries, and nations mythicize their past and their principles and use references, symbols, and images to represent and present themselves. In this vein, the flag of the United States of America is a paradigmatic example of a banner becoming an object of national devotion and a symbol of belonging to a political community.[7]

Political and cultural symbols are deep-rooted elements that express the territorialization of identity. In Europe, beginning in the nineteenth century, such symbols ceased to be exclusively linked to those in power and came to be associated with popular or democratic political and social movements. From that moment on, all such movements have created their own symbols. This is the context in which a cultural identity movement burst onto the scene in Catalunya, particularly starting in the last decades of the nineteenth century. This movement expanded throughout Catalan society, eventually developing into a political movement that advocated for the recognition of Catalunya as a national entity, known as "Catalanism." Accordingly, there is no question that the current independence movement feels itself to be the heir to a social and cultural movement whose roots, like those of movements elsewhere in Europe, can be traced back to the nineteenth century.[8]

Catalanism is a sociologically broad movement, politically and culturally structured, that advocates for the recognition of Catalunya as a historical, cultural, national, and political entity. As has already been stated, it emerged in the nineteenth century as a cultural movement that sought to restore the prestige of the Catalan language and culture, which was what gave Catalunya its identity. Beginning in the late nineteenth century, and throughout the twentieth century, it was also organized as a political movement, with varied goals for Catalunya's political future—as part of a federalist Spanish state, as a region within Spain, or as an independent country.[9]

According to the sociologist Randall Collins, rites and symbols reinforce group belonging and give individuals "emotional energy."[10] Thus, is can reasonably be asserted, regarding Catalunya in the nineteenth century, as elsewhere, symbolic elements became established, and, in time, became part of the corpus of Catalanism.

It should be noted that Catalunya was a nation with a long history, and its own political past had been cut short in 1714. The year 1714 plays a key role in Catalan symbology because it is when the War of the Spanish Succession came to an end. Much of Europe was involved in this war, a conflict between members of two historic dynasties, the Archduke Charles of the House of Habsburg, backed by Catalunya, and Phillip, Duke of Anjou, of the House of Bourbon, who was proclaimed Phillip V in 1700 and accepted as king in the rest of Spain. On September 11, 1714, after a months-long siege, Barcelona surrendered to the Bourbon troops, and Philip V was proclaimed king. The fall of Barcelona meant the end of the war and the military occupation of Catalunya. It also meant the end of the political agreement between Catalunya and the Hispanic Monarchy of the House of Habsburg, which dated from the fifteenth century, and the abolition of Catalunya's governing institutions.[11] Under the new Bourbon monarchy, Spain would become one of the most centralist and forcibly homogenized states in Europe.

As has been stated, this chapter will focus on the symbology of the current independence movement. However, in order to discuss this topic, we must first look back to the Catalanist movement of the late nineteenth century. The emergence of Catalanism marked the beginning of a process, comparable to the Italian *Risorgimiento*, that aimed to recover the identity that Catalunya had lost after the defeat of 1714. Allegory and mythology were at the forefront of these efforts. Symbols from Catalan history that recalled a glorious past were reclaimed and transformed. These included the medieval County of Barcelona, which came to represent all of Catalunya; historical heroes such as Wilfred the Hairy, symbol of medieval Catalunya, said to be the founder of the Catalan nation and creator of the Catalan flag, as will be discussed further on; Romanticism's exaltation of Sant Jordi (Saint George), Catalunya's patron saint since the mid-fifteenth century; and the Catalan language, used as an institutional language under the Catalan-Aragonese Crown and then banned from institutional use after 1714. Another symbol reclaimed during this period was the *Generalitat*, Catalunya's highest institution of government. The *Generalitat* has lived on as a symbol in the Catalanist collective imagination and has been given historical continuity, as it has been formally reinstated whenever Catalunya has managed to regain some form of self-government. This occurred in 1931, during the Second Spanish Republic; the Republican *Generalitat* was abolished by Francisco Franco in 1938, though it continued to exist in Catalunya until the end of the Civil War in 1939. The *Generalitat* was again reinstated in 1977, during the democratic transition, though with functions and powers that were not identical to those of the earlier Republican *Generalitat*. In any case, the *Generalitat* was a centuries-old institution that Catalans saw as the symbol and the recognition of their historical identity.

Throughout the second half of the nineteenth century, the Catalanist movement adopted and came to identify with a variety of elements that would become part of its symbolic corpus: republican movements that advocated for the abolition of the monarchy and the establishment of a federalist state; popular songs that made reference to an epic past or contained Romantic invocations of the Catalan homeland; the identification of Catalunya with certain articles of clothing traditionally worn in rural areas, such as the "*barretina*,"[12] with a somewhat bucolic look; the popularization of group dances, particularly the *sardana*, adopted as the national dance of Catalunya;[13] the creation of public spaces symbolizing Catalanness, such as the mountain of Montserrat and the enthronement of the Virgin of Montserrat and the tombs of those killed in 1714 in the city of Barcelona; and the emergence of great poets like Jacint Verdaguer who extolled the quintessential aspects of Catalunya. In short, a meaning of "Catalanness" was created, with room for a diverse cross-section of Catalan society to identify with the concept: religious, secular, conservative, progressive, intellectual, urban, rural, and so on.

Romantic intellectuals drew on sources from the seventeenth and eighteenth centuries to reclaim and re-narrate revolutionary episodes from the wars fought between Catalunya and the Spanish Crown in that period, presenting them as signs of the will of the Catalans to survive as a nation in the face of Bourbon absolutism. Without making anything up, they popularized and used the evocative power of the past to arouse consciousness. In the first three decades of the nineteenth century, Catalanist intellectuals enshrined the date of September 11, 1714—which marked the fall of Barcelona to Bourbon troops, and thus the defeat of Catalunya—as the "end of the Catalan nation." Using the symbol of the phoenix, they commemorated the defeat of 1714 in order to express Catalunya's ability to rise as a nation from its own ashes.

The new political and social movements that emerged beginning in the early twentieth century inevitably had to create their own symbols, symbols that conveyed the idea of collective demands and claims, in keeping with the new era. They felt themselves to be heirs to the cultural movement of the late nineteenth century, and they reclaimed and transformed historical symbols, giving them new meanings, and created new ones.[14] It is undoubtedly necessary to look back to the Catalanism of the late nineteenth century, which had no intention of breaking away from the Spanish state, and to the first political movements of the early twentieth century in order to identify and understand the symbolic imaginary of the independence movement. However, simple observation shows that the current panorama is significantly different: some symbols have disappeared, others have evolved, and new elements have emerged.[15]

From the mid-twentieth century on, two key elements stand out: efforts to strengthen the position of the Catalan language and Catalanist political action. In the realm of culture, the aim was no longer simply to advocate for the use of the Catalan language, which had survived in family and colloquial contexts despite being banned from official use, but also to "standardize" and "normalize" it, restoring its role as an academic and scientific language in keeping with the new industrialized society. The Catalan language thus became a political instrument, a means of giving structure and cohesion to modern Catalan society, and an essential vehicle for strengthening and giving visibility to its culture.

In the realm of politics, beginning in the early years of the twentieth century, a series of parties were founded that shared the objective of obtaining some degree of self-government. The furthest advancements in self-government were the autonomy statutes of 1932, 1979, and 2005. There were also markedly pro-independence parties, though they were a clear minority in this period. All of these political parties, like the current independence movement, adopted the historical symbols of Catalanism and created new symbols in accordance with their own ideologies and approaches.

## The National Anthem

Identification with the national anthem did not originate with the contemporary independence movement. Rather, since it was first adopted in the nineteenth century, the Catalan anthem has maintained its emblematic power, first within Catalanism, and later within the independence movement.

Anthems contribute to social cohesion and produce collective emotion.[16] Music itself is a notable element of social union. A song, rhythm, or melody can recall memories of past events and lead the listener to reexperience sensations that cannot be repeated. A national anthem goes a step further, providing a unique moment in which the old and the young, women and men, the rich and the poor, country folk and city folk can join in singing the same song. Gender and social status do not matter; it is a moment in which everyone comes together to invoke a common idea through the singing of an anthem. As Esteban Buch has noted, music, conceived of as a language of passions, is the symbol and the instrument of a utopic social order in which subjective emotion contributes harmoniously to the establishment of the group.[17] Catalunya's official national anthem is called "*Els Segadors*" ("The Reapers"). The poet Jacint Verdaguer wrote it down in the late nineteenth century, gathering fragments of popular songs, passed down through oral tradition, that recalled the revolt of 1640.[18]

In 1640, social grievances against the Hispanic Monarchy sparked an uprising in Catalunya, which would lead to the proclamation of an independent republic the following year. In the spring of 1640, peasants who were harvesting wheat with the tools used for this task—sickles—rose up against Castilian authorities and soldiers stationed in Catalunya, who were quartered in private homes, abusing and taking advantage of everyone and everything, including their hosts. This initial virulent popular discontent coincided with the conflict between Catalan political authorities and the Hispanic Monarchy over the latter's attempts to consolidate power despite Catalunya having its own laws and institutions. These social and political conflicts converged, leading to a war in which Catalunya allied itself with France against the Hispanic Monarchy. In return for French military assistance, Catalunya would be constituted as a republic, as occurred fleetingly in 1641. The conflict became part of the Thirty Years' War, but lasted beyond the Peace of Westphalia, eventually concluding with the Treaty of the Pyrenees (1659), a peace accord in which the Hispanic Monarchy ceded to France the Catalan territories to the north of the Pyrenees—the counties of Rosselló, Conflent, and Vallespir, and part of the Cerdanya. Perpinyà, then the second-largest city in Catalunya after Barcelona, became French. Catalunya kept its own political institutions, but from that point on the Hispanic Monarchy exercised significant control over them.

Numerous popular songs emerged from the revolt of 1640, among them "*Els Segadors.*" What had been an erotic song become a combative song and a call to resist and return Catalunya to a state of plenitude.

What is remarkable about the Catalan national anthem is that it dates from such an early period and has endured up until the present day. There are two principal reasons for this endurance. Firstly, nineteenth-century Catalan society adopted the song and made it its own. Secondly, once it had been adopted and began to be sung in public, Spanish authorities began to persecute and ban its performance. From 1882 to 1892, the song's lyrics drew closer to the definitive version, eventually established in 1897 by Emili Guanyavents, and it became increasingly popular. In 1897, the song was banned for the first time by the governor of the province of Barcelona, who saw the entire lyrics, and especially the chorus—"*Bon cop de falç, defensors de la terra, bon cop de falç*" ("A good blow of the sickle, defenders of the land, a good blow of the sickle")—as a glorification of the fight against the Spanish state and a claim to nationhood.

The anthem was repeatedly banned, beginning in last years of the nineteenth century and during the twentieth-century dictatorships of Miguel Primo de Rivera and Francisco Franco. These prohibitions served to reaffirm the status of "*Els Segadors*" as a clandestine protest song. It was only logical that, with the coming of democracy after Franco's death in 1975, the song would eventually be established as Catalunya's official anthem in 1993.

In the twenty-first century, "*Els Segadors*" remains Catalunya's official national anthem and has been fully assimilated as such in Catalan society. It has even been recorded with mostly English-language lyrics by the American heavy metal band A Sound of Thunder.

Concurrently, the independence movement has progressively adopted "*L'Estaca,*" written in 1968 by singer-songwriter Lluís Llach, as a protest song. The lyrics call for the people to work together to bring down a "stake," a metaphor for the Franco dictatorship.[19] Over the years, the song has taken root in Catalunya and has also been adopted as a protest song elsewhere in the world, with translations in multiple languages.

### Mass Demonstrations

One of the most identifying characteristics of the modern independence movement has been the peaceful use of public spaces. Although mass demonstrations do not constitute a symbol in and of themselves, in the context of the independence movement, organizers have transformed them into an instrument that does have symbolic connotations. Throughout the history of Catalunya in the twentieth and twenty-first centuries, citizens have taken to the streets insistently and peacefully, making clear demands for self-government and, more recently, independence.[20] In political terms, this longing for liberty has been symbolically concentrated on the date of September 11. The events organized each year on the occasion of this commemorative holiday have attracted increasingly massive participation, creating a specific tradition of protest that is clearly distinct from all others.

Every nation has a national holiday. As we have seen, Catalunya, as a historical nation, has adopted September 11 as its holiday to commemorate the events of 1714.

In 1901, after Catalanist and republican parties did very well in the municipal election in Barcelona, the first large demonstration was held in the streets of the city. It was to be the first in a series of demonstrations, interrupted only by the repressive policies of the authoritarian regimes of the generals Primo de Rivera (1923-1930) and Franco (1939-1975).

The largest demonstrations have inevitably been held during periods of significant political exceptionality and social tension. The first such demonstration following the death of the dictator Franco took place in 1976. Spanish authorities, still left over from the Franco regime, banned the commemoration of September 11 in Barcelona, and the event was held in nearby Sant Boi de Llobregat, in front of the tomb of Rafael de Casanova, one of the symbolic heroes of 1714. The following year, a million people took to the streets in Barcelona. It was the beginning of a new era.

In 1980, with the political "Transition" underway in Spain and institutions of regional self-government reinstituted, the first legislation passed by the new Catalan *Parlament* was to designate September 11 as Catalunya's national holiday (known as "*la Diada*"). In the ensuing years, the celebration became increasingly institutional, taking on a ceremonial form that did not include the more activist demonstration. The September 11 demonstration became an event organized solely by openly pro-independence groups, with limited participation.

This situation changed in 2012. In an atmosphere of institutional confrontation and in the context of the recently launched "process" to achieve independence, the mass demonstration with the slogan "*Catalunya, nou estat d'Europa*" ("Catalunya, a new state in Europe") revealed the scope of the movement and the pro-independence drift of Catalan political parties. From that year on, a series of increasingly large demonstrations were held each year on September 11, reaching a peak of two million participants. In 2013, civil organizations proposed the "*Via Catalana*" ("Catalan Way"), a human chain stretching about four hundred kilometers along Catalunya's Mediterranean coast, which symbolically emulated events organized in the Baltic countries during their independence process from the former Soviet Union. The successful organization of this mass demonstration demonstrated the independence movement's ability to continue to gain support, and the event became a symbol in its own right. Further calls to demonstrate on September 11 have likewise elicited massive participation, now with the goal of attaining an independent Catalan republic—another symbol. Thus, in 2018 the slogan was "*Fem la República catalana*" ("Let's make the Catalan Republic").

Other symbolic elements that have been incorporated into these demonstrations of popular opinion include human towers (*els castells*), which are themselves one of the most genuinely representative elements of Catalan identity.[21] The building of *castells* is a leisure activity whose existence has been documented since the eighteenth century. It was highly popular in republican and Catalanist circles beginning in the latter half of the nineteenth century. The values associated with *castells* were emphasized in Romantic poetry: strength, balance, bravery, and common sense; in short, the activity brought together the ideal values of a people. Beginning in the final decades of the twentieth century, the building of *castells* spread to all of Catalunya, thus serving to unite youth from a variety of backgrounds.

### L'Estelada (The "Starred" Flag)

The flag with which the independence movement identifies is known as the "*Estelada*" (the "starred" flag). It was created in 1907 and is a version of Catalunya's official flag, called the "*Senyera*."

The *Senyera* consists of four red vertical stripes on a yellow field. Unlike many other European flags, including those of France, Germany, the United Kingdom, and Spain,[22] the origins of the *Senyera* date back to the twelfth century, when it was part of the coat of arms of Ramon Berenguer IV, Count of Barcelona. It became clearly accepted as the flag of Catalunya in the nineteenth century when the cultural Romanticism of the period chose to make it the political symbol of the Catalanist movement. At the end of the nineteenth century, the flag with the four stripes began to be displayed at all sorts of meetings and events, and to be used as an identifying element among a certain segment of the press and in the emblems of social and cultural organizations. By the turn of the century, the *Senyera* had been fully adopted by Catalanism, and it was used throughout the twentieth century, at times being banned and persecuted, before becoming the official flag of Catalunya in 1979.

The pro-independence version of the *Senyera* is the result of the admiration of Catalans living in Cuba for the country's successful fight for independence from Spain. After Cuba finally achieved independence in 1902, with help from the United States of America, the five-pointed white star on a blue field featured on the Cuban revolutionary flag was adopted by Catalans, who added it to the *Senyera*.[23] The Cuban flag had itself been inspired by the flag of the United States, in which each five-pointed star represented one of the states that were fighting for independence from Great Britain when the design was adopted in 1777.[24] For the Cubans, a single white star, which had been a symbol of liberty since the French Revolution, was enough. The blue background symbolized brotherhood. Three blue stripes, one for each department on the island, on a white field completed the flag.

Thus, the *Estelada* was the result of the local Catalan community's affinity with the Cuban fight for independence, inspired by its symbology at a time when the Spanish Empire was collapsing. This new flag became the undisputed emblem of the Catalan independence movement, though it was initially embraced and used exclusively by Catalan communities in Latin America.[25] In fact, the "*Grop Nacionalista Radical*," founded in Santiago de Cuba in 1907, was the first to adapt the *Estelada* as part of its image.

The Catalan pro-independence flag spread slowly in Catalunya itself. In the first years of the twentieth century, Catalans saw it as a strange symbol, and it was not until the First World War (1914-1918) that the *Estelada* definitively took root as a symbol when it was used to internationalize Catalunya's political demands. A small number of Catalans promoted the participation of Catalan volunteers in the French Foreign Legion with a view to subsequently obtaining international support for the fight for political recognition.[26] At an event held on September 11, 1915, three Catalan soldiers enlisted in the French Legion laid an *Estelada* at the feet of the statue of Rafael de Casanova. The *Estelada* began to be widely accepted and circulated beginning in 1915. Francesc Macià, who was to become president of the *Generalitat* in 1932, adopted it as the logo of *Estat Català* ("Catalan State"), the political party he founded in 1922.

The *Estelada* was adopted, beginning in 1922 and in the 1930s, by pro-independence groups who aimed to use the public display of this symbol to clearly show the difference between Catalanists who sought some degree of self-government, but not the creation of a Catalan state, and the fight for full independence.

During the Franco dictatorship, the *Estelada* was banned, and a new version of the flag emerged. This new version was created to show the ideological differences within the independence movement, underscoring the communist basis of the fight for national liberation. Instead of a white star, the new *Estelada* featured a red star. Later, the blue background triangle became white; it was subsequently changed to yellow.

In the twenty-first century, the *Estelada*, in its different versions, has been unquestionably ubiquitous at all public events, beginning with the first mass demonstrations in 2010. It has also been on constant display on the balconies of many homes. The *Estelada* has become the most visible symbol of the independence movement. In this century, it has always been used in association with peaceful demands for the right to vote in a referendum.

### "Les urnes": Ballot Boxes as a Symbol

The latest major symbol of the independence movement to emerge was the ballot box. The clandestine operation that made possible the October 1, 2017, referendum, despite major difficulties that included explicit prohibitions by the Spanish government, is known as "*operació urnes*" ("operation ballot boxes"). Organizers managed to provide 2,343 polling stations located throughout Catalunya with 6,500 ballot boxes.

Since 2010, political and social debate in Catalunya has centered on the right to self-determination and independence. Up until this point, Catalanism had largely and pragmatically accepted the administrative framework of autonomy statutes for Spanish regions, known as "autonomous communities." The debate surrounding these statutes has been continuous in Catalunya; supporters of independence have always believed they do not go far enough, while anti-Catalanists have seen them as facilitating the ulterior ambitions of separatists. Nonetheless, since 1979, Catalunya had enjoyed a certain degree of self-government within the framework of the Spanish constitution, within the limits set by the autonomy statute in force at the time.

There has always been controversy surrounding this statutory framework. Whenever statutory text agreed upon in Catalunya has been brought before the Spanish Parliament for final approval, lawmakers in Madrid have drastically pared it down. This has produced constant political tensions, as well as a collective mood of disappointment in Catalan society, which has perceived that the sacrosanct result of the people's will—that is to say, the exercise of democracy through the act of voting—was being questioned.

Catalunya has a longstanding tradition of "*pactism*." The first Catalan "constitutions"—pacts between the Hispanic Monarchy and Catalan society—dated from the fifteenth century, and in the ensuing centuries their defense became one of the primary symbols of Catalan sovereignty. At the same time, it is important to bear in mind that Catalunya's relationship with the monarchy has historically been difficult, and for this reason, support for a republican form of government has been predominant among those who longed for the return of self-government in Catalunya and unanimous among supporters of full independence. In 1641, during one of the most serious conflicts between the king and Catalunya's institutions of government, a fleeting and dubious Catalan republic was declared, with the backing of the king of France. As we have seen, the song that would become the national anthem, "*Els Segadors,*" originated from this conflict. Although it lasted only seven days, the ephemeral republic of 1641 became a myth, and an objective over the course of the nineteenth and twentieth centuries. Proof of its persistence as a myth can be seen in the decision of early twentieth-century urban planners to name one of Barcelona's main streets after the man who proclaimed it, Pau Claris.

In the twentieth century, pacts with successive Spanish governments to gain some degree of self-government, as well as disagreements, were frequent, and the ballot box consistently played an important role in sustaining these demands. In 1914, the *Manucomunitat,* which brought together the governing bodies of the four Catalan provinces, was constituted. The words of its president, Enric Prat de la Riba, clearly stated what it was and what it meant: "The *Mancomunitat* is everything as a symbol, but it is nothing as a power." For the first time since 1714, Catalunya had gained an institutional instrument, albeit a very limited one—a political body covering all of the Catalan territory. This was of enormous symbolic importance.

A further step was taken in 1931, at the beginning of the Second Spanish Republic. In the municipal elections that led to the proclamation of the Republic, the recently constituted political party *Esquerra Republicana de Catalunya* (Republican Left of Catalunya), which advocated for the constitution of a Catalan republic that would retain some form of relationship with Spain, did remarkably well in Catalunya's municipalities. Here another symbol of Catalanism and the independence movement, in this case, a person comes into play: Francesc Macià. After learning of the results of the municipal elections, Macià proclaimed the Catalan republic for which he and many others had been fighting for years: "In the name of the people of Catalunya, I proclaim the Catalan State, under the regime of a Catalan Republic, which freely and in all cordiality desires and requests the collaboration of the other peoples of Spain in creating a Confederation of Iberian peoples [. . .] At this time, we raise our voice to all free states of the world in the name of liberty, justice, and international peace."[27] These words, mythic as well as epic, summarized the aspirations of the independence movement of the first decades of the twentieth century, and became one of its most valuable symbols. However, the most symbolic of the sentences pronounced by Macià in April 1931 was undoubtedly the following: "Catalans: Interpreting the sentiment and the longing of the people that has just given us its vote, I proclaim the Catalan Republic as a state that is part of the Iberian Federation."

The proclamation of the Catalan Republic was, once again, a symbolic gesture, and as such it was never actually constituted. Political pacts between republican parties led to the creation of a state defined in the new Spanish Constitution as an "integral state," thus avoiding both federalist and centralist models.

The first statute approved after the dictator's death was rolled out between 1980 and 1990, and the limits of autonomous government soon became apparent. This led to discussion of the need for a new statute. On September 30, 2005, the Catalan *Parlament* passed a new statute that was more ambitious than the previous one. The preamble referred to Catalunya's historical rights and the exercise of its inalienable right to self-determination. Symbolically, it stated that, reflecting the sentiment and the will of Catalan citizens, it defined Catalunya as a nation. This statement broached the endless nation/state debate, and the text was drastically amended when it was debated in the Spanish Parliament in Madrid. Nevertheless, pragmatism won in Catalunya, and the new text was approved. After the new statute had been passed by the Spanish Parliament and approved by Catalan voters in a referendum, the most conservative political parties in Spain arbitrarily challenged certain parts of the text in court as unconstitutional. The decision to challenge the new statute brought tensions between Catalunya and Spain to a level not seen since the end of the Franco dictatorship.

Years later, in 2010, a ruling by Spain's Constitutional Court further distorted the text that had been approved. Catalan authorities and political parties reacted in unison. In an unprecedented political move, they asked citizens to demonstrate under the slogan "*Som una nació, nosaltres decidim*" ("We are a nation, we decide") to preserve Catalunya's pride, self-worth, and sense of dignity. The mass demonstration held in Barcelona, symbolically led by all the men who had held the office of president of the *Generalitat* since the beginning of the post-Franco Transition, marked the start of the Catalan "process" for the right to self-determination.

This process was to be characterized by ballot boxes. Starting in 2009, a series of informal, local, popular consultations on the question of independence had been held. The first Catalunya-wide consultation, also unofficial, was held on November 9, 2014. According to data provided by the *Generalitat*, 2.3 million people participated, and more than 80 percent of them voted in favor of Catalunya becoming an independent state. The independence movement reaffirmed its commitment to winning at the ballot box, and the results of the subsequent Catalan parliamentary election corroborated the will of the people to decide their future, given the stance on independence of the parties that won.

In the ensuing months, the combination of an attentive civil society and political parties governing with a plurality of seats, whose platforms included the peaceful fight for independence, made possible the October 1, 2017, referendum organized by the Catalan government. This referendum became a symbol of the right of Catalunya's citizens to decide their future—whether they wanted to remain part of Spain or become an independent country. The vote was banned by the Spanish government and the Constitutional Court, but the day was seen as the culmination of a process that demanded the right to vote on Catalunya's political future. More than two million people voted in favor of independence.

The principal image transmitted by the media was that of police violence and of voters defending ballot boxes, an image that has become a reference.

On September 6, 2017, the *Parlament* passed the Law on the Referendum on Self-Determination, which was immediately blocked by the Constitutional Court. This is not the place to discuss the soundness of the law, but it does show that the independence movement did not contemplate any means other than democratic channels for achieving its objectives. The political situation at the time and Spanish government's refusal to enter into any sort of dialogue with Catalunya led to differences between the two sides reaching a breaking point. In accordance with laws passed by a majority of the Catalan Parliament, but after a significant number of members had abandoned the chamber, on October 27, the speaker of the *Parlament* issued a symbolic proclamation, with no practical effects, of the "Catalan Republic," using the following words: "In the free exercise of the right to self-determination, and in accordance with the mandate received from the citizens of Catalunya, we constitute the Catalan Republic, as an independent and sovereign state, under the rule of law, democratic and social."

What had happened—besides the passage of the aforementioned laws—in order for the speaker of the *Parlament* to consider herself authorized to make such a proclamation? The answer is simple: the referendum, held without the authorization of the Spanish government, on October 1.

The events of October 1, 2017 will undoubtedly have a place of honor within the symbology of the independence movement in the future, for two reasons: the firm will of the Catalan people to participate in a democratic referendum to determine their political future, and the violence carried out by a democratic Spanish government against citizens who were ready to express themselves democratically.

On October 1, 2018, a large demonstration was held to mark the first anniversary of the referendum, with the English slogan "Self-determination is a human right." A ballot box led off the demonstration.

## Continuity or Change?

Starting in October 2017, the symbols of the independence process inundated the urban landscape of cities and towns. *Estelades* on balconies were soon joined by the color yellow following the jailing of pro-independence leaders. These symbols elevated the allegorical battle to an indisputable dimension of ideological confrontation. Symbols, both old and newly created in the twenty-first century, themselves became an object of reflection as never before in the history of Catalunya.

Catalunya has the particularity of having recently added new symbols in its fight for self-determination. The symbology that was created in the late nineteenth century has endured up until the present, and along the way other elements have been added. Some have emerged only to quickly disappear, but others have come to stay, including the song "*L'Estaca*" and the ballot box.

It remains to be seen whether "*L'Estaca*" will remain a protest song in the future. Today, the Catalan independence movement has adopted it as its own and identifies with its lyrics. The fact that it has been used by political and social movements elsewhere in the world has made it all the more powerful.

The ballot box is a new symbol that is particularly powerful because it represents the culmination of democracy, the act of voting. Without the violent intervention of the Spanish government, using its police forces, to stop a peaceful voting process, ballot boxes might not have been adopted as a new symbol by Catalan society. It was the defense of ballot boxes, and the symbolism of having to defend them in order to exercise the right to vote, that turned them into a new symbol that can be expected to endure over time.

In any event, the defense of Catalunya and its essence, as well as the commitment to understanding, will remain. Because, as the musician and political exile Pau Casals recalled in the speech he gave when he accepted the United Nations Peace Medal in 1971:

> I'm a Catalan. Today Catalunya is a province of Spain. But what has been Catalunya? Catalunya has been the greatest nation in the world. I'll tell you why. Catalunya has had the first Parliament, much before England. Catalunya had the beginning of the United Nations. All the authorities of Catalunya in the eleventh century met in a city of France, at the time Catalunya, to speak about peace. In the eleventh century. Peace in the world and against, against, against, against the wars, the inhumanity of wars . . . This was Catalunya.[28]

## NOTES

1 Without a referendum on the question, it is impossible to given exact numbers, but the votes obtained in municipal and regional elections by parties that declare themselves to be pro-independence are enough to venture this estimate.

2 "*Òmnium Cultural*" is an organization founded in 1961 with the aim of promoting the Catalan language and defending Catalunya's national rights. It was in charge of organizing the demonstration held in Barcelona on July 10, 2010, with the slogan, "*Som una nació. Nosaltres decidim.*"

3 The "*Assemblea Nacional Catalana*," founded in 2011, is a political organization with a broad scope that has the goal of achieving independence for Catalunya.

4 *Parlament*: we will use the Catalan term to refer to Catalunya's regional parliament.

5 *Generalitat*: currently, Catalunya's institution of self-government, to which we will refer further on.

6 For a discussion of some of these actions and their consequences, see Montserrat Guibernau, "Prospects for an Independent Catalunya," *International Journal of Politics, Culture, and Society* 27 (2014): 5-23, https://doi.org/10.1007/s10767-013-9165-4.

7 See Henry Tudor, *Political Myth* (London: Pall Mall, 1972); George L. Mosse, *The Nationalization of the Masses: Political Symbolism and Mass Movements in Germany from the Napoleonic Wars Through the Third Reich* (New York: Howard Fertig, 1975); Eric Hobsbawm and Terence Ranger, *The Invention of Tradition* (Cambridge: Cambridge University Press, 1983); Ernest Gellner, *Nations and Nationalism* (Ithaca: Cornell University Press, 1983); Anne-Marie Thiesse, *La Création des identités nationales. Europe XVIII<sup>e</sup> -XX<sup>e</sup> siècle* (Paris: Seuil, 1999).

8 For a discussion of the consolidation of new national identities in nineteenth-century Europe from an anthropological perspective, see Josep R. Llobera, *Foundation of National Identity: From Catalunya to Europe* (Oxford-New York: Berghahn Books, 2004).

9 A summary of the history of Catalanism can be found in Albert Balcells, "Catalanism and national emancipation movements in the rest of Europe between 1885 and 1939," *Catalan Historical Review* (2013): 85-104, https://www.raco.cat/index.php/CatalanHistoricalReview/article/view/268024/355605.

10 Randall Collins, *Interaction Ritual Chains* (Princeton-Oxford: Princeton University Press, 2004). For an analysis of Collins's theories in line with the interpretation used here, see Marta Rizo, "Interaction and emotions. Randall Collins' micro sociology and the emotional dimension of social interaction," *Psicoperspectivas* 14, no. 2 (2015): 51-61, http://dx.doi.org/10.5027/PSICOPERSPECTIVAS-VOL14-ISSUE2-FULLTEXT-439.

11 Agustí Alcoberro, "The war of the Spanish Succession in the Catalan-speaking Lands," *Catalan Historical Review* 3 (2010): 69-86, http://revistes.iec.cat/index.php/CHR/article/viewFile/37024/pdf_49.

12 A distinctive red and black cap, the end of which fits snuggly around the head of the wearer.

13 The *sardana* was endlessly exalted by prominent intellectuals and poets, including Joan Maragall.

14 See the collective volume, Daniel Venteo, ed., *Símbols del catalanisme* (Barcelona: Enciclopèdia Catalana, 2019).

15 See Giovanni C. Cattini, "Myths and symbols in the political culture of Catalan nationalism (1880-1914)," *Nations and Nationalism* 21, no. 3 (2015): 445-460.

16 Xavier Maugendre, *L'Europe des hymnes dans leur contexte historique et musical* (Sprimont: Mardaga, 1996).

17 Esteban Buch, *Beethoven's Ninth: A Political History* (Chicago: University of Chicago Press, 2003).

18 Agustí Alcoberro, "Els Segadors," in *Símbols del catalanisme*, ed. Venteo, 154-157.

19 Steven Forti, "'L'estaca': Transnational Trajectories of a Catalan Antifascist Song," *Popular Music and Society* (2020), https://doi.org/10.1080/03007766.2020.1820781.

20 At different moments in the twentieth and twenty-first centuries, large demonstrations were held in support of a statute of autonomy (April 24, 1932; September 11, 1976; February 11, 2006; July 10, 2010). In July 2011, another large demonstration was held in Barcelona in support of the right to leave behind limited self-government under the Spanish system of "autonomous communities" and aspire to full independence.

21 Human towers can also be found in other countries, including India. They represent the epitome of collaborative effort and teamwork and are featured in most commemorative and festive events all over Catalunya. On "*castells*," their history, and their relation to the independence movement, see Mariann Cavzi, "Catalunya's human towers: Nationalism, associational culture, and the politics of performance," *American Ethnologist* 43, no. 2 (2013): 353-368, online.

22 Giovanni C. Cattini, "Myths and symbols in the political culture of Catalan nationalism (1880-1914)," *Nations and Nationalism* 21, no. 3 (2015): 445-460.

23 Josep Maria Solé Sabaté, "La bandera independentista neix a Cuba," *Revista de Catalunya* 52 (1991): 44-52.

24 Arnaldo Testi, *Capture the Flag: The Stars and Stripes in American History* (New York: University Press, 2010).

25 Antoni Segura and Josep Maria Solé i Sabaté, eds., *Catalunya al món. La presència catalana al món: segles XIX i XX* (Barcelona: Generalitat de Catalunya, Departament de Vicepresidència, 2008).

26 Joan Esculies and David Martínez Fiol, *12.000! Els catalans a la Gran Guerra* (Barcelona: Ara Llibres, 2014).

27 Translations into English can be found in Agustí Colomines i Companys, "Representing Catalan National Identity. Catalunya during the Spanish Second Republic and the Civil War, " *Journal of Catalan Studies* (2008), 65-85; Jaume Sobrequés i Callicó, *History of Catalunya*, trans. Neil Charlton, Barcelona: Editorial Base, 2012, 99-100.

28 United Nations Day on October 24, 1971. https://www.youtube.com/watch?v=TMp1LcJLTmU.

# 11

# Catalunya: The Challenges of Catalanism

## (or "A chronicle of the overflow of Catalanism")

*Salvador Cardus i Ros*

### Preamble

I consider it essential, in order to make an adequate reading of the following lines, that the following considerations be taken into account:

1. When looking at an ongoing conflict, in which democratic quality, respect for citizens' civil and political rights, or the freedom and dignity of peoples are at stake, it is not only difficult to separate an academic perspective from personal commitment, but could even be considered morally and politically unacceptable to try to do so.
2. Speculating on future scenarios at times of great uncertainty—such as June 2019—involves the risk that, at the time of publication of this book, there may have been major changes in expectations, and it will have become obsolete. We have tried not to fall for what Pierre Bourdieu called the "temptation of prophesy," but have inevitably concluded with some ideas with an uncertain future.
3. Finally, although it is not the issue about which I am writing, it should never be forgotten that the conflict between Catalunya and Spain is a local expression of current global challenges: the crisis and obsolescence of political parties as we have known them; democratic crisis due to the weakening of classic functions of the state, such as ensuring security or protecting domestic markets; crisis of political culture, especially as caused by the emergence of the social networks. In this sense, the Catalan case is not a rarity or an exception, but rather one more expression of a global crisis, or, in any case, an advanced expression of what will take place in many other political areas.

## Chronicle of an Overflow

I have subtitled this contribution "A chronicle of the overflow of Catalanism." Which is a way, in fact, to announce the death of Catalanism and, in particular, Autonomist Catalanism as born along with the 1979 Autonomy Statute. But in even a broader sense, Catalanism as we had known it since the late nineteenth century and in the strictest sense—as a process of national reconstruction and at the same time linked to the will to take part in the regeneration of Spain—it practically no longer exists apart from in the nostalgia of some old politician feeling down, or some chronicler bent on saving the unsalvageable.

Of course, two paths to an unlikely resurrection of political Catalanism remain open. One would be a miraculous return to constitutional Autonomism from before the 2010 Constitutional Court ruling, in an unheard of case of time-machine travel. The other would be a type of separatism that is more comfortable in making its way than reaching its final destination. I will refer to these two possibilities. Or, rather, to what I consider to be two impossibilities.

As stated above, Catalanism, as a political project, was knocked on the head by the reform of the statute that began in 2004 and failed in 2006. This is a remarkable case of what in sociology we call "the undesired consequences of social action," a process with paradoxical consequences. What was supposed to revitalize Autonomism for a further twenty-five years, as some of its defenders said, in fact precipitated[1] its demise.

We could examine the precedents for the agreement to reform the statute. Which was a reform that Jordi Pujol—the first president of the Autonomic Generalitat de Catalunya (between 1980 and 2013)—would never have carried out because he knew well the risks that opening that Pandora's box would lead to; in Catalan it is called "the box of thunder." But it is also true that the plan prepared by the conservative think tank FAES (Foundation for Analysis and Social Studies)—and activated thanks to the absolute majority obtained by José María Aznar in 2000, the conservative leader of the People's Party—left little room for impassive regional Catalanism. Pasqual Maragall, Socialist president of the Generalitat de Catalunya in 2003, saw this clearly, trusted the electoral promises made by the leader of the Spanish Socialist government, Rodríguez Zapatero, and went ahead with the rest of the parties with whom he had formed the coalition government (Esquerra Republicana de Catalunya—ERC—and Initiative for Catalunya Verds—ICV) and with the reluctant participation of the center-right coalition, Convergence i Unió (CiU). The result was clear: (a) "the filing down" of the Catalan Proposal for a new Statute, in the words of the president of the Constitutional Commission of the Spanish Parliament,

Alfonso Guerra, as "confessed" in Barakaldo in May 2005 while negotiations were taking place; (b) the surrender of the leader of the opposition in the Catalan Parliament, Artur Mas (CiU), accepting the "filing down" in Madrid in January 2006, meaning the PSOE betraying its own Socialist Catalan leader Pasqual Maragall; (c) the expulsion from political life of the main movers of the reform, first from the Catalan government with a hasty end to the tripartite of Pasqual Maragall (PSC), Josep Lluís Carod-Rovira (ERC), and Joan Saura (ICV) in November 2006; and, finally, (d) the judgment of the Constitutional Court (June 2010) which, in real terms, broke the constitutional pacts of 1978, as Spanish professors of constitutional law at the University of Seville Joaquín Urías and Javier Pérez Royo pointed out.

The so-called "procés d'independence," therefore, was reborn on the death of Catalanism. This beginning is often linked with the 2010 Constitutional Court ruling. But it is a mistake to still think of the traditional mechanisms of political dynamics, or to think that this is a reactive movement from top to bottom. No: the popular movement in favor of independence began during the same debate about the statute itself, a relevant fact because it tells us its true age: fourteen in 2019. The motto at the start of the process—"*tenim dret a*" (we have the right to decide), led by the platform Dret a Decidir (PDD), set up in December 2005—expressed it well. A motto without too much legal value, but as is often said now, with a great capacity for empowerment. In this sense, it would be unfair not to cite the first major gesture of symbolic emancipation enacted by popular consultations—organized by popular initiative and practically outside political institutions—held between 2009 and 2011 in more than five hundred municipalities, with the participation of 800,000 Catalans, and with nearly four thousand public promotional[2] events. It was the first liberating gesture of brazen and democratic disobedience. So broad was the popular awareness—of the fact that the reform of the statute had failed—that it began well before the Constitutional Court's sentence, five years earlier. I place the key moment of the psychological change on December 28, 2006, with the publication of Joan Sol's article "*Plantem cara*" in the AVUI newspaper, where he suggested moving on after the failure of the objectives of that statutory reform. A few months after a referendum which, despite institutional efforts, had fallen slightly below 50 percent participation, it had already been found that unilateral interference with the school curriculum—imposing one more weekly hour of Spanish at all levels—and the intention to breach budgetary agreements had failed. It was obvious that this filed-down statute would not meet any of the promised objectives.

### The Hypothesis of the Reaction to Attempts to Humiliate

It is not the direct object of this contribution, but to speak about these challenges with some basis I must cite my hypothesis about the nature[3] of the change that uncovered the grassroots response in favor of independence. In summary: with regard to the attempt to humiliate Catalunya over the failure of the statute and thus definitively end the "Catalan question"—I have a remarkable collection of provocations made in public by senior Spanish political leaders—instead of continuing in what had been the usual victim's role played by autonomist Catalanism, there was a kind of awakening that has been analyzed by authors in what they call a *theory of humiliation.* I speak, among others, of German psychology professor at the University of Oslo Evelin Lidner,[4] French political scientist Bertrand Badie,[5] and British historian Dennis Smith.[6] From my point of view, the fundamental thing is that reactive attitudes were abandoned, and the initiative was taken by imagining a process of national emancipation based on four clear expectations: radical democratization; economic prosperity; social justice; and international presence and recognition. And this provided a proactive account and attitude that overflowed the Autonomist establishment.

The analysis of the hatching of independence is yet to be carried out, and the gender factor will have to be considered in a special way, with the incorporation into the political debate of women, mostly in the public events that took place during those years. A presence culminating with presence in the two main organizations that boosted civil society: Muriel Casals's and Carme Forcadell's Òmnium Cultural and Assemblea Nacional Catalana, respectively.

### The Characteristics of the Process

But let us return to the death of Catalanism and the challenges caused by the overflow of separatism. I believe that time will say—whether successfully or not—what the future challenges are, and it will be necessary to take into account various characteristics that I will summarize.

1. "*El procés*" (process), or movement in favor of independence, a bottom-up movement, was not based so much on political awareness as on the naturalization of the so-called "right to decide." That is, this "right" had become "taken for granted." So, no strong ideological adscription to ideological independence has been necessary. If I can put it this way, it is an aspiration without separatists (neither lifelong ones, nor converts). This is my "as if" theory: in the same way that Spanish, French, British, and American people defend the independence of their own countries. That is, even celebrating their Independence Day, but without recognizing themselves as "separatists." The same thing is true here.

2. In fact, this assumption of a right to decide was initially a formula with less political weight than the "right to self-determination." Which has made the claim more "natural," more popular, and less dramatic. Unawareness of the magnitude of the change in perspective—and its implications—is what has made the aspiration especially strong. And for that reason, it has been shared by 80 percent of the population. Many of the new "separatists" are convinced that they had always been separatists.
3. In that sense, there is nothing strange about the war against independence for the Unionist parties—especially Ciudadanos, the most aggressive of them—and focusing on combating the naturalization logic mentioned above. They have tried to impose the image of a divided, fractured Catalan society, polarizing conflict in the public sphere as a mechanism of "denaturalization." They aimed to force an "increase in awareness" that would defuse the "spiral of silence" favorable to independence, and were almost completely unsuccessful in that. In fact, they have only achieved media echo because of the bluntness of their propaganda and agit-prop actions, obtaining support in Spain but with little follow-up in Catalunya.
4. While the "change" for independence took place in 2003-2007—well before the economic crisis, and long before 2004, when Convergencia moved over to separatism—this leap was possible due to a slow process in national identification, which began in 1980 (see figure 1). Specifically, identification with Spain, "feeling only Spanish, or more Spanish than Catalan," had fallen by approximately from 40 to 10 percent over forty years.

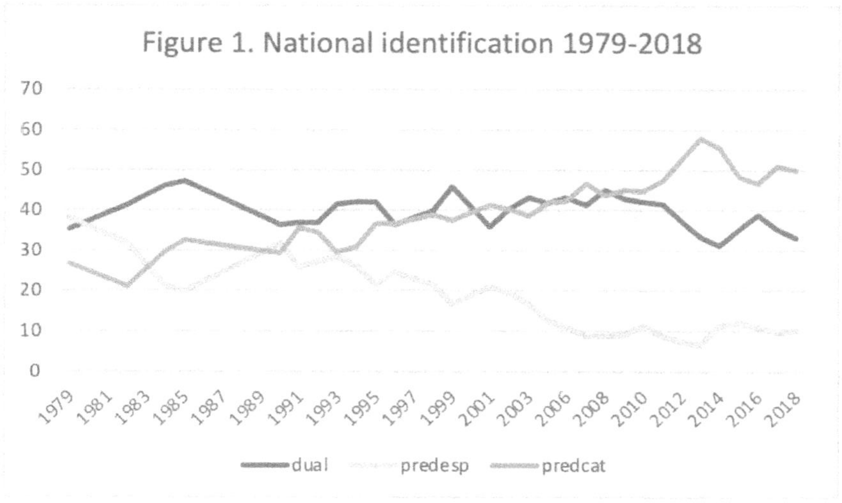

5. The Spanish state's response to this aspiration—opting for an authoritarian, contemptuous, and repressive attitude—only reinforced it rather than deterring it. I believe that until 2014 the state could still have overcome secessionist will with a positive proposal, as the British had done in Scotland. The breakage of the emotional bond with Spain was by now resounding and irreversible, at least for 50 percent of Catalans.
6. The definitive shift in favor of independence cannot be explained without taking into account the traditional mass media's loss of information hegemony—with most of their audience being conservative people favorable to unity with Spain—to the social networks. Firstly, because that brought about a break with the dominant narrative. Secondly, because the latter have been used as instruments of organization by civil society, and with mobilizing effects. And thirdly, because they have built an efficient channel of transmission of new symbols, of denunciation of repression, and, above all, of humorous response to challenge the threats of the state.
7. The current political situation has sometimes been described as a "non-situation" because of the high degree of uncertainty and its constant, accelerated transformation. There is incessantly a continual dissolution and reconfiguration of the political map in each call. Elections are held in situations of normalcy, with leaderships held as political prisoners or in exile, in contexts of political repression or with serious government instability in Spain.
8. With regard to what support for independence is, it is worth ending the confusion of: (a) referencing electoral calls that do not ask about independence; (b) not knowing what support would be in a situation of fair play, i.e., with a pre-debate for and against, without threats of retaliation, and with a commitment to accepting the result (perhaps one day this may have to be asked in polls); and (c) taking into account that, although opinion polls show support for independence in the total voting-age population—not those involved in the elections—stable at 48 percent (see figure 2), voting for independence parties has not stopped growing over each electoral call, in any area (see figure 3).

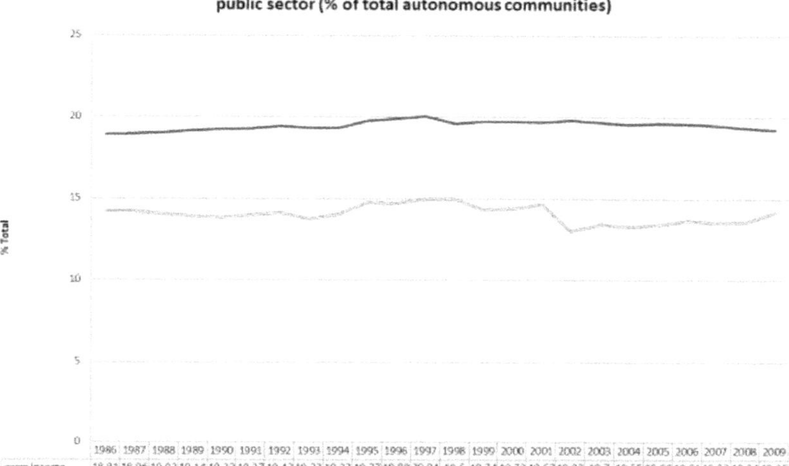


| | 1986 | 1987 | 1988 | 1989 | 1990 | 1991 | 1992 | 1993 | 1994 | 1995 | 1996 | 1997 |
|---|---|---|---|---|---|---|---|---|---|---|---|---|
| Income | 18,91 | 18,96 | 19,02 | 19,14 | 19,23 | 19,27 | 19,43 | 19,33 | 19,32 | 19,77 | 19,88 | 20,04 |
| Expenditure | 14.2 | 14.18 | 14 | 13,9 | 13,8 | 13.98 | 14,1 | 13,73 | 14,02 | 14,78 | 14,68 | 14,98 |

| | 1998 | 1999 | 2000 | 2001 | 2002 | 2003 | 2004 | 2005 | 2006 | 2007 | 2008 | 2009 |
|---|---|---|---|---|---|---|---|---|---|---|---|---|
| Income | 19,6 | 19,74 | 19,73 | 19,67 | 19,83 | 19,7 | 19,55 | 19,66 | 19,61 | 19,53 | 19,34 | 19,25 |
| Expenditure | 14,98 | 14,32 | 14,4 | 14,64 | 12,98 | 13,41 | 13,28 | 13,41 | 13,66 | 13,53 | 13,55 | 14,14 |

Figure 2. In favor and against independence, Source: Elaboració pròpia amb dades de: ICPS 1001-2007 i 2011-2012; UOC 2008-2009; CEO 2015-2018

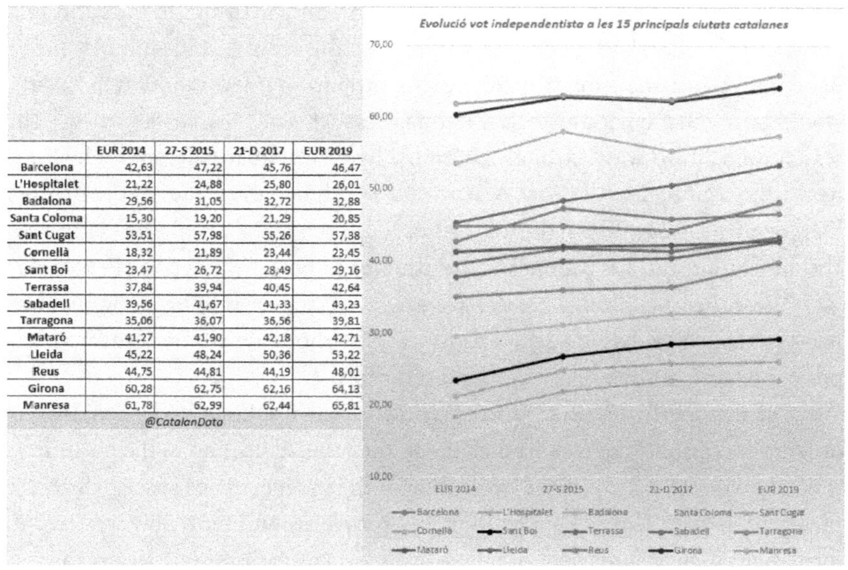

| | EUR 2014 | 27-S 2015 | 21-D 2017 | EUR 2019 |
|---|---|---|---|---|
| Barcelona | 42,63 | 47,22 | 45,76 | 46,47 |
| L'Hospitalet | 21,22 | 24,88 | 25,80 | 26,01 |
| Badalona | 29,56 | 31,05 | 32,72 | 32,88 |
| Santa Coloma | 15,30 | 19,20 | 21,29 | 20,85 |
| Sant Cugat | 53,51 | 57,98 | 55,26 | 57,38 |
| Cornellà | 18,32 | 21,89 | 23,44 | 23,45 |
| Sant Boi | 23,47 | 26,72 | 28,49 | 29,16 |
| Terrassa | 37,84 | 39,94 | 40,45 | 42,64 |
| Sabadell | 39,56 | 41,67 | 41,33 | 43,23 |
| Tarragona | 35,06 | 36,07 | 36,56 | 39,81 |
| Mataró | 41,27 | 41,90 | 42,18 | 42,71 |
| Lleida | 45,22 | 48,24 | 50,36 | 53,22 |
| Reus | 44,75 | 44,81 | 44,19 | 48,01 |
| Girona | 60,28 | 62,75 | 62,16 | 64,13 |
| Manresa | 61,78 | 62,99 | 62,44 | 65,81 |

@CatalanData



Figure 3. Voting for pro-independence parties in the largest 15 Catalan cities, Source: Jeff Stats

### The Challenges

In short, if we take into account all of these backgrounds, then we are not facing a circumstantial challenge, including that of the soufflé repeatedly mentioned in anti-independence propaganda in Catalunya, which will supposedly deflate and join pro-constitutional forces. In fact, we are in a situation of continual challenge, waiting for some exceptional and decisive fact that resolves the current situation of impasse.

I said earlier that I was referring to "impossible" setbacks to this process. And, first of all, I would not want to belittle the hypothesis of the recovery of autonomist, constitutional Catalanism. Certain residual sectors of formerly moderate nationalism (the European Democratic Party of Catalunya, the result of the transformation of Jordi Pujol's former Convergència Democràtica de Catalunya—PDECat) have been predicted due to the exaggerations of conservative media groups and some of their analysts. In some cases, these are very ambiguous positions, without, for the time being, giving up the principle of self-determination, but advocating a halt in the process. The same short journey—and supposedly in the same ideological space—seems to be the new project of former French prime minister, Manuel Valls, with the foundation of a new party "of Catalan matrix"—according to conservative and unionist newspaper *La Vanguardia*—and which, with the support of important entrepreneurs, would bear a name with historical resonances such as "*Lliga Democràtica.*" The search for a "third way," strongly defended by La Vanguardia, and by the business group calling itself Puente Aéreo—and which had the leader of the defunct Democratic Union of Catalunya, Duran i Lleida, as its visible head—was an absolute failure, as was Manuel Valls's attempt to become mayor of Barcelona.

The other possibility of the return, a separatist but limited, prudent neo-Catalanism is that of a separatism which, without giving up, wants to postpone the secessionist project for the distant future.

On the one hand, there is the argument that it takes a wider majority in order to successfully confront the state. On the other hand, and in the meantime, it would work to take over the hegemony of the independence space, which the president in exile, Carles Puigdemont, and people around him, now scattered in formations such as Junts per Catalunya or La Crida, are disputing. In any case, its strategy would be to get a referendum agreed with Spain, far from the proposals of civil disobedience, defended by the president of Amnium Cultural, Jordi Cuixart, and much of the most combative independence movement.

My view—which I probably mix up with what I want—is that neither the return to autonomism nor putting secession off forever is possible. The former is impossible because of the degree of legal, political, and unconstitutional mistrust. The latter is impossible because no Spanish government is in a position to make even the smallest gesture that would make it possible to rely on any future recognition of the right to self-determination. It should be remembered that Pedro Sánchez was expelled from the PSOE General Secretariat in October 2016 for daring to speak to separatists in order to obtain the presidency of the government, and that in February 2019, he preferred to call an election rather than accepting the start of negotiations with Catalan separatists—qualified by the Spanish unionist press as rebels—in the presence of a mediator.

And if it is not possible to turn back to autonomism, nor move toward an agreed recognition of the right to self-determination, then what is the way out of the current collapse? What is the challenge facing separatism in order to democratically complete or postpone its dream?

I know that you will all quite rightly consider my final conclusion to be a real step in the dark. But, for now, I can see no other ending. Let me explain. A few weeks ago, I published an article in the weekly *La República* (May 25, 2019), titled "*No som Derry, serem Berlin.*" The thesis is two-fold: on the one hand, no one here will "start an Ulster-type situation," as the Unionist parties had announced. After fourteen years of the process, there has been no significant form of violence. And, while Catalan society is more politicized than ever—and therefore more politically polarized around independence—it is no less true that fragmentation is also greater among multiple parties—that is, there are not two clearly defined fronts—and that coexistence has not been affected, beyond the (unanswered) provocations of those who would like to destroy it.

On the other hand, the second thesis is that given the instability of the situation at some point, some event which is now unpredictable and probably even not serious could trigger the fall of the "wall" which, paradoxically, currently binds us to Spain. I am talking about a random fact, a misunderstanding—as in Berlin—of the straw that breaks the camel's back, or of a collective, unstoppable gesture of civil disobedience. By the way, a mechanism such as that explains the triggering of most cases of independence: that of the United States, with the Boston Tea Party in 1773; those in Slovenia and in the Baltic Republics with the breakdown of the powerful USSR. Even the one that the unusual event of Brexit may cause in Scotland.

If so, the challenge facing separatism would be nothing more than to keep prepared and alert for future events. A moment that can only be effective to the extent that it is unpredictable.

## NOTES

1 Cardús, Salvador (2010). *El camí de la independència.* Barcelona: The Bell.

2 Vilaregut, Ricard (2011). Memária i emerging in l'independentisme catala. El cas de la Plataforma pel Dret a Decidir (2005-2010). Barcelona: UAB.

3 Cardús, Salvador (2014). "La humiliació com a factor desencadenant de l'eclosió independentista," in Jaume Sobrequés ed. *Vàrem mirar ben lluny del desert. Actes del simposi 'Espanya contra Catalunya: una mirada històrica (1714-2014).* Barcelona: Centre d'Hist'ria Contemporania de Catalunya (537-551).

4 Lidner, Evelin (2006). *Making Enemies.* Humiliation and International Conflict. CN: Preger Securyity International.

5 Badie, Bertrand (2009). "Le discurs identitaire est expression d'incertitude," *Le Monde International* (November 23).

6 Smith, Dennis (2006). "Organisations and Humiliation: Looking beyond Elias," in *Organization.* 8: 537-560.

# Author Biographies

### Iñigo Bullain

Iñigo Bullain (Getxo, 1960), professor of Basque politics at the University of the Basque Country, studied Law at the University of Deusto (Basque Country), post-graduated in European integration at the Europa-Institut of the University of the Sarre (Germany), and obtained a PhD in law at the European University Institute in Florence (Italy). A former European civil servant at the European Commission in Brussels (Belgium), he has taught constitutional and European law at the University of the Basque Country (UPV-EHU) since 1991. He is an author of several books, such as *Revolucionarismo patriótico* (2011), and academic articles on European governance, regional autonomy in Basque, English, and Spanish, and has published a monthly opinion article in the Basque newspaper *Deia* since 2011.

### Salvador Cardús i Ros

Salvador Cardús i Ros (1954) is a doctor in economic sciences and professor of sociology at the Autonomous University of Barcelona. He has been a visiting researcher at the University of Cambridge (Fitzwilliam College), Cornell University, and Queen Mary College of the University of London. He has been a Ginebró Serra Visiting Professor at Stanford University. He has been a permanent member of the Institut d'Estudis Catalans since 2008. As a researcher, he has worked on issues of sociology of religion, the media, immigration, and national identities. He has published more than thirty books, has contributed to more than one hundred collective works, and has written more than sixty prologues and 125 articles in academic and specialized journals. In 2010, he published *El camí de la Independència*. His latest books are *Time and Power* (2016) and *Informe sobre la cohesió social a la Catalunya dels segle XXI* (2020). From 2013 to 2017, he was a member of the Council Assessor for the National Transition of the government of Catalunya, which was dissolved in application of article 155 of the Spanish Constitution.

### Carles Santacana Torres

Carles Santacana Torres (1961) is a professor of contemporary history at the University of Barcelona. His research covers the political history of the Francoist dictatorship, cultural history, and the social history of sports. He has published twenty books and more than 150 scientific articles, as well as making over a hundred contributions to collective books. About his article in the present volume, he published *El franquisme i els catalans. Els informes del Consejo Nacional del Movimiento* (2000), in which he unveiled the secret reports of Falange (the only legal party under the dictatorship), in which they analyzed the evolution of Catalanism and proposed ways to deactivate it. He also provided unpublished documentation on the relations between Catalanism in exile and within the state in two volumes based on the Tarradellas files: *Josep Tarradellas. L'exili (1939-1954)* (2014) and *Josep Tarradellas. L'exili 2 (1954-1977)* (2015). And he analyzed Esquerra Republicana de Catalunya's evolution toward pro-independence in the collective volume *El nacionalisme com a ideologia* (1995).

### Teresa Abelló

Teresa Abelló has a PhD in geography and history. She is a professor of contemporary history at the University of Barcelona (UB). As a researcher, she has been an intern at the Internationaal Instituut voor Sociale Gescchiedenis in Amsterdam and has been a visiting professor at the University of East Anglia, in Norwich. She is currently a member of the History of Culture and Intellectuals Study Group (GEHCI) at UB. Her research has focused on two areas: anarchism and Catalanism. She has published various books and articles on these two subjects. Regarding the former, her main objective has been to analyze the dynamics of the Spanish labor and trade union movement from its beginnings in the second half of the nineteenth century, particularly the anarchist unions, and the connections they had with their international namesakes. This is the topic of her book *Les relacions internacionals de l'anrquisme catala. 1881-1916* (1987), as well as *La CNT. Papers d'exili i clandestinitat* (2013). In her book *El debat estatutari del 1932* (2007), she has analyzed the connections that these groups had with Catalanism, as well as the latter's relationship with the Spanish government.

### Queralt Solé

Queralt Solé (1976), lecturer at the University of Barcelona, has a PhD in contemporary history. Her research focused on repression and political violence during the Civil War and the Francoist dictatorship and the influence of these two periods in the present history of Catalunya. She has focused her studies on the historical analysis of mass graves, Francoist monuments, and gender repression during the dictatorship. She has published several books and numerous scientific articles, such as "Trails of Death. The common graves of the Civil War" (*Journal of Contemporary Culture,* 2008); "The Valley of the Fallen: A New El Escorial for Spain" (*Human Remains and Violence, an Interdisciplinary Journal,* 2017); "Gender and Repression during the Spanish Civil War: Francoist Violence" (in *Legacies of Violence in Contemporary Spain. Exhuming the Past, Understanding the Present,* 2016), and "The Wounded City. The Traces of the Nazi and Fascist Aerial Bombing of Barcelona" (in *Nazi Juggernaut in the Basque Country and Catalunya,* 2018).

### Giovanni C. Cattini

Giovanni C. Cattini (Mantova, 1972) has a degree in contemporary history from the University of Bolonia (1998) and a PhD in history from the University of Barcelona (2006). He is currently a Serra Hunter Fellow in the Department of History and Archaeology (University of Barcelona). His field of study is the Catalan nationalist movement between the eighteenth and nineteenth centuries; however, he specializes in contemporary Catalan Nationalism and intellectual movements. He is the author of several publications regarding the history of intellectuals, cultural identities, and the Spanish Civil War. He has also collaborated with many contemporary history journals. As a researcher, he has taken part in multiple international, national, and local projects. His many publications include: *Historiography i catalanisme. Josep Coroleu i Inglada (1839-1895)*, Barcelona-Catarroja, Afers, 2007; *Prat de la Riba i la historiografia catalana*, Barcelona-Catarroja, Afers, 2008; *El Gran Complot*, Barcelona, Arallibres, 2009 -Italian edition: *Nel nome di Garibaldi. I rivoluzionari catalani, i nipoti del Generale e la polizia di Mussolini (1923-1926)*, Pisa, BFS 2010-; *Joaquim de Camps i Arboix. Un intel·lectual en temps convulsos*, Barcelona, FJI, 2015; with Xavier Fabrès, *Política i cultura: l'ateneisme en la Catalunya contemporània*, Barcelona, AB—DB, 2017; with Àngel Casals, *The Catalan Nation and Identity throughout History*, Bern, Peter Lang, 2020; *Storie di antifascismo popolare mantovano. Dalle giornate rosse alla Guerracivile spagnola*, Milano, FrancoAngeli, 2020.

### Daniel Roig

Daniel Roig i Sanz (Barcelona, 1983) holds a PhD in contemporary history from the University of Barcelona (UB). He is a member-researcher of the Centre d'Estudis Historics Internacionals (CEHI-UB) and is currently an associate lecturer in the Contemporary History and Current World Section of the Department of History and Archaeology at UB. His lines of research include the study of the political, social, and cultural history of the Interwar Europe and World War II, with special emphasis on the history of nationalism and the Catalan pro-independence movement of the period. It's a theme that he examined in his doctoral thesis—*Del Nacionalisme integral al totalitarisme: el catalanisme radical davant l'ascens dels feixismes a l'Europa dels anys trenta (1931-1935)*—and also in numerous publications and academic articles in national and international journals, as well as taking part in different conferences and research seminars on the issue.

#### Xabier Ezeizabarrena

Xabier Ezeizabarrena holds a PhD in law from the University of the Basque Country. He is a lawyer at the Bar of Donostia (San Sebastian) in the Basque Country. He is the director of the Master's Program on Environmental Law at the Faculty of Law of the University of the Basque Country, serving as a professor of the Department of Constitutional and Administrative Law. He is also a lecturer of public law at the University of Deusto. He was a visiting fellow at Oxford (2003), Edinburgh (2009), and Rio Grande do Norte (2013) Universities, inter alia. Since 2019, he is the president of the Parliament of Gipuzkoa (Gipuzkoako Batzar Orokorrak) in the Basque Country.

#### Igor Filibi

Dr. Igor Filibi, professor at the University of the Basque Country (EHU), is the principal investigator (senior researcher) in international relations at the University of the Basque Country. He holds bachelor's degrees in political science and political sociology and two master's in political science and administration (1995) and in European Union (1997). He earned his doctoral degree in 2004, with research focused on the influence of the European integration in the resolution of nationalist conflicts. He worked on the European project EUROREG of the European Commission between September 2004 and August 2007. He currently teaches diplomacy and foreign policy as well as globalization and international relations at the Department of International Relations of the University of the Basque Country. Since January 2006, he also has taught European economic and political institutions for the University Studies Abroad Consortium—USAC (University of Nevada, Reno). He has been published in national and international journals and directed several research projects. He is currently a member of the Consolidated Research Group on Democracy "Parte Hartuz." He has been a member of the Governing Council of the University of the Basque Country. He is currently secretary general of EuroBasque, the Basque Council of the European Movement. His main research topics are European integration and the resolution of nationalist conflicts.

### Xabier Irujo

Born in exile, Xabier Irujo is the director of the Center for Basque Studies at the University of Nevada, Reno, where he is professor of genocide studies. He was the first guest research scholar of the Manuel Irujo Chair at the University of Liverpool and has taught seminars on genocide and cultural genocide at Boise State University in Idaho, and at the University of California, Santa Barbara. He holds three master's degrees in linguistics, history, and philosophy and has two PhDs in history and philosophy. Dr. Irujo has lectured in nearly one hundred American and European universities and academic or cultural institutions. He has published on issues related to Basque history and politics and has specialized throughout his career in genocide studies with a focus on physical and cultural extermination. He has mentored numerous graduate students, and he is the member of the editorial board of four academic presses in Europe and the Americas. Dr. Irujo has authored more than fifteen books and a number of articles in specialized journals and has received awards and honors at a national and international level. His recent books include *Gernika: Genealogy of a Lie* (Sussex Academic Press, 2018), *"Arrasaré Vizcaya". 2000 bombardeos aéreos en Euskadi* (University of the Basque Country Press, 2020), and *Legal History of the Basque Language* (HAEE, Bilbao, 2015).

### Francisco Letamendia Belzunce

Born in 1944, Francisco Letamendia Belzunce has been a labor lawyer from 1969 to 1972, Basque Deputy for the Euskadiko Ezkerra in the Spanish Parliament from 1977 to 1982, professor at the Université Paris 8 from 1982 to 1985, professor of political science at the University of the Basque Country (EHU) from 1988 to 2014, and since his retirement in August 2004, emeritus professor at EHU. He has researched and written on various topics related to Basque politics and political science, specifically about nationalism, capitalism, political ideologies and identity, and political culture. As part of his duty as an emeritus professor, he is currently writing a four-volume manuscript on "Political Culture in the West," published by the University of the Basque Country Press. The first two first volumes are already published, and a third is nearing completion.

### Antoni Segura i Mas

Antoni Segura i Mas (Barcelona, 1952) is a professor of contemporary history and a deputy director (1998-2005) and director (2005-16 and 2018-19) of the Center for International Historical Studies of the University of Barcelona, as well as president of the CIDOB-Barcelona Centre for International Affairs since 2017. Relevant publications of his in recent years include: *Miradas sobre Euskadi* (2004), "El laberint basc: de la ruptura del Pacte d'Ajuria Enea a les eleccions de 2001" (2006), "Un balance del Estado de las Autonomías en España (1976-2002)" (2007), *Euskadi, crónica de una desesperanza* (2009), "L'independentisme tranquil de l'Scottish National Party" (2011), "Catalunya: From Industrialisation to the Present Day" (2011), "Moviments socials, transició democràtica i canvi politic" (2013), *Hablemos de reconciliación. Un encuentro con víctimas del conflicto vasco* (2013), *Crònica del catalanisme. De l'autonomia a la independència* (2013), "Els condicionants de la transició a Catalunya" (2014), "Barcelona cap i casal" (2014), "The End of two-party system in Spain?" (2016), "Regional Financing System, Economic Crisis, and the Independence Movement in Catalunya" (2016), and "La question de la mémoire historique en Espagne et en Catalogne" (2017).

### Alberto Spektorowski

Alberto Spektorowski is a professor of political science at the University of Tel Aviv. His fields of interest are in the intersection of comparative politics and political theory. He wrote widely about the ideology of fascism and the radical right in Europe and Latin America. His books include the edited volume, *Ethnic Challenges to the Modern Nation State* (Basingstoke: Macmillan, 2000), *Argentina's Revolution of the Right* (South Bend, IN: University of Notre Dame Press, 2003), *Autoritarios y Populistas. Los Origenes del Fascismo en la Argentina* (Buenos Aires, Lumiere, 2013), *Politics of Eugenics: Productionism, Population & National Welfare* (London, New York: Routledge Press, 2013), and *From Multiculturalism to Democratic Discrimination: The Challenge of Islam and the Re-emergence of Europe's Nationalism* (Ann Arbor: Michigan University Press, 2020). His articles about the European New Right have been published by *Theory Culture and Society*, *Comparative Political Studies*, and *Journal of Political Ideologies*, among others. Besides his academic activity, Spektorowski was a member of the International Contact Group that facilitated the end of violence, decommission, and finally the dismantling of ETA in the Basque Country, Spain. Spektorowski was an invited professor at Columbia University (New York), the University of Notre Dame (South Bend, Indiana), the University of the Basque Country, Spain, and University ORT Montevideo.

# Index

www.ingramcontent.com/pod-product-compliance
Lightning Source LLC
LaVergne TN
LVHW010053110826
845155LV00028B/323

*9781949805543*